THE VIRTUOUS LIFE IN GREEK ETHICS

There is now a renewed concern for moral psychology among moral philosophers. Moreover, contemporary philosophers interested in virtue, moral responsibility and moral progress regularly refer to Plato and Aristotle, the two founding fathers of ancient ethics. This book contains eleven chapters by distinguished scholars which showcase current research in Greek ethics. Four deal with Plato, focusing on the *Protagoras*, *Euthydemus*, *Symposium* and *Republic*, and discussing matters of literary presentation alongside the philosophical content. The four chapters on Aristotle address problems such as the doctrine of the mean, the status of rules, equity and the tension between altruism and egoism in Aristotelian eudaimonism. A contrast to classical Greek ethics is presented by two chapters reconstructing Epicurus' views on the emotions and moral responsibility as well as on moral development. The final chapter on personal identity in Empedocles shows that the concern for moral progress is already palpable in Presocratic philosophy.

Burkhard Reis is Wissenschaftlicher Mitarbeiter in the project to provide a new German translation of and commentary on Aristotle's *Nicomachean Ethics*, which is being run by Dorothea Frede and sponsored by the Deutsche Forschungsgemeinschaft. He is the author of *Der Platoniker Albinos und sein sogenannter Prologos. Prolegomena, Überlieferungsgeschichte, kritische Edition und Übersetzung* (1999).

THE VIRTUOUS LIFE IN GREEK ETHICS

EDITED BY

BURKHARD REIS

WITH THE ASSISTANCE OF

STELLA HAFFMANS

CAMBRIDGE UNIVERSITY PRESS
Cambridge, New York, Melbourne, Madrid, Cape Town, Singapore, São Paulo

Cambridge University Press
The Edinburgh Building, Cambridge CB2 2RU, UK

Published in the United States of America by Cambridge University Press, New York

www.cambridge.org
Information on this title: www.cambridge.org/9780521859370

First published 2006

Printed in the United Kingdom at the University Press, Cambridge

A catalogue record for this publication is available from the British Library

ISBN-13 978-0-521-85937-0 hardback
ISBN-10 0-521-85937-9 hardback

Note: For reasons of style, the conventional 'he', 'him', 'himself' have on occasion been used to express both genders.

Contents

Contributors

JAMES ALLEN Professor of Philosophy, University of Pittsburgh

JULIA ANNAS Regents Professor of Philosophy, University of Arizona

SUSANNE BOBZIEN Professor of Philosophy, Yale University

CHRISTOPH HORN Professor of Philosophy, University of Bonn

BRAD INWOOD Professor of Classics and Philosophy, University of Toronto

DAVID KONSTAN Professor of Classics, and Comparative Literature Brown University, Providence

MARY MARGARET McCABE Professor of Ancient Philosophy, King's College London

CHRISTOF RAPP Professor of Philosophy, Humboldt University, Berlin

DAVID SEDLEY Laurence Professor of Ancient Philosophy, University of Cambridge

GISELA STRIKER Professor of Classical Philosophy, Harvard University

JAN SZAIF Privatdozent für Philosophie, University of Bonn

Preface

On 5 July 2006 Professor Dr Dorothea Frede will celebrate her 65th birthday. Professor Frede, who has held a chair of Philosophy at the University of Hamburg since 1991, is one of the outstanding scholars in the field of Ancient Philosophy, with a high reputation in Germany and the international academic community. She has published widely on Plato, Aristotle and the Hellenistic philosophers. She has also conducted research on Heidegger and phenomenology, Rorty and Davidson. Currently she is president of the German Society for Ancient Philosophy (GANPH). Recently she has been appointed Mills Visiting Professor at the University of Berkeley, a position she will take up in 2006. Professor Frede's birthday will also mark the end of her official activities in Hamburg. Friends and colleagues in Germany, England, the United States and Canada would like to use this occasion to offer her this volume and thereby to express their gratitude for her academic contributions and her friendship over the years. The title of this collection of eleven papers on ancient Greek ethics thus refers to the common topic of all contributions as well as to the honorand herself.

As editor I would like to thank everybody who has been involved in the production of this book, first of all Stella Haffmans for her assistance in preparing the final typescript and the indices. Special thanks are also due to Mena Grünefeld, Ute Haffmans, Christoph Helmig, Eva Horváth, Brad Inwood, Christof Rapp, Reinold Schmücker, Andreas Schubert, Euree Song, Hans-Walter Stork, Jan Szaif, Roland Weidle, Jan Wiebers, Anja Wolkenhauer and, in more than one respect, to Gisela Striker. For technical support I am grateful to Daniel Deckers and Raffael Schaller. Without constant supervision by Dr Michael Sharp, my commissioning editor at CUP, the book would not have come out in print. The same holds true for the valuable comments supplied by an anonymous reader and the patience of Bernard Dod, the copy editor.

Ancient authors and works are referred to according to the abbreviations listed in the *Oxford Classical Dictionary* (3rd edition, Oxford 1996) and the *Greek-English Lexicon* of Liddell, Scott and Jones (9th edition, Oxford 1940), with the notable exception of Aristotle's *Metaphysics*, which is abbreviated as *Met.* Long and Sedley's *The Hellenistic Philosophers* is abbreviated as LS.

Introduction

Over the last decades, moral philosophers have become increasingly interested in questions that modern ethics had been neglecting since the seventeenth century: What does it mean to have a moral character? How can such a character be acquired and developed? What is the link between character and responsibility? Since a morally valuable character trait is traditionally called 'virtue', the new focus on moral psychology is typically combined with a renewed concern for the virtues. Some participants in the debate have proposed 'virtue ethics' as a third type of normative ethics next to theories in the Utilitarian and Kantian traditions. Those who argue that a substantial account of virtue can be assimilated into the existing types tend to use virtue ethics as a remedy for certain defects characteristic of morality as understood by modern philosophers. However, what the different positions in the debate on moral psychology share is the constant and explicit reference to the way moral philosophy was practised by the ancient Greeks.

Ancient Greek ethics sets out to teach the good life as a whole without being confined either to justifying moral principles and values, as in modern ethics of duty since the Enlightenment, or to resolving moral dilemmas, as in much contemporary analytic philosophy.[1] Virtue (*aretē*) is one of its key terms. In order to clarify what the Greeks have to say on virtue, moral education, the emotions and related issues, historians of ancient philosophy have started revisiting their sources with greater scrutiny than ever before. Yet recognizing the voices of a remote past as a philosophically challenging inspiration requires a sovereign command of the sources as well as a sound familiarity with contemporary problems. Both are virtues of *Dorothea Frede*'s, who, over the years, has made essential contributions to the clarification of ancient thought not only in reconstructing the history of fundamental philosophical concepts but

[1] Cf. D. Frede 1997: 1.

also in demonstrating their fruitfulness for the present. Hence this volume in honour of Professor Frede's work addresses a field where the achievements of the Greeks have become a popular starting point for systematic consideration.

The volume presents eleven contributions that testify to the standards and preferences of current research on ancient Greek ethics and 'the virtuous life' as seen by its proponents.[2] These are, as any well-informed reader would expect, primarily Plato and Aristotle. Inclusion of one Presocratic and one Hellenistic philosopher, Empedocles and Epicurus respectively, gives a taste of the attractions of thinkers working before and after the two great giants of ancient philosophy – despite the fragmentary textual transmission that every reconstruction of their doctrines has to cope with.

There is one striking difference between the contributions on Plato and on Aristotle. Whereas the latter are directly concerned with reconstructing and interpreting ethical doctrines, the former cannot avoid discussing matters of literary presentation. This is due, of course, to the dialogue form of Plato's works. Plato deliberately abstains from expressing any views in his own name. Following the lead of his teacher Socrates, he seems to be convinced that moral progress, in his own words 'the care for one's soul', has to begin with liberation from error. Liberation from error is what many of Plato's dialogues are about, in a twofold sense. In the narrative dimension Socrates refutes his interlocutors' unjustified claims to knowledge, and in the performative dimension Plato invites and exhorts the reader of the dialogues to change his mind and indeed his life.

Three telling examples of this are analysed in the articles by *James Allen*, *Julia Annas* and *David Sedley*. Each of them discusses a different phenomenon. Allen explores the inconclusive but nonetheless instructive series of arguments in the early dialogue *Protagoras* relating to the unity of the different traditional virtues.[3] Annas examines more or less disguised hints at positive doctrines of an ethical nature in dialogues such as the *Euthydemus*, *Theaetetus* and *Alcibiades* where Socrates on the surface seems primarily concerned with arguing from others' views rather than expounding his own.[4] Last but not least comes a treatment by Sedley of the 'sub-Socratic' character of the doctrinal content of Agathon's speech in the *Symposium*. Sedley considers its function as a philosophical and literary device for highlighting the progression reached in Socrates' speech on love, which immediately

[2] Debts to the seminal publications of Professor Frede are numerous and will be acknowledged in the footnotes.

[3] For the part of the dialogue not covered by Allen's analysis see D. Frede 1986.

[4] Annas' article is intended to continue the discussion begun by D. Frede 2002.

follows.[5] With the *Republic* we reach the classic presentation by Plato of what is generally accepted to be his own mature thought on ethics. *Mary Margaret McCabe* presents a thorough analysis of how dialectic, his preferred method for approaching the edifying cognition of the forms, is ideally supposed to work if we follow its description as well as its application in the *Republic*.[6]

By way of contrast, the four articles dedicated to Aristotle's ethics can address their subjects much more directly. *Christof Rapp* proposes a new interpretation of the famous and obscure doctrine of 'the mean relative to us', which forms part of Aristotle's definition of ethical virtue (*EN* 2.6, 1106b36–1107a2) and continues to perplex even charitable readers. Rapp's interpretation takes this doctrine as a purely conceptual truth and thus escapes the problems involved in construing it as a rule or practical guideline for decision-making. That Aristotle is not in principle opposed to general rules is what *Gisela Striker* and *Christoph Horn* purport to show against the self-proclaimed Aristotelianism of contemporary particularists.[7] Striker points to the concept of 'universal justice' and to Aristotle's *Politics* as an indispensable supplement to the *Ethics*, Horn focuses on what Aristotle calls both a part of justice and superior to justice, namely 'equity' (*epieikeia*). Similarly challenging is the project pursued by *Jan Szaif*, who hopes to resolve two notorious problems in the coherent reconstruction of Aristotelian eudaimonism: (1) What are we to make of Aristotle's praise of the life of theory (*EN* 10.6–8) if we refuse to disregard the claim that practical activity according to the ethical virtues is a worthwhile choice for its own sake, rather than just a means for allowing theory to be put into practice? (2) If, according to Aristotle (as well as Plato), acting virtuously serves the interest of the agent, what about the common view that social virtues are outwardly directed, in the sense that they primarily benefit not the virtuous agent himself, but another?

In response to the second problem, contemporary virtue ethicists usually maintain that happiness in the sense of *eudaimonia* cannot be defined independently of morality and moral value, e.g. by compiling a list of non-moral goods or biological traits of the human species.[8] This view is certainly in line with Socrates, Plato, Aristotle and the Stoics regardless of their different anthropological or metaphysical commitments. However, a collection of papers on the virtuous life in Greek ethics cannot afford to exclude theories that treat the virtues as only instrumental and regard

[5] This speech is discussed by D. Frede 1993b.

[6] On that issue see also D. Frede 1999.

[7] e.g. McDowell 1979 and 1996; Wiggins 1997.

[8] e.g. Hursthouse 1999.

happiness as devoid of any moral value. Such is the doctrine of Epicureanism. In order to meet the demands of morality, Epicurus has to construct a concept of pleasure (*hēdonē*) which is ultimately presented as the goal of life, but in a very particular way, remote from the term's popular and vulgar associations. As a result we obtain, as it were, a non-subjectivist version of hedonism. But how is one to distinguish between genuine and apparent pleasures? *David Konstan* argues in his article that pleasure and pain are taken by Epicurus as irrational affects (*pathē*). These affects function as criteria in that they infallibly inform us about the affective value of things in the world – whether they are to be pursued or shunned. It is the addition of false belief that, in the course of individual and collective history, has produced so many and such severe obstacles to happiness – most of all empty or irrational fear; obstacles that only (Epicurean) philosophy can remove, recommending among other things a life in accordance with the traditional virtues.[9]

Epicurean ethics can very well be seen as paradigmatic of ancient ethics in general when it comes to questions of moral responsibility and moral development (as opposed to virtue, where its stance is more idiosyncratic). It is a revealing side-effect of the character-based view of ancient ethics that agents can be held morally responsible and thus praised or blamed even if they could not have acted otherwise.[10] All that is needed to justify praise and blame is causal responsibility.[11] *Susanne Bobzien*'s contribution offers an account of the sophisticated way in which Epicurus managed to defend the notions of moral responsibility and moral development on the basis of his materialistic ontology. According to Epicurus – and in this respect he does indeed agree with his classical predecessors and Stoic contemporaries – the function of ethics does not consist in 'developing or justifying a moral system that allows for the effective dishing out of praise and blame. . . . It takes praise and blame for action as in principle

[9] It is left to the reader to decide whether this approach to ethics and its underlying materialism is more attractive than those adopted by Plato and Aristotle who, by the way, both come up with their own distinctive answer to the challenge of contemporary hedonists. On Plato's theory of pleasure see D. Frede 1985 and 1993a. A detailed account of Aristotle's theory will be found in the new German commentary on the *Nicomachean Ethics* that Dorothea Frede is currently working on. See also D. Frede 2006 and her forthcoming contribution to the XVIIIth Symposium Aristotelicum in Venice, July 2005.

[10] Aristotle, for example, by and large considers agents as morally responsible as long as the action in question was carried out in the absence of force or ignorance (*EN* 3.1).

[11] Since the latter seems to be compatible with deterministic world views, a closer analysis of its precise meaning can be of value even for a modern perspective. Ancient debates on the compatibility of fate with human responsibility were triggered by the Stoic version of determinism, on which see the overview in D. Frede 2003.

justified, based on the rationality of the agent. But praise and blame are not themselves a topic of ethics. Human failure is taken into account only as a starting point for moral progress . . .'[12] If *Brad Inwood* is right, the same attitude can be ascribed already to Empedocles, who, in a very different context, preaches the transmigration of the soul as a punishment for some primal sin. In regarding individual awareness of this sort of personal identity as a necessary condition for moral improvement, this Presocratic thinker in the Pythagorean tradition all of a sudden turns out to stand at the beginning of a powerful intellectual movement which inspires moral philosophers even today and is likely to continue to do so in the future.

[12] Bobzien below, p. 229.

CHAPTER I

Dialectic and virtue in Plato's Protagoras

James Allen

A visit by Protagoras to Athens is the dramatic occasion for the conversations depicted in the *Protagoras*.[1] Protagoras is a celebrity, staying as a guest at the house of Callias, where a large company has gathered. Among the more notable characters present are Critias and Alcibiades, the sophists Prodicus and Hippias, and the two sons of Pericles, Paralus and Xanthippus (314e3–316a5). Socrates is induced to join the gathering by Hippocrates, a young man so eager to meet Protagoras that he has roused Socrates from bed before dawn in the hope of persuading him to use his entrée to secure an audience. Once inside, speaking on behalf of the younger man, Socrates asks Protagoras what Hippocrates could expect to learn should he become his student (318a). The answer – though it is put in various ways – is virtue. And the first sustained discussion is set in train by the doubts Socrates expresses about whether virtue is the kind of thing that can be taught (319a9–320c2).

The so-called great speech is Protagoras' response (320c2–328d2). When it is over, Socrates declares himself convinced that virtue can be taught. He is, however, still troubled by one small question (329b6–d2). This question is the occasion for a new sequence of arguments that occupies the rest of the dialogue apart from a procedural dispute (334c9–338e7) and a substantial digression in which the interpretation of a poem of Simonides is discussed (338e8–349a7).[2] It is not only the subject of the discussion that changes after Socrates' little question is posed but also its form. Socrates praises Protagoras as a master of two forms of *logos*: continuous orations of the kind one might expect to hear from a distinguished speaker like Pericles and of which the great speech is an example, and asking and answering

[1] On the dramatic date see Manuwald 1999: 79–82, who thinks some time towards the end of the 430s BC most likely.

[2] A full interpretation of the dialogue would have to explain the contribution made by this discussion, but I shall have nothing to say about it here. On this section of this dialogue see D. Frede 1986.

questions briefly, that is, though the term is not used in the immediate context, dialectic (329b; cf. 334e).[3]

My aim is to examine the dialectical part of the dialogue – or that part of it that remains when the discussion of Simonides is removed, as it too might be viewed as a species of dialectic – by attending in selective detail to the individual arguments and the overall structure of the sequence to which they belong. My thesis is that the first four arguments in which Socrates attempts to establish that the virtues are more closely related than Protagoras wishes to allow, though they accomplish some valuable, characteristically dialectical, tasks by revealing problems in the position Protagoras is defending, suffer from defects that Socrates and Protagoras must recognize and overcome if they are to achieve a better understanding of the question in dispute and make progress towards its resolution. The most important of these defects is a failure to explain or illuminate. Even when they are cogent, the arguments do not impart an understanding of the conclusions they establish. This is not true, or is less true, of the last set of arguments, which begin at 351b4 with an apparent digression about the relation between pleasure and the good and the impossibility of voluntary wrongdoing and conclude with a new argument that courage is identical with wisdom, the conclusion that Socrates had tried and failed to establish in the last of the first four arguments.

One might, then, speak of a progress from merely dialectical arguments toward demonstrative or didactic argument. This characterization must remain a rough one, however. I do not mean to suggest that the dialogue relies on an understanding of demonstration as explicit or detailed as Aristotle's. And the progress itself is partial and incomplete. One of the premisses that plays a crucial part in the last argument is that the good is pleasure. As has often been noted, this is hardly something Plato or Socrates is likely to have accepted. Witness, for example, the argument of the *Gorgias* and the brusque way in which the conception of virtue for which the hedonism entertained in the *Protagoras* provides a basis is dismissed in the *Phaedo* (68e–69b). What is more, as I shall argue, the discussion in the *Protagoras* is so presented as to emphasize the fact that this proposition never loses the status of a dialectical concession. What we have, I believe, is an argument that illustrates some of the features that a truly explanatory argument bearing on this issue would have without being one. The aporetic note on which the dialogue ends is fully justified; Socrates' call for further

[3] *dialegesthai* is used in a quasi-technical sense of discussion by question and answer at 335a9–c1 and 336b8–d3.

investigation is not an empty gesture (361c). It is also part of my thesis that the first set of arguments contribute to the progress in this direction not only by raising problems for Protagoras and embodying deficiencies that must be remedied, but also by introducing elements that are put to use in the more satisfactory arguments that succeed them.

I. PROTAGORAS' THESIS

Socrates' little question is about how the virtues, justice, holiness and temperance, which Protagoras has already mentioned in the great speech, and wisdom and courage, which Protagoras is now happy to add, are related (329b6–330a2). Is virtue one thing of which they are parts, he asks, or would it be better to say that it is a single thing for which 'justice', 'temperance', 'holiness', 'courage', and 'wisdom' are different names? (cf. 349b1–5). It is, of course, not a little matter at all – this is an exceedingly simple case of Socratic irony – yet it is a perfectly natural issue to raise in the context. In the course of the great speech, Protagoras has already spoken of 'the one thing in which all citizens must share if there are to be cities . . . justice, temperance, holiness and that which taken together make up what I call a man's virtue' (324d7–325a3).[4]

Protagoras undertakes to defend the thesis that the virtues are parts of a whole. The particular form of the view that he will uphold is illustrated with the aid of an analogy. Socrates offers Protagoras a choice between viewing the virtues as parts of a whole in the way the parts of a face – the mouth, nose, eyes and ears – are parts of it; or parts in the way portions of gold are parts of a mass of gold (329c5–d8). The parts of the face mentioned here are sense organs, and it appears to be this aspect of theirs that is the basis of the analogy. Protagoras agrees that they are distinguished by differences in power (*dunamis*) (330a6; cf. 349b4–5, 359a6–7). The whole of which they are parts, then, appears to be less the face than sensation as a whole or the perceptual system.

The senses share a common purpose or function. To put it very crudely, they furnish the human being or animal to whom or to which they belong with information about his or its environment, but they do this in different ways and by means of distinct powers. Political virtue or virtue complete, on this analogy, consists of parts or component virtues with a common purpose – roughly making political communities possible by making their

[4] Protagoras speaks of 'a *man's* virtue' here, but a few lines later he says that anyone who lacks it, man, woman or child, must be made to acquire it (325a7).

members able to participate in and contribute to common life – but each of them advances this purpose in a very different way. It is possible to lose one sense organ or the use of it while the others remain unaffected, and Protagoras accepts that the analogy holds in this respect as well: one can, he insists, possess one of the virtues without having the others, and there are human beings who are brave but unjust, others who are just but not wise (329e5–6).

A question not yet explicitly posed is whether it is possible by exercising one virtue to perform an action that one of the other virtues forbids. Is it possible, for example, by acting courageously to act unwisely, intemperately, unjustly or in a way that is unholy? If we push the analogy with the senses hard enough, Protagoras' choice of this analogy might imply a very strong view about the independence of the virtues. Each sense is exercised in relation to an entirely different kind of object. Such a view plays an important part in the argument of the *Theaetetus* (184e–185a). If the virtues are like the different senses in this way as well, each having its own entirely independent sphere of operation, then there will be no risk that in exercising one virtue one might offend against another.

2. THE FIRST ARGUMENT: JUSTICE AND HOLINESS (330B8–332A3)

The point of departure for Socrates' first argument is Protagoras' strong claim that none of the virtues is like or such as the others in its power or in other respects (330a). It is unlikely that in making this claim, strong as it is, Protagoras is committing himself to a view as extreme as the one described above. Most likely, he is not entirely sure how independent he takes the virtues to be. One of the purposes of Socrates' questioning, then, will be to force him to clarify his view on this point.

Socrates' first question is whether justice is something or a certain thing (*pragma ti*). The force of this question is not entirely clear. It is sometimes supposed that Socrates is talking about the attribute or form of justice, something like what he has in view in the *Euthyphro* when he speaks of the form itself by which all holy things are holy, or the form by looking to which and by using which as a paradigm one is able to distinguish holy from unholy things (6de). If so, when Socrates goes on to ask Protagoras whether justice is just, he is asking whether justice, i.e. the attribute or the form justice, is predicated of itself. This may be right, but, in common with others, I am inclined to suppose that the justice at issue is the virtue, i.e. the state of character that just people have and unjust people lack.[5]

At this point, there is a curious and possibly significant change in the form of Socrates' remarks beginning with the question whether (the virtue of) justice is itself just (330c2–5). Up to this point, Socrates has put questions directly to Protagoras. Now he asks Protagoras what the two of them should say if a third party were to ask them a question; he then says how he – Socrates – would respond, and he asks Protagoras whether he would do the same.

The next pair of questions that Socrates poses in this way are about whether holiness is also something and, if so, whether it is holy. For his part, Socrates says that he would answer that it is something and is holy, and Protagoras readily agrees that he would do the same (330d5–e2). After having Protagoras confirm his thesis, viz. that no one of the virtues is like or such as another, Socrates proceeds to pose questions with a view to discovering whether this thesis commits Protagoras to denying that holiness is such as to be just and justice such as to be holy (331a7–b8). Here the fact that Socrates is not putting the question directly to Protagoras, but asking him how he would respond were someone else to put the question to him, may be significant. For in his question the imaginary questioner suggests that, if holiness is not just and justice is not holy, then they must be unjust and unholy respectively.[6] And this will follow only on certain assumptions that it cannot be taken for granted that Protagoras accepts. There is no general rule that would permit us to infer, for any subject S and predicate F, that the contrary of F belongs to S from the fact that S is not F, though, when restricted to certain subjects S and predicates F, such an inference will be perfectly legitimate (cf. Aristotle, *Cat.* 10, 11b38–12a9).

Perhaps Socrates' aim in posing these questions indirectly in this way is to avoid committing himself to this questionable inference and to put the burden on Protagoras to say whether or not the inference is valid in the present case and why. If so, Protagoras does not rise to the challenge. Later in the dialogue he will distinguish between things that are beneficial to human beings, harmful to them and neither beneficial nor harmful to them (334a3–5), and maintain that some pleasures are neither good nor bad (351d4–7). And depending on how independent he takes the virtues

[5] On this point see Penner 1973: 39–42, who helpfully cites *Laches* 190b–c.

[6] At 330c5 and 330d5 Socrates, or rather the figure Socrates imagines posing questions, has already treated just and unjust and holy and unholy as exclusive and exhaustive alternatives. Is the questioner already guilty of confusing contraries and contradictories, or should these pairs be understood as contradictories here, before the more fine-grained distinction of 331a9–b1 (as Taylor 1991: 113 suggests)?

of justice and holiness to be, it is open to him to do the same here by maintaining that holiness, though not just, does not offend against justice and is therefore not unjust, and that justice, though not holy, does not offend against holiness and is therefore not unholy. (It is safe to assume that the position that justice is unholy and holiness unjust is out of bounds; otherwise it would be impossible for these virtues to form any kind of unity, including that which Protagoras has been calling the virtue of a man.)

Instead Protagoras says that matters are not so simple and that he is not obliged to concede that justice is holy or holiness just. This seems to show that he rejects the suspect inference (331b8–c2). Yet, rather than saying so explicitly and explaining in more detail what he takes the relation between the virtues of justice and holiness to be, he tells Socrates that, if he likes, they can assume justice is holy and holiness just (331c2–5).

This elicits a strong objection from Socrates: 'it is not "if you like" or "if you wish" that I want to see examined and refuted, but you and me' (331c6–7). The point is not that it is only the sincerely held convictions of an interlocutor that are worthy of dialectical examination. Twice later in the dialogue Socrates examines a view that is not held by Protagoras, who merely undertakes to say what others would say (333c3–6; 352d3–353b6). Rather it appears that Protagoras is at fault because he now proposes to abandon the view that he had undertaken to defend without saying whether he has been compelled to do so by the argument. If he is permitted to do this, it will be unclear what we have learned from that argument.

In response to this challenge, Protagoras is willing to admit that in some way or other any two items are like or such as one another, even opposites and the parts of a face, and that in this way the virtues of justice and holiness can be viewed as alike (331d). Socrates asks whether it is only in this way, by sharing some small point of similarity, that justice and holiness are alike (331e4–6). Protagoras thinks not, but he insists that they are not similar in the way that Socrates thinks they are either. The first argument, then, ends in something of a muddle. It seems to have become clear in the course of it that Protagoras is unwilling to subscribe to the most extreme claims about the independence of justice and holiness, but it remains unclear what the argument has shown and precisely what Protagoras is willing to concede.

Much of the blame belongs to Protagoras, who is plainly reluctant to be refuted. But as we have seen, Socrates' questioning has not always been as straightforward as it might be, and if Protagoras feels as though traps are being set for him, it is not without cause. We should also note that Socrates shows, and will continue to show, a tendency to overstate the results to which he is entitled. He invites Protagoras to respond to the question whether holiness is just and justice holy by agreeing that justice is either the same thing as holiness or most like to it of all things (331b4–7). And in the course of the next argument he refers back to this argument as though its conclusion had been that justice and holiness were pretty much the same thing (333b5–6). But even if holiness is like justice in being just and justice like holiness in being holy – something that, as we have observed, may not have been established – this does not require that they are identical or nearly identical.

It may even be that Socrates' impatience to secure this stronger result prevents Protagoras from making the concessions he should make or would be willing to make. If the way in which Protagoras supposes that Socrates thinks justice and holiness are alike is by being identical or nearly identical, rejecting this may be compatible with allowing that justice is holy and holiness just.

3. THE SECOND ARGUMENT: TEMPERANCE AND WISDOM (332A5–333B6)

The next argument is about the virtues of temperance and wisdom. In some important ways it is an improvement over the previous argument. Socrates puts his questions directly to Protagoras, who answers each of them unequivocally. In the end, though not without reluctance, he concedes that a conclusion at odds with his position follows. Nonetheless, I should like to suggest that, though to a lesser extent and in a more subtle way, Socrates is guilty of the same tendency to overstate the results to which he is entitled and to ask more of the argument than, properly understood, it can really give. Thus though the argument further undermines Protagoras' original thesis about the independence of the virtues, it does not do so to the extent that Socrates supposes.

'Temperance' is the received translation for *sōphrosunē*, which tradition, much strengthened by Aristotle, conceives as the virtue governing behaviour in relation to bodily pleasure. 'Self-control' or 'moderation' are also favoured translations. Later in the dialogue, Protagoras treats ἀκολασία, license or intemperance, as its opposite (349d7). But *sōphrosunē* also means soundness of mind or good sense.

The argument hinges on two principles. According to the first, each thing has only one opposite. The second is a principle of coordination, according to which something done in a certain way, say F-ly, is done by or with (the instrumental dative or ὑπό or μετά with the genitive) F, and what is done in the opposite way is done by or with the opposite of F (332c1–2; cf. a8–b1, b5–7, d3–4, d6–e3). The argument begins with Protagoras' concession that folly (*aphrosunē*) is the opposite of wisdom (332a5–7). Socrates proceeds to build a case for the conclusion that acting foolishly and acting temperately are opposites, which Protagoras concedes (332b). It then follows, by the principle of coordination, that that by or with which what is done temperately is done, viz. temperance, is the opposite of that by or with which what is done foolishly is done, viz. folly. But as Protagoras has already agreed that each thing can have only one opposite and that the opposite of folly is wisdom, he is under pressure to agree that wisdom is the same thing as temperance. He must, as Socrates explains, either give up the claim that each thing has only one opposite or the claim that wisdom and temperance are each parts of virtue, different and dissimilar in themselves and in their powers in the way that the parts of a face are different from each other (333a1–b3).

The scope of the coordination principle on which so much depends is unclear. At first it seems to apply to something like dispositions or faculties and the actions to which they give rise, e.g. the virtue of temperance and temperate actions. But Socrates also gives as examples: what is done strongly and the strength with which it is done, what is done weakly and the weakness with which it is done, what is done speedily and the speed with which it done and what is done slowly and the slowness with which it is done (332b7–c1). And this suggests that Socrates may have in mind a more general metaphysical principle of coordination between acts done F-ly and the form or attribute F. Though Socrates does not explicitly say so, he may think it applies to the sample opposites he mentions: the noble and the base, the good and the bad, the high (in pitch) and the low (in pitch) (332c3–8). If this is so, and the argument is about the attributes foolish, wise and temperate, or could be applied to them, we would then be faced with the result that what it is to be temperate is what it is to be wise, which I have been assuming is unwelcome, rather than the desired conclusion that the virtues of wisdom and temperance are the same.

In any case, there is already a problem with Socrates' argument that acting temperately is the opposite of acting foolishly. Socrates asks Protagoras if he thinks that when human beings act rightly and beneficially they are temperate in so doing (332a7–9). Protagoras is happy to agree. He also readily agrees that it is by temperance that they are temperate. What is more, he is also willing to accept that those who act incorrectly act foolishly and are not temperate in so acting and that, therefore, acting foolishly is the opposite of acting temperately (332b4). The inference marked by 'therefore' is open to question, however.[7] Does the fact that acting foolishly is incompatible with acting temperately require that if one acts foolishly one is thereby acting intemperately? If so, it is not on the strength of a general principle that would allow us to conclude that one behaves in the way that is opposite to F-ly if one is behaving not-F-ly, though it may be true that temperance and intemperance are so related that if one is behaving not-temperately one is behaving intemperately.[8] Nor does it seem to have been shown that if one acts, but not temperately, one thereby acts foolishly.

With the aid of some plausible assumptions, the argument can be made to yield the result that all and only those who act not temperately act foolishly, which might be thought to be close enough if to behave in a way that is not temperate is to behave intemperately.[9] But even if one can be intemperate if and only if one acts foolishly and be temperate if and only if one acts in the way contrary to this, viz. wisely, this does not show that being temperate is the opposite of being foolish and it does not follow that acting foolishly is the same thing as being intemperate or that acting wisely is the same thing as being temperate. Though one can be temperate if and only if one behaves wisely and be intemperate if and only if one acts foolishly, each member of the pair, being temperate and acting wisely, and each member of the pair, being intemperate and acting foolishly, may be distinct from the other and have its own opposite.

For purposes of comparison, suppose that all and only those who act in a way hateful to the gods are impious and that all and only those who act in a way dear to the gods are pious. One could, then, act in a way opposite or contrary to piously, i.e. impiously, if and only if one behaves in a way hateful to the gods, but behaving impiously would not on this account be the same thing as behaving in a way hateful to the gods, and it would not be behaving in a way hateful to the gods that is the opposite of behaving piously, but behaving impiously.

If, as I suspect, the considerations that Socrates has assembled will actually support only a conclusion about the coextensiveness of wise and temperate behaviour, Protagoras assents too readily when he agrees that acting foolishly is the opposite or contrary of acting temperately (332b4–5). The principle of coordination will establish only that as all and only wise behaviour is temperate, each instance of such behaviour must be by or with

[7] Vlastos 1956: XXIX, n. 19.

[8] An idea which seems especially plausible if one follows Taylor 1991 in translating *sōphronōs* as 'sensibly'.

[9] Cf. Taylor 1991: 124–5.

both temperance and wisdom; it will not establish the identity of wisdom and temperance.

If Socrates once again overstates the results to which he is entitled, it is nonetheless true that the more modest argument to which he is entitled undermines Protagoras' claim about the independence of the virtues. Even if the virtues of temperance and wisdom are not the same, it now seems that one can be present only if the other is and each exercise of one must at the same time be an exercise of the other. Nonetheless Protagoras is within his rights if he is dissatisfied with the argument and puzzled about why the conclusion Socrates wants to draw should be true.

4. THE THIRD ARGUMENT: TEMPERANCE AND JUSTICE (333B7–334C6)

The next argument begins without a pause. It will break down before a conclusion can be reached. Socrates begins by asking whether it is possible for a human being acting unjustly to be temperate in so acting (333b). Protagoras is firmly of the opinion that it is impossible, though he acknowledges that many people think otherwise. Unlike the original question about the parts of virtue, this question is plainly about whether an action which displays one virtue can offend against another by displaying the corresponding vice.

In response to Socrates' next query, Protagoras says that he should like to have the argument directed against the view of the many people who think it is possible to be temperate in acting unjustly *first*.[10] Socrates makes it a condition for his participation that Protagoras answer on behalf of those who hold this view. 'As long as you answer,' he says, 'it makes no difference to me whether they are your beliefs or not. For it is the thesis itself that I am most concerned to examine, though most likely I the questioner and you the answerer will be examined as well' (333c6–10). There is nothing odd about this arrangement. Quite generally it is both the thesis and the answerer's defence of the thesis that are put to the test in dialectic. Aristotle recognizes a form of dialectic in which the questioner undertakes to uphold the thesis of another person as that other person would uphold it (*Top*. 8.5, 159b27–35). The answerer's function is to conduct the discussion so that he is defeated, if he is defeated, not through his own weakness, but through

[10] It is curious that the alternative Protagoras rejects would presumably require Socrates to attempt a refutation of the view that it is not possible to be temperate in committing an injustice, which he presumably shares with Protagoras. Protagoras' request that the argument be directed against the view he rejects *first* is also odd, as it suggests that he expects that the argument will then be directed against him and his view.

the weakness of the thesis (*Top.* 8.4, 159a20–4). The refutation of a poorly defended thesis tells us nothing about the weakness of the thesis, just as the failure of an incompetent questioner to secure a refutation tells us nothing about its strength.

But Socrates may intend something more by his remark, namely that the examination of the view held by many will have implications for Protagoras' own views about the relations between the virtues. If so, this would be another way in which the argument serves as a kind of rehearsal for the discussion of pleasure and *akrasia*, in which Protagoras answers on behalf of the many although the views of theirs that are under examination are ones that he explicitly rejects. And this might also explain why Protagoras bridles at the direction the argument takes, a development that is otherwise surprising since it is not Protagoras' own view, but one which he firmly repudiates, that stands to be refuted. Another possibility, compatible with the first, is that Protagoras objects, perhaps justly, to Socrates' style of arguing.

After agreeing, for the sake of argument, that someone acting unjustly may in so doing be temperate, Protagoras agrees that by being temperate he means to think or reason well and that reasoning well in such a case is deliberating well regarding the injustice in question (333d6). Next Socrates asks whether it is if agents performing an injustice fare well or if they fare poorly that they deliberate well. 'If they fare well,' Protagoras replies. It is Protagoras' response to Socrates' next question that brings the discussion to a halt. Socrates wants to know whether things beneficial to human beings are good. Protagoras takes the opportunity to hold forth on the variety and multifariousness of the good, apparently a favourite theme of his and one much to the taste of the audience gathered in Callias' house, who break into applause (334a2–c8). Socrates complains that the answer is too long. Protagoras objects that it is not for Socrates to set limits to the length of the answers he is permitted to give. The discussion gives way to the procedural dispute, which is followed, after an agreement to pursue a new subject is reached, by the discussion of Simonides' poem.[11]

5. THE FOURTH ARGUMENT: COURAGE AND WISDOM (349A6–351B3)

At the end of the discussion of Simonides' poem Socrates suggests that they return to what he regards as more fitting subjects and a more seemly form

[11] There has been much discussion of the argument broken off here and whether Protagoras' disquisition on the good is a distracting irrelevance or not. See McKirahan 1984 for a reconstruction of the argument which views Protagoras' remarks as a sensible attempt to forestall Socrates' next move.

of discussion (347c). In the next argument Socrates attempts to establish that courage – the virtue that has not yet been the subject of an argument – is identical with wisdom. It is set out rapidly and elliptically. Parts of it lend themselves to different readings, the choice between which has dramatic consequences for the interpretation of the argument as a whole. It is, however, conducted in the cooperative spirit that Socrates has just called for. And though it fails, it is an instructive failure, as it inspires Socrates to construct a new and more promising case for the identity of wisdom and courage, though one that is not without problems of its own.

The discussion begins with Socrates' summary of the position that Protagoras had taken in response to the little question posed after the great speech (349a9–c5; cf. 329b6–d8, 359a4–7). Protagoras' position, as summarized by Socrates, was that corresponding to each of the virtue terms is a separate being, each with its own power and not such as the others. Protagoras declines to take up Socrates' suggestion and to pretend – for that is what it would be – that he took this position in order to put Socrates to the test. Instead he proposes to defend a revised position that yields some ground to Socrates. He now maintains that the items they have been discussing are all parts of virtue, but that the four already discussed are quite similar, while courage is very different from the others (349d2–4).

Protagoras has, then, conceded that stronger versions of the independence thesis have been undermined. He does not, however, agree that the four virtues so far considered are identical with one another, which, as we have seen, Socrates sometimes seems to think his arguments have established.

According to Protagoras, one can find many people who are most unholy, intemperate, or unwise and yet exceptionally courageous (349d4–8). Though the point is not made explicitly, it appears that, in maintaining that many people who lack the four parts of virtue other than courage, indeed have the corresponding vices, are courageous, Protagoras is not simply saying that these states can belong to the same person at the same time, but that this person may perform acts that display courage while they offend against the other virtues by displaying the vices opposed to them.

The argument sets out from two propositions to which Protagoras readily assents (349e1–8).

(1) The courageous are bold.

(2) Virtue is something honourable (*kalon*).

Proposition (1) appears to treat as equivalent the claims that people who are courageously disposed are boldly disposed and the claim that actions displaying courage display boldness. Proposition (2) is affirmed with considerable enthusiasm by Protagoras. Unless he is mad, he says, it is the most honourable thing there is, and when asked whether it is wholly honourable or in part honourable, in part shameful, he asserts that it is wholly honourable. It too appears to imply corresponding claims about persons and actions. But if a person with a vice has a shameful characteristic and an action displaying a vice is thereby shameful, the fact that each virtue is wholly honourable cannot imply that the actions to which it gives rise cannot also be shameful in some respect and that persons who have it lack any shameful characteristics. Presumably a courageous action or person need be honourable only insofar as he or it is courageous.

Socrates proceeds to pose a series of questions about whether people with expert knowledge display boldness in activities belonging to the sphere to which their expertise relates, expert divers in diving, expert cavalrymen in cavalry operations and so on. Quick to recognize a classic Socratic induction, Protagoras volunteers the general truth for which Socrates is building a case (350a6–8): 'If this is what you seek, the knowledgeable are bolder than those without knowledge and bolder after they have learned than before.' Socrates then asks whether Protagoras knows of people who are ignorant of forms of activity like those already mentioned, but who nevertheless act boldly in them. 'Indeed', says Protagoras, 'only too boldly' (350b3). 'Are these bold people then also courageous?' is Socrates' next question. Protagoras thinks not, as courage would then be something shameful in this case since these people are mad.

Presumably the reasoning here is based on proposition (2). As a wholly honourable thing, the virtue of courage must give rise to behaviour that is honourable. It need not be honourable in every respect, but the boldness which is an essential characteristic of courage cannot fail to be honourable. Boldness due to madness is shameful and therefore not honourable. Therefore this boldness cannot be courageous or a product of courage. Note that Protagoras sees this remark as a clarification of his first claim, not as correcting or replacing it. The first claim, according to which those with knowledge are bolder than those lacking it and bolder than they were before they acquired it, was meant, it transpires, to hold other things being equal or in the absence of further qualification. Protagoras' attention was concentrated on dangerous tasks that fall under different forms of expertise and the contribution made by the relevant expertise to the boldness with which the task is performed – with all other factors excluded. Mad people might attempt a task requiring expertise that they lack with as much or more boldness as an expert, but this does not undermine Protagoras' point.

Though it is not explicitly stated, it seems that both Socrates and Protagoras suppose that being done knowledgeably is sufficient to prevent a bold action from being shameful (viewed simply as a display of boldness). This means that being done in ignorance is a necessary condition for an act of boldness to be shameful as such. The way Protagoras answers Socrates' question makes it seem as if he also thinks that being done in – technical – ignorance is a sufficient condition to make a bold action an instance of shameful boldness. If this were so, then all and only ignorantly bold actions would be instances of shameful boldness. If we suppose, plausibly enough, that acts of the kinds that we are concerned with are either performed ignorantly or with knowledge and that bold acts that are not shameful must be honourable (cf. 360b), then all and only bold actions that are performed knowledgeably are honourable. If all and only honourably bold behaviour is courageous behaviour, then it is plausible to suppose that knowledge is what makes such behaviour honourable and therefore courageous and that, as what makes courageous behaviour courageous, knowledge is courage.

It is this line of reasoning that Socrates seems to express in very compressed form. 'These who are bold in this way are not courageous but seem mad, but *there* (ἐκεῖ), on the other hand [i.e. among those who are bold but not in this way], the wisest are the most bold, and being most bold are most courageous. And according to this argument, wisdom would be courage' (350c1–6). The superlatives are presumably here to suggest that in episodes of honourable boldness the boldness is proportional to the level of knowledge, so that knowledge can be viewed as somehow causing honourably bold, and therefore courageous, behaviour.

It now emerges that Protagoras did not think that acting ignorantly was sufficient to make a bold action shameful. It only looked this way because he was attending to a certain kind of case that contrasts most sharply with bold action that has its source in expert knowledge. His remarks would have been clearer had he said that 'other things being equal' or 'with other factors removed from consideration', facing dangers without the knowledge that allows an expert to reduce or eliminate the risk is mad and therefore shameful. It now appears that, on his view, it is possible to act boldly in a sphere about which one lacks expert knowledge without being mad and without acting shamefully. Indeed it is precisely this kind of action that is courageous. And he maintains that Socrates has failed to show that courage is the same thing as wisdom from the premisses that he has conceded. He illustrates his objections with an analogous argument for the conclusion that strength is wisdom (350d6–351a4).

Protagoras says that he would agree that those who know how to wrestle are more powerful (*dunatos*) than those who lack this knowledge, and the former are more powerful after they have learned than before learning. It emerges that he also thinks that madness can make people powerful as it can make them bold. But he does not think that the cases of power that remain after those due to madness are removed from consideration are all due to knowledge; some are, but others have their source in strength, which is distinct from knowledge. Just as not all cases of power that do not spring from madness are cases of strength, so too not all cases of boldness untainted by madness are cases of courage. Strength, unlike knowledge and madness, is a matter of nature and the good nurture of bodies; courage a matter of nature and the good nurture of souls (351a3–4, b2–3). Thus strength is a source of powerful behaviour to be set beside, rather than identified with, knowledge, and in the same way courage is a source of bold behaviour to be set beside knowledge and not identified with it.[12]

At any rate, this is the conclusion Protagoras seems to be driving at. It has to be admitted, however, that his own statements are less than ideally clear. It may be that Plato wants us to see not only the faults in Socrates' argument, but Protagoras' imperfect grasp of them. Protagoras begins by saying that, though he was asked whether the courageous are bold and agreed that they were, he was never asked whether the bold are courageous and would have said that not all are (350c7–d1). It is technically true that this question was never put to him. But the answers that Protagoras has given make it perfectly plain how he would have answered it. Since he thinks that some bold behaviour is not courageous because, being tainted with madness, it is not honourable, he must suppose that not all bold behaviour is courageous. And Socrates' argument does not rely on the illegitimate assumption that all bold behaviour is courageous. It relies on the more plausible, though still illegitimate, assumptions that bold behaviour that is not shameful is honourable and courageous and that such behaviour is convertible with knowledgeable behaviour.

Equally odd is Protagoras' apparent claim that the analogous argument goes wrong by assuming that the powerful are strong when it is only true, and has only been conceded, that the strong are powerful (350e6–8). As we have seen, the suspect step is to suppose that cases of power that are

[12] If all confident behaviour that is not shameful is honourable, as the argument gives us reason to believe, courage is a type of honourable boldness but not the only one. If courageous action is convertible with honourable bold action, then there must be some bold behaviour that is neither honourable nor dishonourable.

not tainted by madness are all episodes of strength and convertible with episodes of powerful behaviour due to knowledge.

Perhaps the way that Socrates presents his argument has contributed to the confusion. Recall that he said: 'These who are bold in this way are not courageous but seem mad, but *there* (ἐκεῖ) on the other hand [i.e. among those who are bold but not in this way] the wisest are the most bold, and being most bold are most courageous' (350c1–5). Here Socrates does seem to think that, in cases untainted by madness, the bold are courageous. Protagoras was not given a chance to say whether he agreed, and as we have seen, he does not. If Protagoras' objection is that he is unfairly being credited with accepting the principle that the bold are courageous under these restrictions, he is on firm ground. But if this is what he means to say, he has been exceptionally unclear about it.

Quite apart from these problems in the argument, the conclusion at which Socrates seems to be driving is highly suspect. If courage is knowledge, it would be very odd if it were to be identified with a form or forms of technical expertise. Problems are raised for this idea in the *Laches* (192e–193c). What is more, forms of specialized expertise would, like courage as Protagoras conceives it, fall foul of the argument found in the *Meno*, according to which, as a good, virtue must always benefit (87e–88d; cf. *Euthydemus*, 280b–281e).

6. PLEASURE AND *AKRASIA* (351B4–358A1)

Socrates plunges into a new argument immediately. For excellent reasons, it has been the object of a great deal of attention. Among other things, it contains the first sustained systematic discussion of *akrasia*. It also lays the foundation for a renewed assault on the relation between wisdom and courage. After a short transitional passage, in which Prodicus, Hippias and possibly others join the conversation at Socrates' invitation (358a1–359a1), discussion of this question resumes between Protagoras and Socrates. And this time, Socrates succeeds in winning Protagoras' – grudging – assent that courage is wisdom. This argument is, and is intended to be seen as, an advance over the first argument. In what follows I shall focus on the contribution the section on *akrasia* makes to the final argument about courage and wisdom.

The argument begins with Socrates' attempt to secure Protagoras' assent to the proposition that to live pleasantly is good and to live painfully bad (351c1). Protagoras is happy to agree that living pleasantly is good provided that the pleasure is taken in things that are honourable. This is not what

Socrates meant. 'Are pleasures good insofar as they are pleasant and pains bad insofar as they are painful?' he asks. Protagoras demurs (351c4–7): 'it seems safer to me, considering not only the present answer but also the rest of my life in its entirety, to reply that there are some pleasures that are not good, some pains that are not bad, others which are and a third class that are neither good nor bad' (351d2–7). This is an unexceptionable view, which admirers of Aristotle will likely applaud. By putting his answer in this way, Protagoras has made it absolutely plain that he is moved not just by dialectical caution lest, by conceding this point, he be compelled to contradict his thesis about the virtues, but also, and especially, by strong and sincere conviction. Nevertheless he pronounces himself willing to examine the question, which he takes to be whether pleasant and good are the same thing (351e3–7).

But the expected inquiry does not come, or does not come in the expected form. Comparing himself to someone, perhaps a physician, who examines a man to see if he is healthy and fit by looking first at his face and then his back and chest, Socrates asks Protagoras to expose another part of his mind by saying where he stands with regard to knowledge. Perhaps the implication is that Protagoras' responses so far show him to be healthy so far as his attitude towards pleasure is concerned. In any case, Socrates goes on to explain his meaning: does Protagoras share the view of the many, according to which knowledge is nothing strong and not the leading or ruling element (*hēgemonikon*)? On this view, as Socrates explains, it often happens that, though a person has knowledge, he is not ruled or guided by it, but is instead directed by something else, sometimes passion (*thumos*), sometimes pleasure, sometimes pain, sometimes love, often fear. In sum, says Socrates, they think of knowledge as a slave that is dragged in every which way by these items (352b2–c2). The alternative is to suppose that knowledge rules a human being so that someone who knows what is good and bad can be compelled by nothing else to act otherwise than as knowledge bids (352c2–7).

The latter is Protagoras' view and Socrates' as well (352c8–d4). Socrates now proposes that he and Protagoras make common cause by attempting to persuade the many that they are wrong about the occurrence which they call being bested or defeated by pleasure and failing on that account to do what one knows is best (352e4–353a2). Asked why they should waste their time investigating the view of the many, Socrates replies that it will aid them in their inquiry about courage and how it is related to the other virtues (353a6–b2).

Embedded in the case against *akrasia* is an argument for the thesis about pleasure that Protagoras had declined to accept. But like the whole case of which it is a part, this argument turns on premisses that are admitted because they are the views of the many, not because Protagoras accepts them *in propria persona*. This point is relentlessly emphasized. Over and over again, Socrates asks Protagoras whether the many would say such and such when questioned, and Protagoras' answers are about what they would say.[13]

With the collaboration of Protagoras, Socrates shows that, when the many speak of a pleasurable action as bad, it can only be because the pleasure it affords is outweighed by the pain it causes and that, when they speak of a painful action as good, it can only be because the pain it gives is outweighed by the pleasure it causes (353c1–354b6). Protagoras then agrees that it is only by reference to pleasure and pain that the many are able to call anything good or bad; of the actions open to someone, the one that will cause the most pleasure or least pain is good, the one that will cause the most pain or least pleasure bad (354b6–c3).

These results are then used to show that the many's view that it is possible for someone not to do what he knows is best is absurd, as nothing in reality answers to the many's description (355a6, b4, d1). An action that is in fact bad can only be so because it is painful or more painful than the right one on the occasion, right because it is the most pleasant or least painful of the actions available to the agent. To know that an action is bad is to know that it is more painful or less pleasant than an available alternative. To say that pleasure was the motive of a person who took this action despite its known badness, then, is nonsense. Someone who is moved by pleasure and knows what is best, i.e. most pleasant, will take that action.

To have knowledge, it now appears, is sufficient to ensure that one will act as is best, i.e. in the way that is most pleasant. If someone does not do what it is best to do, it cannot be because he is overcome by pleasure, but only because he is ignorant of what is most pleasant and therefore best (357d3–5, e1–2).

Socrates' point is open to misunderstanding here. One might think that being ignorant with regard to a certain question is a matter of not being knowledgeable about it, so that someone who judges falsely concerning it, someone who has no view at all and someone whose judgement is true

[13] 353d6–e3, 353e8–354a1, a7–b1, b5–6, c2, d3, e2, 356c2–3, e3–5, 357a3–5, b3–5, 358a1.

but not well enough secured to qualify as knowledge all count as ignorant. Some commentators have therefore thought Socrates goes beyond what has been established in his conversation with Protagoras about what should be said to the many when, in the transitional passage, he says: 'if the pleasant is the good, then no one who either knows or believes that actions different from the one he is performing are better continues doing what he is doing if the others are possible' (358b7–c1). But surely, these commentators object, what has been established is that knowing that an action is best is sufficient to make an actor choose and perform it, not that believing that it is best is sufficient.

The explanation, I take it, is that attention has been focused exclusively on two opposed cases: judging correctly that an action is best *because one knows what is best* and being ignorant *in virtue of having a false opinion about what is best.* In the transitional passage Socrates easily secures everyone's assent to the claim that ignorance is to have a false opinion and to be in the wrong about matters of the greatest consequence (358c4–6). It is critical to the final argument that the coward's mistaken choice of action be the result of ignorance in this sense, that is, that the coward's false belief that an action is best, most honourable and most pleasant be sufficient to make him take that action and that this false belief be the only explanation for his taking it rather than the action that is in fact best. Questions about the effect on action of judgements which, though true, do not qualify as knowledge – judgements of the kind discussed in the *Meno* (96e5–98a8) – drop out of consideration; for the purposes of this argument, the only way to judge correctly is to have knowledge.[14]

If this suggestion is on the right lines, if someone knows or thinks an action is best, he will take it, and every time someone takes an action, it will be because he knows or thinks it is best. If people are to act reliably for the best, then, they must have knowledge; and Socrates goes on to say something about the kind of knowledge that will eliminate errors about the relative magnitude of pleasures and pains. What is required is a kind of measuring art, which will compensate for the errors that arise when present pleasures and pains are compared with future pleasures and pain, errors that are akin to those which affect efforts to judge the relative sizes of objects at different distances from the observer (356c4–b2).

These results appear to depend on taking pleasure to be the good (cf. 358b7). But what is the status of this assumption? Though he tries to get Protagoras and the other sophists to accept it, Socrates never commits

[14] Cf. Gulley 1971; on the underlying issues, see Segvic 2000: 27–30.

himself to this view.[15] The distance he maintains stands in stark contrast to his open avowal of the view that knowledge cannot be dragged around like a slave (352d3–4). As we have seen, Protagoras is also unwilling to commit himself to it (351d2–7). If this remains Protagoras' view, the question arises why he is made so uncomfortable by a result that ultimately rests on premisses which he rejects. But even if, as much evidence suggests, Protagoras does come round to hedonism in the transitional passage, there remains a question about what force the argument should have for us, or for those of us unpersuaded by hedonism.

These questions are best tackled while examining the transitional passage and the final argument about courage and wisdom for which it prepares the way. But there is a clue in the discussion that may bear on the issue. Though it is elaborated in connection with the assumption that the best available action is the one productive of the most pleasure, there are hints that the case that the one thing that is necessary to act as is best is knowledge can be generalized. Socrates suggests that if faring well (*eu prattein*) lay in selecting longer rather than shorter lengths, our salvation (*sōtēria*) would be the art of measuring length (356c8–e3); if it lay in the selection of odd and even numbers, it would be arithmetic (356e5–357a3).

Apart from pleasure, none of the items considered stands a chance of being the cause of faring well. If we could be confident that pleasure was the only item that belonged both on the list of possible causes of faring well and on that of possible objects of a measuring art, then doubts about whether pleasure is the good would tend to undermine the results Socrates goes on to draw. But it is far from clear that we can impute such a view to the author of the *Protagoras* or to the character Socrates. And at least since Aristotle, readers of the dialogue have supposed that the problems that Socrates raises for *akrasia* do not disappear if one gives up hedonism. If Protagoras does not accept that pleasure is the good, he may nonetheless be troubled by the results of the final argument because it depends less on a commitment to hedonism than on a more general understanding of virtue which, as a believer in the power of knowledge, he is not in a position to reject.

7. THE TRANSITIONAL PASSAGE (358A1–359A1)

The transitional passage begins: 'These are the things we should have said responding to the many, but I ask you, Hippias and Prodicus, along with

[15] This claim is not entirely uncontroversial. For a brief recent discussion, see Annas 1999: 167–71.

Protagoras – for let the discussion be common to you as well – whether you think what I say is true or false' (358a1–4). After securing an enthusiastic answer to his question – 'the things said seemed true to everyone' – he continues: 'Do you therefore agree that pleasure is good, pain evil?' At Socrates' invitation, Prodicus takes the lead in answering: 'Prodicus agreed and so did the others' (358b3). But when Socrates says, 'I ask you whether you think what I say is true or false', is he asking whether it is true that these are the things he and Protagoras should say to the many or is he asking whether, apart from being what he and Protagoras should say, these things are also true? If the former, the 'therefore' in the second question is illegitimate.[16] So perhaps the second question is meant to clear up the ambiguity. If Socrates' interlocutors think that a proposition P that he proposes to put to the many is true, then they must agree that P.

Who is included among the 'others'? Certainly Hippias. I wonder if it may also include the large group of onlookers, whom Plato has referred to before as 'those present' (334c8, 337c5–6, 338b3, e3–4) and, on one occasion, as 'the others' (342a5; cf. 314c2). Does it include Protagoras? Or has Protagoras fallen silent?[17] In marked contrast to the dialogue with the many, the answers to the questions in the transitional passage are characterized in a bewildering variety of ways. Narrating the dialogue, Socrates says 'it seemed so' (358b7); 'it seemed so to all' (358c3, 6; 359a1); and once 'it seemed so to all of us' (358d5). Certainly later in this passage Protagoras seems happy to be included, as we can see from a minor dispute about whether the 'expectation of evil' defines fear and terror, as he and Hippias think, or fear alone, as Prodicus supposes (358d8–e1).

Yet if Protagoras is one of the others who goes along with Prodicus, and he understands the change in the type of questions Socrates is asking, he has casually abandoned the dialectical distance he maintained all through the preceding conversation and reversed the solemn pronouncement of 351d2–7. This would be a strange development for several reasons. The lack of ceremony with which Socrates gets Protagoras to acknowledge that he has changed his mind here would contrast sharply with the scrupulous care he took to determine exactly where Protagoras stands when discussion of the virtues is resumed after the conversation about Simonides, and with the precision with which Protagoras specifies which part of his earlier view about the relation of the virtues he is prepared to abandon and which

[16] Stokes 1986: 213, followed by Manuwald 1999: 416.

[17] Zeyl 1980: 257, thinks so, but that his silence constitutes tacit assent.

part he retains (349a7–d8). And although Protagoras did profess himself willing to consider whether pleasure and the good are the same (351e3–7), it would be odd for him to express his change of heart by falling in behind someone else, and Prodicus of all people. Up to this point, Plato has tended to treat Socrates and Protagoras as though they were on a higher level than the other sophists.[18] When last invited to contribute, in the discussion of Simonides' poem, Prodicus blundered rather badly and had to be corrected by Protagoras and Socrates.[19] What is more, when discussion of courage and wisdom resumes, Protagoras makes his answers in terms of what has been agreed and what follows from what has been agreed (360e5), in a way that suggests he still regards the premisses of the argument as dialectical concessions.[20]

Still, Protagoras may accept hedonism in the transitional passage. The predominance of evidence seems to favour this.[21] And there are several reasons why Plato might have had Protagoras behave in this way. Perhaps he wanted to show Protagoras letting the mask slip and revealing that he was a hedonist all along. Or Protagoras could have been persuaded of the truth of hedonism. More plausible, to my way of thinking, is the idea that Plato is here showing the weakness of Protagoras' grip on the argument. His willingness to follow Prodicus would then be Plato's way of emphasizing this. Plato must have had a reason for bringing Prodicus back into the conversation. But whatever Plato's exact intentions may have been in this passage, I should like to suggest that he meant, among other things, to emphasize the questionable standing of the hedonistic premiss.

[18] Cf. Gagarin 1969.

[19] The interpretative problem arises because Simonides faults Pittacus for saying that it is hard to be good (339c3–5) although, in the same poem, he himself says that for a man to become truly good or truly to become good is hard (339b1–3). Protagoras sees a contradiction here, and Socrates undertakes to acquit Simonides of inconsistency (339c7–d10). To this end, he makes several proposals, At one point, he enlists Prodicus as the acknowledged expert on word meanings. Perhaps, Socrates suggests, in Simonides' dialect the word 'hard' means something like 'bad', so that the fault imputed to Pittacus is that of saying it is bad to be good (341b5–e6). Prodicus obligingly agrees. Protagoras says this is nonsense, and Socrates agrees, observing that the very next line of the poem, 'this prize [being good] is god's alone', proves that it cannot be right. Socrates resorts to the implausible face-saving expedient of saying that Prodicus must have been joking and agreed only to test Protagoras (341d7–9). Prodicus is depicted here as excessively eager to please and desperately anxious to enter the discussion.

[20] Note, for instance, when asked whether we agreed that all honourable actions are good, Protagoras says yes and adds that he has always thought so (359e7–10; cf. 358b6), but a few lines later, when asked whether what is honourable and good is also thereby pleasant, he says only that it was agreed (360a3).

[21] Manuwald 1999: 416 concludes that the evidence suggests that Protagoras is among the others who follow Prodicus' lead.

8. THE FINAL ARGUMENT: COURAGE AND WISDOM AGAIN (359A2–360E6)

At this point, one might wonder whether another argument is really necessary. It was agreed in the discussion of *akrasia* that 'good' and 'pleasant' can be freely substituted for each other when specifying the ultimate object of choice (355b5). It is agreed in the transitional passage that the points already conceded commit the participants in the discussion to agreeing that every action directed (correctly) at pleasure is honourable, and if honourable then good (358b4–6). Protagoras will soon affirm that he is committed by the agreements already reached to accepting that every honourable and good action is pleasant (360a3). And we seem to have discovered that the one thing necessary to ensure the choice of actions that are pleasant, honourable and good is knowledge.

If virtue is a state of character that issues in actions that are honourable, and therefore good and pleasant, the materials for a proof that virtue is knowledge are to hand. If we follow Protagoras in conceiving of courage as a state due to nature and the good nurture of souls whose contribution to complete virtue is to stiffen resolve in the face of danger, one way of interpreting the results reached so far would be to say that courage has been shown to be superfluous as the virtue of wisdom is enough on its own. The alternative is to preserve courage as a virtue by conceiving it as a form of knowledge.

It is this alternative that Socrates will pursue, and one purpose of the last argument is to reveal this. But it also serves to illustrate the progress in argument that I have argued Plato aims to depict in the dialogue. The earlier arguments about the relations between the virtues relied largely on highly abstract principles that made no special reference to virtue, virtuous action or human good and what we might call Protagoras' intuitions about the relations between virtue terms or concepts. I have argued that it is not always clear what the considerations assembled in these arguments actually establish, and that even when it can be determined what they show, they typically fail to provide Protagoras or the reader with an understanding of why it should be true.

Explaining his motives at the end of the dialogue, Socrates says his aim has been to investigate the attributes that hold good of virtue and what virtue itself is (360e7–9). Characteristically he urges a renewed attack on the question what virtue itself is as the best way of clearing up questions about its attributes. But though this task remains to be accomplished, the discussion of *akrasia* has provided at least the beginnings of an understanding of virtue, virtuous action and human good and their systematic relations. It contains gaps, arguably huge ones, and it rests on assumptions that are provisional. Nonetheless it is enough for us to begin to see what an argument about the relations among the virtues put together in the light of an understanding of virtue and the good might look like. This last argument contributes to the understanding of its conclusions at the same time as it establishes them. And by including ingredients that were less than illuminating when they first appeared in earlier arguments, it shows how such argumentative techniques can be put to work in a genuinely illuminating argument.

An important part is played in the last argument by the definition of fear as the expectation of evil, which is accepted in the transitional passage (358d5–e2). Fear entered the discussion in the first argument about wisdom and courage, where Protagoras said the courageous are willing to face dangers from which the many recoil in fear (349e2–3). The definition of fear is immediately brought into connection with the results of the discussion of *akrasia*. If what was said there is true, it is agreed, no one makes for that from which he expects evil, that is, what he fears (358e2–359a1). Protagoras therefore agrees that the common view that the courageous make for what is such as to inspire fear and the cowardly for what inspires confidence cannot be right; no one makes for what he believes to be fearful, but rather for what inspires confidence, i.e. everyone makes for that from which he expects good (359c5–e2). But, observes Protagoras, the courageous and the cowardly make for opposite things, the courageous towards war and the cowardly away from it (359e3–5).

It is now agreed that the courageous make for what is honourable and therefore good (e6–10). This, I take it, is an application of the principle agreed to in the first attempt to establish the identity of wisdom and courage, according to which virtue is an honourable thing (349e3–8). Since it is honourable, the actions to which it gives rise or in which it is displayed must also be honourable. In that argument, however, Protagoras held that it is possible to act courageously while acting foolishly or so as to display another vice. In order to accommodate this position, it was necessary to suppose that an action could be honourable insofar as it displayed courage while being shameful in other respects. In the light of the position explored in the discussion of *akrasia*, according to which there is a single uniform standard of the good, and the agreements it has inspired, this is no longer plausible. For an action to be good, it must be the best available according to this measure. If it is not, then it is not honourable either. And if it is not honourable, it is not the product of courage or any other virtue. Courage can only be displayed in actions that are unqualifiedly honourable and good.

Socrates reminds Protagoras that, if what the courageous make for is honourable and good, it must according to what has been agreed also be pleasant (360a3). But it seems that relation between virtue and good and honourable actions could survive even if hedonism were abandoned, provided that the view of the good that replaces it is of the same general form. Cowards in sharp contrast to the courageous avoid what is honourable, good and pleasant. According to what has been agreed, however, they cannot do so knowing that it is honourable, good and pleasant (360a4–7). The courageous man's views about what to expect evil from, i.e. his fears, and what to expect good from are honourable, while the coward's fears and views about what to expect good from are shameful (360b).

It is now agreed that that through (διά) which cowards are cowards is cowardice. Despite the change in preposition, this is an echo of the coordination principle already used in the discussion of temperance and wisdom (cf. 332b). But it is not the highly abstract principle of unknown scope that figured in that argument, but a principle based on a conception of how states of character cause the behaviours for which they are responsible. And it is applied to the relation between cowardice and cowardly behaviour insofar as it is cowardly, not to cowardly behaviour insofar as it bears an attribute that may only be coextensive with cowardice. On the basis of what has gone before, it is now easy to see that it must be through ignorance of what is and is not to be feared that cowards perform cowardly actions. Reasoning by opposites, which was also employed in the argument about wisdom and temperance, yields the result that courage, as the opposite of cowardice, must be knowledge of what is and is not to be feared. There the fact that each thing has only one opposite was used to show that if two apparently different things, namely wisdom and temperance, were both opposite to one thing, namely folly, they must be the same thing. Here, on the basis of an understanding of what cowardice is, namely ignorance of what is and is not to be feared, it is shown that courage, as the opposite of cowardice, must be identical with the opposite of cowardice so understood. That is, it must be knowledge of what is and is not to be feared.

If the argument of this paper is on the right lines, the *Protagoras* is intended, among other things, to depict a progress in argument. Some of the progress is simply an improvement in cogency. But I have argued that it also includes an advance from what I called merely dialectical argument towards demonstrative or didactic argument. This is an Aristotelian way of putting things; a more Platonic way would describe the advance as a progress within dialectic. The earlier arguments are dialectical in the Aristotelian sense because they rely on principles of the utmost abstractness and generality without taking into account the special features of the matter under discussion, namely human nature and action. They serve to reveal problems with the position Protagoras undertakes to defend, but they are not equal to the task of imparting an understanding of why things should be as they show they are on those occasions when they do succeed in establishing a conclusion. The later arguments differ by coming to grips with the subject under discussion. When the general principles employed in the earlier arguments reappear, it is in the context of a conception, however partial and tentative, of human character and conduct that makes it possible to understand the conclusions reached with their aid and why they should be true – or rather why they should be true *if* the conception of human nature and action on which they depend is correct. The aporetic note on which the dialogue ends warns us not to take that conception as the last word on the subject.[22]

[22] I am grateful to David Berger and Constance Meinwald for very helpful comments on an earlier draft.

CHAPTER 2

Ethics and argument in Plato's Socrates

Julia Annas

I. SYSTEMATIZING SOCRATES

Socrates is a figure in all of Plato's dialogues except the *Laws*; and in all the dialogues in which he occurs, Socrates illustrates something important to Plato about philosophy and the way it should be pursued. However, as soon as we try to think of Socrates as an intellectual personality unified across dialogues, we run into the need to take an interpretative stance.

There has recently been increased focus on the radically different lines taken by developmentalism, which sees Plato's works in terms of an overall development of thought between dialogues, and unitarianism, which leads us to approach Plato in terms of themes across dialogues. In this paper I aim to continue in a constructive and friendly way a debate on this issue with Dorothea Frede, hoping to develop a point of debate between us in a (relatively) new direction. It is a pleasure to offer this paper to Dorothea, whose work on Plato has excited and benefited us all.[1]

Developmentalists see progress from Socrates as negative arguer to Socrates as positive expounder. As far as this development is concerned, we can separate off those dialogues where Socrates takes part only in a short introductory conversation, and the rest is carried on by somebody else, like the Eleatic Visitor or Timaeus. When we look at *Sophist*, *Statesman*, *Timaeus* or *Critias* we find that Socrates' presence in these dialogues is important, but not central to the issue of this development.

In *Phaedo*, *Republic*, *Symposium* and *Phaedrus*, we find Socrates expounding ideas central to our understanding of Platonism: the distinctness of soul from body, the elevating nature of love, the contrast of philosophy

[1] I presented 'What are Plato's "middle" dialogues in the middle of?' (Annas 2002) at a conference in Washington, DC, at which Dorothea replied, defending the virtues of a more developmental approach and also criticizing some claims in Annas 1999. Our resulting contributions to Annas and Rowe 2002 benefited from mutual discussion as well as comments from readers and participants at the conference. The present paper continues my conversation with Dorothea in what I hope is a positive way.

and rhetoric, the centrality of Forms for knowledge and for an adequate account of reality. In others, however, we find him arguing against the claims of others, showing them that their views are confused and they lack the ability to 'give an account' of them. A fairly uncontroversial list of these dialogues is: *Euthyphro*, *Apology*,[2] *Crito*, *Charmides*, *Laches*, *Lysis*, *Hippias Minor*, *Ion* and *Protagoras*. Those who think that the *Hippias Maior* and/or the *Clitopho* are by Plato put them in this group.[3] What Socrates is doing in these dialogues is arguing *ad hominem* in the precise sense: arguing only from the claims made by the interlocutor himself rather than claims of his own, thus showing the interlocutor that he has problems just from holding his own position, independently of Socrates' own views. We have here, in fact, the difference between the sceptical Plato and the doctrinal Plato of the ancient traditions.[4]

Some dialogues appear to be 'mixed' between the two. *Cratylus* and *Philebus* contain stretches of *ad hominem* argument; but it is reasonable to put these dialogues as a whole on the doctrinal side, given that the positive views are not merely what take up most of each dialogue but are what the dialogue is centrally about, while the passages of *ad hominem* argument are very brief.[5] The *Gorgias* and the *Meno* are often seen as 'transitional' from the dialogues of negative argument to those of positive exposition.[6]

Developmentalists cope with this by partitioning Socrates into two: the Socrates who argues *ad hominem* and the Socrates who expounds. This partition can go with a range of views as to who the arguing Socrates is; Socrates the main figure in dialogues can be divided into either the historical Socrates and Plato, or early and later (usually 'middle') Plato. The thought is still that Socrates sometimes argues against others and sometimes expounds

[2] Which is not a dialogue; but this has not been widely taken as a problem for putting it in this group. The same holds true for the *Menexenus*.

[3] *Parmenides* part 1 arguably belongs here, with Parmenides in the Socratic role and young Socrates in the role of the premature dogmatist, but I will not argue the point here. I take no stand here on the minor dialogues like *Lovers* and *Theages* whose authenticity is disputed.

[4] This is a clear distinction, more useful in the present context than an appeal to some modern account of 'Socratic *elenchus*', given the utter lack of agreement on what *elenchus* is.

[5] Here I agree with D. Frede 2002: 29, 'There is one mini-*elenchus* in a long expository discussion (*Philebus* 20e–21d). Though the brief refutation comes at a crucial point in the discussion, it is quite insufficient to justify Davidson's claim that the *Philebus* signifies Plato's renunciation of the theory of Forms and a return to the Socratic method.' Not only does Socrates argue from the views of his interlocutor only briefly, his procedure in no way distinguishes the dialogue; it is the ideas that Socrates puts forward about pleasure which dominate the work.

[6] In the *Meno* the change of approach is strongly marked. The *Republic* also contains a well-marked change of approach, from Book 1 to the rest of the work; various interpretations of this have been given, but all tend to emphasize that the switch underlines the point that the *Republic* as a whole is characterized by positive claims.

Platonic views, but these activities are not readily unifiable to give us a single intellectual personality, and so should be seen as stages of a development.[7]

What I am calling the partition between Socrates the arguer and Socrates the expounder is not, of course, the same as the distinction often drawn between the Socrates of so-called 'early Plato' and the Socrates of 'middle Plato' by scholars who think that this marks a distinction between two philosophical systems. What I have introduced is not this distinction, but one between *ad hominem* reasoning on the one hand and exposition of doctrine on the other. The partition underlies most versions of the distinction, however, since positive doctrine can be ascribed to the Socrates of 'early Plato' only in ways that are indirect and indeterminate by comparison with the straightforward exposition of doctrine by Socrates found in 'middle' Plato.

2. ISSUES ARISING WITH THE *EUTHYDEMUS* AND *THEAETETUS*

There is a nagging problem with the developmentalist idea that arguing from others' views and expounding doctrine are such different forms of philosophical activity that we must locate them in two distinct philosophical personalities. In both *Euthydemus* and *Theaetetus* Socrates is the central figure. Not only does he argue *ad hominem*, this is prominently a theme of the dialogue. In the *Theaetetus* Socrates presents himself as a barren midwife, who helps others to have ideas and test them rather than producing his own. In the *Euthydemus* Socrates' way of arguing with the young Cleinias, encouraging his search for wisdom, is contrasted with that of the sophists, who merely want to win. In both dialogues there is a heavy emphasis on the importance of the philosophically appropriate method. In both cases this is found to be a method which encourages the respondent to have ideas and to engage in testing them rigorously.

Both dialogues, however, contain prominent passages which are as positive and expositional as anything in the doctrinal dialogues. In the *Theaetetus* 'digression' we find claims like the following:

Let us try to put the truth in this way. In God there is no sort of wrong whatsoever; he is supremely just, and the thing most like him is the man who has become as

[7] In this discussion I am focusing only on the issue of *ad hominem* argument versus exposition of doctrine. There are obviously very many differences of style between different dialogues, and also of personality in the less intellectual sense: in some dialogues Socrates is witty and ironical, in others eloquent, in others aggressive, and so on. There are also very obvious differences of content between dialogues where Socrates appears as an erotic figure, competing with sophists or in other contexts.

just as it lies in human nature to be . . . There are two patterns set up in the world. One is divinely and supremely happy; the other has nothing of God in it, and is the pattern of the deepest unhappiness. This truth the evildoer does not see.[8]

In the *Euthydemus* we find Socrates claiming that,

for a man who thinks he ought to get [wisdom] from his father much more than money, and not only from his father but also from his guardians and friends (especially those of his city and elsewhere who claim to be his lovers), and who begs and beseeches them to give him some wisdom, there is nothing shameful, Cleinias, nor disgraceful if, for the sake of this, he should become the servant or a slave of a lover or of any man, being willing to perform any honourable service in his desire to become wise.[9]

The positive assertions are ethical in content, and in the case of both dialogues the passages bring out a strong ethical drive. The *Euthydemus* passage is strongly marked as a protreptic to pursuing wisdom and so virtue; the reader cannot help seeing the young, unformed boy Cleinias as choosing between the course Socrates points out and the crowd-pleasing of the sophists. The *Theaetetus* passage was of course famous in the later ancient world as the proof text for ascribing to Plato the view that our final end is becoming like God; the passage is a powerful encouragement to detach ourselves from worldly concerns and pursue a counter-intuitive, more profound course. The *Euthydemus* can be read as a collection of sophisms, and as an amusing but devastating attack on non-philosophers who try to get into the business of argument,[10] and it is these things, but it is also a passionate defence of the pursuit of virtue, and hence of philosophical wisdom, in a competitive society impressed by flashy show. The *Theaetetus* can be read as an exercise in epistemology, and it is, but it is also a passionate defence of the value of pursuing virtue and hence philosophical wisdom in a competitive and hostile world.

In both cases the philosopher's way of arguing is represented both as aiming at truth, and as caring for the soul of the person participating in argument; these concerns are contrasted with those of people who argue for the sake of winning, or for worldly success, with no concern at all for the ethical improvement of the people they are arguing with. In both dialogues the philosopher's method is presented as that of *ad hominem*

[8] *Tht.* 176c–e, tr. Levett, rev. Burnyeat in Cooper 1997.

[9] *Euthd.* 282a–b, tr. Sprague in Cooper 1997. Socrates asks for Cleinias' assent to this, but it is not seriously in doubt. He also points out that the claim depends on wisdom's being teachable, which has not yet been established, but is satisfied, at least for present purposes, by Cleinias' ready assertion that it is (282c).

[10] Not just the long-dead fifth-century sophists, but contemporaries of Plato like Isocrates.

argument, something which in the *Theaetetus* is taken up and commented on at length in the figure of the barren midwife, as well as being remarked upon several times in the course of the dialogue.[11] In both cases this is part of a strongly marked protreptic towards virtue and wisdom.

But there is something distinguishing these dialogues from other dialogues, often labelled 'Socratic', where we see an equally clear contrast between Socrates' ethically oriented questioning of others and the pontificatings of pompous worldly people like Hippias, and where the contrast is also underlined, in dialogues like *Ion* and *Hippias Maior*, by Socrates' use of a form of argument which takes the interlocutor's position and shows him that he has problems just from holding this position, regardless of Socrates' own views. What, then, is different in the *Euthydemus* and *Theaetetus*? There are passages in these dialogues which do more than urge us to pursue wisdom and virtue by contrasting them with shallow worldly success. These passages are on first reading hard to understand, and they become much more comprehensible in the light of doctrinal dialogues like the *Republic*. To understand them fully we seem to need more theoretical background than is given in the dialogues themselves.

There are two examples of this in the *Euthydemus*, which I present in order of importance. Firstly, it has been argued by Myles Burnyeat that the sophists' arguments about not-being (283a–287d) do not show that Plato is himself hampered by a crude approach to the issues later superseded by the analysis of the *Sophist*. Rather, the *Euthydemus* shows the disastrous effects of bad reasoning on an issue where Plato is already aware of his own more satisfactory answer; the *Sophist* lays out the answer, but the *Euthydemus* more indirectly shows us the danger of playing irresponsibly, as the sophists do, with ideas which require serious treatment.[12]

The second, more dramatic example is the passage at 290b–291a. The callow youth Cleinias claims that generalship cannot be the skill being currently sought, since it is a kind of hunting, and hunters hand their prey over to people better at making use of it. It is, he says, the same as the way intelligent geometers and astronomers and calculators (who are in their own way hunting down results) hand their results over to dialecticians, who know how to make use of their discoveries. 'Did *Cleinias* say all this?' asks Crito, breaking in from the frame dialogue. When Socrates asks in

[11] The most famous midwife passage is 148e–151d. Cf. 161b, 184b, 210b–d.

[12] Burnyeat 2002: 65, 'The *Sophist* gives a straightforward presentation of the puzzles of false statement and their solution. The *Euthydemus* prepares us for this, without competing with the *Sophist*, by showing two people in action controverting the possibility of false statement in the presence of the young. In that context, their bad reasoning verges on the wicked.'

return whether he believes it, Crito says strongly that he does not. Could it have been Ctesippus? suggests Socrates, and when the idea is at once rejected he says that he certainly heard the claim, perhaps from a 'superior being' (*kreitton*) who was present. That sounds right, responds Crito.[13] Here, as Burnyeat reminds us, 'Plato wrote both Cleinias' remarks . . . and the . . . paragraph where Crito refuses to believe that such advanced thinking could have come from anyone but a superior being (e.g. Socrates).' Burnyeat adds, 'I read this as a deliberate cross-reference to the *Republic*, presupposing readers who know that work.'[14] We find a very marked and deliberate commentary on the point that Cleinias is not a plausible source for the point about dialecticians, Crito making it clear that he cannot believe the account offered. The reader's attention is drawn to the dramatic inconcinnity.

Can we then not understand the *Euthydemus* unless we are already familiar with the *Republic*? There is a continuing divergence of opinion, especially over this passage, which indicates that it is possible to make some sense of it without importing understanding of the *Republic*, while it remains puzzling for people not familiar with that work. Perhaps, however, we should consider the thought that this is not a mistake on Plato's part, or mere inadvertent clumsiness, but something he intends. Beginners in philosophy can appreciate the force and ethical purpose of Socrates' methodology, and they are given examples of the kind of result philosophical reasoning can lead to when practised seriously and in a positive vein; but these examples cannot be fully understood until the reader has himself pursued philosophical reasoning in such a positive vein, and read the theoretically much more ambitious and dense central books of the *Republic*. Thus the passage can be fully understood only when we can refer back to the *Republic*; but, as with the puzzles about falsity, we can also read the passage as a deliberate indication of something fully comprehensible only after some further work, from a different kind of dialogue.[15]

In the *Theaetetus* we find, as noted, the claim that '[t]here are two patterns set up in reality. One is divine and supremely happy; the other has nothing of God in it, and is the pattern of the deepest unhappiness. This truth the

[13] I agree with the widely shared view that Crito has Socrates in mind here, while Socrates is more modestly ascribing the thought to some divinity of an unspecified kind.

[14] Burnyeat 2002: 63, n. 46. Cf. Hawtrey 1981: 127–9.

[15] Even after we have read the *Republic* we can still see the point of the reference to a subject that is not made fully comprehensible by its context. Thus we are not supposing that Plato is posing a problem to which he has the answer, while keeping it 'up his sleeve' for the reader to guess at. The relation of the passages is more complex than that.

evildoer does not see . . . For this he pays the penalty of living the life that corresponds to the pattern he is coming to resemble' (176e–177a).[16]

This passage is typical of the problem that the 'digression' raises. We seem here to have a reference to what in the *Republic* are called Forms, the objects of philosophical dialectic. Whether or not they are (and problems are standardly raised about the paradigm of evil), the 'digression' seems to resonate with ideas that we find in the central books of the *Republic.* We find that to come to a proper view of what is good and bad, what are worthwhile and worthless ways of life, we need to turn utterly away from the views about these things prized in our society. The philosopher tries to draw his interlocutor higher up, like philosophers drawing people up out of the Cave, and he does so by turning the discourse away from individual concerns to asking what happiness and misery are themselves – and doing so in the context of kingship (175b–d).

We find a continuing stand-off between scholars like Cornford, who insist that the 'digression' is reaffirming, against Protagoras, the ideas of the *Republic*,[17] and those who take the dialogue to be self-standing and interpret the 'digression' without reference to any other dialogue.[18] (Indeed, the view that the dialogue is self-standing is often conjoined with the view that the dialogue is in some ways critical of positions established in the *Republic.*) Again, the fact that both types of interpretation are viable and defensible suggests that Plato may have allowed for this. We can make sense of the 'digression' without referring to the *Republic*; but referring to that dialogue allows us to make more and better sense of it. We can relate this to the point that Theaetetus is, like Cleinias, a promising and eager learner, who is in the process of having false and confused views removed, in a way preparing him to go on to further, more positive philosophical thinking. The reader, like Theaetetus, is given an example of something that needs further study and work to be grasped properly. After reading the *Republic* the reader can more fully appreciate the passage and the ideas alluded to in it.

Both these dialogues combine, in a way which is strongly underlined, the point that Socrates argues *ad hominem*, from the interlocutor's premisses

[16] Tr. Levett, rev. Burnyeat in Cooper 1997.

[17] Cornford 1957: 83, 'The whole digression is studded with allusions to the *Republic*, and in the course of it the moral Forms are plainly, though unobtrusively, mentioned.' On p. 89 he specifies, 'the allusions to the allegory of the Cave, the passage about the true meaning of kingship, happiness and justice'.

[18] Burnyeat 1990: 37 points out that these two readings of the 'digression' go with what he calls Reading A and Reading B of the dialogue (roughly, a doctrinal and *ad hominem* reading of Socrates' arguments in the dialogue respectively). A doctrinal reading of the 'digression' is compatible with a reading of type B of the dialogue as a whole, if we stress its status as a digression, and thus not part of the dialogue's argument.

rather than his own, *and* the point that Socrates has a strong and positive ethical message; further, this is one which is not just put forward as part of a general contrast with worldly and pompous people but actually makes reference to ideas that are developed explicitly and at length in the doctrinal dialogues. As a result, these dialogues do not fit a story of development from 'early', negative dialogues to 'later', more positive dialogues. We find Socrates the arguer *and* Socrates the expounder as part of the same Socrates within a single dialogue. With the *Theaetetus* in particular, Socrates, on many developmental views, becomes schizophrenic; the intellectual midwife with no offspring of his own also turns out to be someone who retails deep metaphysical truths confidently and at length.[19]

On the story whereby Plato develops from a writer who presents Socrates as arguing against the views of others to someone who uses Socrates as the mouthpiece for positive positions, where do these dialogues fit? Standard developmental stories have nowhere to put the *Euthydemus*, and until recently have dealt with the *Theaetetus* by ignoring the 'digression' passage. And, quite apart from its role as a problem for a developmental account of Plato, what we find in these two dialogues is of enormous importance in its own right: we find Socrates *both* arguing *ad hominem* against the views of others *and* emphasizing a positive ethical project. We also find some results of Platonic philosophical thinking, which in their contexts indicate that the philosophical wisdom developed in progress towards virtue will take a specific form: it will be what is called dialectic in the *Republic*, and the objects which it grasps will be the Forms that we find in the doctrinal dialogues. Socrates the arguer is also Socrates the expounder of doctrine.

If we take this idea seriously we are led to (at least) two points. One is that these two dialogues show us particularly clearly why *ad hominem* argument need not be seen as a stage prior to positive, doctrinal theorizing; the two can be seen as parts of the same enterprise. When Socrates puts forward claims about Forms or dialectic, he need not be seen as having renounced, or moved on from, arguing against others; and when he argues against the views of others he need not be thought to be doing this from nowhere; the midwife of ideas can have plenty of his own, but keeps them separate

[19] I have emphasized this particular difficulty in Annas 1999: ch. 1. Sedley 2004: 13–15 claims that Plato 'was, not unlike Hare, concerned to present his own corpus of work so far as possible as the unfolding of a single project'; I am unconvinced by his interpretation of the *Theaetetus* as an attempt to do this. Hare is an unfortunate choice of model for Plato in this respect, as no serious account of Hare's thought would accept his claims never to have changed his mind on philosophically important matters.

from the examination of those of others.[20] We have two dialogues in which we see exactly this combination. When we face the issue of where in the corpus to put these two dialogues, we see that, rather than being misfits on a supposed time line, they fit well into a corpus which can reasonably be seen as a whole, with dialogues grouped thematically.[21]

The second point relates to Frede's reasonable objections to unitarian readings of Plato. She objects in particular to the Middle Platonist kind of unitarian approach on three grounds: they treated Plato's ideas as monolithic doctrine, something requiring a selective approach; they thought of it as 'a cycle of wisdom that could be entered anywhere', and they thought of Plato as a superhuman figure who could never be wrong. We have to agree, of course, that adulatory and uncritical readings of Plato are unlikely to be fruitful, but thinking seriously about the above passages in the *Euthydemus* and *Theaetetus* may lead us to find a spark of interest in the notion of a cycle as opposed to a straight line. It is an interesting feature of ancient discussions of reading Plato's works that they are innocent of the modern assumption that there is such a thing as *the* order in which to read the dialogues, the main issue being, which it is.[22] It is important not to exaggerate the idea, and of course I would not suggest that we see Plato's entire corpus as a strongly unified monolithic structure. But the systematic difficulty of fitting either of these dialogues into a linear developmental picture suggests that sometimes Plato may have regarded two dialogues as mutually enriching, rather than simply going from the less to the more theoretically developed. We can read the *Euthydemus* before the *Republic*, as an encouragement to the kind of philosophical thinking developed in the longer work; the reference to dialecticians indicates, without fully explaining, the kind of thinking that will be required. After we have read the longer work we can return to the *Euthydemus* and understand that passage better. Further, we can continue to appreciate the protreptic force of the dialogue, and its contrast between Socrates and the sophists, after we have seen the fuller sketch of philosophical development. Each reading of one of the dialogues deepens our appreciation of the other.

Similarly with the *Theaetetus*: the 'digression' recalls the *Republic* in a way that is kept distinct from the dialogue's arguments, for these rule out

[20] This idea is expanded on in Annas 1999: ch. 1. Cf. Sedley 1996: 79–103.

[21] To forestall a still common misunderstanding: what is being rejected is the hypothesis of an overall negative to positive development in Plato's thought; it is of course highly plausible that on some issues Plato's thought developed over time, as Frede stresses in D. Frede 2002: 30–1, 33–4. So this is an argument only against one simple form of overall developmentalism.

[22] Annas 1999: 27 with nn. 44 and 45 for references.

unacceptable accounts of knowledge, leaving open what the true account is. Plato may, as Cornford thought, be pointing back to the *Republic* to remind us of the positive account he has already worked out, and which is taken to be waiting for those who come to understand, through the *Theaetetus*, why the wrong accounts will not do. Or the differences between the 'digression' passage and the *Republic* may indicate that the desired true positive account may differ from that worked out in that dialogue; some of the *Theaetetus*' arguments may indicate that Plato is critical of some of his own ideas as well as those of others. I shall not try to adjudicate this issue here. On either interpretation, working through the *Theaetetus* will greatly increase the reader's appreciation for the positive theory of the *Republic*, and working through the latter will improve our appreciation of indications in the *Theaetetus* of a sharpened sense of some difficulties – with issues of perception, for example. As with the *Euthydemus*, there is no one single 'reading order' for the two dialogues which exhausts their relation; in neither case do we find a simple development.

3. CONNECTING WITH THE *ALCIBIADES*

We may also find that taking the problems of these two dialogues seriously gives us a better approach to understanding the *Alcibiades*, neglected since nineteenth-century scholarship deemed it spurious.[23] For, as Nicholas Denyer has recently reminded us, 'the most serious difficulty for defenders of the authenticity of the *Alcibiades* is the difficulty of fitting the dialogue into what is nowadays the mostly widely accepted account of Plato's literary career' (meaning a developmental account).[24] The *Alcibiades* combines things which elsewhere are kept apart (if, of course, we ignore the *Euthydemus* and *Theaetetus*).

In the *Alcibiades* we find a very heavy emphasis on *ad hominem* argument and its nature. Socrates distances himself from long speech-making at 106b,[25] asking Alcibiades to answer questions. There follow long, carefully spelled-out exchanges (106b–118c) in which Socrates shows Alcibiades that he lacks knowledge on the subjects on which he expected to dominate

[23] Recent scholarship has tended to revert to the ancient acceptance of the dialogue. I argue for its authenticity in Annas 1985: 111–38. Smith 2004: 93–108 rejects authenticity, with arguments which I have tried elsewhere to meet.

[24] Denyer 2001: 20.

[25] This is not in conflict with his giving the long speech at 121a–124b, since that is informing Alcibiades of what he needs to know (almost certainly with much irony, given Alcibiades' later relations with Sparta and Persia), not an attempt to persuade Alcibiades that he needs Socrates, which is what Alcibiades is expecting at 106a.

Athenian politics. The subjects he knows are of no use for politics and he has no specific expertise to offer (106c–109a); he lacks understanding of justice and injustice (109a–113c), and even of what is and is not expedient (113d–116d). Alcibiades is thus reduced to admitting, like other interlocutors, that he is ignorant of what he thought he knew. Socrates emphasizes at length (112d–113b) that Alcibiades' discomfiting admissions are *his*; Socrates has merely questioned him, and it is Alcibiades, the answerer, who has made the admissions. I have been the questioner, Socrates stresses, and you the answerer, so which of us is it who said what was said? It seems to be me, admits Alcibiades (113b).

Socrates also spells out some other points – for example, that there is nothing wrong with repeating an argument if there is no need for a different one. At 113e Socrates chides Alcibiades for wanting a new argument, as though the previous, 'used' one would not do. When Alcibiades finally admits that he feels flummoxed because of constantly shifting his ground (116e), Socrates points out that he is in the state of continually changing his views because he is ignorant on matters about which he thinks he does have knowledge. This is the state which leads to his contradicting himself once he starts answering Socrates' questions.

Here we find spelled out with more care and length than in other dialogues, since Alcibiades is an absolute beginner in philosophy,[26] the working of Socratic *ad hominem* arguing. Socrates points out that Alcibiades has answered questions about his own views, not those of Socrates; the recognition of his confusion that ensues is due to his being unable to defend his own views. The dialogue illustrates how particularly devastating it is to realize that your views can be demolished without the intervention of anyone else's views.

But this is not only consistent with, but forms a fitting prologue to,[27] Socrates leading Alcibiades to accept some positive views of Socrates' own. Firstly, he gets him to see the importance of 'caring for himself', an ethical protreptic central also to the *Apology*.[28] Far from being in a position to tell other people how to live their lives, Alcibiades has to realize that he does not know how to live his own, since he has simply absorbed views about what

[26] Presumably a reason why the dialogue was popular in late antiquity as an introduction to Plato's works: having Socrates explain what he is doing makes it easier for the reader to understand what is going on in other dialogues.

[27] In the way envisaged by Plutarch, *Quaest. Plat.* 1; see Annas 1999: 21–3.

[28] The notion of *epimeleia* is introduced at 119a and 120c, and developed in the passage at the end of the dialogue about caring for what is really you, rather than merely something belonging to you (cf. 128b ff.). It is the care of the soul, rather than bodies and belongings, that Socrates urges on his fellow Athenians at *Ap.* 29d–30b.

to do and what kind of person to be uncritically from his environment. He has to learn how to *live* his life, organizing it in line with critical reflection.

Further, Socrates leads him to see that the self he should care for is not what he carelessly assumed, the socially embodied self identifying with his status and possessions. It is not even the beautiful body he is so proud of. Rather, it is the soul, the conclusion he is forced to accept at 130e. True care of himself, and true love on the part of others, will concern the soul, not the body (132b). To live well and be happy Alcibiades must thus pursue wisdom and virtue,[29] a conclusion he heartily accepts at the end of the dialogue.[30] False beliefs about himself and what matters have been removed, clearing the way for the acceptance of true views, which, at any rate at the beginning stage, have to be presented by Socrates.

At the end of the dialogue we find a puzzling query at 129b: how can the itself itself (*auto to auto*) be discovered? This is the way we can discover *ti pot'esmen autoi*, what we are ourselves. However we interpret this passage, it surely requires recognition of the point that we find here the Platonic use of *auto to* to indicate that what is under consideration is a Form. Just as we find *auto to ison* in the *Phaedo* because we are thinking about *equal*, so we here find *auto to auto* because what we have in mind is *what it is* for someone to be *autos*.[31] Socrates then argues that Alcibiades *autos*, himself, is really his soul, and moreover the reasoning part of his soul, and that, contrary to what we intuitively accept, his body is like his money, something that is not really him himself at all, but merely something belonging to him.

Moreover, just as an eye sees itself in the best part of another eye, namely the part by which the eye sees, so a soul best knows itself by 'seeing' itself in the best part of another soul, namely the wisdom which makes the soul good. This is the most divine part of the soul, which resembles God, and someone trying to understand it and hence God and wisdom,[32] will come to know himself as well. After the expansive pedagogy of the main part

[29] Especially since self-knowledge is in this dialogue identified with *sōphrosunē* (131b, 133c).

[30] Like Cleinias in the *Euthydemus*, Alcibiades responds well to Socrates, but his subsequent career emphasizes the importance of staying the course and working at becoming wise and virtuous, as opposed to temporary enthusiastic conversion.

[31] Denyer 2001 *ad loc.* holds that it is more generally whatever it is which explains our use of *auto*, in a way not limited to persons and talk of the 'self'. While I agree that talk of the 'self' can be misleading here, I take it that the passage is in fact about the way in which we can use *autos* of a person; otherwise it is obscure why finding this would enable us to find 'what we are ourselves (*autoi*)'.

[32] 133c4–6. This is a disputed sentence; '(understanding) everything divine, namely God and wisdom' is the MSS reading. Hutchinson in Cooper 1997: 592, n. 29 accepts the alternative reading *thean* for *theon* and translates, 'everything divine – vision and understanding'.

of the dialogue, it is striking to find so compressed a thought, which is barely understandable without bearing in mind the ideas, familiar from *Phaedo* and *Republic*, that our real self is our reason, and that reason is divine.

This whole passage makes use of ideas which need further study to be properly understood, and which are given such further study in doctrinal dialogues like *Phaedo* and *Republic*. We might well ask why Alcibiades, who is such a beginner in thinking philosophically that the most obvious moves have to be spelled out for him,[33] is introduced to such difficult and profound ideas. One obvious answer is that Alcibiades is, after his initial shocked recognition that he is in a bad way and in need of help, introduced to ideas which he can make some sense of, but cannot properly understand without further study. The reader is left to reflect that Alcibiades never did come to understand these ideas properly, because after his initial keen conversion he never did apply himself with tenacity to caring for himself in the right way – that is, by seeking real wisdom and understanding; the reader, by contrast, is encouraged by this failure to persevere in their own case. The point is brought home at 130d, where Socrates remarks that they have not in fact investigated *auto to auto*, but merely *auto hekaston ho ti estin*, that is, what Alcibiades, or any person, actually is; this is put in sharp contrast to what belongs to them.[34] The investigation of *auto to auto*, which would lead to something like a Form, cannot be done without more sophisticated philosophical inquiry.

4. MUTUALLY ENRICHING READINGS

We have, then, three dialogues in which we see Socratic arguing against the views of others as one aspect of a unitary philosophical activity which also includes exposition of doctrine. Moreover, they suggest that with some dialogues there is no way to read them which fits a story of simple overall development. The *Euthydemus*, for example, comes 'before' the *Republic* in that Socrates embodies and praises a method of arguing which aims at truth mainly by exposing others' pretensions and mistakes, rather than expounding systematic doctrine. But it also comes 'after' the *Republic* in that only after reading the *Republic* do we understand the nature of the positive

[33] As at 108c–d, where he has to be pushed to come up with the generalizing term *mousikē*.

[34] Compare *Symp.* 199d4–e5, where Socrates asks about *auto touto pater*, whether *ho pater esti pater tinos ē ou*, and then asks whether *adelphos, auto touth'hoper estin, esti tinos adelphos ē ou*? These are questions about a father *qua* father and brother *qua* brother.

philosophical thinking which is described in that work, and merely referred to without explanation in the *Euthydemus*.[35]

The dialogues in which we get these 'cross-references' to ideas more fully explained elsewhere are those in which the *ad hominem* nature of Socratic arguing is most stressed. This makes sense. If we were to take the major feature of Socratic arguing to be merely that no positive conclusion is reached, it would indeed seem strange how arguing about what virtue is not, or what Alcibiades does not know, could form part of a coherent unity with bold metaphysical claims about what virtue is, or about what he needs to know. But once we are clear, as these dialogues in particular show, that Socrates is arguing *ad hominem*, showing the interlocutor what is wrong with his views, we can see how Socratic argument might make *us* properly aware of *our own* sorry intellectual state in a way that prepares us to receive truths about virtue and wisdom. And it is in this context that we, along with Cleinias, Alcibiades, Theodorus and Theaetetus,[36] are introduced to some of Plato's ideas, in a way which enables us to make some sense of them, but also encourages us to the further study needed to achieve anything like adequate understanding of them.

The way these dialogues combine emphasis on the *ad hominem* nature of Socrates' arguing with his exposition of not merely positive ideas but ideas which manifestly need further study to be correctly understood should, I think, encourage us in the project of unifying some of the dialogues in thematic ways. This falls short of a *generally* unitarian reading of Plato as a whole; as Frede has reminded us, such a project may turn out to rest on a general approach to Plato's philosophy which is disturbingly uncritical in various ways. Moreover, the way I have suggested that we approach the problematic passages in these three dialogues should in no way encourage an overall approach which ferrets out passages to be better understood in the light of other dialogues. I have suggested a way of reading passages

[35] I have said nothing about date of composition. The stylistic division of the dialogues proposed by Kahn 2002 puts *Euthydemus* in Group One and *Theaetetus* in Group Two (along with *Republic*; so much for the common assumption that it is stylistically obvious that the *Theaetetus* belongs with post-*Republic* dialogues). Kahn unfortunately does not consider the *Alcibiades*. Denyer 2001: 152 suggests that it 'was written not before, and not too long after, the events of 361', when Athenians would recognize the reference in 116d8 to obscure Peparethos, briefly in the news in that year. Denyer 2001: 20–6 however rejects attempts to argue from style to chronology, or to fit the *Alcibiades* into a view about Plato's philosophical development. I agree with the increasing wariness about arguing from style to either chronology or philosophical development.

[36] The interlocutor for the 'digression' is Theodorus, a point which is underlined (since the 'digression' opposes Protagorean views, while Theodorus is Protagoras' friend, there is some irony, especially since Theodorus, being a mathematician, should have been more critical than he is of Protagoras' 'measure' view). Presumably, however, Theaetetus is also taken to be a beneficiary of thought about the alternatives offered in the 'digression'.

which Plato himself has made prominent, forcing us to recognize them as problematic. It would be perverse to extend this way of reading to passages where there is no such prominent difficulty in the context.

Euthydemus, *Alcibiades* and the 'digression' in the *Theaetetus* are all passages displaying what I have called ethical drive. They not only depict an ethically crucial choice, they clearly suggest that the reader think about this choice in their own life. By referring to ideas which can be fully understood only by the reader of the doctrinal dialogues they indicate the direction in which we will go if we make the right choice to pursue wisdom and virtue. If we return to these dialogues after the doctrinal dialogues (or, of course, if we read the doctrinal dialogues first) we will have a deepened appreciation of the significance of the choice presented to and encouraged in the reader.

This paper is not intended as an argument 'for unitarianism', since we lack a clear sense of what that is; almost certainly it is a cluster of views, like the developmentalism with which most of us have been familiar for many years. The considerations I have put forward help to unsettle the presumption of a single overall development in Plato's thought, but also to indicate that this need not lead to the 'contention that all his dialogues can be read in an open and experimental way as though they might have been composed at any time and in any order', a view which Frede warns us against.[37] Rather, rejecting overall developmentalism as a framework may lead us to look more carefully at points where Plato's own procedure indicates that dialogues may be related not as marking simple progress but as mutually enriching reading for the person spurred to pursue wisdom and virtue.

[37] D. Frede 2002: 28.

CHAPTER 3

The speech of Agathon in Plato's Symposium

David Sedley

I. AGATHON AS SOCRATIC CONDUIT

It is a familiar pattern in Plato's definitional dialogues that the individual definitions are proposed and examined in an ascending order of quality, seeming for that reason to move towards the correct, Socratic definition. Whatever gulf may remain between the last non-Socratic definition in the sequence and the usually elusive one that Socrates himself would approve,[1] the progression offers an optimistic perspective on the value of dialectic.

In Plato's *Symposium*, the series of speeches about Love that culminate in Socrates' own seem to me to be contrived by the author to run in a similarly ascending order. This is not the occasion to argue such a claim systematically with regard to all the early speeches, but I shall later take the opportunity to support it with examples. And in more direct support, it is worth pointing out that in Socrates' climactic speech it is only the two immediately preceding speeches whose content is picked out for critical discussion in the light of insights supplied by his erotic counsellor Diotima. Although Socrates deplores all the preceding speakers for not caring sufficiently about truth (198d3–e4), he does not go so far as to accuse any of their speeches of being altogether devoid of it, and it seems clear enough that the final two, those of Aristophanes and Agathon, from his point of

This paper is built out of ideas that I put together for a seminar on the *Symposium* organized by Robert Wardy and Richard Hunter at Cambridge in 2004. My thanks to all participants in that seminar, and to members of the Helsinki Classical Association in 2005, for helpful discussion, and for further written comments to Robert Wardy, Seth Schein, Burkhard Reis and Frisbee Sheffield. It is an especial pleasure, as well as a ground for trepidation, to be able to dedicate the paper to Dorothea Frede, whose publications and example have set such a dauntingly high standard for new work on Plato.

[1] Curiously, the one case where the correct definition undoubtedly *is* reached is also the one case where the preceding definitions, proposed and refuted, have not been given in increasing order of quality: Polemarchus' definition of justice in *Republic* 1 will prove to have if anything more in common with Socrates' own than does that of Thrasymachus, which follows it. But I think few would dispute that classic definitional dialogues like *Laches*, *Euthyphro* and *Theaetetus* follow the pattern I have described.

view do have the merit either of being nearer to the truth, or at any rate of discerning and addressing some of the right issues.

Thus Aristophanes, in the speech located two before Socrates' own, has advocated the idea of love as the search for one's missing other half. The remarks which Socrates recalls from Diotima address what is (as Aristophanes himself notices, 212c4–6) unmistakably that same thesis: 'One account has it that it is those who are seeking half of themselves that are in love. But my account says that love is neither for a half nor for a whole unless, my friend, it is *good* – since people are willing to cut off even their own feet and hands, if what belongs to themselves seems to them bad' (205d10–e5). The Socratic viewpoint here does at least deem the Aristophanic theory worthy of discussion, but also of criticism: such theories may be right (it is implied) that love is focused on completion of the self, but they miss the key point that it is the self's *good* that love seeks.

Agathon's speech, the very last one before Socrates' own, fares rather better than this. Agathon, it turns out, did make a series of errors, but some of them were the very same errors as had been made by the young Socrates, before he gained the benefit of Diotima's insights. And although in his own speech Socrates will, with a kind of transferred irony, report Diotima as speaking disparagingly of his younger self (209e5–210a4), the now proven philosophical promise of that youthful Socrates makes it hard to doubt that he is intended to represent, at the very least, potential understanding. If so, that same potentiality is being associated with Agathon, or at any rate with ideas, common to him and to the young Socrates, that he is found voicing in his speech. What then are these ideas?

First, Agathon emphatically believes Love[2] to be beautiful, a contention to which he devotes nearly half his speech. So too did the young Socrates, until he was corrected on the point by Diotima's demonstration that Love is in fact neutral between beauty and ugliness (201e3–7):

> What I said to her was little more than a variant of what Agathon has just said to me: that Love was a great god, and was beautiful. And she refuted me with the same arguments with which I refuted Agathon, showing that according to my own assertion Love is neither beautiful nor good.

Socrates' direct reference here ('what Agathon has just said to me') is to what Agathon said in the cross-examination which he faced after his own speech

[2] Like translators of the *Symposium* into most modern languages, I can find no alternative to constantly shifting between the capitalized name 'Love' and the common noun 'love' in the course of this paper. See the full discussion of the issue by Castagnoli 2001: 46–9. It would have been simpler, from that point of view, if the paper were in German.

and as a prelude to Socrates'. But his thesis, refuted there, was not formally restated during the cross-examination itself. Instead, back-reference was there made (199c4–5 and 201b9–10) to it as a primary contention of Agathon's preceding speech, where he had indeed discoursed eloquently on the theme that love is supremely beautiful. Although he was wrong, as it turns out, he was making a mistake that even an inexperienced Socrates might make.

A second point on which Agathon's error mirrors Socrates' is the question of love's proper object. Agathon assumed love to be love of beauty (197b5), and of the beautiful (197b8). Moreover, in the subsequent cross-examination Socrates was willing to allow him that same assumption as a 'reasonable' hypothesis[3] (201a2–10), in order to refute him on the first thesis: the reason why love cannot be beautiful is that, if it is a desire for the beautiful and hence also a love of beauty, it must at present lack what it desires, namely beauty. In due course, Socrates will recount how he himself had to be disabused by Diotima of that very same assumption that love is love of the beautiful. More correctly, she explained to him, 'love is not of the beautiful, as you think it is' (206e2–3, cf. 204d3); rather, love is to be analysed as a desire for one's own everlasting good,[4] and the form taken by this happy self-perpetuation that love seeks is not 'the beautiful' as such, but 'procreation in the beautiful' (206e4–5). Despite this very subtle correction, it should be clear that identifying the beautiful as love's object is presented as considerably better than a half-truth. Indeed, it is a sufficiently close approximation to the truth not just to have been believed by the young Socrates, but also to be employed by the mature Socrates as a dialectical premiss in his argument against Agathon, an argument he regards as coming to an irrefutably true conclusion (201c8–9).

A third mistake made by both Agathon and the young Socrates was to assume that Love, the power which causes individuals to love, is a god. This

[3] For this idea of a reasonable hypothesis, see 201a8–10: '"And it is at least reasonable (ἐπιεικῶς) for you to say so," said Socrates. "And if this is correct (εἰ τοῦτο οὕτως ἔχει), Love would be precisely love of beauty, not of ugliness."'

[4] Despite Diotima's clear assertion here, many interpreters (e.g. those listed by White 1989: n. 3) take good and beautiful to be identical in the *Symposium*, so that this change would in a sense not represent an actual correction of the earlier thesis. I do not believe that that is Plato's view. Diotima's substitution of 'good' for 'beautiful' at 204e1–2 is a change to a different premiss, and not an alternative way of formulating the same premiss (cf. White 1989: 156). To the best of my knowledge good and beautiful are nowhere identified in Plato's dialogues, apart from the highly dialectical passage at *Prt.* 358a1–360e8, where *all* positive values, including the pleasant, are being made identical. In lists of Forms, Good and Beautiful are regularly listed side by side as distinct. In so far as a relation between them is assumed, it is the asymmetric one that beautiful is truly predicable of good (e.g. *Ly.* 215d2; *Symp.* 201c2; *Ti.* 87c4–6; cf. *Phlb.* 64e5–65a6), but as far as I am aware never vice versa. For further arguments, see White 1989.

time the truth, that Love is in fact a daimon, is brought out not in Socrates' cross-examination of Agathon, but in Diotima's reported cross-examination of the young Socrates (201e3–203a8). Her correction, formally theological in content, will thereafter metamorphose into a basic thesis in moral psychology: love – along with all desires, including philosophy, the desire for wisdom – has its essence in creative *lack*, rather than in actual possession of the good it seeks. That is what assimilates it to the role of intermediary daimons rather than of paradigmatically blessed gods. Agathon failed to appreciate this, but in doing so he was once more replicating the error of the young Socrates. And in getting clear about the nature of Agathon's and Socrates' error, we as readers are reliving Socrates' own progress towards his current state of enlightenment.

It appears, then, that the views unreflectively assumed by Agathon are non-accidentally close to those represented by the speaker Socrates. We may risk calling Agathon's views 'sub-Socratic', and this motif tends to confirm the 'crescendo' interpretation advocated above: it is the Socratic respectability of the speeches that successively grows as they converge on Socrates' own.

By 'Socratic' I do not in this context mean to single out philosophical views traceable back either to the historical Socrates or to the semi-historical Socrates portrayed in Plato's early dialogues; I use the term within the constraints of the dramatic fiction, to designate views held by the Socrates of the *Symposium*. Thus if Agathon's speech is sub-Socratic, that is because it gestures towards the views shortly to be expounded by the speaker Socrates. But as a matter of fact the unqualified identification of the beautiful as love's proper object, assumed by both Agathon and the young Socrates, had a perfectly good pedigree in Plato's early 'Socratic' dialogues, having been formally endorsed by Socrates himself at *Charmides* 167e7–8. This suggests at least some degree of identification between on the one hand the young Socrates who met Diotima and on the other the figure called Socrates who had been constructed as the protagonist of Plato's early dialogues.[5] And if so, the refinements which Diotima taught Socrates will represent a newer and more Platonic set of insights.[6] Since her refinements culminate in a

[5] This bears a partial comparison to the very young Socrates of Plato's *Parmenides*, widely agreed to represent, not the historical Socrates, but the views put into the mouth of the speaker 'Socrates' in preceding dialogues such as the *Phaedo*.

[6] That Plato's own views can be, with due caution, read off from the arguments he puts in the mouth of his main speaker remains the default assumption, despite a number of recent challenges, and I shall assume it here. I have set out my own position on this in several places, of which I cite here just Sedley 2003: 1–2.

description of direct communion with a transcendent Form, that element of mature Platonism cannot easily be doubted.

Not only is the sub-Socratic character of Agathon's speech amply confirmed by its content (more on this shortly), but as a matter of fact readers were carefully prepared for it early in the dialogue, back at 175c6–e6. Socrates has arrived late at the banquet, after standing for a long spell in the neighbours' porch, locked in thought. Agathon, the host, invites the late arrival to sit at the empty place next to him, joking that in that way he can hope to absorb some of the new wisdom that Socrates has hit upon during his meditation. Socrates obliges, remarking how fine it would be if thanks to mere juxtaposition wisdom could pass by osmosis from the fuller vessel to the emptier, as when water is siphoned through a strand of wool. But his stated reason for this wish is that he, not Agathon, would then have been the beneficiary of their sitting together: his own wisdom is feeble, open to challenge, and dreamlike, whereas Agathon's is great and glorious, as testified by his recent victory in the dramatic contest. This characteristic pairing of Socratic irony and the Socratic disavowal of wisdom leaves us the readers in little doubt that the very reverse is true: of the two, it is Socrates who has much the greater and more authentic wisdom. We should therefore not be surprised if their sitting together at the banquet turns out with hindsight to symbolize an intellectual osmosis in which Agathon will sound as if some of Socrates' outlook has flowed into him, albeit without a matching level of understanding.

I do not mean to suggest that the osmosis represents any actual process of intellectual cross-fertilization postulated by Plato. Contrast the speakers Nicias in the *Laches* and Critias in the *Charmides*, who likewise propound Socratic-sounding theses without fully understanding them, but have learnt them from their previous contact with Socrates in dialectical situations. There is no suggestion in the *Symposium* that Agathon is propounding overtly Socratic ideas acquired in any such way. Rather, the play on the osmosis theme symbolizes for the reader the fact that Agathon will function in the text as an unwitting and passive conduit[7] of ideas preparatory to Socrates' own. That his role in this regard is orchestrated purely by the author, and not, as it might have been in a definitional dialogue, partly by

[7] Anyone reluctant to believe that Plato would play such a game can usefully compare *Euthd.* 290b1–291a7: there young Cleinias, won over to philosophy for the first time just pages earlier, suddenly voices ideas so strongly reminiscent of the metaphysical middle books of the *Republic*, and hence so incongruously placed in his mouth, that the frame dialogue breaks in for Crito to check with Socrates whether it can really have been the youngster who said these things, and Socrates himself begins to wonder if it wasn't instead some god (see above, chapter 2, pp. 36–7).

interaction between the discussants, is itself signalled by the utterly accidental reasons determining this culminating sequence of speeches:[8] Agathon's speech is preceded by Aristophanes' only because the latter was delayed by hiccups, and followed by that of Socrates only because of Socrates' late arrival and the chance circumstance (175c6–7) that a place remained free next to Agathon. Yet it is precisely that sequence – Aristophanes, Agathon, Socrates – that will prove to be vital to the crescendo of ideas with which the dialogue's philosophical message emerges.[9] There should be little doubt that the author's voice is the dominant one here.

2. THE PRIORITY OF DEFINITION

The impression that this mysterious intellectual osmosis has occurred can be tested by examining the declared methodology of Agathon's speech. After an opening announcement that his aim is to eulogize love itself, and not just, as he alleges the previous speakers have done, love's human beneficiaries, Agathon sets out his method (195a1–5): 'For any eulogy on any subject, there is only one correct method: to use one's speech to explain what its subject is like and what sort of things he is cause of. That is the way in which we too ought to eulogize Love, speaking first about what he himself is like, and secondly about his gifts.' This concern with the correct sequence of questions to answer easily gives the impression of being a studiously Socratic piece of methodology,[10] all the more so because Socrates himself in the opening words of his own speech will praise it (199c3–6): 'Actually I thought you made a fine beginning to your speech, Agathon my friend, when you said that your first job was to show what Love is like, and after that his works. This beginning I entirely approve.' But Socrates' approval is itself not without a tinge of irony. For Plato's readers knew well that the 'what is it like?' question is in reality the *second* one a true dialectician would ask, only after establishing the identity of the item in question. This cardinal point is stressed in the *Gorgias* (462c10–d2) and *Meno* (71a1–b8), among other dialogues: according to the Socrates of the *Meno*, to ask what virtue is like, for example whether or not it is teachable, without first establishing what it itself is, would be as hopeless as to ask what Meno is like, for example

8 On this see especially Clay 1975.

9 It is equally significant that Alcibiades' position as the concluding speaker is the result of another chance cause, his arriving late and drunk after the other speeches have been delivered. But that falls outside the scope of my paper.

10 Cf. Allen 1991: 42, 'This conforms to Socrates' procedure in other dialogues' (followed by an explicit comparison to the *Meno*'s methodology).

whether he is beautiful, before one has the least idea who Meno is. Agathon was absolutely right (for reasons concerned with causality, to which we will come later) to raise the 'what is it like?' question before going on to ask the further question about love's effects; but in not first asking what love is, he was inevitably giving a defective account.

Since Agathon is making a rhetorical speech, and not engaging in dialectic, it might have seemed that he is hardly at fault for not applying full dialectical rigour. But even rhetoric can be practised either well or badly, as Plato's Socrates is at pains to insist in both the *Gorgias* and the *Phaedrus*. Indeed, the most frequently cited version of his Priority of Definition principle is one that opens Socrates' own first attempt at a rhetorical speech in the *Phaedrus* (237b7–c4): 'Concerning every topic, my boy, there is but one beginning, for those who are going to deliberate well: you must know what it is that you are deliberating about, or else necessarily go altogether wrong. But most people don't realize that they do not know each thing's essence . . .' And a definition – here too one of love – follows. Likewise in the *Symposium*, the signals are clear: we are being invited to notice not just the merits of Agathon's method but also its defects.

Similarly to the Socrates of the *Phaedrus*, Socrates' informant Diotima, albeit likewise not speaking in an undilutedly dialectical voice, will proceed in the canonical order that readers of earlier dialogues have learnt to think of as methodologically proper, starting with a definition. Indeed she will do so twice over, once in figurative genealogical terms, and once more in the language of moral psychology. Her progression from asking genealogically *who Love is* to asking definitionally *what love is* itself mirrors the methodological analogy set up in the *Meno* between the questions (a) who Meno is, and (b) what virtue is. In the first, genealogical phase, Diotima will start by explaining who Love is: by genus he is a daimon, and specifically he is the son of Poverty and Plenty. This procedure already mimics in genealogical language the Platonic dialectical method of definition by genus and differentia.[11] Only after that semi-formal identification will Diotima, still in this first phase, add what Love is like: he is a lover in relation to the beautiful, at once an impoverished vagrant and a philosopher, and so on (203c3–e5). In the second phase, she will develop a more properly philosophical (if still informal) definition of *what* love is – it is the desire to bring about one's own everlasting good by procreating in the beautiful (204d1–207a4). And only thereafter will she go on to detail love's actual procreative effects

[11] Quite apart from its later development in Plato's method of collection and division, definition by genus and differentia was already used by Socrates in his own definitional proposals in early dialogues like *Gorgias* (462b3–465e1) and *Euthyphro* (12d5–7).

(207a5–212a7). In both phases, the definitional stage precedes the further questions about love's properties or effects.

In this light, Agathon's method is not yet fully Socratic. Rather it is, to repeat my preferred formula, sub-Socratic. By inviting us to compare Agathon's methodology with that of Socrates' speech, Plato has encouraged us to notice and appreciate – what we otherwise would be likely to miss – the latter's tacit respect for that fundamental principle, the Priority of Definition.

3. LOVE AS THE DESIRING SUBJECT

Thus armed, we can shift our attention to the doctrinal content of Agathon's speech. To bring this into a suitable focus, it will help to start with a look at its Socratic counterpart in the ensuing speech, which comes out especially in Socrates' opening cross-examination of Agathon. One of the controlling hypotheses of that cross-examination is that love itself is the proper subject both of the verb 'to love', and of such functional equivalents as 'to desire' (200a, 201b). The same point will be more formally stated by Diotima at 204c1–3: love is properly to be identified with 'what loves' (τὸ ἐρῶν), not 'what is loved' (τὸ ἐρώμενον).

Why so? We are, I am convinced, here being confronted with a fundamental thesis of middle-period Platonic metaphysics, one most fully articulated and put to work in the Last Argument of the *Phaedo* (102a9–107a1).[12] If you possess some property accidentally, contingently or ambiguously, you do so because of something in you which possesses it inalienably and essentially. For example, as a human being you are – temporarily – alive, thanks to the presence in you of something which is inalienably and essentially alive, a soul. These chairs are contingently and ambiguously odd in number, thanks to the presence in them of something, the number 5, which is essentially odd. You are contingently and relatively hot because of the presence in you of fire, which is essentially hot.[13] In each case the immanent item is the primary bearer of the predicate: it is only thanks to soul being alive and fire being hot that you too possess these predicates. It is only

[12] D. Frede 1978 is the best guide I know to this argument.

[13] Likewise, you are large only ambiguously and unstably, being large in relation to a dwarf but small in relation to a giant, but you are so thanks to the presence in you of your own largeness, which is essentially and unambiguously large (102a11–103a3). I relegate this example to a footnote because it is the most controversial of those discussed in the *Phaedo*, too obscure in itself to shed much light on the *Symposium*. Less formally but more illuminatingly, on the other hand, note also 77e4–8: Simmias and Cebes are a little bit afraid of death, despite Socrates' reassurances, because of the presence in them of an inner child which is inherently afraid (Young 1988).

thanks to 5 being numerically odd that the chairs are too. It seems clear to me that the same principle is at work, in Socrates' speech, with regard to desires.[14] If you happen to love chocolate, we might say by way of illustration, that is due to the current presence in you of a passion (chocoholism) which is essentially, in its own nature, a passion for chocolate. That passion is the primary bearer of the predicate 'loves chocolate', whereas you are only its derivative and quite possibly fickle and impermanent bearer. In the *Phaedo*, these primary bearers of properties are endowed with a causal function: they are causes of the attributes they bring about in us.[15]

Within the *Symposium*, this same metaphysical principle is first unveiled, it seems to me, not in Socrates' speech but in the one that immediately precedes it. Agathon's opening words there (194e5–195a3) are that the speeches so far have been remiss to the extent that, instead of eulogizing the god Love himself, they eulogized the good effects in human beings of which he is the cause. To rectify this, Agathon will turn to praising the 'cause', Love as such. And in doing so he repeatedly and emphatically develops the same causal theme. In particular, note the sentence in which he sums up his main contentions (197c1–3): 'Since this god was born, it is from love of beautiful things that all goods have come to be for both gods and men. Thus it seems to me, Phaedrus, that it is by being himself in the first place most beautiful and best that Love is thereafter the cause to others of further beautiful and good things.' This observes the causal principle, so prominent in the *Phaedo*, that a cause must itself possess the same property as it brings about in something else: it is only hot things that can make you hot, for example. It is at the same time a prime example of the further refinement of that principle, regularly credited to Plato in antiquity, that

[14] An alternative way of reading Socrates' remarks, favoured by Castagnoli 2001, is to take 'Love loves . . .' as Pauline predication: to say that love loves would then be reducible to the truism that people who love love. The view I am myself defending makes the former the *cause* of the latter, and therefore decidedly not reducible to it. Here is not the place to launch a criticism of Gregory Vlastos' 'Pauline predication' thesis, so let me limit myself to citing *Resp.* 507d10–e1, where 'sight' is the subject of the verb 'to see', but cannot be reduced to a reference to people who see, because it is there explicitly distinguished from them. Castagnoli's is a masterly analysis of the passage, but it does have the drawback, which its author does not shirk, of threatening to make Socrates guilty of conscious fallacy in an argument underwriting his and Diotima's main philosophical contentions about love. I believe that my preferred reading avoids any such drawback.

[15] As a matter of fact, the 'subtle' items mentioned at *Phd.* 105b6–c6, including fire in relation to heat, are not there explicitly called 'causes' (I owe the point to Dominic Bailey). But (a) the original question to which they are said to provide an alternative, 'subtle' answer as distinct from the earlier 'safe' answer was a question about causation (100c9–e3); and (b) immanent largeness, which (see n. 13) functions analogously to them, is explicitly a cause: its causality is expressed at 102c2 by τῷ μεγέθει, this dative construction being one of the *Phaedo*'s regular ways of expressing causation (see Sedley 1998: 115).

'the cause is greater than the effect': whatever makes you hot has to be not only hot, but hotter than it could ever make you.[16] And it is precisely those twin causal principles that underlie the metaphysical thesis to which I have already referred: if you desire something, your doing so is secondary to, and caused by, the presence in you of the relevant desire, itself the primary subject of the desiring.

Agathon, in observing these principles, is showing a more Platonic understanding of causality than any preceding speaker has done. In particular Phaedrus, to whom the above remark is addressed, in his own speech failed to manifest comparable causal insight when at 178c2–3 he said of Love, 'It is by being the oldest [of the gods] that he is the cause of the greatest goods for us.' Unlike Agathon, whose words stand in effect as a correction of his,[17] Phaedrus has not begun to understand the descending likeness relation that binds cause to effect.

The advance in understanding that Agathon represents is, relative to the overall progression of the dialogue, anything but casual. For one thing, it is precisely this enhanced appreciation of causal structures that makes Agathon, and not for example Phaedrus, the appropriate interlocutor for Socrates' cross-examination at 199c3–201c9. It is because Agathon has recognized love itself, and not lovers, as the true subject of the verb 'to love' that Socrates can successfully take him through the following argument:

1. (199d1–e8) Love necessarily has an object.
2. (200a1–4) Love desires that object.
3. (200a5–e6) What a subject desires, it necessarily at that time lacks.
4. (200e7–201a1) Therefore love lacks its object.
5. (201a2–10) According to Agathon, love's object is beautiful things, and hence, more specifically, beauty.
6. (201b1–5) Therefore love lacks beauty.
7. (201b6–8) What in all respects lacks beauty is not beautiful.
8. (201b9–12) Therefore love is not beautiful (conclusion 1).
9. (201c1–3) Everything good is beautiful.
10. (201c4–7) Therefore [since love lacks all beautiful things, as implicit in 4–5] love also lacks all good things (conclusion 2).

Although this argument is, like virtually any interesting philosophical argument, open to criticism, it does not seem to me to be, or to be intended to be seen as, obviously faulty. The apparent slippage occurs in step 7

[16] Makin 1990–1.

[17] 178c2–3 (Phaedrus): πρεσβύτατος δὲ ὤν, μεγίστων ἀγαθῶν ἡμῖν αἴτιός ἐστιν. 197c1–3 (Agathon): . . . πρῶτος αὐτὸς ὢν κάλλιστος καὶ ἄριστος, μετὰ τοῦτο τοῖς ἄλλοις ἄλλων τοιούτων αἴτιος εἶναι.

(201b6–8), '"What is lacking in beauty *and in no respect possesses beauty*, do you call beautiful?" "No I don't."' The clause which I have emphasized here requires and assumes a matching understanding of step 6 as 'Therefore love *in all respects* lacks beauty.' Once that is granted, the conclusion at 8 does indeed follow from 6 and 7, since if, contrary to 8, love were in some way beautiful, there would necessarily be at least one respect in which it did not after all lack beauty, contrary to 6. The pressing question, however, is whether Agathon had good reason to grant Socrates the additional clause.

It is here that Agathon's complicity in the Platonic causal theory is vital. Certainly if all that were meant by steps 5 and 6, that love desires beauty and therefore lacks beauty, were that *people who love* desire beauty and therefore lack beauty, there would be room for insisting on all kinds of qualifications. People desire some beautiful things but not others, which they may already possess. Likewise, they lack beauty in some respect, for example beautiful thoughts, but may possess it in others, for example bodily beauty. Or they may possess beautiful things, e.g. oil paintings, without themselves possessing those things' beauty. But because love itself is the subject, such qualifications are not called for.[18] Compare once more the numerical oddness of five chairs. If we pick the chairs as our subject, although odd in some respects they are liable to turn out to be even in others, for example in respect of the number of their components or colours. But so long as we concentrate on the number 5 itself, we will find no respect whatsoever in which it is even. The number 5 as such is unambiguously and inalienably odd, and incapable of being in any way whatsoever even. Likewise, although lovers may both possess and not possess beauty, the desire whose presence in them makes them lovers is, as such, entirely without beauty, because its very essence lies in that absence of beauty at whose rectification it aims. Hence Agathon was, from a Platonic point of view, quite right to allow Socrates' argument its understanding of the lack in which love consists as an unqualified lack.

To translate this abstruse metaphysical point into the graphically personalized terms that Diotima will shortly make familiar, in so far as love is present in you, it makes you too, by proxy, a bearer of its own essential predicates; and in doing so it does *not* make you beautiful, but rather makes you a vagabond, vacillating between poverty and plenty, and acutely conscious of what you lack. It is, then, by the usual Platonic causal principles, this unstable intermediacy and sense of lack, rather than beauty, that

[18] I am grateful to Robert Wardy for this point.

constitute love's own defining properties. The metaphysically based argument embodied by Socrates in his cross-examination of Agathon is the formal counterpart of this fundamentally psychological depiction.

I submit, then, that the progressive convergence of the speeches on authentic Socratic insights is not merely a piece of literary architecture on Plato's part, but is in addition essential to our philosophical understanding of the dialogue. It is only through the lens provided by Agathon's speech that we can ourselves, like Agathon, become full partners in Socrates' dialectic, sufficiently immersed in Platonic thought to follow his full reasoning.

4. LOVE AND GOODNESS

Emboldened by this finding, I shall hasten on to the other main part of Agathon's speech. Following its programmatic introduction, the first of its two main sections (195a7–196b3) has been devoted to demonstrating that Love is supremely beautiful. The theme of the second main half (196b4–197b9), preceding a final summing up (197c1–3) and extravagantly Gorgianic peroration (197c3–e5), is that Love is also supremely good.

Love is emphatically 'good', *agathos*. Greek at this date had no abstract noun for 'goodness' cognate with the adjective *agathos*, and instead standardly used *aretē* for the purpose. *Aretē* is more familiarly translated 'virtue' (sometimes 'excellence'), and is the regular philosophical word both for 'virtue', understood like the English 'goodness' as uncountable, and for 'a virtue', a count noun applicable to the individual species of goodness. Justice and courage, for example, are 'virtues' (*aretai*) in this latter sense, parts or species of 'virtue' or 'goodness' in the former sense.

Agathon, in showing Love to be supremely good, undertakes to speak of Love's *aretē* (196b5). He proceeds to do so by showing how it manifests each of the four cardinal virtues, although the relevant use of *aretē* as a count noun nowhere shows up in his discourse, making it probably more accurate for us to think of them as the four parts of a unitary 'goodness'.[19] The four qualities in question are, in order of their appearance here, justice, moderation (*sōphrosunē*), courage and wisdom.

I shall not dwell at length on the familiar puzzle that in Plato's middle-period dialogues (*Phd.* 69c1–2; *Resp.* 4.427e9–10; cf. *Alc.* 121e6–122a1) the list tends to be restricted to these four, and to omit piety despite its prominent inclusion in earlier dialogues as a fifth virtue. But it is at least worth pointing

[19] Nor indeed does *aretē* function as a count noun in any of its 22 occurrences in the *Symposium*, with the possible exception of 180a4. Thus the tendency to treat it as a singular item is a feature of Plato's thought in this dialogue, not of Agathon's speech in particular.

out that Agathon speaks as if the list of four is known to be exhaustive: 'I have spoken about the god's justice, moderation and courage, and it remains to talk about his wisdom' (196d4–5). He might be thought to have omitted piety simply because this is a purely human virtue, not one that gods could possess. On the other hand, to attribute such virtues as courage and moderation to a god is odd as well (cf. Aristotle, *EN* 1178b12–13, 15–16), yet he seems to have no hesitation about doing so. Hence he does appear to be confidently restricting the number of cardinal virtues to four, and thereby to presage the argument of *Republic* 4, where Socrates and his interlocutors are so confident of it as to assume, to the astonishment of many readers, that as soon as they have identified the wisdom, courage and moderation of the ideal city, whatever good quality remains will necessarily be justice (427e9–428a1). If Agathon's tacit adoption of the same restricted list has been deliberately planted here by the author, it is once again a hint to us that some of Socrates' present wisdom has overflowed into Agathon. Agathon, then, is speaking with a sufficiently Socratic (or Platonic) voice for it to be worth tracking his ideas and seeing what will become of them in the hands of Socrates himself.

I shall consider only briefly the first three virtues. Love is *just*, argues Agathon (196b6–c3), because it never involves coercion: love neither yields to coercion nor coerces anybody, the latter because those driven by love are *ipso facto* acting in accordance with their strongest wishes; and any arrangement that involves free consent on both sides must be just.[20] Second, love is *moderate* (196c3–8), because moderation is control of pleasures and appetites,[21] and love exerts exactly that – in the sense, presumably, that all other pleasures and appetites, such as our desires to eat, drink and sleep, have to take second place to love when it is in charge. Third, love's *courage* is attested by the myth of Ares' passion for Aphrodite (196c8–d4): if one leaves aside Love himself, then Ares is the bravest of the gods; yet Love mastered Ares; so Love must be the bravest god of all.

If there is a serious content running through these attributions, it lies in the theme that virtue is a matter of non-coercive control. This has obvious enough resonances with the theory of virtue, in both city and soul, developed in (once again) *Republic* 4, and tends to confirm the impression already noted that, thanks to his physical proximity to Socrates,

[20] For all its obvious shortcomings, this argument is at least backed up at some length by Agathon's attempt to set straight the mythological record (195b6–c6, 197b3–9): all the violent and coercive things that the gods did to each other in the early dysfunctional phases of their family life were, he maintains, the work of Necessity, not of Love, who had not been born yet. See further the Appendix.

[21] 196c4–5, a definitional formula almost identical to that at *Resp.* 4, 430e4–6.

some mature Platonic thought about virtue has filtered through into Agathon.

However, the treatment of these three virtues by Agathon is light-hearted, to say the least. At the close of his speech he will remark, 'Let this speech of mine be dedicated to the god, Phaedrus. I've done my best to ensure that it had its share of fun, and its share of moderate seriousness too' (197e6–8). His treatment of the first three virtues is probably the leading candidate for the 'fun' part, and it might be unwise to squeeze its content any harder for further philosophical hints.

It will be more fruitful for us to concentrate, as Agathon himself does, on the fourth virtue, wisdom (196d4–197b3). That love is wise is the point he is most at pains to emphasize. If we work through his explanation of this with Socrates' speech in mind, we cannot but be struck by Agathon's constant focus on *productive* wisdom, under three headings: poetic production, animal reproduction and craftsmanship. All three of these are forms of *poiēsis* or 'production', the first two explicitly so called (196e5, 197a1), the last only implicitly, although Agathon's failure to make it explicit will later be rectified by Diotima (205c1–2). Indeed, it is hardly an accident that Agathon's repeated focus on Love as the cause of *poiēsis* is as a whole an anticipation of one of Diotima's most prominent themes. I shall return to this shortly. Before that, we must consider what in Agathon's eyes makes Love a wise producer.

First of all (196d6–e6) Love is, like Agathon himself, a poet. This is inferred from the alleged fact that love makes everybody a poet (in the literal sense of this word, 196e4–6). Love could not pass this gift to us if he did not himself possess it to an even higher degree, according to Agathon. Once more (cf. section 3 above) Plato's double causal principle is implicit: what makes you F must itself be F, and indeed more F than it makes you.[22] To this extent, authentic Platonic thought is being called on here.

On the other hand, readers will quickly recognize that Agathon, by making his own poetic métier a leading paradigm of wisdom, is from Plato's point of view radically de-intellectualizing wisdom itself. Poets' lack of real understanding is a theme well known to any reader of, for example, the *Ion* or *Republic* 10. It is a theme to which I shall return shortly.

Secondly (196e6–197a3), Love exercises his creative wisdom in the reproductive activities that are manifest right across the animal kingdom. Third

[22] The causal language (cf. Sedley 1998: 115) is at 196e2, ποιῆσαι. The text does not explicitly add that Love must be a greater poet, or more poetic, than he makes us, but strongly implies it by the words, 'This god is a wise poet, so much so as to make another a poet too,' thus apparently anticipating the appeal to the principle, 'The cause is greater than the effect', that underlies 197c1–3.

(197a3–b3), Love is the leader of the manufacturing crafts, whose greatest practitioners have always been inspired by him. This is illustrated mythologically by examples of gods – Apollo, the Muses, Hephaestus, Athena and Zeus – whose signal successes in various crafts were driven by passionate desire.

With this third and final case, 'love' has been broadened out from its specifically erotic connotation so as to range indifferently over all creative desires. This mode of enlargement has a partial antecedent in the speech of Eryximachus, where love was similarly presented as a universal principle extending far beyond interpersonal passion. But Agathon has gone much further than that. In perfect parallel to his broadening of 'love', by progression through his three examples of production he has extended *poiēsis* too, from specifically 'poetic' production to the entire genus of creative activity. The double move, treating 'love' and *poiēsis* in parallel, is a prominent and detailed anticipation of Diotima's speech (205b4–d9). The very same point about *poiēsis* is one that she will herself articulate with a surprising excursion into semantic theory, explaining that sometimes what is most properly the name of a whole genus is used instead with specific reference to one of its species. *Poiēsis*, literally 'making', connotes any kind of production, but its name has been hijacked by one small group of its exponents, the poets. (In English we might more easily illustrate this same point with the example of 'composer'.) And she will explain that semantic shift precisely in order to bring out a corresponding shift in the word 'love': it too, she maintains, properly designates all creative desire, and we should not be misled by its conventional restriction to one species of such desire, erotic desire in relation to an individual.

Plato has artfully contrived the two speeches so that Diotima is formally theorizing what Agathon has already done *de facto*. Agathon, starting from the link of sexual love to specific kinds of production, widened it into a link between passionate desire in general and creativity in general. Later, Diotima is credited with the linguistic theory that makes sense of what Agathon has in fact already done. The semantic broadening which she advocates is meant to be, on the one hand, a proper restitution of the two words' basic meanings, and on the other the disclosure of a universal law about creative desire in general, a law hitherto only half-known to us through one prominent species of the genus, sexual passion.

In Diotima's hands, all of Agathon's examples will be subsumed under this broader law. Properly redefined, love is a mortal being's desire to secure its own everlasting good by deriving a kind of immortality from the process of procreation in the beautiful. All drives to creativity that occur in mortal beings can serve this end in lesser or greater measure: biological reproduction, the quest for everlasting fame, artistic creation, virtuous benefactions in the political or educational arena, and above all philosophy, the passion for wisdom.

Most of these cases have already been anticipated by Agathon – a vital structural parallelism, to which I shall return shortly. But what is decidedly lacking from his account is the last, philosophy. Agathon's view of wisdom (*sophia*, the goal of philosophy) is a deeply unphilosophical one, and the same might be said of his treatment of virtue in general. From a Socratic or Platonic point of view, Agathon is far from grasping the role of intellectual understanding in human goodness.

At the end of her account of intellectual ascent, Diotima will revive the theme of virtue. One who by an ever-widening activation of love has ascended all the way to the point of achieving a kind of intellectual union with the Form of Beautiful will 'give birth, not to images of virtue, since he is not laying hold of an image, but to realities, since he is laying hold of what is real; and, having given birth to real virtue and nurtured it, to him it belongs to become dear to the gods, and to him, if to anyone, to become immortal' (212a3–5). Much can be, and has been, written about the possible meaning of this portentously eloquent climax. What is on offer is after all nothing less than the attainment of immortality, and the privileged route to it appears to be graduation from producing images of virtue to producing real virtue. What does this amount to? In *Republic* 10, 600e5, 'images of virtue' (εἴδωλα ἀρετῆς, the identical expression) are virtuous actions performed by individual good people, their metaphysical status nevertheless being that of imperfect imitations of the Forms of the virtues; below these images there stand, as mere external imitations of them, the artistic descriptions of them produced by poets. If we assume that that passage of the *Republic* is meant to inform Diotima's words, we may take it that she is implicitly ranking three kinds of attainment: at the lowest level (if only by implication), stands poetic production; above that, virtuous conduct; and at the top of the hierarchy, intellectual grasp of the Forms of the virtues, which is made possible by direct communion with the Form of Beautiful. That the successful philosophical inquirer might be credited with the first of these is not even contemplated, for where the philosophical ascent starts is already well above that level. What he is envisaged as doing in his ascent is, rather, to progress via the generation of virtue in individuals (210a4–c6) all the way to a full intellectual understanding of the Forms underlying this (210c6–212a7). If that final intellectual attainment is the likeliest of all to confer immortality, as Diotima predicts, the 'immortality' in question may be linked to the permanence of this highest kind of knowledge, compared with the transience of all lower cognitive states.[23]

However, even if I am right that *Republic* 10 is the text that ultimately offers the most precise commentary on Diotima's meaning, the question remains to be asked, what within the *Symposium* itself equips readers to make any significant sense of Diotima's closing allusions?[24] And the most plausible answer appears to me to be: Agathon's speech. But to see why, we must approach this through the series of speeches leading up to it.

That love promotes virtue has been an insight recurrently displayed in the speeches. For Phaedrus, the first speaker, however, it does so not directly, but by activating the sense of honour, making lovers ashamed to manifest cowardice or any other vice in the presence of their beloved. This treats the causal relation of love to virtue as what Plato would consider an inappropriately indirect one, driven by what in his developed tripartite psychology is the intermediary 'spirited' part of the soul, rather than by reason.

The second speaker, Pausanias, not only sees love as a spur to virtue (184c4–d3), but also understands enough Platonic ethics to be able to call on the distinction between on the one hand things with intrinsic value, whether positive or negative, and on the other hand morally neutral items, capable of being used either well or badly (180e4–181a6, recalling *Grg.* 467c5–468c8). This distinction, however, he has proceeded to misapply by ranking love with the neutral items, thus missing the essential good-directedness of all love that Diotima will later bring out. That same duality has remained a keynote of the ensuing speech by Eryximachus (see especially 188d4–9).

The fourth speaker, Aristophanes, offers an aetiology of love as the search for one's own missing half, one which captures something the others have failed to understand about the essential focus of love on the enhancement of the self, but which also, as we saw earlier, faces criticism from a Socratic point of view for overlooking the essential focus of love on the good.

[23] Diotima's closing words associate the prospect of immortality with the gods' special favour towards the highest intellectual achievers. On the surface then, it seems to me, she must be understood as indicating the very rare privilege of apotheosis: not merely the self-prolongation by proxy that is available to all mortal natures (207c9–208b6), but the attainment of an immortal *nature*. It is, I suggest, only below the surface that her words are to be decoded as alluding to the permanence of an intellect's understanding of the Forms. Among the transient lower cognitive states with which this contrasts even 'sciences' or 'pieces of knowledge' (ἐπιστῆμαι, 207e5–208a7) are listed, but these as described do not sound as if they are meant to include philosophers' knowledge of Forms.

[24] I assume in any case that, as the stylometric evidence suggests, *Republic* 10 postdates the *Symposium* and is glossing it retrospectively. But my main point is to do with the internal integrity of the *Symposium* as a text, independently of chronological considerations.

Seen against this backdrop, Agathon's speech has moved further in the right direction. For he alone has made its relation to goodness part of love's very essence. Moreover, as we have seen, he has importantly anticipated the Socratic account in the following way. He has recognized in familiar 'love', conventionally understood as passionate desire focused on another individual, no more than one manifestation of a human drive to production which is better understood when universalized to embrace an entire genus of productive desires. Whatever incipient insights Plato may be asking us to notice in the preceding speeches, none of them is nearly as close as this one is to Socrates' own eventual analysis of love.

Nevertheless, Agathon's account of love's goodness is imperfect. First of all, to make love itself virtuous is a version of the error committed by the young Socrates: for love consists not in goodness as such, but on the contrary in a *lack* thereof (201c4–5). More relevant to our present concern, however, is the following defect. Although Agathon, in associating love with virtue, rightly allots the greatest emphasis to the most fundamental virtue, wisdom, his understanding of wisdom is itself from Plato's point of view a seriously impoverished one. When the feted poet Agathon starts by vastly overrating the value of poetic production among love's intellectual outcomes, readers familiar with such dialogues as the *Ion* are already being alerted to this blinkered overestimation. The same de-intellectualization continues when he associates love's virtues with biological reproduction, and then with the crafts – the former, because, as we will learn from Diotima (207a5–c1), biological self-perpetuation is a universal but very low-level manifestation of love, the latter because, as Socrates learnt when he questioned the craftsmen in the hope of uncovering their wisdom (*Ap.* 22c9–e4), craft knowledge does not bring with it any important kind of understanding. Agathon also emphasizes that creative passion in the crafts is rewarded by fame (197a3–6), and here again Platonic readers will recognize an inherently non-intellectual value, fame being, in the terms of Plato's mature tripartite psychology, a goal of the spirited part of the soul, not the reasoning part. Only the very last craft listed by Agathon, the ruling craft (assigned to Zeus at 197b3), begins to sound intellectually respectable enough to count as any kind of 'wisdom' in Plato's eyes.

Yet these forms of production coincide almost perfectly with the range of manifestations of love's work that Diotima catalogues *before* she turns to the ascent. For she too illustrates the power of love with the examples of biological reproduction (207a5–208b6, 208e1–5), seeking fame (208c1–e1), poetic creativity (209a4–5, d1–4), and virtue as manifested above all in political benefactions (208e5–209c7, 209d4–e3).

When the philosophical aspirant has finally given birth to 'real virtues', even the highest achievements included in that pre-ascent catalogue have now been left behind, reclassified as nothing better than 'images of virtue'. As Rowe well puts it:

> If this interpretation is right, all those 'great achievements' referred to in the earlier passage – those of Homer and Hesiod, Lycurgus and Solon – are written off as insubstantial; but so they must be, by implication, in any case, since Homer and the rest lack the vision of true beauty that enables the philosophical lover to procreate true virtue. And that is the usual, uncompromising verdict of Plato's Socrates on all poets, politicians, and others who operate without devoting themselves to the philosophical search for truth.[25]

I think this is exactly right. But the demotion of these fine achievements, hymned by Diotima, to that lowly status remains a paradoxical outcome, and at first sight places a considerable strain on the reader. The reason for this, it seems to me, is that it is not Diotima, but *Plato*, who has conveyed the demotion to us. And he has done so, not by the internal dynamics of Diotima's speech, but by laying the groundwork in the cumulative effect of the earlier speeches. These have, as we have seen, developed a steadily improving picture of love's relation to virtue, one which, starting from utterly non-Platonic beginnings, has culminated in Agathon's half-truths about love's promotion of wisdom and the rest of virtue. It is by thinking back to Agathon's concluding depiction of 'wisdom', still no more than a pale ghost of the Platonic truth, that readers can recognize the intellectual impoverishment that makes even love's highest non-philosophical achievements mere 'images' of the philosophical understanding in which real virtue resides.

5. CONCLUSION

In emphasizing how well-informed Agathon's philosophical intuitions are, for all his speech's residual limitations, I am aware of going against the overwhelming tendency of the modern literature, which is to treat his speech as little more than a vacuous show of rhetorical self-promotion.[26] The

[25] Rowe 1998: 201.

[26] A rare exception is Stokes 1986: ch. 3 ('Socrates and a tragic poet'), the only previous full-length study of Agathon's role in the *Symposium* that I have so far tracked down (although there have been some valuable discussions devoted to his cross-examination by Socrates, including Payne 1999 and Castagnoli 2001). It certainly does have the merit of taking Agathon seriously, not however, as I do, by starting from the common ground between him and Socrates, but by placing them in extreme opposition, thus in effect interpreting the whole of Socrates' speech as a critique of Agathon.

elements of parody[27] that are undoubtedly present in this speech, as indeed they are in the others, should not blind us to the philosophical progress that it represents. The sub-Socratic content of Agathon's speech, far too dense and systematic to be dismissed as accidental, serves a complex purpose. It constructs an Agathon sufficiently in tune with Socrates' insights to become a fruitful interlocutor in his ensuing elenchus – as fruitful an interlocutor, indeed, as the young Socrates had once been to Diotima. It prepares the ground for Socrates' speech by rehearsing what will prove to be some of its pivotal themes, most notably the intimate causal link of love to virtue and the parallel broadening of 'love' and *poiēsis* from their familiar specific senses to their hidden generic senses. By vaunting its own recognizably second-best methodology, and securing Socrates' partly ironic approval for this, it points us towards what we might otherwise never notice, the philosophically superior methodology that underlies Diotima's speech. And finally, by exhibiting the dialogue's most advanced non-Socratic account of love, it enables us to work out why, when all is said and done, Plato's own deeply philosophical understanding of love raises the subject to an entirely new level.

In introducing the idea of Agathon as an unwitting conduit for Socratic ideas, I attached significance to a prominent piece of symbolism in the opening scene of the dinner party. To conclude, let me highlight a matching piece of symbolism in its closing scene (223b1–d12). As dawn approaches, only Socrates, Aristophanes and Agathon are still awake. Socrates is trying to persuade the two playwrights that the expert at writing tragedy must be an expert at writing comedy too. The comic poet Aristophanes finally nods off, and soon after him so does the tragic poet Agathon. Only Socrates, who has in effect been trying to fuse their two métiers into one, is still going strong.

The potential meaning of this celebrated scene is hardly likely to be exhausted by any one decoding,[28] but let me nevertheless point out how satisfyingly it maps onto the interpretation I have been advocating.

Socrates' speech, I have argued, looks back to those of Aristophanes and, more especially, Agathon, the two speeches closest to it not only in time but also in philosophical content. With Aristophanes Socrates shares in fact just one idea, that love is at root a quest to enhance the self. What Aristophanes is seen to have omitted, namely that this must be the promotion of the self's *good*, has been foreshadowed by Agathon with his imperfect appreciation of

[27] Well brought out by Hunter 2004: 71–7.

[28] Among many valuable contributions to the scene's understanding, Clay 1975 remains something of a landmark.

Love's essential relation to goodness. Socrates' own account of love unifies both elements. But Aristophanes' contribution is swiftly marginalized, and in the end Agathon's many incipient insights are left behind too. The Socratic whole, raised to a new level by Diotima's teaching, proves to be incommensurably more than the sum of these two parts.

In the closing scene, when Socrates propounds his argument for unifying the work of the two poets, and continues to develop it while Aristophanes and Agathon in turn fall away, is this not a dramatic re-enactment of the interrelation between their three speeches?[29]

APPENDIX: LOVE AS THE YOUNGEST GOD

In insisting that Love is the youngest god, Agathon explicitly corrects Phaedrus' speech, according to which Love was on the contrary among the oldest. As quoted by Phaedrus at 178a9–c2, Hesiod made Earth and Love the very first divine generation after the initial advent of Chaos (*Theog.* 116–22); and similarly in Parmenides' cosmogony, although Necessity was the dominant goddess (cf. his fragment B 10), the very first new deity that she 'devised' was Love (B 13). In both poets, we may add, Love's early arrival was followed by further divine generations.[30] Hence both Hesiod and Parmenides really did rank Love as one of the oldest deities. Phaedrus is right on the exegetical point.

Contrary to an impression regularly given by editors and translators, it seems clear to me that Agathon challenges Hesiod's and Parmenides' actual genealogies, not Phaedrus' interpretation of them. His objection to these two poets is that such extreme seniority would entail that Love must already have been operative as an interactive force among the gods early enough to be responsible for the terrible things they inflicted on each other in the first generations. His words at 195c1–5[31] require to be translated counterfactually: '. . . and the ancient goings-on concerning the gods, of which Hesiod and Parmenides speak, were due to Necessity and

[29] One might add the following implication. Aristophanes did not, any more than any other comic poet, write tragedies, nor did Agathon, any more than any other tragedian, write comedies. Hence, by Socrates' implication (backed in other ways by such dialogues as *Ion*), neither of them is a real expert at his genre, as he might be if he composed in both genres. If so, their fusion into a single poet would offer to raise their work to a new level, one of genuine expertise. This mirrors the way in which the combination of Aristophanes' and Agathon's insights, in Socrates' own speech, ushers in an entirely new level of understanding.

[30] In Parmenides these included War and Discord, according to Cicero, *Nat. D.* 1.28.

[31] τὰ δὲ παλαιὰ πράγματα περὶ θεούς, ἃ Ἡσίοδος καὶ Παρμενίδης λέγουσιν, Ἀνάγκῃ καὶ οὐκ Ἔρωτι γεγονέναι, εἰ ἐκεῖνοι ἀληθῆ ἔλεγον· οὐ γὰρ ἂν ἐκτομαὶ οὐδὲ δεσμοὶ ἀλλήλων ἐγίγνοντο καὶ ἄλλα πολλὰ καὶ βίαια, εἰ Ἔρως ἐν αὐτοῖς ἦν.

not to Love, *<as they themselves would say> if they were speaking the truth*. For castration and imprisonment of each other, and numerous other acts of violence, would never have happened if Love had been among them.' All the translations I have consulted render the clause italicized above as conveying a presumption of fact, with such renditions as 'assuming that what they said is true', as if Agathon were claiming that Hesiod and Parmenides actually *said* that the early history of the gods was the work of Necessity, not of Love, and have simply been misreported by Phaedrus. This is open to challenge not only on linguistic[32] but also on exegetical grounds. Although it might have worked as an appeal to the authority of Parmenides, it will hardly do for Hesiod. 'Necessity' (ἀνάγκη) occurs just twice in the *Theogony* (517, 615), where it is not the name of any discrete divine power. Given that Agathon in any case does not offer either a new citation of Hesiod or a reinterpretation of the lines quoted by Phaedrus, it seems most unlikely that he is claiming Hesiodic backing for his rewriting of divine history. Rather, he is contradicting Hesiod's story: when those terrible goings-on occurred, Love cannot yet have been born, as Hesiod falsely claims he had.[33]

If I am right about this, when soon after (197b5–7) Agathon recapitulates what he has maintained here, he means:[34] '. . . before that [the arrival of Love], as I said at the outset, it was due to the sovereignty of Necessity that the many terrible things happened to the gods that are said to have happened (ὡς λέγεται).' The translations I have consulted, although rightly leaving the point as ambiguous as the Greek does, allow and in some cases encourage[35] one to understand the last part as amounting to '. . . it was

[32] The imperfect indicative ἔλεγον expresses an unfulfilled condition. If instead it were a historic imperfect referring back to the time when the poets said it or (Bury 1932, citing Rettig and Stallbaum) when Phaedrus quoted them as having said it, the shift to the imperfect from the present λέγουσιν in the preceding line would be anomalous. Besides, the way in which the second sentence of the quoted passage explains the first lies in the fact that their respective 'if . . .' clauses are equivalent in content: 'if they were speaking the truth' = 'if Love had been among [the gods]'. The latter clause (εἰ . . . ἦν, c5, again with imperfect indicative) is counterfactual, as this time all the translators agree, and that tends to confirm that the former is too.

[33] An alternative possibility (kindly pointed out to me by Seth Schein), which may even underlie some of the current translations of the sentence, is that εἰ ἐκεῖνοι ἀληθῆ ἔλεγον amounts to '. . . if they were [past indicative] telling the truth *about the terrible goings-on among the gods*' – that is, about the castrations etc. themselves, not about Necessity or Love being their cause. The reason for doubting this alternative is (in addition to the point about tenses raised in the previous note) the implausibility of Parmenides' having written about these divine castrations etc., whereas he has actually been cited as naming Love as a primary cosmic force, making this – the theme that he manifestly does share with Hesiod – the far more likely candidate for 'truth'.

[34] πρὸ τοῦ δέ, ὥσπερ ἐν ἀρχῇ εἶπον, πολλὰ καὶ δεινὰ θεοῖς ἐγίγνετο, ὡς λέγεται, διὰ τὴν τῆς Ἀνάγκης βασιλείαν.

[35] Castagnoli 2001: 66–7 translates 'mentre prima succedevano, come ho detto, molte cose terribili tra gli dei, a quel che si dice, a causa della sovranità di Ἀνάγκη', which properly preserves the ambiguity, although in commenting he speaks of 'lotte tra gli dei raccontate da Esiodo e Parmenide nei loro poemi, e a lor dire causate da Ἀνάγκη'.

due to the sovereignty of Necessity that many terrible things happened to the gods, as Hesiod and Parmenides say it was.' Again, nothing in the text forces us to read him in this latter way, as invoking the poets' authority for his own thesis that Necessity, not Love, was the culprit. I believe that he is, on the contrary, rejecting their authority.

This result is not of merely philological significance. Yet again, it reveals the sub-Socratic character of Agathon's speech. Recall *Euthyphro* 5e2–6c9, where Socrates declares himself unable to believe the stories the poets tell about strife between the gods, and *Republic* 2, where a similar dismissal of the poets' many falsehoods about the gods is developed at considerable length. That repudiation of the poetic tradition – a fundamental Platonic theme, stemming ultimately from Xenophanes – is the negative complement to Plato's positive conviction that the gods are essentially and perfectly good. And this latter conviction in turn provides a key premiss of Diotima's speech, when she is proving Love not to be a god: unlike Love's, a god's being, she insists, is characterized by complete happiness, beauty and goodness (202c6–12). How close has Agathon come to that insight?

On the one hand Agathon has turned out to be, like Plato's Socrates, taking the bold step of rejecting the poets' authority when they attribute moral failings to the gods. On the other hand, unlike Socrates he does not go so far as to doubt that those terrible events can ever have happened. He denies that one particular deity, Love, can have permitted them, but is nevertheless perfectly willing to contemplate such strife among the gods in the absence of Love and under the influence of Necessity. It is not clear whether this 'Necessity', the governing force in Parmenides' cosmogony, represents for Agathon, as an entity of the same name does for Plato himself in the *Timaeus*, the material necessity that has been 'persuaded' by divine reason into cosmic concord. But at all events, by allowing Necessity to dominate the gods and to generate discord among them, instead of being itself kept under their benign control, Agathon is once again falling short of a truly Platonic level of understanding.

CHAPTER 4

Is dialectic as dialectic does? The virtue of philosophical conversation

Mary Margaret McCabe

I. A CHRISTENING?

Republic 7, it appears, is the christening ceremony for dialectic. For here, we might say, is the moment when Plato appropriates the expression '*dialektikē*' as a term of art, to mark out the pinnacle of his own philosophical method. Indeed, it all seems deliberate, even emphatically technical:

> 'So, then, do you call "dialectician" the person who grasps the account of the being of each thing? Surely you will not say that someone who has no account, to the extent that he is unable to give that account to himself and to another, has understanding of it?'
> 'How could I say so?' he said.
> 'So likewise for the good: someone who cannot distinguish the idea of the good in account by marking it off from everything else, and who cannot get through all the tests of what he thinks as if through a battle, nor is eager to test it according to the way things are, rather than according to opinion, and who cannot progress through all these things without his account collapsing – such a person you will surely say, knows neither the good itself, nor any other good.' (534b3–c5)[1]

> 'So you would legislate, would you, that they should most of all receive that education through which they would be able to ask and answer questions in the most knowledgeable way?'
> 'Yes, I would so legislate – and you with me, too.'
> 'So do you suppose,' I said, 'that dialectic lies at the top for us, like a coping-stone on our studies, and that there is no other subject that should rightly be put higher than it, but that it provides now the end to our inquiries into education?' (534d8–535a1)

It is a pleasure to me to offer this paper to my dear friend Dorothea (in the hope that the pleasure will not be too deplorably mixed, for her). It was first delivered at the Leventis Conference on the Form of the Good, organized by Terry Penner, March 2005. I am immensely grateful to the participants in that conference for their comments and suggestions, especially to Terry Penner, Tim Chappell (my commentator), Lesley Brown, Chris Gill, Thomas Johanssen, Vasilis Politis, Christopher Rowe, George Rudebusch, Dory Scaltsas; also to Jonathan Lear, John Cleary, Owen Gower, Alex Long and Jimmy Doyle, to an anonymous commentator for CUP, and also, especially, to Verity Harte.

[1] Translations are my own.

. . . and insistent on the name:

'And so when someone attempts, by conversation, to arrive at what each thing itself is, by means of reason[2] without any of the senses, and does not stop until he grasps what is the good itself, by thought itself, then he is at the very end of the intelligible, just as then the man in the cave came to the very end of the visible.'
'Absolutely,' he said.
'Well, now. Do you not call this journey "dialectic"?' (532a5–b4)

. . . and notice the frequency of the term *dialektikos* in the six Stephanus pages 531–7, compared to its complete absence elsewhere in the *Republic.*[3] That supports both the technicality, and the claim that this is the point of its introduction as Plato's own term of art.[4]

What is more, the expression's genealogy is marked. For Socrates has worked up to this moment from the beginning of the discussion of the greatest learning ('You have often heard that the idea of the good is the greatest learning . . .', 505a2–3) by a series of variations on the theme of conversation, *dialegesthai* (a word not in fact as commonplace in the Platonic dialogues as one might expect).

The first variation plays at 454a, where Socrates inveighs against the dangers – and the temptations – of antilogic or disputation, the art which deceives people into thinking they are having a proper argument, when in fact they are only practising eristic.

'It is a notable power, isn't it, Glaucon, that antilogic has?'
'Why?'
'Because,' I said, 'many people seem to me to fall into it quite involuntarily, and to think that they are not disputing, but conversing. This is because they are unable to consider their subject by dividing into forms – instead, working just on the name of the thing, they pursue the contradiction of what has been said, and treat each other competitively, not as in a discussion.' (454a1–9)

Antilogic is unable to consider (*episkopein*) the subject under discussion by virtue of the proper distinctions.[5] Having a proper discussion, by

[2] The expression *logos*, notoriously difficult to translate, reappears in these passages to describe both the faculty by which dialectic is done (as here) and the content of what dialectic says (as 'account' in the previous passages). The word *dialegesthai* itself is cognate with *logos*, of course. It is, as I shall argue, significant that the conception of dialectic here bridges both the faculty of reason and its content. For reasons of space I eschew here, however, further discussion of *logos*.

[3] See Brandwood 1990.

[4] We might distinguish, as Lesley Brown suggests to me, dialectic's conception, at *Men.* 75d, from its christening, here.

[5] This 'dividing into forms (types? *eidē*)', however it may be related to the method of collection and division of later works (*Phaedrus*, *Sophist*, *Politicus*, *Philebus*, see Stenzel 1940; Gomez-Lobo 1977; McCabe 2000; Silverman 2002) is at least systematic in some way: see below.

contrast, avoids getting caught up in sophistical difficulties (as, for example, by virtue of the dropped qualifiers in the preceding discussion of sameness and difference of natures among men and women) by making the right distinctions; this is done by conversation (*dialegesthai*) and discussion (*dialectos*). 'Conversation' here, then, has a normative force: not just any old talk, but conversation and discussion conducted along the right lines and with the right precision.[6]

Conversation of the philosophical kind pervades the cave, too. From the very beginning, the prisoners are imagined having a conversation even when they are tied down (515b4). And the release and the ascent from the cave resound with the language of philosophical discussion – and philosophical discussion with Socrates, at that (notice the gloomy prediction that someone who tries to release the prisoners from their darkness would be killed, so long as he could be caught, 517a). So when the prisoners are released they are shown one of the objects carried behind the wall; and they are asked what it is – but they are in *aporia* about it, and cannot answer (515d5–7). Their journey upwards – which Glaucon agrees to call dialectic (532b4) – is characterized by their increasing ability to reject what they see before them (532c) and to resist fixed assumptions (533c) in favour of being able to give an account of what they are considering (533c).

Indeed, this feature of philosophical conversation is taken to be true, not only of the prisoners as they emerge, but also of Socrates and Glaucon themselves. The discussion of antilogic, of course, was provoked by the position they had both reached in the argument; and repeatedly the conditions associated with *dialegesthai* apply to the interlocutors themselves. At 528a Socrates exhorts Glaucon to conduct his conversation with the right sort of people: those who 'accept that in these subjects an organ of each person's soul is purified and rekindled – an organ which is destroyed and blinded by other pursuits – whose preservation is more important than that of a thousand eyes, since only by this organ is truth seen' (527d7–e3). He should do this, indeed, for his own sake; and it is for his own sake that he should ask questions and answer them: this is how the arguments should be made (528a). The process of conversation, thence, starts to work in exactly the prescribed way. At 532d Glaucon vacillates[7] in his response to what Socrates says; and then, when he asks Socrates to tell him the whole story

[6] It is a matter of moral character, too; see 538–9.

[7] Notice the way this works: he thinks it is hard to accept what Socrates says; and hard to deny it. The terms of assent and dissent will reappear in the account of the silent dialogue; see further below. On the importance of *aporia* see e.g. Matthews 1999, and Politis 2004b.

about dialectic, Socrates strikingly warns him that he is not yet ready to follow that far (533a). Glaucon needs a bit more philosophical conversation before he may see the good: and he should have known it, for Socrates had already told him that they might only see the good through an analogy (506e).

The emphasis on philosophical conversation throughout the central books of the *Republic* might, then, make us hardly hesitate, at least on a careful second reading, when – in advance of the formal account of *dialektikē* in book 7 – Socrates announces that it is the 'power of conversation', *hē tou dialegesthai dunamis*, that will allow us to touch, or to view,[8] the topmost intelligible part of the divided line (511b4, 511c5). Conversation, we might then think, proceeds *to a conclusion*; and it does so by overturning, or confirming, the assumptions upon which its earlier stages rested (511b, 533c). It is an old question just how that is supposed to work.

The features of conversation urged in the setting of the *Republic* are reinforced in the description of the divided line: that conversation allows us to treat our assumptions with proper caution; and that it is, somehow, a method of proceeding in philosophical inquiry. In particular, we might think, five aspects of the conception of conversation would be indispensable to the philosopher as he moves up the line:

- a *logical* aspect: the question and the answer represent two sides of a case, and the imagined conversation takes place as the two points of view play off against each other (examples at 525e–526a, 529a). This play-off has a compulsive side: these kinds of opposition demand resolution.[9]
- a *psychological* aspect: the philosopher is puzzled by these oppositions; he remains agnostic, suspends judgement about which side of the case he proposes to take while he considers the matter. His agnostic stance is a sense of puzzlement, of *aporia*, in his soul, and the considering is something he does in his soul: e.g. at 524e5.[10]

[8] I shall return to these perceptual metaphors in what follows: I here translate *theōreisthai* as 'view'; the word is notoriously tricky, however, see e.g. Nightingale 2004.

[9] We may readily see why, from Glaucon's vacillation at 532d: he cannot both assent and dissent, on pain of contradiction. See Politis 2004a on the nature of aporematic argument; and McCabe 2005b on one of Plato's detailed accounts of the nature of contradiction. The element of compulsion is emphatic in the discussion of philosophical progress, 515e1, 525d6, 526b1–2, 529d1.

[10] Compare the muddle the released prisoner gets into when he is forced to evaluate the impressions he gets at different stages in his ascent, along with a principle of interpretation (the later impressions are more significant than the former) at 515d. The idea that puzzlement may be philosophically productive, of course, lies behind Socrates' disavowal of knowledge – which is not to be confused with scepticism: see e.g. *Ap.* 20–3.

- a *sequential* aspect: conversations are conducted in such a way that the answer is relevant to the question, and the next question to that answer. The notion of a conversation, that is, has an order, a proper sequence built in (compare Socrates' repeated insistence on doing things in the right order, e.g. at 527b, 528d, 535a).[11]
- an *epistemological* aspect: the philosopher takes a synoptic view of both sides of the case at once: he both entertains the opposed views, and he considers their relative merits.[12] This synoptic view, that is, is reflective, or second-order; and it has both sides of the conversation within its scope (this is exemplified by Socrates' own reflective procedures, for example at 529a–b; and see the ringing claim at 537c, that the dialectician is someone with a synoptic view).
- *normativity*: you can do this kind of conversation well or badly; or fail to do it at all (see e.g. 525d, 527d, 528a, 531e–532a, 538–9).

These conversations may be conducted, indeed, not just between two parties to a philosophical debate, but within the soul of the speculating philosopher. Notice a passage to which I shall return: at 523b ff. Socrates describes the way in which the reportings of the senses cause the soul to be at a loss about what perception is saying, and to consider (*episkopein* again, 524b4–5) whether the senses report one thing or two. Soul *asks questions of itself* (524e5–6); by this means the soul will be turned towards, and come to *touch*, being and truth (525b), and will have a discussion (*dialegesthai*, 525d5–6, 526a2) of the numbers themselves.

This internal conversation, we might further think, fits with Plato's account of thinking as the 'soul's silent dialogue' in *Theaetetus* and *Philebus* (*Tht.* 189–90; *Phlb.* 38c ff.; and see *Soph.* 263e).[13] Does that comparison allow us to answer the old question, how philosophical conversation is to reach a conclusion? For just as the soul, in silent dialogue with itself, is able to come to a single view (it 'says the same thing', *Tht.* 190a3); so the philosopher engaged in the conversation of dialectic – whether with himself or another – might be able to resolve the question at the end of the discussion; by virtue, perhaps, of his synoptic view. Something, then, about his epistemological state, or his epistemic capacity, will explain the way that philosophical conversations get somewhere, and do not merely continue

[11] There is an obvious normativity here: consider an exchange of views in which neither side pays any attention to what the other says; here the two parties may talk at cross-purposes and, in extreme cases, fail to have any conversation at all.

[12] Compare the reflections on the drawings of Daedalus at 529e, and on the absurdity of their claims to give clues to the truth. Compare also Socrates' brusqueness with Glaucon's suggestion of a short-cut at 523d–533a.

[13] See D. Frede 1989; Burnyeat 1990; Dixsaut 1997; McCabe 2000.

to vacillate, as Glaucon does, between two different points of view. That is what we might think, at any rate, if we read the soul's silent dialogue back[14] into the *Republic*'s account of dialectic. But the *Republic* has something else up its sleeve.

2. THE FORM OF THE GOOD

Quite right, too, you might say. For after all, the soul's silent dialogue has only a limited account to give about just why I might reach a conclusion, or why its outcome might constitute knowledge – this is one of its problems as a model for epistemology.[15] More broadly, it is hard to see why a philosophical methodology analogous to conversation would ever appeal, since there is no guarantee that – as such – it would produce truth as its output. After all, why should I not ask myself all sorts of questions; deliberate on the answers; and end up, as Socrates insisted, with a consistent set of beliefs – and still be comprehensively *wrong*? How can Socrates' sort of inquiry provide itself with independent support? Meno pressed the point: he demanded that Socrates show just how we might begin our inquiries into knowledge and truth; and how, if we ever reach the end, we are to know that the end is what we have reached (*Men.* 80d).[16]

In the face of this kind of difficulty, the *Republic*'s account of dialectic has what we might think an appealing answer: the form of the good. Consider again just how Socrates describes the end of the dialectical journey (even although what he says is still hedged about by disclaimers to Glaucon): that the soul suddenly *sees* the form of the good (517c); or it *touches* the unhypothesized beginning (511b). The form of the good, of course, is the source of everything good and fine; as a consequence of seeing it, the dialectician is able to give an account of everything; then to get clear all the connections between things, and thus to have a complete account of all the things that he treated as provisional on his way up the line (see 516b). The form of the good, on this account, answers the second limb of Meno's paradox by suggesting that while the *process* up the line may be conducted by conversation and investigation, its *verification* is provided by the dialectician's *view* of the good. For the good is independent of him, and therefore it provides an independent justification of his

[14] There is, I fear, an issue of the chronology of Plato's dialogues here; I ignore it here, save to assume that *Theaetetus*, *Sophist* and *Philebus* were written (perhaps considerably) later than the *Republic*.

[15] Indeed, the soul's silent dialogue is not offered as a model of knowledge; instead, it gives us either a view of the psychology of *thinking*, or of the mechanics of *judging*. Still it is normative: there are good and bad judgements or decisions.

[16] On this see especially Scott 1995; Scott 2005.

knowledge; consequently it allows the rest of his system to be objectively confirmed.

A view of *Republic* 6 and 7 has long been popular that takes what happens at the top of the line to be explained in terms of some special epistemic access which the soul has to the form of the good.[17] Consider, for example, Cornford's remark: 'The apprehension of the Good is rather to be thought of as a revelation which can only follow upon a long intellectual training . . .',[18] which he follows up by talking of the philosopher's 'immediate knowledge of the Good'.[19] Or:

> The backwards regress is said, vaguely, to end in apprehension of an unhypothesized beginning: the Form of the Good. Plato does not elaborate, but since the Good is the first principle, there must be nothing more basic in terms of which the Good can be explained or defined. Knowledge of it will have to consist in some sort of intuition.[20]

More recently, Nightingale emphasizes the connections between what occurs at the top of the line and the sexual imagery of both *Republic* (e.g. at 490a–b) and *Symposium* (210e, which connects the visual and the sexual imagery): 'both metaphors portray the apprehension of truth as a receptive activity.'[21]

This view has many variants, and many different accounts of how we should cash Plato's metaphors. But fundamentally it supposes that the relation between the philosopher and the form of the good is precisely *not* given by the process of philosophical conversation. Instead, by contrast, the good is thought to affect the soul. In particular, this is often taken to be the point of the perceptual metaphors throughout these pages of the *Republic*:[22] that the good is quasi-perceived by the soul (whether by quasi-touch or quasi-sight). When perception happens, moreover, on this view

[17] But n.b. the detailed and persuasive dissent of Fine 1990 to the common view that in the *Republic* someone's state of mind is determined by the objects they encounter. In what follows I recant what I said in McCabe 2000: ch. 7 that the form of the good acts on the passive mind of the philosopher.

[18] Cornford 1941: 208, and see Cornford 1965.

[19] Cornford 1941: 208, n. 2. Cornford is brisk, however, in dismissing Neoplatonist interpretations of the *Parmenides* which press the idea of a mystical union between the Intellect and its objects (1939: 131–3). Cross and Woozley are more reluctant, but still concede that 'presumably the hypothetical method has to be supplemented in the end by intuition' (1964: 252). Robinson characterized this as the 'intuition-theory' of the upward path (1953: 172–7); but he is inclined to gloss intuition in terms of confirmation, rather than as an unmediated grasp of what is known.

[20] Heinaman 2003: 377 here rightly emphasizes the epistemological problem with which the intuition theory is meant to deal.

[21] Nightingale 2004: 116; and see her programmatic remarks at 109–14.

[22] Both tactile and visual imagery is used: seeing: 511a1, 516a5, 517c1, 519c10, 519d2, 520c4–5, 526e1, 526e4, 527e3; touching: 511b4, 511b7, 525c1; and the imagery of unmediated contact, grasping: 524e1, 529d5, 529e5, 532b1.

the perceiver is acted upon by the object perceived: the agent, as it were, of perception is the object, the perceiver is the patient.[23] So it would be the soul's passivity to the form of the good – or, to put it a different way, *the directness of the presentation* of the form of the good to the soul – that would provide the verification at the end of the dialectical process.

The claim that these presentations are direct, that they are somehow or other 'raw feels', could make two quite different points, however. On the one hand, we may wish to emphasize the *rawness* of the feel, the unmediated affection of perception by its object. In such a case, the verification is provided by the causal relation between object and perceiver: the fact that the object just does act on the perceiver (and that when it does so, the perceiver actually perceives the object as it is) is what guarantees the truth of the perception. On such an account, perception must make no contribution, do no work, of its own. This rawness, then, carries a realist or objective assumption along with it – that as a matter of fact there is an object which rawly determines this feel. On the other hand, the emphasis in a raw feel may be rather on the *feel*: on the fact that a raw feel is so subjective, so much in the private experience of the feeler, that it is inaccessible to anyone else. Here, too, perceptual experience is unmediated in some way; if there is something that it is like for me to see red, that is somehow directly available to me – and, more to the point, not to you. That gives my feel a claim to truth; but none to objectivity.

If the form of the good is to perform a role as the unmediated source of truth at the end of the dialectical process, then, it had better do so raw, rather than by virtue of the fact that it is felt. The privacy of a subjective feel cannot, at least, perform this role in the account of knowledge in the *Republic* – for the very issue in that account is how the objective realities of the world (sensible or transcendent) are rendered accessible to the soul. In what follows, therefore, I shall consider whether Plato postulates events which are in the objective sense intellectually raw; and not whether he supposes that what is intellectually raw is privately felt by its subject.

If the intellect receives it directly, the form of the good would be a foundation twice over: it is the foundation, the source, of the goodness in the world; and it is the foundation of the dialectician's knowledge. It is not the dialectician who must verify his views, but the form of the good which

[23] That this could be a Platonic view is confirmed by the theory of perception offered in the discussion of Protagorean relativism at *Tht.* 154–5; on the complex issues that arise about that passage and its sequel, see Cooper 1970; Burnyeat 1976; Burnyeat 1990; M. Frede 1987. Notice, also, the role the language of perception and sight may play in the account of recollection at *Men.* 81c6, to exempt the process of prenatal learning from a vicious regress.

does it for him by appearing to him directly, unmediated and objective. Meno's second limb may be thought to have been shod.

The price of the shoes, many have thought, may be too high: for it is fixed at the theory of forms (and we may be too parsimonious to pay it). It looks, furthermore, like an extreme version of that theory: where the highest flights of knowledge are explained just by the ineffable – by what is 'beyond being in authority and power' (509b9–10), and by the direct action of the ineffable on the mind of the philosopher (that it is his *mind* has then little to do with it). Thence there is a second price, concealed in this account of dialectic itself. For it seems to commit Plato to two rather different views of the relation between philosophical conversation and what happens at the top of the line.

First, he may need to make a psychological claim, that:

(i) philosophical conversation will *as a matter of fact* open the 'eye' of the soul to the forms.[24]

Should we find this persuasive, in the absence of any actual cases? And even if it is persuasive, it suggests that the progress up the line, all the way to, and including, the top, is somehow psychologically continuous. The construal of the soul's view of the form of the good that I have just elaborated, however, requires discontinuity, since it requires the verification of an inquiry to be different in causal structure from the inquiry itself.

Second, on this interpretation, Plato would claim that:

(ii) philosophical conversation is *replaced*, at the summit of the line, by the affection of the soul by the form of the good.

This discontinuity may itself be problematic; for it suggests that at the very top of the line cognition is *determined* by its objects. We might object that any account of the divided line which has cognitive states determined by their objects interferes with the thought that philosophers will (in the ideal situation) be better kings than those who find the lower reaches of the line or the cave familiar. After all, if the philosopher-king is to be any use to us on his return to the cave, he had better include the objects of the phenomenal world in the scope of his knowledge;[25] his superior cognition cannot be

[24] e.g. at 527d. See D. Frede 1999. How should we cash the thought at 518c that the eye moves *with the whole body*, or that the whole soul moves with the eye of the soul? I shall return to this below, section 6.

[25] Or, better, his understanding: I shall return to this issue below, section 5. See e.g. Burnyeat 1981; Nehamas 2004.

restricted to the world outside the cave if he is to be a king. Somehow it is his cognitive state that makes him better than us at dealing even with the sensible world; so his state of mind, his cognitive state, cannot just be determined by the objects he encounters.[26]

These two claims invite quite different construals of the nature of philosophical progress: the first that it is continuous from inquiry to verification, the second discontinuous. This, as well as general considerations about Plato's account of the philosopher-king, might invite us to wonder whether the role of the objects at different stages of the line is more complex, in each case, than a direct encounter; from the topmost section down.

Objections to the thought that the good is just directly experienced by the soul may be reinforced by the descent down the line. For here Socrates repeatedly speaks of the soul's activity of contrasting and comparing, of establishing a systematic set of connections between different parts of knowledge (511b, 517c, and compare 531d, 537c7).[27] That activity, for sure, bears its similarity to philosophical conversation on its linguistic face, especially in the way in which the soul negotiates the tension between assent and dissent by 'syllogizing' (516b, 517c) or by taking a synoptic view (537c2, 7). This may put further pressure on the idea that what happens at the top of the line is somehow or other quite different in kind from what happens elsewhere; and it puts that pressure by virtue of the emphatic interest in the setting as a whole on the discursive ways of philosophical conversation.

So: are we easily convinced of the thought that the ways of the intellect might alter sharply as we come to the experience of the good? Must we agree that the form of the good only appears to us after we have done some philosophical talking? Is this all just too easy to wrap up in the language of seeing of a mystical sort? Let me put the point in a different way: if the *end* of dialectic is something essentially non-discursive, quasi-experiential, why take the trouble to call this *dialectic* at all? Is the christening of dialectic just misconceived?

Well, perhaps christenings are like this anyway; it does not matter, if I call my daughter Poppy, that she does not end up pink and crinkly. Proper names (and so christenings) behave in rather more rigid ways than definite descriptions, and we should not be perturbed that Plato chooses this route to coming up with a term of art for his very own philosophical method. Its name (like my daughter's) makes some obeisance to its ancestry

[26] The exact significance of this issue is disputed; but see Annas 1981; Fine 1990; D. Frede 1999.

[27] On the mathematization of this, see Burnyeat 2000.

(in dialectic's case, Socrates' ways of inquiry; in Poppy's case, her great-grandmother). So, many have supposed, the christening of dialectic is not meant to give us a description, just to mark out, with a privileged name, the best possible way of doing philosophy. Dialectic, as Robinson remarked and as others have regularly repeated after him,[28] is the name Plato uses at any time for his best philosophical method.

Is that right? It may be true of what happens after the *Republic* (although I have my doubts about that[29]); but it is hard to defend for the *Republic* itself, for two reasons. First, the eventual use of the expression *dialektikē* is carefully anticipated in the conditions for philosophical conversation, for *dialegesthai*. It is hard to comprehend why the outcome of all this fuss is a name which has no real resonance for the method to which it applies. Second, if philosophical conversation is not essential to dialectic as a whole, but only to its preliminaries, the verbal connection between dialectic as conversation and dialectic as whatever happens at the end of the philosopher's endeavour merely serves to emphasize an uncomfortable tension within the methodology described in the central images of the *Republic*. Must we just accept that this is an unfortunate feature of Plato's account of philosophy?

That would be a counsel of despair. Instead I shall make three suggestions to invite the conclusion that philosophical conversation is indeed essential to Plato's methodology, through and through. My first suggestion (section 3 below) revisits the question whether the deliverances of perception are merely passive and thence non-discursive. I argue, instead, that the evidence of the *Republic* – especially of those passages where Socrates and Glaucon seem to be speaking *non-metaphorically* – supports the view that perception, too, is a part of the internal conversation of the soul; and that it fulfils this role by delivering reports that have propositional content: so its reports are not unmediated.

[28] Robinson 1953: 70.

[29] See McCabe 2000. Outside the *Republic* the expression *dialektikos* turns up in *Phaedrus* (266c, 276e), *Sophist* (253d–e), *Politicus* (285d, 287a), and *Philebus* (17a) in (otherwise notorious) contexts where we might reasonably understand it as a term of art, directed at a knowing readership. It also appears in three other dialogues: *Meno* (75d), where it is used as a condition of philosophical conversation; *Cratylus* (390c, 398d) where it reminds us that the dialectician is the expert in asking and answering questions, and has the dialectician operating as the overseer of other skills; and *Euthydemus* (290) in a context which appears deliberately designed to recall the *Republic* (see McCabe 2001, and also pp. 36–7 above). All of this evidence is consistent with the *Republic*'s offering us a christening: a christening with the conception of dialectic as philosophical conversation firmly in mind; and where the technicalities of dialectic are worked out more carefully (but still, I claim, as conversation of some kind) in later works, *Phaedrus*, *Sophist*, *Politicus* and *Philebus*.

My second suggestion (section 4), consequently, denies that at the top of the line the soul should be imagined as the merely passive recipient of an unmediated 'seeing' of the form of the good. Not only should we understand ordinary seeing in a discursive manner, I argue, but also the notion of the 'spectacle' of the good is itself discursive, because it is synoptic and second-order.

Thirdly (section 5), I suggest that when the form of the good operates as the cause of everything else, the soul sees it *as* the cause: and this special 'seeing as' ensures the content of the soul's understanding, its reflectiveness and its claims to unity. This move, moreover, insists on the realism of what is thus understood. So it avoids the complaint that dialectic is inconclusive without having the verification of dialectic's conclusions done by something intellectually raw. The *Republic*'s model of dialectic, therefore, incorporates a rich account of the psychology of the philosopher with its objective validation by the form of the good.

This, in turn, explains just why the philosopher's state of soul is virtue: the completion of the philosophical journey demands not only the right object of his knowledge, but the right and ordered state of soul. In closing, therefore (section 6), I offer a speculation on an issue beyond the scope of this paper. Why is dialectic focused on the good? It is not, surely, merely of instrumental value, not merely to provide the philosopher with the ability to make accurate choices (and so to achieve the best result every time); such a role for the good would be tendentious. Instead, Plato claims that the philosopher knows the sovereign good; and this knowledge is transformative of his life just because it is the source of value for him. Understanding the good, therefore, incorporates both the psychological and the metaphysical conditions for dialectic: the role of philosophical conversation is essential.

3. SEEING FINGERS

The central books of the *Republic* are much taken up with images and metaphors – and it is the cashing of these metaphors which causes so much trouble.[30] Pervasive is the use of verbs of seeing, looking and

[30] Burnyeat 2000: 55 is surely right to suggest that whether or not a given expression is metaphorical in these passages of the *Republic* may well be a matter of perspective, in the sense that something may look metaphorical when viewed from an early stage in one's philosophical (mathematical) education, but turn out to be literal when viewed from a more advanced stage of philosophical understanding. However, the interpreter still faces the challenge of working out which aspects of an apparent metaphor are salient.

grasping to describe the activities of the mind;[31] but is the implication of this terminology that the mind works (or works at the crucial topmost stage of the line) as if it were passively perceiving?

One passage in the midst of the extended images of sun, divided line and cave, however, seems to be largely non-metaphorical: the contrast between perception and intellection amplified at 523a–525b. This passage shows, I shall argue, that so far from perception being a rawly direct affection of the perceiver by the sensible object, the deliverances of perception are propositional – even complexly so – in content.[32] As a consequence, the parallel between perception and intellection urged throughout the middle books of the *Republic* may not demand a non-propositional account of intellection either; no more than perception is intellect rawly affected by its objects. This, I shall argue further, extends the significance of philosophical conversation for Plato's account of dialectic.

Socrates' argument proceeds by considering what study 'drags thought to being' (523a2–3). Some things 'in perceptions' do not call the intellect to reflection (*episkepsis*) because they are adequately judged by perception.[33] This happens when the perception does not 'result in' (*ekbainei*) the opposite perception at the same time. But there are things which do 'order thought to reflect' (*episkepsasthai*) because perception 'makes nothing sound' (523b3–4). For when there is the opposite perception at the same time, the mind is called to reflection; in these cases perception 'shows[34] one thing no more than its opposite'.

What on earth could Socrates mean? Glaucon attempts a gloss: surely Socrates is talking about 'objects appearing at a distance, and shadow images'? Socrates demurs – and insists that perceptual mistakes or illusions are not at issue here. This little exchange invites us to be careful about what follows; to wonder how – *other than* by mistake or illusion – perception fails.

Socrates begins with an example (523c10 ff.). Consider three fingers, one large, one small, one in the middle. Each appears equally a finger, and sight does not 'signify[35] at the same time' (523d5) that the finger is the opposite of a finger; so the soul is not impelled to ask, of them, 'What is a finger?'

[31] See above, n. 22. [32] See Scott 1995: 83.

[33] Perception makes a *judgement* in the sense of a settled decision between two options, perhaps, or a discrimination already adequately done (so the expression 'judgement' here is importantly *not* merely equivalent to 'belief' or 'opinion').

[34] The same verb is used of what Socrates is doing here in the dialogue: showing Glaucon what he means, 523a5. See also 524a3.

[35] At *Cra.* 436, 'signifying' seems to apply to the announcing of a name; this would fit with my option (d) below, that all that perception does is label an experience.

Contrariwise, sight does not 'see adequately' their largeness and smallness, and cannot discriminate[36] which one lies in the middle. The same account can be given of the other senses. They show such things *deficiently*[37] just because the same sense reports on opposite properties (large and small, hard and soft, sweet and bitter); thus the same sense 'announces to the soul that the same thing is hard and soft as it perceives' (524a3–4).

What exactly happens when perception 'announces to the soul that the same thing[38] is hard and soft as it perceives'?[39] Neither the context nor the terminology allow us yet to choose between the following glosses for what perception is imagined to say:

(a) perception announces that it perceives the same thing as hard and soft; perception says: 'I perceive that the same thing is hard and soft.'[40]

(b) perception announces, as it perceives, that the same thing is hard and soft: 'This (same) thing is both hard and soft.'

36 'It makes no difference to sight', e2. Does this mean that sight cannot discriminate *at all* (which would be decisive for my option (d), below)? Or is the point that sight cannot make the discriminations which reason can do; but that instead, it proffers something 'mixed up together'?

37 There is no claim here that the properties of the objects in question are deficient (that, e.g., the finger that is seen in the middle is not *really* in the middle) – the point made is an epistemological one, about what sight says to the soul.

38 In addition to the problems of interpretation discussed below, there is another: what is 'the same thing' about which perception makes its announcement? Perhaps perception announces something about some individual particular object – a finger, or a stick, or a man. In that case the announcement is imagined to be a *banal* utterance about the ordinary phenomena of the sensible world. Or perhaps perception is here imagined to be making a claim about what it is to be (such and such a thing). This will allow its announcement to be more philosophically *loaded*: what a finger is, it can tell us easily; but what hard or soft is, it confuses. It has been suggested (not least, on the basis of the apparent contradiction which is attributed to sensation, 'the heavy is the light', 524a9–10; see Fine 1993: 56–61; Irwin 1995: 157–62; but White: 1992) that perception is here answering a question which has already been put to it by the soul: 'What is a finger?' 'What is the heavy?' Because perception is limited to sensible properties, it can only answer in those terms. So it might say: 'this is (what it is to be a) finger', or 'this (e.g. being one kilogram in weight) is what it is to be heavy.' This works for explaining what finger is; but with individual perceptual properties, such as heavy or soft, no sensible property (being one kilogram in weight) can offer an answer that is other than confused (being one kilogram in weight might just as well explain what it is to be light). (On this, loaded, model, perception is conceived as a sight-lover, telling us, for example, what beauty is: see 475e ff. There is not, I think however, evidence in the text that Plato supposes all perceptual reports to be like those of the sight-lovers.) I have no space for further discussion of this point here; but perhaps what follows below may contribute. For if perception is imagined to make a report as a result of a question *it has already been asked* (about what something or other is), and so as already engaged in a philosophical discussion with the soul, then the second, loaded, model may be plausible. If, however, the conversation begins *after* perception makes its announcement, it is hard to see that the announcement itself is already engaged with questions about what things are. In that case, as I shall urge below, we should prefer the banal account of the announcement perception makes.

39 The loaded reading described above might prefer that perception 'announces to the soul that hard and soft are the same thing'. The Greek suggests, however, that 'hard and soft' are in the predicate position.

40 So 'as it perceives' is in the scope of what perception is imagined to utter. The word order is inconclusive.

(c) perception announces, as it perceives, of the same thing, that it is both hard and soft. Here perception seems to say two things: 'This is hard,' 'This is soft.'

(d) perception announces, as it perceives, of the same thing, that it is both hard and soft. Here perception may merely label its raw affection: 'hard!', 'soft!' [41]

The first of these possibilities is ruled out by the argument as it proceeds. Self-consciousness is something perception manifestly lacks: this occurs only when the soul begins to puzzle. Still the matter is not clear. Does sensation merely label what it feels (d)? Or does it utter something like a proposition (b or c)? And if the latter, is the proposition simple (c) or complex (b)? The latter question turns further on how to interpret what perception is imagined to *say*: does it say of the same thing (*de re*), both that it is hard and that it is soft; or does it explicitly attribute both properties to the same thing, saying that the same thing is both hard and soft (a *de dicto* reading of 524a)? Of course, if this last is what happens, there is undoubtedly more than raw labelling going on; can the text be further disambiguated between the *de re* and the *de dicto* readings?

The terminology of the passage so far is, I think, insufficient to ground a decision.[42] Scrutiny of the sequel, however, may allow us to do so. Once perception announces to the soul (whatever it does announce), the soul is necessarily[43] puzzled and asks itself: 'What does perception itself signify by hard, since it says that the same thing is soft too, and likewise for the perception of light and the perception of heavy, what is light and heavy, if it signifies that the heavy is light and the light heavy?' (524a6–10). One might be forgiven for supposing that Socrates here imputes a *contradiction* to perception (it says 'the heavy is light'); but perhaps this would be better construed transparently,[44] or otherwise as stating something less

[41] Compare the differing views of Burnyeat 1976, and Cooper 1970, on *Tht.* 184–6, and also M. Frede 1987.

[42] The terminology in the passage for what perception does is varied: it '*shows* this no more than its opposite', 523c2–3; it does not *signify* that the finger is the opposite of finger, 523d5–6; it *reports* perceiving that the same thing is both hard and soft, 524a3–4; it *says that* the same thing (the hard, or what is hard) is soft, 524a8; it *signifies* that the heavy is light and the light heavy, 524a10; sight *sees* the large and the small as something confused, 524c4.

[43] This may show too much, on any reading; does everyone puzzle about the deliverances of the senses? On the loaded reading, however, it might come out true; for then the philosophical conversation has already begun – the soul's puzzlement is inexorable. For other reasons, however – see below – I think this account of what is happening is not persuasive.

[44] They say, of the heavy thing, that it is light. Compare the amplification of this problem following the discussion of *allodoxia* at *Tht.* 188 ff. This expression might be thought to support the loaded interpretation (they offer an account of what heavy is that is also an account of what light is); but the language at this point is not decisive in favour of that interpretation.

logically worrisome (they say 'what is heavy is (also) light' where each of the predicate terms is understood as incomplete: 'heavy compared to a mouse', 'light compared to an elephant'). On either account, however, the deliverance of perception seems to be both discursive (perception is said to *say* something, as well as to *signify* – the latter might be just labelling, but not so, surely, the former in this context?) and complex. For the expressions 'heavy' and 'light' are used of the same thing; and they appear (as the last two clauses of the passage show) somehow *in the same announcement*. The announcement itself is what generates the soul's puzzlement. The contrast between perception and the soul is urged here, therefore, in just one dimension: the affect of puzzlement (suffered by the soul), or its lack (in perception, which just reports). That affect is what causes the soul to formulate a question, 'What does perception signify by the heavy?'

Glaucon responds, and amplifies the collection of metaphors used here to describe the interchange between perception and the soul. The deliverances of perception are announcements, messages, utterances[45] (524a3; the language is picked up again at 524b5); and Glaucon says that they are puzzling, and require *consideration*. The messages are puzzling, but perception itself is not puzzled. The puzzlement is felt, instead, in the soul, for it is the soul that needs to embark on consideration. Then the significance of the difference between what perception does, and what the soul does, is the difference in, if you like, cognitive *stance*, not in the discursive character of what each faculty says. The cognitive stance of perception is mere reportage – reportage which includes judgement (523b2); whereas the soul, appropriately enough, has all sorts of other stances, including the affect of puzzlement, and the ability to have a conversation with its own parts. So perception just delivers the message that this thing is hard and soft; the soul reacts by being puzzled, and then summons calculation and thought to think about the message that has been delivered (524b4–5).

When perception reports, soul invites reason to consider whether 'each of the things announced'[46] is one or two (524b5). If they are two, then each (of the two) will be one; and in that case, each will be separate from (non-identical with) the other – for otherwise they would not be conceived

[45] The Greek is *hermēneiai*, whose cognate verb is often translated 'interpret'. However, Plato often uses this group of words to describe an articulation or an utterance: e.g. at *Tht.* 209a; likewise at *Soph.* 246e the verb describes Theaetetus' taking the role of the reformed giants (he is supposed merely to express their view, not to do any more on his own behalf).

[46] That is, each of the things which figures in the announcement; reason does not check whether there is one announcement or two.

as two, but as one. But as a matter of fact, perception presents, for example, large and small, not as separate, but as mixed up together (*sunkechumenon*, 524c4). It is this confusion of two separate things which soul is supposed to sort out, and to see as distinct (524c7), quite to the contrary of the deliverance of perception. What is it for perception to muddle something up? Here the issue cannot be that perception provides the soul with two messages, which the soul then mixes up together and then needs to separate out. On the contrary, the mixing up is done by perception: it reports *as one* large and small, hard and soft. In that case the report of perception must be not only discursive, but also complex. The soul succeeds in seeing each property *as one* (hence the predicatives at b10–c1), while perception sees large and small not *as* separate, but *as* something mixed up. The complex structure of perception's deliverances falls out from this directly. What perception actually says is, 'This (same) thing is both hard and soft' (option (b) above).[47]

So each report of perception has propositional content: seeing is seeing as, and even bare perception reports a complex situation. That complexity is what causes soul to *wake thought up* (524d). Without it, we should be left with the dull series of distinct pieces of information: 'this is a finger', 'that is a chair'; and without waking thought up, we should be left in confusion: 'this chair is both hard and soft.' What perception does is complex, but banal: the questions arise in the soul after its report. The deliverances of the senses, then, are not represented here as providing purely empirical foundations for thought, foundations different in kind and in mode of access from the comparisons and the puzzles forced on us by the conflicted appearances. Instead, the contrast between sight and what the soul does is offered in terms of the non-reflective attitude of sight (it merely reports the conflict), and the puzzlement the soul feels when it realizes that there is a conflict – that puzzlement is what drags it to think. Socrates' point is then *not* that the soul operates in a quite different, because discursive, medium from perception: indeed, that would render incoherent his account of the failings of perception (and leave insignificant the warning that he is not going to speak of dim and failing sight). Instead, the soul is provoked – puzzled – by the deliverances of perception, and so has something to do: to resolve the puzzle. It is the puzzle itself then – both the puzzle as it appears in the report of perception

[47] If this is a *report*, not an answer to a question, it is, in the terms I suggested in n. 38, banal, not philosophically loaded: the philosophical issues are raised *after* perception delivers its report. It follows, I think, that we should prefer an interpretation that has the subject of perception's report as one of the ordinary individuals of the perceptual world.

(a logical aspect), and the sense of puzzle in the soul (a psychological aspect) – which generates the move up the line towards the full account of what largeness is.[48]

The interaction between perception and the soul, despite the appearance that it is described here in non-metaphorical terms, is dominated by the metaphor of conversation. The conversation is initiated when perception delivers a message to the soul: a message about the way the world is. That message puzzles the soul, and causes it to try to find out what is meant. The soul asks the mind some questions; and the dialogue between soul and mind is directed towards questions such as 'What is the large?' So the report of perception leads the soul to the consideration of being: to consideration of *what it is to be* one, or large, or soft. But the soul is led by perception as discursive, by 'seeing' as 'seeing as'.

Nonetheless, perception's role is to connect the soul with the way the world is. Even although it does not, as I have argued, deliver unmediated, raw foundations for the ratiocinations of the soul, but reports something that the soul finds puzzling, perception is not thereby represented as mistaken. On the contrary, as Socrates' correction of Glaucon's suggestion (at 523b: 'surely we are talking about things seen dimly, or about illusions?') makes clear, perception is still thought of as delivering reports that are somehow true of the way the world is. Perception's contact with reality is the starting point of the conversation in the soul.

The account of the conversation that takes place within the soul has several points of contact with the conversation that is represented in the dialogue itself. Socrates anticipates this parallel at the outset:

> 'I shall try', I said, 'to show how it seems to me. When I distinguish, on my own behalf, between those things which lead in the direction we said, and those which do not, then you must view them with me, and agree or disagree, so that we may see this more clearly too, if indeed it is as I pronounce it to be.' (523a5–8)

The verbs which are used to describe the report of perception and the soul's conversation are used by Socrates to describe what he is doing for Glaucon: he is showing Glaucon what he (Socrates) thinks (523a5, compare 523e7); he invites Glaucon to join with him in viewing or seeing (523a7, 523a10, compare 524e10); he delivers an oracular message (523a8, compare 524b1); they are both invited to see more clearly what the message means (523a8, compare 524a7); and part of that clarification will come through agreement or disagreement with what each other says (523a7, compare 524e5). So the

[48] See Politis 2004a and 2004b.

philosophical conversation represented by the *Republic* itself is analogous to the conversation that takes place in the soul, when it puzzles about the report of perception. This analogy presses the question again: how comprehensive is the conversation of dialectic?

4. THE SOUL'S VIEW (OF THE GOOD)

If perception is discursive, then its role, I claim, cannot be to provide foundations in some special, unmediated way.[49] For what perception reports is already mediated by the propositional nature of its utterance. How, then, will sense-perception serve as an analogue for the quasi-perception of the soul when it reaches the form of the good, or the physical eye for the eye of the mind (e.g. 518c–e)? How can the form of the good be foundational for knowledge if it is not grasped in the special manner we might attribute to quasi-perception, or to intuition, or to something otherwise intellectually raw?

When perception makes reports, such as 'this (finger) is large and small', the soul, reacting to its own puzzlement at the conflict, separates out the two confused claims, reflects on them and thinks about just how to resolve them and to explain the terms used. This dialogue in the soul has a crucial second-order element; for the soul's puzzlement is a result of its noticing a problem with perception's report; and the questions it asks of thought are reflective on the structure and the grounds for perception's message.[50] The soul's questions, that is, include several other (first-order) claims in their scope. Throughout the imagined dialogue, the role of the soul is to take the detached stance of considering the reports and the answers to its questions, as it were from outside. This detachment, therefore, is reflective and second-order.[51]

We might say the same of the soul's silent dialogue:

Socrates: So by 'thinking' do you mean the same thing as I do?
Theaetetus: What do you mean by it?
Socrates: When the soul goes through a dialogue itself with itself about something it is considering. Of course it is in ignorance that I tell you this, but this is how it seems to me. As the soul thinks, it seems to me to do nothing but have a

[49] One might argue that the fact that perception reports the way the world is (save when the organ fails, or is confronted by an illusion) is sufficient for its report to be foundational. In that case, perception's claim to being foundational is not a matter of its being unmediated, but a matter of its being true. I had seen this matter differently (at McCabe 2000: ch. 7); but see D. Frede 1999.

[50] This is most noticeable for a *de dicto* reading of perception's report.

[51] See McCabe 2000: ch. 8 on 'detachment' in this sense.

conversation with itself, asking itself questions and answering them, agreeing and disagreeing. When it comes to something definite, whether after a slow process or swift as a flash, and it now says the same thing and doesn't dissent, we call this its belief. So I call this saying believing, and the speech I describe I call belief, not speech to another nor aloud, but in silence and to itself. (*Tht.* 189e–190a)

The silent dialogue seems to represent ordinary thinking;[52] but its structure bears significant similarities to the dialogue of the soul in the *Republic* in two important respects.

First: in the silent dialogue, as in the *Republic*, there are two parties to discussion: at times this is described as the soul 'talking to itself'; at times as though different parts of the soul take opposite roles, one part assenting, the other dissenting.[53] But the soul takes a third role: of 'wanting to reach a judgement' (*Phlb.* 38c5–7); of 'considering' (*Tht.* 189e7). In that role, the soul seems to have an overview of the whole discussion, and to assess what is going on, since the outcome is represented, in both texts, not as the soul merely *plumping* for one side or the other, but as reaching a thought-out judgement. The forming of that judgement comes about through reflection, through higher-order thought *about* the dialogue that is going on.

Second: the final stage of the silent dialogue, the judgement that is reached, is represented in the *Theaetetus* as the soul 'saying the same thing' (190a3); this occurs when a belief has been reached (or, if the discussion is held aloud, a statement, *logos*, *Phlb.* 38e3[54]). At that stage there is no longer a discussion, no longer any differences of view within the soul – instead, in the metaphor suggested by the *Philebus* account, the journey comes to an end. The finality of this point is expressed in the silent dialogue by there being a single, unified view in the soul: this is the belief.

If we ask just how these accounts of what are, after all, pretty ordinary cognitive episodes – deciding what is under the tree over there, or whether Theaetetus is Theodorus, or the beautiful ugly – bear on the grand business of dialectic in the *Republic*, these two features provide two points of contact. First, thinking seems to have an essential second-order element: and that, as I have suggested, is central to the *Republic*'s dialectic. But the second feature, the unity of the soul's belief at the end of its dialogue, may assist

[52] For discussion see Sedley 2003: ch. 1; Sedley 2004; Dixsaut 1997; Long 2004.

[53] For my purposes here it is indifferent whether this divides the soul, or simply illustrates the soul's taking different positions over time. Notice, again, the theme of assent and dissent, e.g. at 523a7, 525d–e, 529a, 533b.

[54] See above, n. 2: the expression *logos* is normative here.

with understanding the point of the analogy between the final stages of dialectic and perception.

The soul sees the good *after* it is puzzled, *as a result of* reflection on that puzzlement. For as it puzzles, the soul asks, for example, 'What is the one itself?' (525a1); and this question leads it to the contemplation of what is (525a2), or to the grasp of being (525b3) and thence to its grasp of the unhypothesized beginning – the form of the good.[55] The return of the language of 'learning' at this point in the discussion (525a3, 525b1 ff.) points to the connection between this part of the philosopher's activity and the 'greatest learning' of the form of the good, at 505a. But the analogy between what the soul does at this final point, and what sight is said to do, is still at work, too:

> 'But work it out from what has been said before,' I said. 'For if the one is adequately seen itself by itself, or grasped by any other sense, then it would not be something that drags us towards being, just as we said for the case of the finger. Yet if some sort of opposite to it is always seen at the same time, so that it appears no less one than also its opposite, then this will demand someone to judge it, whose soul will be compelled to puzzle and inquire, moving thought within itself, and asking what the one itself is. In this way learning about the one is one of the things that drag and turn us towards the contemplation of being.' (524d8–525a3)

Sight, no less than thought, may provide the soul with something 'itself by itself'; the contrast between sight and thought in this passage is urged, to repeat, not in terms of their objects, but in terms of the puzzling nature, or otherwise, of what perception reports.[56] Soul or thought grasps the 'itself by itself' in the cases where perception reports a puzzle. But perception reports both the uncontroversial cases (the finger) and the controversial ones (hard and soft); so Plato's point cannot here be that thought is veridical just when it is analogous to the passivity of perception to the uncontroversial cases – since, on such an assumption, perception would be passive to the controversial cases, too. Passivity is not the point. Instead, this sequence of argument turns on how thought is able to produce uncontroversial cases (the one itself by itself) from controversial ones, deciphering perception's messages and turning them from the coded versions, which contain an opposition, into uncoded accounts of something 'itself by itself'. The summit of the line, therefore, demands that what the soul says be said in clear.

[55] There are those who say that the form of the good and the unhypothesized beginning are not the same; in what follows it will become clear that, and why, I think they are.

[56] Cf. Fine 1990 on the significance of this for the earlier discussion of the contrast between knowledge and belief, at 476–80.

So perception proper is discursive, and this culminating intellection may be no less so. The intellectual event that occurs at the top of the line may differ from its dialectical precursor, then, not in kind (e.g. as intuition as opposed to reasoning) but in terms laid down by the conditions of dialectic.

First, it differs in psychological structure. At the end of the silent dialogue, the soul 'says the same thing'. At the end of the process of dialectic, likewise, the soul says the same thing; its view is no longer puzzled, vacillating, bothered by conflict. In this, it is like perception which is untroubled, when it delivers its message, by any sense of conflict. In perception's case, this is because it is unable to puzzle; in the case of the intellect the puzzles have been dispelled by the process of dialectic.

Second, the intellect's view at the top of the line differs from the preceding process of dialectic in logical structure. For there are no logical conflicts at the top of the line. Does this imply that quasi-perception presents the soul with something *simple* and unmediated by virtue of its simplicity?

Not so: perception is not simple, and no more is intellection. Socrates suggests that what happens at the summit of the philosopher's emergence from the cave is a spectacle (e.g. at 516b or in the (proleptic) account of the analogy between the form of the good and the sun at 509[57]). Again, if we were still to suppose that perception is unmediated and direct, we might think that the language of spectating here insists that the observer is passive, merely the recipient of what is borne in on him by his mind's eye. But the notion of a spectacle may have a different set of connotations.

To spectate may be an activity, to survey the spectacle, to take it in, integrate it, see how it all fits together into a whole (notably at 508 and 516).[58] This kind of surveying, after all, is the task of the dialectician after he has reached the pinnacle (537c–d): it is directly connected to the dialectic of conversation just because it is reflective, engaged in the second-order consideration of what is before it. This, in turn, is connected to the pervasiveness of the synoptic view; it looks over, looks through and through, it 'syllogizes' (516b9, 517c1, 531d2, 537c and see, for an example, 528d7). The soul's survey is thus definitive, because it is complete and, in just this sense, final (511c2, 517b8, 532b2, 535a1). This completeness of its vision both mirrors and replaces the way in which perception produces its message whole. The soul's vision, on this account, is unitary, and unconflicted – a synoptic view, not simple nor raw.

[57] See 511c8, 516a9, 517b4, 518c10, 525a1, 525c2, 526e6, 532c6; and also 517d5, 529b3.

[58] See Burnyeat 2000.

Once again, the metaphor of conversation is doing important work here. This final stage, where the soul views the whole, imitates the close of a discussion, the moment in the silent dialogue when a belief is finally reached. But the final stage of the discussion can only integrate the whole if the discussion itself is somehow conducted in sequence, connectedly. I suggested that the model of philosophical conversation trades on just such a notion of the sequence of a conversation; it is explicit in these pages of the *Republic* as the giving and taking of reasons (531e4, 533c2, 534b); as the asking and answering of questions (515d5, 524e6, 526a, 528a5, 534d9); as the way in which puzzlement provokes a question and demands an answer – as the entire process of turning the soul towards being. This is what I called the *sequential* feature of conversation; and that sequence is integrated into the final view of the soul.

5. THE GOOD AS CAUSE

But this hasn't said enough, you might reasonably complain, about the *good*, nor about how this final spectacle explains the philosopher's grasp of the truth. At an earlier stage of dialectic the philosopher faces the kind of difficulty urged against Socrates and his method of question and answer. For when someone practises what the *Republic* describes as *dianoia*, he posits principles which are treated as self-evident, and which are coherent with the rest of the system derived from them (510c5–d3). In such a case, there is no independent verification of the system; instead, it is entirely possible that the entire structure of principles and consequences, albeit sequential and coherent, is comprehensively wrong. In the account of the divided line, this difficulty is apparently addressed by the claim that the person practising dialectic treats the hypotheses of *dianoia* as mere starting points, until he can arrive at the unhypothesized beginning. By *touching* this, he is able to verify everything that depends on it (511b4–c2). Somehow, therefore, the philosopher's *touching* of the unhypothesized beginning, the form of the good, provides the verification demanded by Meno: it allows him to know that his conclusion is the right answer to the question with which he began.[59]

How does the ascent to the form of the good offer such verification? In the first place, the move from the system of thought based on hypotheses to the system based on the good may be characterized as a move away from what is true just by virtue of its coherence with its system, to what

[59] See discussion of this issue in Scott 1995: chs. 1 and 2.

is true by virtue of some fact of the matter, independent of the mind of the philosopher. This realist dimension to the philosopher's knowledge is crucial to explaining just why the top of the line is unhypothesized (it is real); and in showing how there would be just one true system which knowledge knows, or understanding understands (reality is, one might reasonably think, unique). But how does Plato make a bridge between the hypothesized system and the one true one?

Here again the version of the process of dialectic against which I have been arguing has an answer: the form of the good is the single and simple item which is responsible for the verification of all the rest. It does so, that account would insist once again, by being apprehended in a quite different manner from everything else: grasped raw and unmediated. But if this is the only way of bridging the divide between hypotheses and the unhypothesized beginning, we are back to the problem with which I began, of a fracture within the method of dialectic itself.

I have argued, however, that Plato's model of perception in these pages of the *Republic* is discursive, not raw and unmediated; and that intellection should be understood analogously. And, indeed, the form of the good cannot be strictly simple; for it is not only the object of intellection, but the cause of everything else, and the source of its intelligibility.[60] Consider the discussion of the light of the sun, which yokes together the faculty of sight and the power to be seen (507e ff.) and is itself seen by what it explains (508b). Likewise, the light of truth which comes from the form of the good, and which explains the intelligibility of what is known (508d), is itself the object of knowledge, the greatest learning (505a). The cause of knowledge and truth, and what it causes, are tied together, and they form (as does the sun for the sensible world) a complete whole.

But the form of the good, of course, also represents something more: it is 'beyond being in authority and power' (509b9–10). This remark, famously, started a tradition of discussions: is the good somehow mysterious, mystical, ineffable? To suppose so, I submit, would take us, once again, away from the carefully wrought discussion of dialectic in the *Republic*. Recall that, so far, the view of dialectic as philosophical conversation presses both the sequential nature of what is discussed, and the synoptic view taken of it by the philosopher. From the psychological point of view, this higher perspective, this second-order thinking is what allows us to understand the complete system, to take an entirely synoptic view. But there is a further demand put on such a sequence by the conversational model: that it be

[60] I am grateful to Vasilis Politis and Christopher Rowe for discussion about what follows.

conducted by the giving and taking of reasons. We may understand this from the objective point of view in terms of the causal structure of what is known. The good is the cause of everything else; and we know just when we grasp that it is so: when we 'see' the good *as* the cause, and of the things it causes. But that grasp can be neither non-discursive, nor of something simple: the cause offers knowledge when we see just what it is the cause of; and knowing the cause is itself complete (on pain of causal explanation becoming regressive), and so authoritative and final. Such an account is also reflective; for we know, not only that the cause is a cause but that our knowledge is a consequence of seeing the causal structure of things. For such knowledge, the second-order perspective is essential.

Think again about the second limb of Meno's paradox: how do we know that we know? The *Republic*'s dialectic is interested both in the psychological aspect of coming to know[61] and in the systematic, objective nature of what is known. We might rephrase Meno's question, therefore, as one about understanding: how do we understand that we understand?[62] If we think of dialectic as conversation, both the psychological and the objective aspects come into view. In its psychological aspect, dialectic takes a synoptic, systematic and reflective view of what it concerns. In its objective aspect, that systematicity is assured by the explanatory structure of causation, itself the object of dialectic's study.

This objective aspect is brought out strongly by the role of perception in Plato's account of dialectic. For while perception is not here construed as raw or unmediated, it does still have a peculiar feature of veridicality. Perception is, in the way that thought is not, unpuzzled, because perception makes its reports wholesale; but it is not thereby *false*. On the contrary (recall Socrates' caution with Glaucon's talk of perceptual errors), perception does indeed connect with the world as it is (507d–508b). When I see, even when my seeing is complex and discursive, my seeing is somehow veridical: seeing a finger, for example, as large and small is still a case of seeing it the way it is – even if that is, on reflection, confused and hard to understand. But the psychological aspect of that seeing is captured by the way in which seeing seems to cross a perceptual threshold: 'Yes, yes, I see it!' In the same way, we use perceptual or physical metaphors in English to capture the crossing of the cognitive threshold when we suddenly understand something we

[61] I avoid calling this 'subjective' in order not to raise a series of epistemological issues that would be out of place here. See above, section 2, on the two ways of understanding the rawness of a feel.

[62] 'Understand that we understand' looks clumsy; but it makes the point that a part of understanding is the second-order element, understanding that we understand. On understanding see, notably, Burnyeat 1981; Nehamas 2004.

failed to understand before – we 'see' it, we 'grasp' it, we 'get' it. From these moments, we are no longer puzzled or confused – but quite sure of what it is that we have understood.

In that case, there is an exact parallel between the untroubled stance of perception when it delivers its report to the soul, and soul's untroubled grasp of the truth when, indeed, it does see the unhypothesized beginning. The essential feature of the analogy, however, is not something about how perception occurs but – as we have already seen – in the cognitive stance adopted by perception: it does not puzzle, it simply states. When the soul reaches the final stage of dialectic, likewise, what falls away is its puzzlement, not its discursive grasp of what it understands. So those moments when we step across the cognitive threshold are not individual events of raw perception or quasi-perception – on the contrary, that sense that we suddenly understand arrives when we see how things fit together, how they are all explained, and when we see, further, that we see it; this is why the form of the good is beyond being in authority and power. The language of perception, construed thus discursively and reflectively, offers Socrates the analogy he needs for the crossing of the dialectician from the process of inquiry to the state of understanding. The process of dialectic is thus continuous up to, and including, its end; for it culminates – as, in a way, it began – in the untroubled satisfaction of 'I see!' And it does so, when what is seen is the explanatory structure of the whole.

6. KNOWLEDGE, UNDERSTANDING AND THE GOOD

You might still complain that there is just not enough about the good in all this: not enough, first, to account for the normativity of dialectic; and not enough to show why the choice of the form of the *good* as the end of philosophical inquiry is anything but tendentious. Even if Plato can show how to do good dialectic, can he show how dialectic is good? The question is a huge one, and well beyond the scope of this paper. I offer, instead, a brief speculation about how philosophical conversation might figure in its answer.

The paradigm of philosophical conversation is normative: it is something that can be done well, or badly. If I am right about its structure, this normativity bears both on the psychological conditions for dialectic and the objective ones: dialectic reaches the truth out there in the world just if and just when the soul of the dialectician is in the right (discursive and synoptic) state for the truth with which it is presented. So for dialectic to be done well it is not enough for it to issue in a reliable and defensible grasp of the truth; for then any method might do, just so long as this end is reached. Nor, however, is our cognition determined simply by the conversations we have, nor the subjective decisions we may make about conflicted points of view. Instead, just as in cases of perception, conflicting appearances invite us to think – not from a standing start, but from something already fully cognitive; and when we reach the end, the end is not a singular event, a vision to which we are passive, but a synoptic view of what is, completely informed by the good. As we move up, and down, through the intelligible world, the interrelation between what is intelligible and our cognition of it is uniformly dialectical. This outcome of philosophical inquiry is rightly seen as understanding, rather than knowledge: for in this way the state of mind of the knower is fully engaged with what is known.[63]

If this is right, then the conversational model is essential to the way in which dialectic hopes to explain understanding. But it still has the appearance of something uniformly epistemological: does it tell us anything more substantial about the good, or about virtue? That seems to be what Glaucon is promised (528a).[64] If we know what it is to do good dialectic, do we also see that doing dialectic is good?

One answer to this question might be that if knowledge is of the good, our knowledge always provides us with the right thing to do. Having knowledge of the good, this answer declares, allows us to be regularly successful (certainly always more successful than without it). The advantage of dialectic, that is to say, is an instrumental one – that it uniformly offers the right answer to ethical questions; and thus supplies happiness (and virtue too, perhaps).[65]

This instrumental account of the importance of dialectic is one which will explain why philosophers should rule (they will always make the best decisions for the state); but it fails to account for why I should care for knowledge; nor why understanding should be what I search for. After all, if my state is ruled by a philosopher-king, his decisions on my behalf will be as good as my own would be; so there is no need for me to trouble myself with learning mathematics, nor with the hard enterprise of philosophical examination; I can simply enjoy the benefits of my ruler's decisions on my

63 Burnyeat 2000: 70 – as the philosopher progresses through and up the disciplines, he gets a more and more integrated vision. 'Someone who has achieved that integrated vision has not only assimilated a vast amount of mathematics. They have assimilated it as a structured whole. And for Plato, assimilation means that your soul takes on the structure of the abstract realm you study.'

64 Notice Socrates' rejection of the instrumental account of the value of learning at 527a–b.

65 This is the tip of a large interpretative iceberg: the nature of Platonic eudaimonism. This should not, in my view, be construed in a thinly consequential way – or even fatly so; but see different approaches by Irwin 1995; Penner and Rowe 2005.

behalf. All I need to know, for happiness, is someone who knows. Once again, this account of the role of the good in my intellectual life is too thin to account for the complexity of Plato's claims for dialectic; notably, it fails to show why the psychological conditions on dialectic are anything more than a pious hope for the philosophical life.

Instead, I suggest, we should attend to the way in which the process of dialectic transforms the soul of the dialectician,[66] and to the way in which this transformation is related to the good.[67] Suppose we find ourselves clambering out of the cave by means of dialectic; we might think that each higher step is *better* than its predecessor, just in the sense that it is nearer to the point when we are actually wise (see 531d). The situation is different after we have seen the good, after wisdom and virtue become the settled state of our souls (if that can ever happen). For from that point everything we do is informed by our understanding. This is not an instrumental claim, about how our virtue, or our knowledge, makes us better at getting goods. Instead, the point is that this state of soul makes valuable the features of our lives,[68] makes them into good lives; for then the good operates as an informing cause.

When our souls understand and are wise, then, the ethical structure of our lives is determined by that wisdom; and the sight of the good at the top of the line is thus transformative. The eye of the soul turns the whole soul with it (518e); after that point, the value of everything is determined by virtue; one thing is *better* than another in this sense (and in contradistinction to the way in which things can be better on the way up the line). Ethical sight, on this view, makes things (actually, really) valuable in the life of the person who sees them, and the virtue of wisdom thus transforms the life of the person who sees the good. That transformation occurs by virtue of the bridge philosophical conversation builds between the soul of the dialectician and the reality of the good.

This, then, is what it is for the form of the good to be reached by dialectic. The form of the good on this account is the sovereign good, the source of all value.[69] Its role as the sovereign good in the life of the dialectician is for it to make value in his soul and his life; and that happens by virtue of his state of soul. For the good to be sovereign for him, that is to say,

[66] Burnyeat 2000: 56, 'For Plato, the important task of ruling is not day-to-day decision-making, but establishing and maintaining good structures, both institutional and psychological.'

[67] See here Nightingale 2004: 116.

[68] This is the point made at *Euthd.* 281: for the virtuous man, poverty is better than wealth for the vicious. Cf. Burnyeat 2003; McCabe 2005a.

[69] On this issue see Korsgaard 1983 (who describes this as the intrinsic good); Williams 2003; Burnyeat 2003; Broadie 2005; McCabe 2005a.

he must satisfy both the objective and the psychological conditions for dialectic. Without that, what seems valuable is an illusion, a dream of the good:

'So, then, do you call "dialectician" the person who grasps the account of the being of each thing? Surely you will not say that someone who has no account, to the extent that he is unable to give that account to himself and to another, has understanding of it?'
'How could I say so?' he said.
'So likewise for the good: someone who cannot distinguish the idea of the good in account by marking it off from everything else, and who cannot get through all the tests of what he thinks as if through a battle, nor is eager to test it according to the way things are, rather than according to opinion, and who cannot progress through all these things without his account collapsing – such a person you will surely say, knows neither the good itself, nor any other good. And if perchance he gets hold of some kind of image of it, he does so by opinion, not by knowledge; and living his present life in dream and sleeping, before he ever wakes up here, he arrives in Hades and sleeps at last.' (534b3–d1)

CHAPTER 5

What use is Aristotle's doctrine of the mean?

Christof Rapp

The current revival of virtue ethics is indebted to Aristotle in many ways: Aristotle clearly states that the virtuous agent displays the right action together with the appropriate motivation; he explicitly connects the concept of virtue with the accomplishment of the best and flourishing life; he formulates a principle that is often used to define the very concept of virtue ethics, namely the principle that the good particular action cannot be defined by general rules, but is rather determined by the way the virtuous person would act; in the same context Aristotle seems to hint at the idea that it is a sort of context-sensitivity that allows us to find and execute the right course of action. Further, Aristotle unambiguously describes the acquisition of virtues as a process of forming and habituating one's character, and last but not least, he outlines his theory of ethical virtue in terms of emotional responses to various situations. Some of these points can be found in other ancient ethical schools as well, but there are characteristics of Aristotle's ethics that make it more attractive for modern ethical theory: his account of virtue does not seem to carry the burden of Socratic intellectualism; it seems to be less dependent on metaphysical background theories than, e.g., Plato's ethics; it does not display the same hostile attitude towards emotions as the Stoic account of virtue; and it seems to be closer to some important common-sense convictions, e.g., that the good life must be a pleasant one and that not even virtue immunizes us against the effects of great misfortunes.

Nevertheless, there is one piece of Aristotle's theory of virtue that modern virtue theorists either politely ignore or severely criticize: the famous doctrine that virtue is a mean between two correlative vices. Bernard Williams even calls it one of the most celebrated and least useful parts of Aristotle's philosophy[1] and adds that this doctrine is better forgotten. Perhaps Williams' verdict could be neglected or relativized if the doctrine of the

[1] See Williams 1985: 36.

mean were just a marginal thesis within Aristotle's general account of virtue, but the contrary is true: the thesis that virtue is a middle state is explicitly introduced as the *differentia specifica* of virtuous dispositions (*hexeis*), and it is also meant to explain what it is for the non-rational part of the soul to be in an excellent condition. If this is the case, Aristotle's account of virtue and the doctrine of the mean stand and fall together. Hence, it must be unsatisfying for all philosophers who are interested in virtue ethics to appeal to an Aristotelian account of virtue on the one hand, but to reject an essential piece of this theory on the other. In what follows, I am going to argue that, though there are many internal problems in this doctrine, we must not regard it as fundamentally mistaken, if we just acknowledge the main function of this theory. I will, however, not spend too much time discussing and rejecting the numerous objections that have been raised against Aristotle's doctrine; instead I am going to highlight some aspects of Aristotle's account of ethical virtues that allow a more charitable reading of the doctrine of the mean.

1. THE PLACE OF THE DOCTRINE IN ARISTOTLE'S ETHICS

As Sarah Broadie has noted, the doctrine of the mean (or, in short, 'the doctrine') often gets a disappointed reception;[2] *disappointment* is a good expression to describe this, because it is primarily a matter of what we have expected; and, indeed, some expectations about the doctrine of the mean turn out to be unjustified. Readers are particularly disappointed when they expect to get a general guideline for action; but it is quite obvious that the doctrine is not intended to give us such a practical guideline. What its real purpose is can be best judged if one looks at the context in which this doctrine is introduced into the ethical theory.

1.1. The broad context

In the *Nicomachean Ethics*, the doctrine of the mean first occurs in the second book, which gives us a comprehensive analysis of the ethical virtues; this second book is preceded by the treatment of happiness in the first book and followed by the discussion of particular virtues in the third and fourth books. The situation in the *Eudemian Ethics* is similar: the first chapter of the second book introduces a definition of happiness before switching to the topic of ethical virtues; the doctrine of the mean is sketched in the

[2] See Broadie 1991: 95.

third chapter of the same book as one element of the general account of ethical virtue. This general account of virtue is followed by an extensive discussion of particular virtues in the third book.[3] The concept of virtue plays a crucial role in the definition of happiness in both treatises: happiness (*eudaimonia*) is characterized as 'the activity of a complete life in accordance with complete virtue',[4] as 'an activity of the soul in accordance with complete virtue',[5] or as 'activity of the soul in accordance with virtue (and if there are more virtues than one, in accordance with the best and the most complete)'.[6] Hence, it is not surprising that Aristotle hastens to substantiate the relatively vacuous definition of happiness with an extended discussion of one of its key terms: 'virtue'. He explicitly says that we will probably get a better understanding of happiness by investigating the field of virtue.[7]

But, whereas everybody has a certain grasp of what the concept of virtue means – since everybody is acquainted with virtues like justice, moderation and courage, etc. – the definition of happiness makes a peculiar use of the same term 'virtue': a first indication is that in connection with happiness the word is mostly used in the singular, while for the common understanding of 'virtue' it goes without saying that there are many of them, so that the plural use is indicated. Also, if we look at the premisses from which the definition of happiness is derived, it would not even be possible to replace 'virtue' by items like 'justice', 'courage' or 'moderation', because these premisses are about the good or best state of the soul and the proper functioning of certain capacities of the soul. According to the respective arguments, happiness is the good or successful activity or actualization of a capacity that is peculiar to the human soul, and the Greek term for virtue, *aretē*, comes in to indicate that not *each* but only the *good* activity of the soul is to be associated with happiness;[8] hence it is clear that what matters in the definition of happiness is the intention of the word *aretē*, namely that it means an *excellent* state, something that functions well and matches the highest standards. This is a possible and not unusual meaning of the Greek word *aretē*, but the singular use, referring to the best possible state in any particular field, is still far from the plural use of the word by which we refer to 'ordinary' virtues like justice, courage, moderation.

[3] Another similarity is that in both treatises the discussion of the voluntary and involuntary is located between the general account of virtues and the discussion of particular virtues.

[4] *EE* 2.1, 1219a38–9. [5] *EN* 1.13, 1102a5–6. [6] *EN* 1.7, 1098a16–18. [7] *EN* 1.13, 1102a6–7.

[8] The connection between the *good* performance and the introduction of the term *aretē* is most obvious in lines 1098a10–15 of *EN* 1.7.

Plato and Aristotle played with this ambiguity of *aretē*, sometimes deliberately jumping from one meaning to the other,[9] and perhaps they even expected that the average reader was inclined to believe that each virtue in the ordinary sense is something *good*, since it is a good trait of character. But of course, from a philosophical point of view, it cannot be taken for granted that the properties that contemporaries and fellow citizens happen to accept as being virtuous simply describe the excellent state of the human soul. Though Plato and Aristotle seem to agree on the point that a proper understanding of virtues must identify them with the good state of the soul, they did not regard this as a trivial point, but were quite aware that it must be argued for. According to the picture of popular morality that Plato drew in some of his dialogues, the ordinary understanding of virtues is vulnerable to the seduction of the Sophists precisely because it fails to make use of the intimate connection between virtues and the good state of the soul on the one hand, and between the good state of the soul and happiness on the other. But once we come to understand that the various virtues are manifestations of a good state of the soul and that a good state of the soul is either identical to or crucial for happiness, the alleged tension between the performance of moral virtues and the conquest of one's own happiness, which seems to be irresolvable on the level of popular morality, more and more disappears. So much is common ground between Plato and Aristotle, though they disagree on some relevant points: for example, the role of knowledge, the partition of the soul, the unity of virtues, etc. But it should be more obvious now that the relation between 'virtue', signifying the excellent state of the soul, and 'virtues', referring to the ordinary and socially accepted praiseworthy personal traits, is a crucial point in every Platonically inspired moral philosophy and that it is just this relation to which Aristotle devotes his undivided attention. Since it is the first sense of 'virtue' that is at stake in the first book of *EN* (i.e. in the definition of happiness) and the latter sense that becomes prominent in the third and fourth books, we are now justified in expecting that the general account of virtue which is developed in between the first and the third book and of which the doctrine of the mean is one indispensable piece will help the reader to understand the link between the excellence of the human soul and the ordinary virtues as we used to know them before dealing with moral philosophy.

[9] As Aristotle does in *EN* 1.7, 1098a17, when he suddenly switches from the singular to the plural.

1.2. The intermediate context

The first book of *EN* is completed by the distinction between two types of virtues, the ethical and the intellectual ones. The list of generally accepted virtues includes virtues of both types. But the ambition of the philosophical account of virtues is to base this division on a certain theory of the human soul. For the previous discussion of happiness has unambiguously shown that happiness is essentially connected with the activity of those capacities that are peculiar to the human soul. The capacity that exclusively belongs to the human soul has already been identified as *logos*, reason, but if the two types of virtue are to be related to typical capacities of the human soul, it is crucial to identify either a division in the concept of reason or a twofold use of the rational capacity. Actually, Aristotle says that either the sense of the phrase '*logon echon*' ('having reason') is twofold – first, what has reason in the proper sense and has it in itself, and second, what is able to listen, to obey or to be responsive to reason[10] – or that one element of the non-rational part[11] of the soul is able to listen, to obey or to be responsive to the part of the soul that possesses reason in itself. This division allows Aristotle to associate the intellectual virtues with the part of the soul that possesses reason in itself and ethical virtues with the corresponding part that does not possess reason in itself but, nevertheless, has a certain share in it, since it can react to what reason says.

So far, so good. But what has to be explained is how virtues can be understood as the best state of the respective parts of the human soul. In the case of intellectual virtues, such as wisdom, prudence, etc., it is easy to see why they manifest the good state of the rational part of the soul: the rational part of the soul is in a good state if it has certain rational or intellectual capacities and if it performs those capacities well. But how can we define the good state of the non-rational part of the soul? To be good, one could say, it must perform its typical capacities well. But what is the criterion for the good functioning of non-rational capacities? As we saw, the part of the soul that is responsible for the ethical virtues is not simply

[10] See *EN* 1.13, 1103a1–3.

[11] In this context, Aristotle does not want to be committed to the assumption of *parts* of the soul in a literal sense: In *EE* 2.1, 1219b32–6, he explicitly says that it does not matter whether we speak of parts or not; what matters is that we can distinguish several capacities within the soul. In *EN* 1.13, he mentions parts (1102a29), but weakens this claim by referring the relevant discussion to the exoteric writings (1102a26–7). Critical remarks about the partition of the soul can be found in *De an.* 3.9 and 10; most of them seem to be directed against Plato's tripartite soul because this model of the soul artificially separates desire from the perceptual capacity.

defined by being non-rational, but by being non-rational *and* being able to listen, to obey or to be responsive to what reason says. Hence, this part of the soul is in a good state if it actually obeys what reason says and if it reacts just as reason would recommend. 'Obeying what reason says' can mean two quite different things: the controlled person (*enkrates*) does what reason says while there are opposing impulses urging him to do something else; or the virtuous person does what reason says, but without having competing or contrary impulses. These are two degrees of obedience, since Aristotle says that in the latter case the non-rational part is more or more easily obedient (*euēkoōteron*[12]) and everything in such a person is consonant with reason (*homophōnei tōi logōi*).[13]

So much is clear by the end of the first book of *EN*. But what does reason want us to do? When is the non-rational part of our soul in agreement with what reason says? It is clear that we cannot understand why the ethical virtues manifest the good state of the non-rational part of the soul as long as these questions are unanswered. The first book does not attempt to comment on these points, but leaves it to the extended discussion of virtue in the second book to develop an answer. And, indeed, when one of the later chapters of book 2 summarizes that discussion, it explicitly mentions 'consonance with right reasoning' as a defining element (2.6, 1107a1).

It is obvious, then, that the discussion of virtue in book 2 of *EN* must explain how ethical virtues can be understood as effects or manifestations of the good state of the non-rational part of the soul. We cannot guarantee yet that it is exactly the doctrine of the mean that has to fulfil this task; however, since the doctrine is essential for the definition of ethical virtues, we can be confident that the doctrine will contribute to the elucidation of this problem.

1.3. The narrow context

Both the *Nicomachean* and the *Eudemian Ethics* introduce the core of the doctrine of the mean with almost the same wording: in everything continuous and divisible there is a greater, a lesser, and an equal amount, and this again means that there is always the possibility of excess, deficiency and the mean.[14] This is a merely conceptual point: in the realm of what is continuous and divisible, 'being good' or 'being right' means that it is not *too much* and not *too little*, so that it must be somewhere in the mean between

[12] *EN* 1.13, 1102b27. [13] *EN* 1.13, 1102b28. [14] See *EE* 2.3, 1220b21–3; *EN* 2.6, 1106a26–9.

them.[15] Hence, we can assume that the doctrine of the mean is introduced to explain what it is for virtue to be the *good* or the *right* disposition; that this is the function of this theory in *EN* can be seen (a) from the way it is introduced in the context, and (b) from a remark that concludes the first sketch of it.

(a) According to the previous chapter, *EN* 2.5, virtues are dispositions (*hexeis*); but since vices are dispositions, too, the subsequent chapter, *EN* 2.6, has to show what sort of dispositions virtues are. The idea that virtues are the good dispositions is developed in two approaches. The first approach (1106a14–24) gives a short version of the *ergon* argument that the reader already knows from the first book. It amounts to the assertion that the virtue of human beings is the disposition that makes the human being *good* and from which they will perform their function *well*. In the next sentence, the transition (1106a24–6) to the second approach, we are told that we already know how it must be understood that virtue makes the human being and his function good (probably from the more extended discussion of the *ergon* argument in the first book) and that the same idea will become clear in the second approach (starting from 1106a26), which outlines the doctrine of the mean. We can therefore conclude that this doctrine is designed to show the sense in which virtue is the good sort of disposition; and the sketchy answer we get is that virtue is a good disposition because it avoids excess and deficiency, where 'excess' and 'deficiency' designate the two ways of failing to be right or good in the field of continuous subject matters.

(b) That the core of the doctrine of the mean is the analytical point that what is good or right in continuous things must be neither be too much nor too little is confirmed by a proverbial formula that Aristotle quotes after introducing the doctrine: 'This is why people are accustomed to say of well-done products that it is possible neither to take away nor to add something.'[16] A similar conviction is expressed in a joke that Aristotle quotes in the *Rhetoric*: '. . . as the man said to the baker when he asked whether he should knead the dough hard or soft: "What? Isn't it possible to

[15] I take this to be the core of the doctrine of the mean, though I am aware that there are other versions of this doctrine and other non-conceptual arguments to support this doctrine. There are two main reasons why I think it is justified to focus on this version of the doctrine: first, it is the version that is given in reply to the question what sort of disposition virtue is, so that this version of the doctrine of the mean is used as *differentia specifica* in the definition of virtue; second, as opposed to the *EN* version, the *EE* version does not need any preparatory empirical steps in order to introduce this version of the doctrine of the mean, which clearly shows that this is the self-contained core of the entire enterprise.

[16] *EN* 2.6, 1106b9–11.

knead it *well*?"'[17] Finally, when Aristotle summarizes the doctrine in *EN* 2.6, he rephrases excess and deficiency with 'going astray', and the intermediate with 'getting it right (*katorthoutai*)'.[18]

1.4. *Summary: the function of the doctrine in its proper context*

Happiness has to do with virtue, since virtue is equivalent to the good state of the human soul and since it enables the soul to perform its proper function well. But how are ordinary virtues, like justice, temperance, courage, etc., related to the good state of the human soul? The popular catalogue of virtues comprises capacities that Aristotle would call 'intellectual' and 'ethical' virtues. The latter are defined as the good state of the non-rational part of the soul; it is due to ethical virtues that the non-rational part of the human soul performs its proper function well. This, again, means that it obeys what reason says; and right reasoning[19] wants the non-rational impulses to be directed to what is right or good. What is right or good cannot be defined by a general rule,[20] but, given that the ethical virtues are about something continuous, there is one constraint that must be met: virtues cannot aim at what is too much or too little. Hence, the mean represents the aspect of rightness, correctness or goodness in the definition of ethical virtues. It does not presume a decision procedure, or method, for determining the right course of action, nor does it presuppose an antecedent metaphysical doctrine or therapeutic technique.

2. CONCEPTUAL VERSUS EMPIRICAL VERSIONS OF THE DOCTRINE

In the previous section we have emphasized that the main purpose of the doctrine of the mean is to circumscribe the rightness or goodness of those dispositions that are in agreement with what reason says. On this reading, the doctrine carries a merely conceptual point: being too much or too little are just two ways of missing the right amount, and 'being in the mean' is just another word for avoiding both directions of failure. This analytical sense of the mean is relevant when it comes to the definition of virtue in *EN* 2.6 and *EE* 2.3, but, unfortunately, the conceptual

[17] *Rh.* 3.16, 1416b31–2. [18] *EN* 2.6, 1106b25–6.

[19] 'Right reasoning' or *orthos logos* occurs, e.g., in *EN* 2.2, 1103b33, and is alluded to in the definition of virtue in *EN* 2.6, 1107a1.

[20] *EN* 2.2, 1104a1–10.

character of the doctrine is obscured by the fact that the *Nicomachean Ethics* also introduces an empirical variation of the same doctrine. In *EN* 2.2, Aristotle argues that the things under discussion are destroyed by deficiency and excess and are preserved by the intermediate state. As an example, he introduces bodily strength, which can be destroyed by excessive and deficient training.[21] Excess, deficiency and the mean clearly allude to the doctrine of the mean; but here they are introduced as factors of preservation, generation and destruction, and this is not just a conceptual matter. Aristotle himself emphasizes that this is something that can be observed (*horōmen*[22]).

As already indicated, it is somehow misleading that the second book of *EN* offers both an analytical and an empirical version of this doctrine. This is probably why scholars thought that the doctrine of the mean oscillates between an analytical model and something else.[23] However, there are some signs that the empirical version is not on an equal footing with the analytical one: (i) The empirical version in *EN* 2.2 does not develop the complete doctrine, which would at least include the concept of 'the mean for us', etc. (ii) *EE* and *EN* substantially agree on the definition of ethical virtue and on the doctrine of the mean, which is one element of the discussion; but the *EE* only offers the conceptual version and includes no equivalent of the empirical variation. Therefore we can conclude that the full doctrine of the mean can be defended without any reference to the empirical conditions of generation and destruction of virtuous dispositions. (iii) The observation that excess and deficiency can destroy virtue are introduced as part of the discussion of how the virtues can be acquired. This discussion precedes the definition of ethical virtue and is not dependent on the fully developed doctrine of the mean. At this point in the discussion, it rather sets the scene for the appearance of the doctrine of the mean in *EN* 2.6; it makes the reader familiar with the general scheme of excess and deficiency and secures the general principle that the traits of our character become similar to the respective activities. (iv) Immediately before the introduction of the empirical variant of the mean, Aristotle warns us against the use of generalizations in the realm of ethics or politics. Though this is true, Aristotle says, we must give our present account the help we can,[24] and he then makes a new start with the observation that excess and deficiency can destroy our bodily and psychic qualities. It is clear, then, that this observation must be

[21] *EN* 2.2, 1104a11–13. [22] *EN* 2.2, 1104a14.

[23] See Williams 1985: 36, 'The theory oscillates between an unhelpful analytical model (which Aristotle himself does not consistently follow) and a substantively depressing doctrine in favour of moderation.'

[24] *EN* 2.2, 1104a10–11.

taken as a rule that holds only for the most part and that the subsequent remarks are rather seen as a starting point for the following discussion. (v) According to the empirical argument, someone who runs away from every dangerous situation becomes cowardly and someone who avoids every kind of pleasure becomes insensate. This, again, clearly argues from the developmental perspective and therefore diverges from the full doctrine of the mean in an important respect: according to the full doctrine, the point is not that we become cowardly or insensate because we avoid dangerous situations or voluptuous temptations; the point is rather that we are driven by non-rational impulses that make us avoid the right measure of danger or pleasure. (vi) Finally, according to the empirical argument, it would be harmful, in any case, to avoid all dangerous situations or voluptuous temptations, while, according to the full doctrine of the mean, it can happen that, under certain circumstances, the right measure actually demands that we avoid all those things.

In general, it does not seem that the empirical and the conceptual versions are simply competing arguments or that Aristotle is basically confused about the difference between these two arguments. It is rather the case that the conceptual truth that deviations from what is good or right in a continuous realm are always deficiencies or excesses provides the basis for all other applications of the doctrine of the mean. Aristotle's argument that virtues are destroyed by excess and deficiency, but preserved by the mean, is just the observable reverse side of the same coin: if all deviations from virtue have the form of excesses and deficiencies, and if, as Aristotle argued at length in *EN* 2.1, the dispositions come about from activities of the same sort,[25] then it actually follows that excessive and deficient activities do not bring about virtuous dispositions.

3. HOW TO APPLY THE DOCTRINE

The doctrine has sometimes been understood as (a) the general prescription to be moderate in all of our actions, (b) the guideline to select only those actions that are equidistant from the opposed extremes, (c) the recommendation to reach a harmonious state[26] of the soul by reducing all emotions to a mean or moderate measure. All these readings regard the doctrine as a practical guideline in one sense or the other; further, they presuppose

[25] *EN* 2.1, 1103b21–2.

[26] The ideal of a harmonious soul, which was defended by Plato, actually recurs in Aristotle; but not in the doctrine of the mean, but in the idea that, in the soul of the virtuous person, the non-rational impulses are consonant with what reason says.

that the agent is consciously trying to hit the mean under the description 'mean'; finally, they all require a positive evaluative statement in favour of moderation, harmony or the mean. Hence they are opposed to our view that the doctrine mainly rests on a conceptual clarification about what it means in the field of a continuous subject matter to be good or right. This opposition between the 'normative' readings on the one hand and the conceptual reading on the other hand raises the question whether there is a practical application of the doctrine at all, if we adopt the conceptual reading. This is an important question; it can even be formulated as a dilemma for our reading: if we answer the question in the negative, it could be objected that Aristotle's discussion of the several types of virtue does apply the doctrine; but if we answer the question in the affirmative, it can be objected that conceptual truths are no more than trivialities, and trivialities cannot be of any practical use. In order to respond to this dilemma, we should divide our leading question into two sub-questions: (3.1) Is the doctrine a practical guideline to action? (3.2) Does the doctrine amount to a sheer triviality? We can block the dilemma if we succeed in showing that, with respect to (3.1), the doctrine cannot be meant as a practical guideline in the sense of a decision procedure, and with respect to (3.2), that, after all, it provides a general scheme or blueprint that guides the exploration of the various virtues.

3.1. The doctrine as practical guideline?

According to the conceptual reading, the doctrine is more or less empty, so that it is hard to imagine how it could ever help us make a concrete decision. Whoever envisages the virtuous agent as using the doctrine to narrow down the room for possible actions by measuring their distance from the opposed excesses implicitly makes use of one of the mentioned readings (a), (b) or (c), and not of the conceptual reading. However, since the conceptual reading is still under examination, in a sense, we should not take the non-informative character of the doctrine for granted in order to argue against its practical applicability.

But there is independent evidence to show that the doctrine was never intended as a guideline for the agent to determine the right course of action. To begin with, some of the examples that have often been regarded as irresolvable problems for a consistent interpretation of the doctrine provide the most serious difficulties for those who understand the doctrine as a practical guideline or deductive rule-case system. The first example is the case about which Aristotle says that not its excess but the type of action itself is blameworthy, as e.g. adultery and murder.[27] Whenever adultery or murder is among the possible actions that are open to us in a particular situation, the doctrine of the mean would be of no use in sorting them out. And, what is more, if we regard the golden mean as the highest maxim from which we can deduce, step by step, the right particular action, adultery and murder would violate our guiding maxim, because they are regarded as blameworthy without being excessive. Further, the golden mean would fail as a practical guide, then, since the user would have to know which actions and emotions are bad by type and not by excess, and if, by mistake, he happened to apply the golden mean maxim to cases that are bad by type, he would even make it worse.

The second example is the case in which the mean is not equidistant from the extremes, but is closer to one of the poles than to the other;[28] for example, in the case of courage, rashness is much closer to the virtue than cowardice. This is a fatal and decisive admission, since, if there are cases in which the right action is closer to one sort of failure than to the other, the recommendation always to choose the middle of the road will be definitely misleading. In a final desperate attempt to preserve the action-guiding status of the golden-mean rule, we could postulate second-order rules that tell us when to apply the rule and when not; but it does not take much reflection to see that this would be a futile project. Some commentators have explained the non-equidistant cases by the concept of 'the mean relative to us' and, indeed, it is true that, according to Aristotle, the relevant mean is not the mean 'in the things', but the mean relative to us and that, within the 'mean relative to us', the principle of equidistance seems to be replaced by a sort of proportionality. But this does not apply to our case: the 'mean relative to us' implies that the right measure must be adjusted to the specific circumstances, while in the non-equidistant cases under discussion it is generally true that one extreme is closer to the mean than the other, regardless of any specific circumstances, and Aristotle even stresses that this situation can derive from the things themselves,[29] and not from the involved agents or circumstances.

So, we cannot help but conclude that these examples disavow the idea that the doctrine of the mean could have been introduced as an action-guiding rule. The conceptual reading can better deal with these exceptions; what matters is that virtues are the *good* dispositions, and if they are concerned

[27] *EN* 2.6, 1107a11–12. [28] See *EN* 2.8, 1108b35–1109a19 and *EE* 2.5, 1222a22–b4.
[29] *EN* 2.8, 1109a5–6.

with continuous things the criterion of being good can be rephrased by the concept of the mean; if not, then not.

Aristotle frankly invokes cases in which the doctrine would be bound to fail, if it were considered as a general guideline for practical decisions. Hence it is very unlikely that he himself regarded the doctrine primarily as such an action-guiding rule. This conclusion is confirmed by Aristotle's well-known theory that general rules or statements cannot determine what is good or right in every particular case, since in the sphere of action and things that bring us advantage or disadvantage there are always exceptions and other instabilities. In many cases, the best that the ethical theory can do is to formulate statements that hold only for the most part (*hōs epi to polu*), but not in general.[30] And since those things that we consider in practical deliberation do not happen by necessity, it is impossible to deduce them from necessary premisses.[31] For these reasons, Aristotle regards it as absurd to model the procedure that leads us to the right action as a sort of deduction from a general rule or maxim.

But even if one grants this background, it could still be objected that, when it comes to the doctrine of the mean, Aristotle just forgets about these declarations of intent and declares moderation or the mean to be the highest moral principle. There are, however, at least two indications that even the doctrine is perfectly in line with the anti-deductive character of Aristotle's ethics: first, one of the most important methodological passages concerning the problem of generalizations[32] in ethics is located right in the middle of the discussion of virtue in *EN* 2 and immediately before the first appearance of the doctrine, so that the formulation of the doctrine seems to be aware of the lessons to be learnt from the methodological remarks. Second, the concluding definition of virtue in *EN* 2.6 formulates, 'virtue is . . . in the mean relative to us, this being determined by reason (*logos*) and by the way in which the *phronimos* (the person of practical wisdom) would determine it.'[33] Here it is clear that the phrase 'mean relative to us' is empty insofar as it does not itself determine the right course of action; what the mean consists in must be determined by the *logos* and the wise person, i.e. by a personal capacity and a qualified person. This is strictly opposed to any sort of rule-based ethics; it is not the correct application of a general rule or maxim that defines the good action, but the particular judgement of the virtuous person. Since Aristotle invokes the virtuous or wise agent

30 See, e.g., *EN* 1.3, 1094b21.

31 See *Rh.* 1.2, 1357a22–33.

32 *EN* 2.2, 1103b34–1104a11.

33 *EN* 2.6, 1106b36–1107a2.

in order to elucidate the occurrence of the mean in the definition of virtue, it is safe to conclude that the doctrine itself cannot be intended to prescribe a concrete decision procedure.

3.2. The doctrine as triviality?

That the doctrine does not prescribe our decisions in particular actions does not imply that it cannot be applied at all. In both the *Eudemian* and the *Nicomachean Ethics* the definition of virtue, which includes the mean as one element, is followed by extended discussions of the various virtues; and these discussions show, among other things, how each particular virtue does fit into the scheme of excess, deficiency and the mean; for some virtues this scheme must be stretched or modified, in some cases it can only be applied in a very loose fashion, but at any rate it cannot be denied that this *is* a sort of application. But in contrast to the sort of application we discussed in response to question 3.1, the crucial difference is that the doctrine is not applied to particular decisions or actions, but to the philosophical exploration of the various ethical virtues; Aristotle's ethics comprises many different levels of generality or particularity. The definition of virtue as a disposition that lies in the mean between deficiency and excess is obviously settled on a rather high level of abstraction and generality. The price the philosopher has to pay for this generality is that the truths formulated on this level are rather vague or, as Aristotle is accustomed to formulating it, just in rough outline (*typōi*) and not precise.[34] In comparison with that level, the detailed discussion of the individual virtues, such as courage, temperance or generosity, is much more concrete, but is still far from the level at which we deliberate how to act in a particular situation. So there is an application of the doctrine, but not as a decision procedure.

But how does the discussion of the individual virtues benefit from the doctrine, if the doctrine is regarded as a conceptual truth? What lessons are to be learned from the relatively modest insight that what is good or right is neither too much nor too little? The least we can say is that the doctrine of the mean structures and systematizes the analysis of the various virtues. First of all, the description of each virtue in terms of the doctrine requires the identification of a continuous scale of emotions with respect to which the specific virtue is the mean. This is a non-trivial step, because it presupposes Aristotle's project (as described above, in sections 1.1 and 1.2) of describing ethical virtues as the good state of the non-rational part of the

[34] See *EN* 2.2, 1104a1–2.

soul so that every virtue must be related to a type of non-rational impulse or desire. Next, the doctrine requires that the multiple ways of missing the virtue or right action be found, identified and ordered according to the two directions of deficiency and excess. This procedure also helps to reveal failures that are not as frequent or not as obvious as the opposed failures are.[35] Further, the reconstruction of the several virtues in terms of the doctrine converts the contingent catalogue of commonly accepted virtues into an ordered system of virtues, in which every virtue corresponds to a certain piece of our non-rational life and every type of failure can be arranged around the respective virtue. This systematization even leads to the identification of means that have not been acknowledged as virtue so far. And, most of all, by analysing and explaining each virtue in accordance with the scheme of excess, deficiency and the mean, we learn how each virtue can be understood as contributing to the good state of the non-rational part of our soul. And this, again, is essential for the function we attributed to the second book of *EN* in section 1.1, namely that the discussion of virtues must show how the various commonly accepted virtues relate to the idea of a good state or excellence of the soul.

4. DEFICIENCY, EXCESS AND THE PROBLEM OF QUANTIFYING VIRTUES

If one adopts a simple quantitative understanding of the mean, it is easy to produce a long list of difficulties for the doctrine. For example, if the doctrine requires that we have neither too much nor too little fear, are we not bound to conclude that we should always feel a moderate amount of fear? Certainly not, since, fortunately, very often there are no threats to be afraid of. And even if we add the clause that we should feel a moderate amount of fear whenever we are faced with threats that are ordinarily regarded as frightening, the resulting doctrine would be still odd; for the average person the presence of a lion would be frightening, but can we infer that the virtuous lion-tamer should feel the same moderate amount of fear? Also, if, as Aristotle says, we feel pity when faced with undeserved misfortune and indignation when faced with undeserved fortune, we expect that the strength of our emotions should be proportionate to the degree of the fortune or misfortune we experience; hence great misfortune deserves a great and not a moderate amount of pity, great undeserved fortune a great

[35] While, for example, people frequently enjoy more bodily pleasures than they should, it is relatively seldom that they seek too few pleasures.

and not a moderate amount of indignation, a severe insult deserves strong and not moderate anger, and so on. Another class of difficulties is usually taken from the examples in which the type of emotion or action itself is blameworthy, as e.g. in the case of envy, murder and adultery. For Aristotle, these things are wrong, no matter whether we do them too much or too little. Some authors have concluded that, since every literal interpretation of the mean leads to such serious difficulties, it must be meant in a mere metaphorical sense.[36] This, again, would reveal a serious inconsistency in the doctrine, since the scheme of deficiency, excess and the mean was precisely justified by the argument that the subject matter of ethical virtue is continuous and divisible in a literal sense.

Now, Aristotle himself warns us against applying a naively quantifying account when he distinguishes the mean with regard to the object itself and the mean 'relative to us' (*pros hēmas*).[37] In the former meaning, the mean is equidistant from the two poles and can be arithmetically determined; in the second meaning, so much is clear, this is not the case. But the concept of a mean that is 'relative to us' brings with it problems of its own. The famous example that Aristotle offers as illustration of this concept (that the appropriate amount of food cannot be the same for all of us, since the well-trained athlete needs more of it than someone who is just starting the training) has received conflicting interpretations so that it is not particularly helpful in itself. This does not make the job of the interpreter any easier. On the one hand, he has to figure out what is meant by the assertion that the virtue is a mean, which, however, cannot be fixed by an arithmetical procedure; on the other hand, he has to show that there are continuous scales in a literal sense to which the ethical virtues refer and which justify the application of the deficiency–excess scheme.

4.1. *An initial problem to deal with*

First, one could be confused by two distinct uses of the mean. On the one hand, the virtue is in the mean between two vices; on the other hand, there is the right amount of a certain emotion that is said to be in the mean between an excessive and a deficient amount of the same emotion or the right action that is said to be in the mean between an excessive and a deficient way to act. In the latter case we can imagine that there is a continuous scale or dimension on which the mean is to be located, while in the former case there is no continuous divisible scale or path that leads from

[36] See Hursthouse 1980/1. [37] *EN* 2.6, 1106a27–8.

a virtue to a vice. Hence, the two means are distinct, though they are, of course, interrelated. They are interrelated because it is by hitting the mean in the latter sense that someone is virtuous, and it is by missing the mean in the latter sense that someone fails to be virtuous. Vices are opposed to each other, and each vice is opposed to its corresponding virtue;[38] the vices are bad and objectionable and virtue is good and desirable; this three-place scheme, according to which two contrary things are both objectionable, only occurs where there is deficiency and excess.[39] Since virtues are good and vices are bad dispositions, there is no continuous transition from virtue to vice.

Sometimes Aristotle says that one vice is closer to the virtue than the opposed vice or that the deficiency is less opposed to the mean than the excess is.[40] At first glance, these constellations could be seen as a counter-example to what we have just explained; but what Aristotle means is not that, as a vice, the deficiency is less bad than the opposed excess. Rather, all these cases can be traced back to deficiencies and excesses within the type of emotion and action the corresponding virtue is responsible for; when, for example, the excessive emotions occur more often than the deficient ones, or when the excessive actions are harder to avoid than the deficient ones, or when the deficient emotions or actions are more similar to the intermediate state than the excessive ones, then we say that the corresponding vice or deficiency is closer to the virtue than the opposed excessive vice.

Therefore, when Aristotle says that the mean is the good or right standard in the field of what is continuous and divisible he is referring to the continuous scales between emotions and between actions, and not between virtues and vices. Consequently, we cannot expect to find genuinely quantitative relations between virtues and vices, but only in the field of emotions and actions.

4.2. *An analogue: the virtue of style*

For the next step of our argument we will use the analogue of a kind of virtue that is much less disputed than the ethical virtue: the virtue or *aretē* of prose style. In *Rh.* 3.2 Aristotle attempts to define the virtue of prose style, which has to be clear and transparent on the one hand and somehow noble and sublime on the other. It must be clear, since it is the proper function of a speech to make something clear, and it must be noble, sublime or dignified, because this is more pleasant and admirable than the

[38] See *EN* 2.8, 1108b11–13. [39] See *Top.* 2.7, 113a5–8. [40] See *EN* 2.8, 1109b1–19.

ordinary way of speaking;[41] and what is admirable arouses our curiosity and attention. So good style in prose speech must be clear but not too banal on the one hand and noble but not too extraordinary on the other.[42] It does not take much reflection, then, to see that the virtue of style is also a sort of mean; and therefore it is, in principle, legitimate to transfer insights from the stylistic virtue to the ethical one. Now, clearness in speech is realized by the use of ordinary words; the noble or sublime tone is effected by the use of unusual words; this second group includes metaphors, which are said to combine clearness, pleasantness and the noble in an optimal way,[43] but also neologisms, poetic words, epithets, foreign words, etc.

This is roughly what *Rh.* 3.2 tells us about the virtue of style. Since there is just one virtue of prose style,[44] the entire constellation is less complex than in the *Ethics*; this simplicity allows us to observe some interesting phenomena. First, an increase in clearness can diminish the degree of 'nobleness', and vice versa. But, for example, does every gain on the side of clearness automatically lead to a loss on the side of nobleness? If we construe the relation between clearness and nobleness as a one-dimensional scale with perfect clearness and perfect nobleness at its poles, so that with every move on the scale towards one of the poles we would depart from the other pole, this would be an inevitable consequence. But philosophically, it would be disappointing, since the analysis of a virtue should help us to understand why the virtue is an excellence or even the best possible state, and not just a lame compromise. But, above all, the simple one-dimensional scheme would not even represent Aristotle's theory of style appropriately; the addition of a certain number of metaphors, for example, increases the noble and admirable aspect without any negative effect on the clarity. Given these phenomena, the mean between clearness and nobleness is not just a matter of one continuous scale; we should rather think of two independent scales for the various degrees of clearness on the one side and of nobleness on the other. Next, too many noble elements would make the style worse, because the nobleness of speech would impede its clarity. This is one reason why excess of nobleness must be avoided, but it is not the only one. If our style is too noble it is no longer appropriate to the typical subject matter of prose style; if this inappropriateness is recognized by the audience, people will be annoyed because they come to think that the speaker is speaking artificially. There are various ways, then, in which nobleness can cause a

41 *Rh.* 3.2, 1404b1–12. 42 See *Rh.* 3.2, 1404b35–7. 43 *Rh.* 3.2, 1405a8–9.

44 This is not the traditional interpretation: Cicero's and Quintilian's doctrine of the four *virtutes dicendi* is clearly developed from an interpretation of Aristotle; but, indeed, there is no chance to read four virtues of style into Aristotle's *Rhetoric*: the plural of 'virtue' does not even occur.

stylistic failure,[45] and it is not always the loss of clearness that makes nobleness excessive. Further, the use of metaphors, we said, does not in itself diminish the degree of clearness. But beyond a certain threshold value, the frequency of metaphors starts having a negative impact on clarity, since the audience gets more and more involved in deciphering all the metaphors. In this case, the excess comes by degrees, but this excess does not start with the first metaphor we use. Finally, it can be, as in the last case, that the number of metaphors spoils the style; this is a clearly quantitative question, but it is also possible that the use of one particular word spoils the style, if it is not appropriate for the given genre of speech, for example when we use poetic words in prose speech. The problem here is not that we use too many of them, but that we use them at all.

These are the phenomena; what can we infer from them? In comparison with the complexity of action and ethical virtue, Aristotle's account of prose style is perplexingly simple; but even here the one-dimensional scheme with one continuous scale, on which there are two poles and the golden mean between them, is of little help. Result 1: First of all we should allow for more than just one continuous scale; some phenomena can only be accommodated if we think of two or more scales or dimensions with one mean each. Hitting the virtuous mean implies, then, that we hit the mean on each scale. Result 2: Next, even if we are faced with continuous scales, we are not committed to think that every move along that scale makes things better or worse: it is thoroughly possible that there is a neutral zone on that scale, so that moves within the limits of that zone do not affect the goodness or virtue in the respective field. Sometimes this neutral zone can be limited by a threshold value up to which increase or loss does not count as failure, but beyond which every further move would make things better or worse.

Result 3: Further, it is not always excessive or deficient quantity that brings about the vices; some things are bad by type, not by excess. This is perhaps the most interesting case, since it is questionable whether it can be accounted for within the frame of deficiency, excess and the mean. For this question, let us return to the example of the use of inappropriately noble words. In this case, we said, it is one single word that could spoil the style so that it is not a certain amount or quantity that makes the difference between right and wrong, but rather a certain quality. Can we still apply the terminological inventory of the doctrine of the mean? Of course, we could

[45] There is just one virtue of style, but many 'vices', in a sense, and not just two: four vices of style are identified in *Rh.* 3.3.

say that in this case the style has become 'too noble' or 'excessively noble'. But, since the phrases 'too much' and 'too little' have a quantitative as well as a normative connotation, we should make clear that we are interested in the genuinely quantitative sense of the phrase 'too noble'.

Result 4: First we can state that, if these inappropriate words are, in principle, unusual, noble or strange, we would say that there is an excess *in the direction* of nobleness; if they are banal, mean or hackneyed we would say that there is deficiency in nobleness or an excess *in the direction* of banality. Thus the basic scheme of two opposed directions of failure remains intact. 4.a: but since there are numerous ways to be either too banal or too noble, the two directions may be just meant to structure a variety of possible mistakes. These are important results, but since we replaced the quantitative vocabulary by 'directions of failure' one could dispute whether this is still a literal or already a figurative way of speaking.

Result 5: Next, even if we use just one inappropriate word of the noble sort, we can say there is 'too much nobleness' in our speech or that the 'degree of nobleness is too high' or the like. It can hardly be denied that some quantitative sense must be involved here. But how is this possible once we assume that it is not the quantity, but the quality that makes the difference? There are (at least) two ways to explain the quantitative character of the above statement. 5.a: The description 'too much nobleness' is not equivalent to 'too many noble words'; hence, it is important to observe that the quantitative aspect has jumped from the means by which a certain effect can be brought about (i.e. the words we use) to something else, say the effect itself or the overall character of the speech. 5.b: Every single inappropriate or qualitatively mistaken word is one (mistaken) word *too many*. By this easy trick we can turn every qualitative mistake into a quantitative one, thus, of course, trivializing the quantitative aspect in such descriptions. We will get back to this problem later.

4.3. *From virtue of style to ethical virtue*

What holds for the virtue of style must also hold for the ethical virtue, since here we are faced with analogous phenomena. Though every virtue is dedicated to one specific section or aspect of our life (courage: dangerous situations in war; moderation: 'temptations of the flesh'; liberality: dealing with money, etc.), it turns out that some virtues must be accounted for by more than just one continuous scale: courage is concerned with fear *and* confidence, moderation with pleasure *and* pain, etc. It is true that, for example, strong fear and strong confidence mutually exclude each other, and it may also be true that the increase of fear and the decrease of confidence are mutually proportional for major parts of the two scales and for most of the cases, but the absence of the one does not automatically imply the presence of the other, so that the corresponding virtue must be modelled with two continuous scales, each having its own standards of rightness. Further, it is sometimes the quantity itself that makes an action or emotion excessive: overspending, overeating, being over-anxious, etc. can impinge on our lives and are fallacious in themselves. But often it is not the extraordinary quantity which is the problem, but the quality of what we do or feel; we get things wrong when we are afraid of the *wrong* things, when we are angry for *negligible* reasons, when we spend money under *inappropriate* circumstances, etc. Also, excessive indulgence in bodily pleasures is blameworthy, where 'excessive' can be described in purely quantitative terms, but up to a certain threshold value there is nothing wrong with our enjoyment of bodily pleasures, such as wine, food and sex.[46]

Given these phenomena, it is not difficult to discover the analogues to the results (1) to (5) from the analysis of good style, and it is fairly clear how these points would affect an elaborated theory of the mean. Also, when Aristotle emphasizes with respect to ethical virtues that it is possible to fail in many ways, while success is possible only in one way,[47] this can refer to the observation that some virtues are better described by two or more continuous scales or dimensions so that we can go wrong with respect to each dimension, while virtue requires that we hit the right mean on each of them; but it can also refer to another observation we have already made, namely that on each scale there are various ways to go wrong, including quantitative as well as qualitative failures. Finally, when we are afraid of the wrong things, get angry for negligible reasons, are generous under inappropriate circumstances, etc., it does not seem to be primarily a matter of quantity, because the failure does not come by degrees but rather involves the wrong quality of emotional response or action. At any rate, getting angry when we should not, enjoying bodily pleasures where we should not, etc., is also a matter of excess, and not getting angry when we should, not enjoying where we should, etc., is a matter of deficiency. As in the field of stylistic virtue, the basic scheme of two opposed directions of failure remains intact. And if it is, in principle, possible to accommodate such qualitative mistakes within the scheme of deficiency and excess, then it is also possible to apply more or less the same analysis to the notorious examples of murder and adultery, since 'adultery', e.g., is the name of a

[46] *EN* 7.14, 1154a8–21. [47] *EN* 2.6, 1106b28–33.

kind of action that, by its nature, always takes place with the wrong person and under the wrong circumstances.

4.4. *Quantitative and qualitative failures as not strictly opposed*

In the last two sections, the distinction between quantitative and qualitative failures became more and more central. Prima facie, this seems to be a crystal-clear distinction: sometimes we are blamed for doing something too often or too seldom and sometimes we are blamed for doing one particular wrong action; also, we can be blamed for being angry with too many people or for being angry with the wrong person. And apparently the doctrine is better suited for the former, the quantitative case.

However, once we take a closer look at the quantitative case, these assumptions become dubious; there are two kinds of problems for the quantitative cases, which can be resolved only if we equate them with the qualitative case. The first problem is that the quantity of an action or emotion can be manifested in many different ways: it can be a matter of felt intensity, of motivational strength, of duration or of frequency, while the frequency, again, can be measured in occurrences, in the number of involved people, the number of occasions, the number of places, etc. Excessiveness in these various respects corresponds to different types of failures. In this sense, the quantitative descriptions that someone is 'too angry' or 'acts too angrily' alone are elliptical. When we blame someone for their excessive anger or for acting too angrily we should, in principle, be able to specify the respect or bundle of respects in which their angry responses were excessive. The second problem reveals another reason why quantitative descriptions alone are incomplete: when someone gets angry on many occasions and with many persons, we may blame them for excessive anger. But how many occasions and persons are in order, and when does it start getting excessive? When we do exceed the average number of occasions or persons? Maybe our angry person is faced with more injuries and insults than the average person; isn't he justified, then, in being angry more often? Obviously he is. The fatal, but inevitable conclusion is that the absolute number or the absolute quantity cannot tell us when things become deficient or excessive. Whenever we have to judge a person's degree of anger, we have to take into account whether he is angry only with the persons who deserve it or with more, whether he gets angry only for respectable and important reasons or also for negligible reasons, whether his reactions are appropriate or exaggerated, he whether his calms down after a reasonable period of time or whether he is unable to get over it, etc. We can conclude then that the ascription of quantitative deficiency and excess in cases like this ultimately rests on the counting of qualitatively specified failures.

This is a striking result, but how can we generalize it? Should we say that there are no genuinely quantitative failures at all, since all quantitative failures can be reduced to the total of qualitative mistakes? This would probably go too far; eating too many apples can be wrong, though there is certainly nothing qualitatively wrong about eating one or two of them (provided that each of them is good or beneficial[48]). But again it is true that there is no absolute number determining when our desire for eating apples becomes excessive. The right quantity is dependent on parameters that are relative to us or relative to everybody who is in the same situation as we are. And just as the qualitative failures must be defined by appealing to the right persons, the right times, the right circumstances, the right ways, etc., the quantitative failures cannot be identified without the appeal to what is right or appropriate in a situation of a certain type. Therefore, the phenomenon of qualitative failures is far from being a counter-example to the doctrine or to a literal reading of the doctrine's quantitative vocabulary; it is rather the case that quantitative failures, such as eating too many apples, are just one special case of violating the standards for right action and behaviour in a given situation, and this completely parallels what happened in the case of qualitative failures. The concept of the 'mean relative to us' must be meant to capture both types of cases: we enjoy too many pleasures either when we enjoy just one or a few pleasures of a type we should not enjoy (as in the case of adultery) or when we enjoy more pleasures than we should. This again would mean that no quantity as such, however high or low, can define what is right or wrong; the transition from the purely quantitative 'much/many' and 'little/few' to the normative 'too much/many' and 'too little/few' cannot take place before we relate these quantities to the already mentioned standards of what is good or right for us in a given situation. In some cases (for example, when we enjoy too many apples), the violation of these standards may come by degrees, but this is by no means crucial for the doctrine itself, since even if the violation happens by just one discrete step, the response or action will be excessive or deficient, and it is exactly this kind of excess and deficiency that the right mean avoids.

48 This sort of proviso is not trivial and lends further support to our claim that quantitative failures depend on what is qualitatively right or wrong. The parlance of failure that 'comes by degree' or that consists in 'doing too many instances of F' actually presupposes that it is no failure to do one or a few instances of F; hence, if we are right in doing one or a few instances of F, we do what we should, how we should, etc.; and this, again, implies a qualitative description of right and wrong. It seems then that even the definition of genuinely quantitative failures cannot do without a qualitative account.

4.5. The introduction of the 'parameters'

When describing the various forms of failures in the previous two subsections we often alluded to the idea that we get things wrong when we fail to do them with the right persons, under appropriate circumstances, etc. This motif occurs in the description of particular virtues, and it seems as if Aristotle wanted to systematize this idea by the introduction of certain 'parameters':

> For instance, both fear and confidence and appetite and anger and pity and in general pleasure and pain may be felt both too much and too little, and in both cases not well; but to feel them at the right times, with reference to the right objects, towards the right people, with the right aim, and in the right way, is what is both intermediate and best, and this is characteristic of excellence.[49]

Obviously, these parameters determine what it means for an emotion to be right or for the non-rational part of the soul to respond in accordance with what reason would say. Perhaps not all of these parameters are important for all emotions, and perhaps they are not even complete (though the parameter 'in the right way' is suited to cover almost everything else that could become relevant), but the least we can say is that the reaction of the non-rational part of the soul must be correct with respect to all *relevant* parameters. Now, if these parameters are agreed to offer criteria for the correctness of emotional responses, one could wonder, as many commentators actually have, whether this account is compatible with the doctrine that right and wrong in the realm of emotions and actions is just a matter of deficiency and excess. Or, to put it the other way round, if we take it for granted that a certain emotion, say fear, is correct if it is neither too strong nor too weak, what use are these parameters requiring that the same fear be directed to the right objects, at the right times, in the right way, etc.?

First of all, if the parameters and the doctrine were competing or even incompatible accounts, it would have been extremely odd to mention both accounts in one single sentence, as Aristotle did in the passage just quoted. Also, the quoted passage strongly suggests that Aristotle introduces the parameters in order to explain what it means for an emotion to be felt not too much or too little, but well. Hence it is plausible that these parameters are meant to shed some light on the concept of the mean, rather than to introduce a competing account. But even if we accept this as a correct description of this passage, it is still open to widely differing interpretations. First, we have to choose between a weak and a strong reading; in the weaker

[49] *EN* 2.6, 1106b18–23, tr. Ross 1984.

sense it would mean that the parameters formulate additional criteria that an emotion must fulfil in order to be in the best possible condition (in addition to the requirement that they must not be too much or too little); the stronger sense would amount to the claim that the right measure of an emotion, whether it is felt too much or too little, can only be assessed by the application of these parameters. One can feel inclined to follow the weaker reading, since we become acquainted with the concepts of deficiency and excess right from the beginning of *EN* 2, while the parameters appear all of a sudden in the text. However, we have to keep in mind that Aristotle announced that he aimed to develop the concept of the 'mean relative to us' and, since at this stage of the discussion it is not entirely clear what this concept implies, the parameters could be taken as a clarification of that point. And indeed, the textual basis of the quoted passage strongly suggests that Aristotle wants to defend the stronger claim, since he introduces the parameters as defining the mean without any further reference to the felt strength or quantity of the respective emotions.

Another interpretational alternative would be this: possibly, the several parameters are meant to define several dimensions of a virtue so that there is a mean and two fallacious extremes for each dimension or scale: 'too many' and 'too few' can apply to the times, to the objects, to the persons, etc. In this account, virtue would require the right, middle quantity of emotion on each scale. Alternatively, we could think not that the right quantity in each respect defines when the parameters are matched, but the other way around, that the parameters define what it means for an emotion to be not too much or too little.[50] Now, the wording of the quoted passage from the *Nicomachean Ethics* clearly supports the second alternative, since the several parameters themselves are not quantified; and also, it seems unclear how to apply the quantification to all parameters (can the right aim, for example, be more or less right?) as the first reading would require. But it could seem that a similar passage from the *Eudemian Ethics* is in favour of the first alternative:

> For the irascible is one who is angry more than he ought to be, and more quickly, and with more people than he ought. The unfeeling is deficient in regard to persons, occasions, and manner.[51]

Here it seems as if the parameters themselves are quantified and are to be represented as separate continuous scales. However, even this passage does

[50] I owe this distinction to Müller 2004: 30–3, who, after a careful discussion, favours the second alternative, as we will do.

[51] *EE* 2.3, 1221a15–17.

not say that the medium quantity of persons, objects, times, etc. would define when each of the parameters is matched. This reading is actually impossible because of the following detail: the irascible is said to be angry with more people *than he should*. But this cannot mean that we should be angry with, say, 30 people a month on average and that the irascible is angry with 40 people a month. It means that the irascible is not only angry with the right people, i.e., those people who deserve our anger, but with more than that. Therefore the passage is not about quantity, but about the violation of what we *should* do or of what the *right* person, the *right* time, the *right* way, etc. is. Thus the *EE* passage agrees perfectly with what we know from the corresponding *EN* passage, the only difference being that the *EE* text brings in the phrase 'more than'. But this difference can easily be explained. In the *EE* passage, Aristotle wants to show that there are always two ways to fail with respect to the several parameters: if we are angry with more people than we should it is excess, if with fewer, it is deficiency. Hence the introduction of the seemingly quantificational phrase 'more than' does not manifest a different attitude to quantity, but is motivated by the confrontation of the excessive and the deficient state, which plays no role in the corresponding *EN* passage. The lesson we can learn from this discussion is that there is no basis for the quantificational reading and that the introduction of the parameters does not preclude the application of the deficiency/excess scheme.

We have good reasons, then, to adopt the second reading, according to which the question of whether we feel an emotion 'too much' or 'too little' can only be assessed by checking whether our emotional responses are right in the sense of the different parameters. Having adopted this reading, there is only one minor exegetical question left: does the violation of each parameter define its own scale of deficiency and excess, or does the violation of all parameters together define one unified scale of deficiency and excess? In the first case, we would have many excesses or deficiencies for every emotion. Exegetically, it seems that our *EN* passage does not pluralize the scale of deficiency and excess for every emotion, but rather aspires to define the 'too much' and the 'too little' by the totality of the parameters. Philosophically, it would make little sense to insist on different scales; if, e.g., the irascible is angry with more people than he should be, at more times than he should, etc., these violations can be seen as manifesting the same, excessive, tendency with respect to anger, while, sometimes, being angry with the wrong people and being angry for the wrong reasons come down to almost the same thing.

In summary, the introduction of the parameters is far from obscuring the doctrine, as some interpreters have maintained; on the contrary, the parameters spell out the qualitative criteria without which the scheme of deficiency and excess could not be applied.

4.6. Conclusion

We are now in a position to get back to the question from the beginning of section 4, whether there is a continuous scale that justifies the application of the triple scheme of deficiency, excess and the mean, if it is clear that the mean cannot be determined arithmetically by equidistance from the extremes. Whenever we blame someone for their excesses or shortcomings, it is because of the number of *inappropriate* emotional responses or actions. 'Inappropriate' can mean that we do things we should not do or that we fail to do things we should do; accordingly, we can classify the mistaken reactions as either deficient or excessive. In accordance with the number of deficient or excessive reactions, we can build a continuous scale stretched out between maximal deficiency and maximal excess; there is no need at all to assume that the 'deficient' and the 'excessive' part of the scale have the same length (even a zero extension of one of the two parts is not excluded), so that the right mean cannot be defined by equidistance from the poles; the mean is a mean just because it is located *between* both parts of the scale and hence belongs to *neither* direction. Some virtues involve more than one scale, in which case it is clear that being virtuous implies the hitting of the mean on all relevant scales.[52] Inappropriate reaction can be a matter of qualitative or quantitative failures, but, as opposed to common expectation, it is neither true (a) that the quantitative failures play a privileged role here, nor is it true (b) that the qualitative failures provide a problem for this account. The only quantity that matters is the quantity of inappropriate responses, not the absolute quantity of, say, the pleasures we enjoy; only when we confuse these two types of quantitative scales can we come to think that failures of the quantitative type, such as overeating sweets, drinking too much ouzo, sleeping with too many women/men, etc., are paradigmatic for Aristotle's account of virtue and vice. But, actually, it makes no major difference for the doctrine whether, for example, our excessive enjoyment

[52] One might find it helpful to represent these various scales as intersecting at their means; this, again, may evoke the idea of a concentric target or node, which is, on the one hand, indeed helpful for modelling the 'multi-dimensionality' of some virtues, but, on the other hand, also misleading since concentricity implies equidistance for all relevant scales.

of bodily pleasures rests on the enjoyment of the wrong things or on the enjoyment of too many things, each of which alone would be good and beneficial.

Taken together, these aspects sketch a consistent reading of the doctrine, including a literal understanding of the terms 'deficiency' and 'excess'. Indirectly, this sketch confirms the result of sections 2 and 3 of our paper. If, as we said, the doctrine formulates the conceptual truth that in the field of continuous and divisible things, to be right, good or correct means to be in the middle between too much and too little, it is not surprising that the relevant continuous scale refers to the number of inappropriate reactions. Had it been, on the contrary, any scale of absolute or natural quantities (e.g. the number of muffins we can eat, the physiological strength of emotions we can feel), it would have meant that either the mean is to be defined by empirically successful values or that the optimal value has to be fixed by some mean-finding procedures, and both alternatives would not have been compatible with the analytical character of the mean.

Finally, in our reading, the definition of what is excessive and what is deficient must refer to the 'parameters', and the good or correct emotional response is given precisely if we feel them with respect to the right people, at the right times, in the right ways, etc. But what the right way or the right time is and who the right people are depend on the type of situation and context in which we act. The concept of a 'mean relative to us' is obviously coined to grasp the idea that the content of these parameters can vary according to the circumstances of the action.[53] The doctrine of the mean does not attempt to determine the individual parameters by a quantitative account of what is good or bad, but it clarifies the conditions under which the impulses of our non-rational soul and the corresponding actions can be said to be good or right. And this is exactly what the context of the doctrine in *EE* 2 and *EN* 2 requires.

[53] This does not imply that the right mean varies according to the subjective condition of the agent: see Brown 1997.

CHAPTER 6

Aristotle's ethics as political science

Gisela Striker

Anyone who has read the first few chapters of the *Nicomachean Ethics* will know that Aristotle considers his treatise on ethics as a contribution to the science of politics. The claim is stated prominently at the beginning (e.g. 1.2, 1094b10–11; cf. 1.13, 1102a7–13); we are reminded of it in the discussion of practical wisdom in book 6 (e.g. 6.8, 1141b23 ff.), and the last chapter of the *Nicomachean Ethics* announces the transition to the inquiry into politics proper – forms of government and the ideal state. But few scholars who have written on the *Ethics*[1] pay more than passing attention to these statements. This is understandable: not only has the treatise on politics come down to us as a separate work; politics also plays hardly any role in the treatises on ethics, and after all, the two disciplines have been treated as distinct since ancient times. Furthermore, ethics has stubbornly remained a part of philosophy, while political science now officially purports to be a social science – one which seems, however, to be largely a combination of history and philosophical theory (much like Aristotle's *Politics*, by the way). Besides, Aristotle's *Politics* may come as something of a shock for readers who begin with the *Ethics*. It is much more obviously a product of its time in history and advocates views that are now thoroughly unacceptable: it defends slavery, assumes the natural inferiority of women to men, and argues for a rather elitist form of government. Finally, it is certainly a disappointment to discover that Aristotle thought his plausible and attractive model of the best human life could be realized only in politics or in

Earlier versions of this paper were presented at the annual Ancient Philosophy conference in Chicago, at the Political Philosophy workshop at Johns Hopkins University in Baltimore, and at the University of California, Los Angeles. I am grateful to Paula Gottlieb for her detailed comments on a very rough first draft, and to the audiences at Johns Hopkins and UCLA for helpful criticism and suggestions for improvement. Dorothea Frede also read an early draft and encouraged me to continue.

[1] I use *Ethics* to refer to Aristotle's ethical treatises in general, i.e. both the *Eudemian Ethics* (*EE*) and the *Nicomachean Ethics* (*EN*). Unless otherwise noted, translations are from Barnes 1984, with occasional minor modifications.

pure research.[2] We can see why Aristotle thinks that politicians should study his theory of the human good, since the aim of a ruler should be to provide the best life for the lucky few who are capable of living it and (therefore) have the right to participate in government. This also explains why Aristotle insists on the necessity of legal rules for education (as already announced in *EN* 10.9, 1179b34). But beyond this, modern readers might be forgiven if they decide that Aristotle's conclusions in the *Politics* don't follow from the premisses laid out in the *Ethics*. The *Politics* contains a large number of false empirical assumptions that a reader of the *Ethics* may safely ignore.

I sympathize with this attitude, even though, on closer inspection, the *Politics* turns out to be less outrageous than one might think. But while Aristotle's political theory does indeed play little or no role in the *Ethics*, one should perhaps keep in mind that Aristotle's plan for two interconnected treatises may have led to some gaps in the first one that may seem hard to understand if one limits oneself to the *Ethics*. I think, in fact, that some recent scholarly controversies may be due to the tendency to consider the *Ethics* as a work that is complete by itself. It seems to me that some of the difficulties that have led to these controversies can be resolved – whether or not one is satisfied with the solution – if one considers the *Ethics* as only a part of the larger enterprise.

I. ETHICS AS AN ARISTOTELIAN SCIENCE

But before I return to these questions, let me first take a look at Aristotle's claim that ethics as a branch of politics is a science in his sense of the word.

One might have some doubts about this on the ground that Aristotle contrasts both ethics and politics with exact sciences like geometry in a famous passage (*EN* 1.3, 1094b11–27; see also 2.2, 1103b34–1104a11) in which he reminds the reader that the subject matter of politics – what is noble and just – presents much variation and diversity; so much so that some people have maintained that it is only a matter of convention or custom. The same is true of goods – the subject matter of ethics. Therefore, Aristotle says, one should be content with an investigation that indicates the truth only roughly and in outline; the subject is such that generalizations will hold only for the most part, and so will the corresponding conclusions. Hence an educated person will not expect strict demonstrations in ethics. Indeed,

[2] It might be worth noting that Cicero still seems to think in the same way (*Off.* 1.69–73). Choosing a profession was presumably not a part of the leisured classes' lifestyle, since they did not usually have to earn a living.

to ask a public speaker for formal proofs would be just as silly as to accept merely persuasive arguments from a mathematician.

It is unclear whether this verdict should be taken to cover absolutely everything that Aristotle has to say later. I find it hard to believe, for instance, that he takes his definition of *eudaimonia* as a rough and ready generalization. On the other hand, the notorious 'doctrine of the mean' is a thesis that offers guidance, if any, only in a vague and general way. I think, in fact, that Aristotle is running together two distinct points in these passages: first, he wants to say that certain generalizations admit of exceptions (such as that wealth is a good thing); second, he also wants to point out that the general theses he argues for are so general that they need to be complemented with a lot of detail to provide any actual guidance for action. This is obviously true of the thesis about the mean, but it could be said also of the definition of the human good. But even if we insisted that all of Aristotle's theory is to be understood in this way, it would not follow that the investigation he is about to begin could not be what he calls a science: a theory that explains a set of more or less agreed facts by finding general principles that will help one understand why the facts are as they are. And a few paragraphs further down (1.4, 1095a31–b8) Aristotle describes his procedure as following the familiar pattern of scientific investigation by starting out from the things 'better known to us' and leading up to principles that are 'better known in themselves'.

One difference between a purely theoretical science like mathematics and a science concerned with action lies in the fact that the second is – in our, not Aristotle's terminology – an applied science that deals with individual cases. Here the analogy with medicine which Aristotle frequently invokes, notably in *EN* 6, can be helpful. Doctors treat individual patients whose condition varies so much that any textbook knowledge will have to be supplemented with experience. But this does not mean, of course, that the general theory of health and illness or of the human body that informs the doctors' diagnoses and therapies is not a science. There remains a gap between the scientific theory and the treatment of actual cases that only extensive experience can bridge – and the same holds for ethics and practical wisdom.

But the most important difference between ethics and the theoretical sciences lies in a point that Aristotle mentions just after the remarks about its lack of precision – namely that the aim of the investigation is not just knowledge, but action (1095a5–6). Here the contrast between ethics and medicine is more significant than their similarity. Both ethics and medicine have an aim that goes beyond finding the truth. But while the good to be achieved by medicine, health, is uncontroversial and largely accessible to observation, as are the individual facts and low-level generalizations collected by the doctors, the facts to be considered in ethics can only be securely grasped by persons who have received the proper education (1.4, 1095b4–7). Aristotle devotes the first book of each of his treatises on ethics to the establishment of a definition of the human good. But he realizes that such a definition will not be sufficient to lead an agent to adopt the proposed conception of the good, and to act accordingly. For unlike an anthropologist who wants to learn about the moral code of a tribe he does not know well – e.g. mafiosi or golf players – students who are to benefit from lectures in political science or ethics must have learned to value the things they recognize as good or noble and see them as desirable ends of action, so that they may use the explanations offered by the science not only as explanations, but also as justifications of their own way of acting. The anthropologist need not adopt the moral code he is studying, while the student of ethics is trying to arrive at a better understanding of his own moral judgements.

The education Aristotle has in mind here has to do, as he explains in book 2 (3, 1104b8–27; see also 10.9, 1179b23–31), with pleasures and pains. That is to say, children are trained by praise and blame, rewards and punishments to like and dislike the right things, as Plato memorably put it. This will lead them to see the right things as good and bad, and to aim at things that are good *because* they are good.

The requirement for a good education marks the difference between a science of action (*praxis* in Aristotle's strict sense of that word) and a productive science, or for that matter a theoretical science as well. Both doctors and botanists have to be keen observers, but they can collect the information they need regardless of their moral character, and there is no principled reason why a child might not begin to study botany by the age of eight. Quite the contrary – he may become a better scientist the earlier he starts. In ethics, however, the facts do not become clear through mere observation of people's behaviour. Aristotle is surely right in thinking that systematic reflection on the values one has been taught to appreciate will not make one a better agent unless one also endorses those values. Ethics, then, is not what we would call an empirical science. While both ethics and empirical science start from a collection of facts that one tries to understand, the peculiar nature of the facts one needs to be familiar with in order to study ethics also explains why one's initial collection of putative facts may turn out to be an incoherent set. Reflection on moral questions may sometimes lead one to revise one's initial judgement, while the observations of doctors and biologists are not usually expected to need revision. I emphasize this because Aristotle has sometimes been accused, on account of his method, of being hopelessly conservative. Yet he himself points out early on that judgements about what is good or noble may be controversial – not, I presume, because he shares the view of those who maintain that there are no facts to be found in this field, but because it may take some reflection to sort out the controversies.

To continue with the outline of the proposed investigation: the plan of the *Nicomachean Ethics* can be compared, for example, with that of the *De anima*. Aristotle begins by establishing a definition of the subject – the human good – and shows that it is supported by the common beliefs (or intuitions, as they are now called) that we already have about it. As with the (second) definition of the soul in the *De anima* (2.2, 413b10–13; 414b19–415a13), he then goes on to analyse the elements that go into the definition: in the case of the soul, the various capacities that define it; in the case of the human good, virtue and action. Since virtue of character is defined as a disposition to make the right choices in accordance with reason, we also get a discussion of choice and deliberation. One would then expect the book on the intellectual virtues, *EN* 6, to shed further light on the notion of 'right reason' – which is indeed what Aristotle promises at its beginning (1, 1138b32–4). After the virtues comes an investigation of the less desirable states of character – self-control, weakness of will and viciousness. The rest of the plan is less clearly tied to the definition, but can be connected to the conditions Aristotle had set out in the first book for any candidate for the human good: pleasure is not only one of the traditional candidates for the human good, it must also be a part of the best life because, as Plato had pointed out in the *Philebus* (21d6–e5), no one would be content with a life devoid of all pleasure. Friendship is relevant because Aristotle had also noted that the good life for an individual will have to include the well-being of his family, friends and fellow citizens as well (*EN* 1.7, 1097b8–11). The final chapters of the *Nicomachean Ethics* return to a question left open in book 1 (7, 1098a16–18) – should we say that the best life consists in activity in accordance with all the virtues, or only with the best among them? – and apparently answers it in favour of the second option: the best virtue, namely excellence in pure theoretical thought, is what makes for the best life. Aristotle notes that his present project has been completed (10.9, 1179a33–5), at least as far as writing can contribute to it, and proposes to proceed to the investigation of legislation and forms of government.

However, in terms of the avowed purpose of making us better agents, most readers might be forgiven for feeling somewhat disappointed. Barring the radical conclusion that we should all try to become philosophers or mathematicians, we seem to be left with very little indeed in terms of advice for acting as we should. This is, of course, because book 6, in spite of its initial promise, has little or nothing specific to say about the content of our deliberations. Aristotle talks a lot about the differences between theoretical and practical reasoning, the latter being exercised in deliberation. Its end is, as he puts it, 'truth in accordance with right desire' (2, 1139a29–31), reminding us of the requirement for a good upbringing; and the general aim of the agent is 'acting well' (*eupraxia*). What he does not tell us is just how we determine what constitutes 'acting well' in each particular situation. So it is understandable that many of Aristotle's readers have argued that the apparent gap must be filled by what we already have.

2. PRACTICAL REASONING: RULES OR NO RULES?

With apologies for oversimplification, let me outline the solutions that have been proposed in the last few decades. They fall roughly into two types: the first and most widely accepted view is that practically wise people's deliberations and decisions will be guided by their conception of the human good. There is an ongoing controversy over whether this means that they must have studied the *Ethics* to acquire the relevant clear and specific conception of the best human life, or whether this conception is largely implicit, arising initially from their (good) upbringing and becoming more articulate over the course of their life[3] – a process that would no doubt be helped along by a study of the *Ethics*, but that would not presuppose it. If we assume the more plausible second version of this interpretation, the suggestion is that, according to Aristotle, a good education would lead a young man (*sic* – that is, after all, what he is talking about) to opt for a life of virtue – as opposed to, say, honour and glory, or pleasure (see *EN* 1.5) – and to have acquired an attachment to the relevant values, so that he takes pleasure in virtuous activity and detests viciousness. Such a person would have a fairly good idea of what counts as virtuous or evil action in his society, and this would enable him to see, in each particular situation, 'what the practically wise man would choose'. So he would set himself the right aims – say, defending his country, contributing to public enterprises, helping the poor – and then figure out the right way of achieving them. This, then, is what Aristotle has in mind when he claims that the good and wise person will act 'for the sake of the noble'.

[3] For these different interpretations see Cooper 1975; Broadie 1991; Kraut 1993.

The second proposal comes from interpreters who tend to see Aristotle's ethics as a kind of polar opposite of modern theories of morality, and Kant's theory in particular.[4] Their view is that there is *no* gap in Aristotle's account of practical wisdom. Aristotle does not think that the good person's deliberations or decisions rely on any kind of rule, or on a blueprint of the kind provided by his own account of the human good. Though one might still say that the good person's decisions *express* their conception of the best life, this conception is not explicitly invoked in any deliberation, being entirely the result of their good upbringing. After all, Aristotle compares the wise person's deliberative ability to perception informed by experience (see *EN* 6.8, 1142a23–30; 11, 1143a35–b14). Decisions, just like perceptions, concern particulars, and this is taken to mean that the virtuous man will simply 'see' what needs to be done, without appeal to any rules. So defenders of this anti-Kantian view insist that Aristotle offers no rules or standards of rightness for decisions because he thinks there can be no such thing.

It seems to me that neither party to this dispute can be entirely right. For the first view is open to another objection, less frequently mentioned in this context: it is not at all clear how an Aristotelian conception of the best life – whether articulate or implicit – could help one in figuring out what should be done. Aristotle's version of eudaimonism is not a theory like utilitarianism in which we can use the conception of the good to find out what is right, simply because Aristotle's conception of the human good includes moral virtue. The agent who wants to do the right thing will hardly be helped by the advice that he should do what the virtuous person would do, since what he wants to know is precisely what it is that the virtuous person would do. If Aristotle's account of the human good only tells him to do what virtue requires, this is not much better than being told 'in case of doubt, do the right thing'.

But before we conclude that therefore the opposite party must be right, we should remember that Aristotle also keeps referring to the wise person's knowledge of 'the universal' (that is, as his examples indicate, the universal premiss of a practical syllogism). He tends to illustrate this by his woefully trivial examples of practical syllogisms, typically taken from medicine, like this one: All heavy liquids are bad; this is a heavy liquid . . . (6.8, 1142a20–3). Presumably the conclusion is that I should not drink this liquid. To use an example that looks more like moral reasoning: suppose I see that someone has been injured in a car accident. I reason like this: People who are injured

[4] The most vigorous exponent of this view is John McDowell – see e.g. McDowell 1996.

need help; in particular, they need to see a doctor; so, let me take this person to a hospital. It might plausibly be argued that most of us would indeed 'see' immediately that the accident victim should be taken to a hospital. But one might equally plausibly retort that this is because we know, quite generally, that accident victims should be assisted, and that they need medical help. And this kind of general rule is surely what an agent would appeal to if asked to justify or explain their action. It is difficult to understand how, on the 'no rules' view, there could be any meaningful controversy about the rightness or wrongness of specific ways of acting. I should hesitate to ascribe such a view to an author who clearly thinks that questions about what is good or bad, just or unjust can not only be discussed but also, in most cases, correctly answered.

What I want to suggest instead is that Aristotle does not spell out the universal premisses of practical deliberation because he takes it to be obvious what they must be – namely the rules of *justice* in the wide sense in which, as Aristotle tells us in *EN* 5, justice is 'complete virtue in relation to others'. Aristotle believed that most if not all of those rules can be found in the laws of a well-ordered city, and the Greeks traditionally understood justice in this wide sense as obedience to law (*to nomimon*, 1129a34, b11–25).

Here is how Aristotle introduces his distinction between general and specific justice:

> Now 'justice' and 'injustice' seem to be ambiguous, but because the homonymy is close, it escapes notice . . . Let us then ascertain the different ways in which a man may be said to be unjust. Both the lawless man and the grasping and unfair man are thought to be unjust, so that evidently both the law-abiding and the fair man will be just. The just, then, is the lawful and the fair, the unjust the unlawful and the unfair . . .
>
> Since the lawless man was seen to be unjust and the law-abiding man just, evidently all lawful acts are in a sense just acts; for the acts laid down by the legislature are lawful, and each of these, we say, is just. Now the laws in their enactments on all subjects aim at the common advantage either of all or of the best or of those who hold power, or something of the sort; so that in one sense we call just those acts that tend to produce and preserve happiness and its components for the political society.
>
> And the law bids us do both the acts of the brave man (e.g. not to desert our post or to take flight and throw away our arms) and those of the temperate man . . . and similarly with regard to the other virtues and forms of wickedness, commanding some acts and forbidding others; and the rightly framed law does this rightly, and the hastily conceived one less well.
>
> This form of justice, then, is complete virtue – not absolutely, but in relation to others . . . And it is the most complete form of virtue, because it is the actual exercise of complete virtue . . . Justice in this sense, then, is not a part of virtue but virtue in its entirety. (*EN* 5.1, 1129a26–1130a9)

Aristotle's distinction between general justice in this wide sense and the specific virtue he discusses in *EN* 5 – what we might call fairness as opposed to selfish greed (*pleonexia*) – has not attracted a lot of scholarly attention in recent debates, and one has to admit that Aristotle himself does not make much use of it. Indeed, one might argue that the lines between general and specific justice get blurred even in book 5 itself, once Aristotle turns to questions of what he calls 'political justice' in ch. 7; and as far as I know, the *Politics* does not even mention the distinction. The opening chapter of *EN* 5 may well be one of many instances of implicit criticism of Plato: Aristotle notes that while greed is traditionally described as the contrary of justice,[5] it is actually not the case that every instance of injustice is a case of greed. Plato sets out the traditional contrast between (allegedly natural) selfishness and justice at the opening of *Republic* 2 (358b–367a), but what he then defends in the rest of the book is not only fairness, but moral virtue as a whole – righteousness, as one might call it with a slightly antiquated term. Remember, for example, that justice is defined in book 4 as each part (of society as well as of the soul) doing its proper job, which shows that justice presupposes the other virtues. What is at issue in the *Republic* is indeed justice as lawfulness or obedience to the law – the notion of justice attacked by Thrasymachus in book 1. But justice in this wide sense is a matter of politics, as is the law. As Aristotle puts it succinctly in *Politics* 1.2, 'justice is a political thing. For it is the order of the political community; and a judge's verdict is a determination of what is just' (1253a37–9, tr. GS).[6] So in the *Ethics* Aristotle limits himself to a discussion of the virtue of fairness, leaving the discussion of justice as determined by the law for the treatise on politics. But what the law (if good) prescribes is precisely morally good conduct, as the lines preceding this passage show: 'For man, if perfected, is the best of animals, but when separated from law and justice, the worst of all; since armed injustice is the most dangerous, and he is equipped at birth with the arms of intelligence and virtue, which can be used for the best as well as the worst ends.' I suggest that if there is a term in the Greek vocabulary that corresponds to our 'morality', it is *dikaiosunē*, not *aretē* (virtue) or even *kalon* (noble or fine).[7] It is after all

[5] Before Plato, see the fragment *On Truth* by the sophist Antiphon (DK 87 B 44); for Plato, *Grg.* and *Resp.* 1–2.

[6] ἡ δὲ δικαιοσύνη πολιτικόν· ἡ γὰρ δίκη πολιτικῆς κοινωνίας τάξις ἐστίν, ἡ δὲ δίκη τοῦ δικαίου κρίσις. The text is difficult, and some editors (notably Ross 1957) have emended it. My translation is an attempt to capture what I take to be the point Aristotle wants to make.

[7] Here I am indebted to Irwin 1986, though I want to go beyond Irwin in claiming that 'justice' in the sense of obedience to law actually is Aristotle's term for what we now call morality. It seems unfortunate to me that in making his case against Bernard Williams' claim that there is no such notion in Aristotle, Irwin draws almost exclusively on the *Rhetoric* rather than the *Politics*.

generally acknowledged that the Greek word *aretē* covers more than what we would call moral virtue – I suppose this lies behind the recent tendency to translate it as 'excellence'. The same is true of *kalon*, translated as 'noble' or 'fine' in the context of moral philosophy, 'beautiful' in the context of aesthetic evaluation. Aristotle agrees with Plato's view that the aim of the true politician is to make the citizens 'good and obedient to the law' (*EN* 1.13, 1102a7–10). He tells us that the law prescribes conduct in accordance with all the virtues (5.1, 1129b19–25, quoted above; also 1130b22–4) – not, of course, by telling the citizens to act temperately or courageously, but by prescribing ways of acting that require courage or temperance. Courage, for instance, consists not simply in facing dangers, but in facing them for a noble reason such as defending one's city. Temperance consists not simply in refraining from pleasure, but in not pursuing pleasure when doing so would cause harm – in the case of adultery, the harm would be done to another person, in cases like drunkenness, to ourselves by making us unable to function as reasonable and responsible agents. In this way, the law also indicates what counts as 'the mean' or what one ought to do (*hōs dei*) in certain types of situation. In other words, if there are principles of morality to be found in Aristotle's works, they should be looked for under the heading of justice, not practical wisdom.

Now legislation is clearly a part of politics proper, and it can be done well or badly. As Aristotle says in *Politics* 3 (1277b7–32), in the best city – and only there – the virtue of the good man will coincide with that of the good citizen. Hence the place for a discussion of moral principles is presumably not the *Ethics*, but the *Politics*.

I cannot here enter into a detailed discussion of what Aristotle has to say about justice in the *Politics*, but what he says about the aim of good legislators in both the *Ethics* and the *Politics* seems to me to confirm the view that he sees morality as a matter of the order of society and the relations between citizens. In the opening chapter of *EN* 5, Aristotle asserts that legislators prescribe action in accordance with all the virtues. In the *Politics*, this claim is supported by the argument that the end of the civic community is 'living well' (*Pol.* 1.2) – and we already know from the *Ethics* that this means leading a life of virtue. This point is taken up again in 3.9 (1280b7–12), where Aristotle rejects the idea of law as a mere contract aimed at guaranteeing protection from mutual harm, but not concerned with making the citizens good and just people. As I have already suggested, legislators or rulers will try to achieve this aim by giving their citizens reasons to act for noble ends. For example, a citizen would be expected to contribute to the common good – not just by paying taxes, but also (in ancient Athens) by financing dramatical performances or erecting public monuments, thus exercising the virtues of generosity or magnificence. Again, citizens will have to serve in the army and go to battle to defend their country, which requires courage and bravery. Their ability for practical reasoning will be developed in an education that teaches them both to be ruled and to rule – and ruling over equals is seen by Aristotle as the highest exercise of practical wisdom. In this way, then, engaging in the activities of a citizen enables the members of a community to lead an active life in accordance with virtue – as laid down in Aristotle's definition of the human good. It is true that in *EN* 6 (8, 1141b29–1142a10), after having said that political expertise and practical wisdom are the same disposition (though not the same 'in being', i.e. in definition), Aristotle mentions that the label 'practical wisdom' is usually thought to apply only to the wisdom exercised in looking after one's own individual affairs, because politicians tend to be seen as busybodies. But he immediately adds: 'but no doubt one cannot run one's own life well without some expertise in household management or without some form of government', and notes that how one should manage one's own life is an open question that should be investigated (1142a10–11). This may be a rare concession to the view that one could also lead a good life without being involved in the political life of the city, but in the *Politics* Aristotle clearly thinks that acting on a larger scale is more admirable. The only exception is the intellectual virtue of pure theoretical thought, which requires little or no cooperation. But even here Aristotle says explicitly that the rulers must provide room for it (*EN* 6.13, 1145a6–9).

The aim of making citizens virtuous is also implicit in the requirement that legislators must seek to establish (civic) friendship among the citizens. This friendship manifests itself in intermarriages between families and shared activities of citizens such as religious ceremonies, which show the citizens' decision to lead their lives in common (*Pol.* 3.9, 1280b35–9).

The relation between justice and friendship is perhaps best illustrated in a slightly paradoxical passage from *EN* 8:

> Friendship would also seem to be what holds states together, and legislators would seem to be concerned about it even more than about justice. For unanimity seems to be something like friendship, and this is their main aim, while they fend off civil conflict most of all as being a kind of hatred. And when people are friends they have no need of justice, while when they are just they need friendship as well; and the highest form of justice is thought to hold between friends. (1, 1155a22–8)

This passage might seem at first to speak against the identification of morality with justice, but I think the contrast which Aristotle appears to draw first between justice and friendship, then to deny again by saying that friendship is the highest form of justice, is actually meant to be the distinction between morally correct conduct – which is all that the law can prescribe – and the moral attitude of a person who accepts justice as a good and hence goes beyond what the law requires. Friendship includes, but goes beyond, mere moral obligation, one might say, remembering that for Aristotle the truly virtuous person is the one whose inclinations are in perfect harmony with their sense of duty.

One might protest at this point that morality has a much larger scope than legislation (and vice versa, of course). Aristotle does occasionally acknowledge this, as e.g. in *EN* 10 (9, 1180a34–b2), where he says that it makes no difference whether the laws are written or unwritten. But the insouciance of this remark should remind us of two historical facts: first, that the Greek word *nomos* means both 'law' and 'custom', and second, that the discipline of jurisprudence either did not exist or was at best in its infancy when Aristotle wrote. It is no accident that 'jurisprudence' is a *Latin* word. Even though in speaking of legislation Aristotle must surely have been thinking of officially enacted laws, he may not have spent much time asking himself what kinds of things should or could be prescribed or prohibited by law, and what should – whether for reasons of principle or of practicality – be beyond the scope of legislation. Like Plato, Aristotle considers the law as a means of moral education – education, that is, for those who are capable of seeing the point of the rules, coercion for those who are allegedly unable to control their base impulses (*EN* 10.9, 1180a4–5). Law and custom, then, will provide some rules of morality. But neither of these offer rules that can be applied 'mechanically', as is sometimes suggested by anti-Kantians. Again like Plato, Aristotle is acutely aware of the fact that legal rules are generalizations that will not always fit all the relevant features of a particular situation. Legislators aim at the common good and at harmony among the citizens, and they formulate their laws with these aims in mind. But they cannot provide for all possible circumstances in advance, and so the application of the law – as any judge or lawyer knows very well – requires more than a reading of books. This is why Aristotle insists on the need for experience. What he has in mind is not the kind of experience – systematic empirical observation – that forms the basis of skills and theories and can be passed on to others, but rather personal experience that will help one to find the appropriate response in a given situation. This is what is needed to act 'at the right time, on the right occasions, in relation to the right persons, for the right reason, in the right way' (*EN* 2.6, 1106b21–2) – all the qualifications Aristotle attaches to his formulation of the 'mean'. The analogy with medicine holds here, too: a well-educated young person who begins to be an independent agent is in a situation similar to that of a student of medicine who begins his internship. This kind of experience is indeed not codifiable. Each person has to acquire it for himself – not in the absence of rules, but because it is needed to apply the rules in the right way. Young people who have been brought up in the right way will have acquired some knowledge of what counts as good and right, and they will also have formed emotional attachments to these values that will enable them to notice the morally significant features of a given situation. When Aristotle says, as he does with respect both to medicine and to ethics, that experience without theory is better than theory without experience, he is clearly thinking of personal experience. (For medicine see *Met.* 1.1, 981a12–24; for ethics, *EN* 6.7, 1141b14–22.) It is because of their personal experience that we 'ought to pay attention to the undemonstrated sayings and opinions of experienced and older people or of people of practical wisdom no less than to demonstrations', as Aristotle says, 'for having acquired an eye from experience, they see aright' (*EN* 6.11, 1143b13–14). One might be surprised to find unargued experience placed on the same level as scientific demonstration, but Aristotle is acknowledging a familiar fact: namely that although experience may rank below scientific knowledge in the order of understanding, it also vastly exceeds the scope of what we can explain, and even what we can clearly articulate. The comparison of experience in this sense with perception is very much to the point. We do not study psychology to make some sort of sense of what others do, and we do not study decision theory to weigh the consequences of different ways of acting. One result of such experience is what Aristotle calls *epieikeia* (equity or decency) in book 5 – the ability to see when and why strict adherence to the letter of the law would be a mistake. In other contexts we might call it tact, or patience, or psychological astuteness – abilities that depend on a sense of the character of a person or the special features of a situation, and that go beyond what is captured by general rules. So practical wisdom, like medicine, will be guided by general rules, but – also as in medicine – these rules have to be supplemented by personal experience. Even if we consult others – experts or friends, as the case may be – our decisions will in the end depend on our overall judgement of the circumstances and the persons affected by our actions, and this part cannot be covered by any textbook.

To return now to the controversies I mentioned above: it seems to me that those who maintain that Aristotle deliberately offers no rules at all are concentrating exclusively on the part played by personal experience, while those who think that deliberation must be guided by the agent's conception of the final good overlook the crucial role of justice in moral deliberation. What distinguishes Aristotle – and, for that matter, other Greek philosophers – from modern authors like Kant is not that he thinks there can be no rules of morality, but that he does not clearly distinguish between moral and legal rules, and therefore definitely sees moral rules as rules of society. One might perhaps find a precursor of the modern distinction in the difference between written and unwritten laws, and an even clearer approximation in the Stoic distinction between the laws of universal reason that apply to all human beings as opposed to the specific legal codes of actual states. But it took many more centuries before morality could be described as autonomy in the modern sense – giving laws to oneself.

If I am right about the place of general justice in the larger scheme of Aristotelian political science, it should be clear that the aim of becoming better agents will not be achieved by reading only the *Ethics*. This also means that individual morality, according to Aristotle, cannot be studied in isolation from the political framework in which we live as agents. Only in the best city will the virtue of good men in general coincide with the virtue of the best citizens, and hence the best life can only be realized in the best social order. It follows that it is probably a misunderstanding to see the *Ethics* as a book that is meant to advise its readers about their individual 'rational life plans', to use Rawls' phrase. One might be led to think so because of the remarks in the opening chapters of both the *Eudemian Ethics* and the *Nicomachean Ethics* about the usefulness of knowing what *eudaimonia* consists in, and in particular the line in the *Eudemian Ethics* (1.2, 1214b10–11) which says that 'it is a sign of great folly not to have one's life organized with a view to some end'. It is not very clear from the context in which these remarks occur what kind of end Aristotle is thinking of, but I suspect he may mean not much more than that one should have a clear idea of what one values most in life – virtue or pleasure, as the traditional alternatives tended to be presented by the Greeks, with the Platonic addition of pure theoretical thought.

Aristotle's general account of the best life for humans can hardly provide much in terms of individual decisions. What Aristotle sets out in both his treatises could be better described as the conditions that make a good human life possible. This general theory is of importance primarily for the politician and legislator who can have a direct influence on the organization of the lives of his fellow citizens. Now Aristotle may very well have thought of his audience as consisting of potential legislators, but even apart from that, he is no doubt right in thinking that systematic reflection on this topic may make every one of us better as moral agents. Even if one does not need to refer to the general theory in every deliberation, both one's actions and one's life plan (if one has one) will be influenced by this kind of reflection. Furthermore, even a good education will probably not provide one with a lot of insight about how the various things one has learned to value hang together, or how they should be ranked. Understanding this may well serve to strengthen the moral character of people who are already inclined to think and act in the right way. Education and the law provide, as it were, the facts which an Aristotelian science sets out to understand and explain, and I think that both the *Ethics* and the *Politics* serve precisely this purpose. By showing us why we have good reason to think that moral virtue is essential to a good human life or why good rulers should act in the interest of the common good and try to foster a spirit of friendship among the citizens, and how they might go about doing that, we gain a better understanding of what might be good or bad in our own lives and communities, and that, one hopes, might also contribute to making us better agents.

So a prospective student of Aristotle would be well advised to attend both halves of the course on what Aristotle calls, at the end of the *Nicomachean Ethics*, 'the philosophy of human affairs' (*hē peri ta anthrōpeia philosophia*, 10.9, 1181b15).

CHAPTER 7

Epieikeia: *the competence of the perfectly just person in Aristotle*

Christoph Horn

For many readers of the *Nicomachean Ethics* it is surprising how highly Aristotle values a capability which he calls *epieikeia* or *to epieikes*, an expression usually rendered by 'equity'. In the short chapter *EN* 5.10, he characterizes it as a perfect moral competence which overrides even justice. At first glance, one might suppose that Aristotle does nothing more in this passage than report several traditional commonplaces (*endoxa*). But on a close reading, there can be no doubt that his account is strongly affirmative. The reason he gives us for this affirmation is that while *to epieikes* is itself a form of justice, at the same time it goes beyond justice, since it enables the person who possesses it to improve written law when it is in need of correction or when written law is incomplete. Thus *to epieikes*, he says, can even be used as an equivalent of 'good' (*anti tou agathou*), for what is more equitable (*epieikesteron*) is always the better. What is called equitable, Aristotle continues, is a form of justice, but it is even superior to justice (1137b1–2 and 8–11). According to Aristotle, the riddle of how equity can simultaneously transgress justice and be a form of justice finds a simple solution: *to epieikes* is the second part of justice which supplements the first part, or the law. Both are species of a unique genus justice, but *to epieikes* is the better one of them (1137b11–13). Since Aristotle sometimes identifies justice with lawfulness (especially in *EN* 5.1, 1129b11–14), the virtue which rectifies law must in a sense transcend justice. One must also add that Aristotle characterized justice as 'complete excellence to the highest degree' (*teleia malista aretē*, 1129b30).

Moreover, there are numerous passages in the *Nicomachean Ethics* and in the *Politics* where Aristotle provides descriptions of a person called 'the equitable' (ὁ ἐπιεικής). It is no surprise that *ho epieikēs* is among humans what *epieikeia* or *to epieikes* is among competences: the perfect level of moral goodness. Aristotle repeatedly applies the expression to any kind of praiseworthy abilities, as he himself realizes and points out (*EN* 5.10, 1137a34–b2). In several texts, we find the words *epieikēs* and *spoudaios* (the standard term for the morally perfect person) used more or less interchangeably.[1] An explicit identification with the expression *phronimos* is given at *EN* 6.11 (1143a25–35). Aristotle informs us that the *epieikēs* is entirely committed to the truth (1127b3); the equitable never does anything wrong or bad, or anything about which he must be ashamed (1128b21). He acts for the sake of the moral good (1168a33–5), and he feels self-love in its highest and most appropriate form, i.e. as love for his own intellect (1169a16). The *epieikēs* is friendly, lenient, and benevolent towards all people with whom he interacts, including those unknown to him.[2] He tends to take less of a good which is in high demand than he is entitled to, especially if this relinquishment leads him to the possession of a higher-order good.[3] In the *Politics*, the expression *hoi epieikeis* is used to signify citizens of excellent character (e.g. 1281a28). A government guided by these decent people would rule without making mistakes and hence would be highly desirable (1318b32–1319a4).

Several scholars have argued that we should distinguish carefully between the competence called *epieikeia* or *to epieikes* on the one hand and the person called *ho epieikēs* on the other.[4] Prima facie, there is indeed a considerable difference: the first means an ability to interpret, to rectify, and to supplement written laws, the second signifies a personal ideal centred on the tendency to practise grace, mercy and leniency. To put the difference in the words of Constantine Georgiadis, there seems to be 'a lack of correspondence between the value-equitable . . . and the virtue-equity'.[5] Apparently, these two features are derived from two different historical traditions: the first arises out of a legal context defining the relationship between legislator and judge, the second comes from a popular appreciation of forgiveness and indulgence. These two features seem to be quite difficult to reconcile: being a good interpreter of written laws may have little or nothing to do with making concessions – in many cases, a professional judge may even feel compelled to increase the severity of a punishment. Conversely, practising mercy in many cases implies the neglect of both the letter and the spirit of the law. To be sure, a merciful and benevolent person is not always the best interpreter of a given juridical problem and vice versa.

[1] See e.g. *EN* 1166a10–23 and 1175b24–8.

[2] *EN* 4.6, 1126b21. *Epieikeia* seems to be the aspect of benevolence contained in all ethical virtues insofar as they concern other people; cf. *EN* 6.11, 1143a31–2.

[3] *EN* 5.9, 1136b20–2 and 5.10, 1137b34–1138a3.

[4] See e.g. Dirlmeier 1956: 584 and Gauthier and Jolif 1970: vol. 2, 432–3.

[5] Georgiadis 1987: 165, 'The problem is, however, that this rectification has a different meaning in each case. The rectification of the legally just in the case of value-equitable does not entail a concessive spirit but only the filling out of the gaps in the law. Conversely, the concessive spirit of virtue-equity does not entail any filling out of gaps in the law.'

Nevertheless, we find in Aristotle's account of equity an apparent tendency to unify both features. At the end of *EN* 5.10, he declares that the equitable person is he who simultaneously gives adequate legal interpretations and applies an appropriate measure of leniency (1137b34–1138a3). Interpreting and correcting the law here means to relativize it by considerations of mercy. Aristotle characterizes him as someone 'who is no stickler for justice in a bad sense but tends to take less than his share though he has the law on his side' (. . . ὁ μὴ ἀκριβοδίκαιος ἐπὶ τὸ χεῖρον ἀλλ' ἐλαττωτικός, καίπερ ἔχων τὸν νόμον βοηθόν, ἐπιεικής ἐστι, 1138a1–2).[6] This clearly is an attempt to reconcile the two traditional features. The same holds true at *Rh.* 1.13 where corrections of the written laws are described only from the perspective of a merciful interpreter. So there are good reasons to follow the interpretation advanced by Jacques Brunschwig, who tries to moderate the contrast stressed by Georgiadis.[7] I will come back to the question of a possible unity of the two features of equity at the end of this essay.

But before we can propose a possible solution for this, we have to face a major problem: what kind of knowledge or competence does Aristotle have in mind when he describes the perfect virtue of *epieikeia* and its bearer? In ordinary Greek, the term *epieikeia* simply means something like 'appropriateness', 'suitability' and 'reasonableness'. During the history of its application in moral, political and legal contexts from the times of the *Iliad* up to Euripides, it became an expression of increasing importance and with more specific meanings.[8] In Aristotle, manifestly, it is used both as a non-technical expression to signify different personal excellences and as a semi-technical term to describe a perfect attitude of an individual in juridical and moral questions. Whatever the precise place of *epieikeia* and the *epieikēs* may be in Aristotle's moral and juridical thought, we have sufficient reason to assume that it is a very important one. But what sort of ability or competence is meant? In some passages, it is clear that the expression signifies both a moral and a cognitive ideal. In *Rhetoric* 1.13, e.g., Aristotle discusses a case in which someone 'is guilty of a criminal act according to the written words of the law, but he is innocent really (*kata de to alēthes*), and it is equity that declares him to be so' (1374a34-b1).[9] This remark seems to imply that *epieikeia* enables one to identify what is really just and what is not.

[6] Unless otherwise indicated, the *Nicomachean Ethics* is quoted from Ross 1984, with occasional minor modifications.

[7] Brunschwig 1996.

[8] A short historical analysis of the sources is provided by Brunschwig 1996.

[9] Quotations from Aristotle's *Rhetoric* are after Roberts 1984.

1. THE CHALLENGE OF A PARTICULARIST READING

What, then, is the truth that is known to the *epieikēs*? The competence of *epieikeia* consists, as Aristotle declares in *EN* 5.10, in rectifying the kind of justice established by the law (*epanorthōma nomimou dikaiou*).[10] The insufficiency of written law is due to the fact that each enactment speaks generally whereas, at least in some cases, it is not entirely possible to do so. The decisive passage runs as follows:

About some things it is not possible to make a general statement which shall be correct. In those cases then in which it is necessary to speak generally but not possible to do so correctly, the law takes the usual case, though it is not ignorant of the possibility of error. And it is not wrong to do so: for the shortcoming is not in the law nor in the lawgiver but in the nature of the thing. Since the subject matter of the practical is like this from the outset . . . About some things it is impossible to lay down a law, so that a particular decree is needed. For when the thing is indefinite, the rule also is indefinite, like the leaden rule used in making the Lesbian moulding: the rule adapts itself to the shape of the stone and is not rigid. So too a decree adapts itself to the particular facts.

I quote this passage (*EN* 5.10, 1137b14–19 and 28–32) from the translation of David Wiggins, who takes it as evidence for his particularist or incommensurabilist view of Aristotle's moral philosophy.[11] According to Wiggins, what Aristotle wants us to see is that 'the subject matter of the practical is by its nature both indefinite and unforeseeable'. No agent can anticipate the situations in which he has to act, no agent knows how to deal with conflicting commitments, or what it will take to persist in a given commitment.[12] So there is no common ground for agents to apply one single rule of practical deliberation, e.g. a norm of maximization.[13] A similar interpretation can be found as early as 1979 in John McDowell's seminal article 'Virtue and reason'. In his account of moral particularism and Aristotle's supposed adherence to it, he explicitly refers to *EN* 5.10, 1137b19–24, to support his

10 *EN* 5.10, 1137b13–14. 11 Wiggins 1997: 61–2.

12 Wiggins tries, as he says, to make speculative sense of our condition to act 'in a world for whose countless and not exhaustively classifiable contingencies no Decalogue or code of practice or statement of objectives could ever prepare them' (61).

13 Wiggins 1997: 62 in particular defends the Aristotelian view against an instrumentalist theory of practical rationality: 'It [i.e. philosophy] must attend instead to the various ideas that give the however essentially contestable content of reasonable agents' conceptions of the good. *Pace* the received misinterpretations of Aristotle, the main business of practical reason is ends and their constituent, not instrumental means. For an Aristotelian, the idea that a self-contained part of the concept of rationality can be bitten off and studied in value-free fashion as the rationality of means, leaving the rest, that is ends, to the taste or formation of individual agents, is a delusion, and a gratuitous delusion at that.'

claim that the virtuous man in Aristotle cannot act on the basis of strict generalizations.[14]

With respect to the views of Wiggins and McDowell, one may object that it is a legal context, not the more general area of practical deliberation, in which Aristotelian *epieikeia* is discussed. However, as Aristotle shows an exceptionally high esteem for *epieikeia* and transfers it to various contexts, we may reasonably expect its treatment to be quite telling for the entire project of Aristotelian ethics. At first glance, the reading advanced by Wiggins and McDowell seems to be attractive: Aristotle tells us in the passage that a strict generalization of laws is impossible (*ouk hoion*). For him this is a matter of principle, which lies 'in the nature of things' (*en tēi phusei tou pragmatos*), since the 'matter of practical questions' (*hē tōn praktōn hulē*) does not allow comprehensive generalizations. Aristotle concedes that it is sometimes necessary to provide abstract legal formulas, but it seems that when he says this, he is thinking of a mere practical or social necessity, not an objective one. Moreover, he maintains that the lawgiver is not ignorant of the *aporiai* which threaten as a result of generalizations; through foreseeing his mistakes (*ouk agnoōn to hamartanomenon*), however, the legislator formulates the enactments regarding only the usual case (*to hōs epi to pleon*). Hence his legislative act needs to be supplemented by some particular decree (*psēphisma*). Aristotle adds that a rule (*kanōn*) corresponding to something indefinite must itself be indefinite (*aoristos*). This is an important remark, since it doesn't seem to indicate an indefinite variation of general rules, but rather their relinquishment. Finally, Aristotle illustrates the problem under consideration by the use of a comparison: the procedure of *epieikeia* resembles the method used by Lesbian masons who utilize a leaden rule which can adapt itself to the form of the stone. Whatever the precise technical background of this method may be, it is clear that what is meant is a procedure to pile irregular stones on the top of one another by finding out which stone will fit next.[15] So the person who practises *epieikeia* is someone who can deal with situations which do not allow the application of invariant and rigid norms. In contrast to a general rule, a decree adapts itself to the particular facts of a given situation.

All this seems to support the idea that practical reason is, for Aristotle, concerned only with particular cases, not with abstract rules. Strict and

[14] See McDowell 1979: 336, 'If one attempted to reduce one's conception of what virtue requires to a set of rules, then, however subtle and thoughtful one was in drawing up the code, cases would inevitably turn up in which a mechanical application of the rules would strike one as wrong – and not necessarily because one had changed one's mind; rather, one's mind on the matter was not susceptible of capture in any universal formula.'

[15] See Gauthier and Jolif 1970: vol. 2, 434 and Sorabji 1980: 261.

comprehensive generalizations are impossible; creating abstract formulas always amounts to committing mistakes. For practical purposes, it may be unavoidable to adopt such rules, but their shortcomings must be constantly rectified by particular decisions. Taking Aristotle's text seriously seems to lead to the interpretation of the defect under discussion as a principal one, not as anything accidental. It cannot be repaired by widening the scope of a law, i.e. by applying it to further cases or by refining its criteria. To say that law is defective since a strict generalization is impossible must mean that general rules cannot be given with regard to practical questions at all. On the contrary, the situation resembles, as the text contends, that of someone who has to build a house with irregularly formed stones. When Aristotle says that a rule concerning something indefinite has to be itself indefinite, this seems to be the end of all rule-following anyway. So one could easily be persuaded to accept the particularist conclusion that, for Aristotle, laws can have no more generality than rules of thumb. Let us call this the *rule-of-thumb interpretation* of *epieikeia*. One can add that Aristotle, as we have seen at the beginning of this essay, maintains the superiority of equity to written laws. *Epieikeia* is even better than justice, as he claims forcefully. The consequence seems to be that, for Aristotle, a particularist account of moral and legal philosophy is superior to a generalist one.

Modern moral particularism can take many forms. A widespread and quite attractive version may be traced back to Wittgenstein's criticism of moral practice as a sort of rule-following. What Wittgenstein wanted to refute is the concept of the agent as being guided by a general principle which can rationally be applied to various situations. An agent learns, according to Wittgenstein, how to act in typical situations by being introduced to certain practices. There are no general moral principles which are appropriate for all similar cases. Rather, there has to be a genuine perception of all situations as being radically different from each other. In this tradition, many particularists make a claim for a systematic vagueness of all situations in which we act. According to them, there can be no single rational solution for this principal lack of definiteness. Differing situations are incommensurable, and it is only possible to make a decision with regard to each of them from case to case or through the guidance of socially accepted standards and of specific perceptions.[16]

There is a sense in which a particularist account of agency may be a truism: no one can correctly assess individual cases without taking careful

[16] Systematic and historical accounts of particularism are given by Chang 1997, Hooker and Little 2000 and Dancy 2004.

notice of the particular circumstances in which they occur. But taken in this sense, particularism is clearly compatible with generalism of rules; therefore, it is not helpful to understand it in this way. How should one put, then, the boundary between the two positions? For our discussion of Aristotle's *epieikeia*, that which makes a decisive difference is the answer to the question of how we should interpret the procedure of bringing together rules and cases. Does this involve an *application of rules*, or a *transcendence of rules*? Does context-sensitivity, in a given situation, lead to refined and specified laws or to their relinquishment? In the first case, one can easily imagine a historical author who discusses problems of adjustments of given laws or questions the establishment of a new one, without being inconsistent with generalism. Hence, one has to distinguish precisely between difficulties in applying rules to cases and difficulties which lead to a substantive particularism – i.e. a position that claims a fundamental incommensurability of general principles and situations. Now, can we find something of the latter kind in Aristotle?

As is well known, there are at least three basic kinds of evidence for Aristotle's affinity to a certain form of particularism. The first is a sort of pedagogical contextualism which manifestly plays a role in Aristotelian moral and political philosophy. The person considered to be perfectly able to determine questions of justice is, according to Aristotle, brought up in an ideally just society. He has internalized the traditions of his *polis* and, therefore, always acts in complete accordance with the standards of his city's laws.[17] Learning to be good means to identify and to imitate those people who are socially accepted as good people. It means to learn by examples and by imitation. Aristotle connects this contextualist view at least once explicitly with the concept of *epieikeia*. In a passage of the *Politics* dedicated to musical pedagogy, Aristotle points out that 'since music is a pleasure, and virtue consists in rejoicing and loving and hating aright, there is clearly nothing which we are so much concerned to acquire and to cultivate as the power of forming right judgements, and of taking delight in good dispositions (*tois epieikesin ēthesin*) and noble actions' (8.5, 1340a14–18).[18] A second broadly discussed contextualist element in Aristotle is his repeated claim that moral philosophy can be nothing more than an inexact discipline. Because of the variability of its objects and the context conditions of agency it is unable to reach the generality and exactness of mathematics or theoretical philosophy. Generalization in ethics is possible only to the degree

[17] For a strong contextualist reading of Aristotle's pedagogy see MacIntyre 1981: ch. 12. A more neutral account is provided by Sherman 1989: ch. 5.

[18] Quotations from the *Politics* are after Jowett 1984.

of judgements *ut in pluribus*.[19] Persons who lack experience, e.g. young men, cannot have practical knowledge at their disposal (*EN* 6.8, 1142a11–13). Concerning *epieikeia* it is worth noting that Aristotle refers twice to his standard formula *hōs epi to polu* to characterize its job: *epieikeia* is the ability to act in a field where only rough generalizations are possible.[20] Aristotle stresses the need for a faculty of perception and judgement, and this seems to be clearly contextualist. The third contextualist element is Aristotle's famous comparison of the person who is able to find the morally right option with an archer able to hit the target (*EN* 1.2, 1094a22–6). This craft analogy seems to imply that the sort of competence under discussion is a practical capacity based on experience and exercise rather than a kind of theoretical knowledge. In *EN* 2.6, in one of the central explanations of what it means for moral virtue to be something intermediate, he tells us that such emotions as fear, confidence, appetite, anger etc. 'may be felt both too much and too little, and in both cases not well; but to feel them at the right times, with reference to the right objects, towards the right people, with the right motive, and in the right way, is what is both intermediate and best, and this is characteristic of virtue. Similarly with regard to actions also there is excess, defect, and the intermediate' (1106b20–3). The virtuous person is thus able to determine the right emotions and actions by adapting their behaviour to the current circumstances. A further passage which seems supportive of Aristotelian particularism is *EN* 2.9, 1109b14–26. The issue there is the problem of how to find the appropriate mean concerning pleasure. Aristotle declares that it isn't easy to determine the right line of demarcation in the application of an abstract principle (*ou radion tōi logōi aphorisai*, 1109b21). This difficulty holds true, he adds, for all cases where perceptibles are involved. That seems very close to the picture that Aristotle draws of the competence of the *epieikēs*.

Two albeit minor statements do not fit into the particularist reading of the passage quoted from *EN* 5.10; in fact, they even contradict it. Firstly, Aristotle explicitly limits his insufficiency thesis; he says that the problem caused by overgeneralized laws is a matter only of 'some cases' (*peri eniōn*, 1137b14), not of all. Secondly, though we are told that the shortcoming of written law is a principal one, nevertheless it is not of universal significance, for there are cases for which a law can successfully be formulated: the 'standard cases' or 'for the most part' (*hōs epi to pleon*, 1137b15–16). Both

[19] The most important passages are *EN* 1.3, 1094b13–27; 1.7, 1098a26–32; 3.3, 1112a34–b11; 9.2, 1164b27–1165a18. The meaning of this claim is widely discussed, e.g. in Nussbaum 1990: 54–105 and Anagnostopoulos 1994: chs. 6 and 7.

[20] *EN* 1137b15–16; *Rh.* 1374a31.

remarks go in the same direction; the second is even stronger since it speaks only of 'usual situations'. Both imply the opinion that rules *can* provide us a completely adequate way to guide our conduct. The two statements apparently presuppose that valid cases of using rules do exist (and not just a few at that), even if abstract rules do not cover the whole field of practical reality. How do we have to interpret this residue of cases not covered by existing laws? One might argue as follows: if there are examples in which laws or rules are appropriate, but not comprehensive, then it seems as if *epieikeia* is precisely needed to enhance or advance the range of written laws. Taken this way, it may be understood as a capability which does not replace, but instead expands generalized enactments by including non-standard cases which the lawgiver did not have in mind when he formulated the rule. So we come to a second way of interpreting Aristotelian equity which does not presuppose moral particularism. In this alternative interpretation, *epieikeia* is able to apply general rules to given cases even beyond the legislator's horizon by adequately enhancing or amplifying existing enactments. One may speak of an *enhancement interpretation* of equity. Central difficulties that could be solved by such a capacity, then, would be the following: firstly, no written law can exhaustively describe all relevant circumstances that define a situation. A faculty to judge is thus needed in order to subsume a given case under the appropriate rule and in order to correctly apply a given rule to present cases, especially in situations in which several rules must be taken into consideration or in which a rule can be applied only to a certain degree. Secondly, no legislator can foresee all the problems that may occur in a society. A faculty like *epieikeia* is thus advantageous to compensate for the gaps in the existing legal code. Finally, there may be aspects related to public interest or to 'natural law' that may be of overriding importance; hence the application of law must sometimes be relativized by more fundamental goods.

Epieikeia can thus be seen in two considerably different ways. Either it is a faculty to judge on radically singular and unique cases and to construct, if necessary, some rough guidelines (rule-of-thumb interpretation). Or it is an applicative faculty to judge according to a given rule even if this rule has to be supplemented by additional aspects (enhancement interpretation). I would like to call the first the 'incommensurabilist' and the second the 'applicationist' view. If one adopts the first reading, Aristotle wishes to argue that no abstract and general rules of justice exist, for all persons have to act under conditions which are specific and incommensurable to one another. Equity is necessary and sufficient for cases beyond general or written rules. According to the second interpretation, Aristotelian *epieikeia* is necessary and sufficient for rule-case deliberations, i.e. for problems concerning the application of given rules and their possible enhancement to non-standard cases. But general laws or enactments are perfectly possible.

Which of these two descriptions is it that Aristotle provides by characterizing equity? The problem of how to understand *epieikeia* in *EN* 5.10 leads us to a central problem concerning the interpretation of Aristotelian moral philosophy: is Aristotle a particularist or a generalist? Is there evidence to support the view advanced by Wiggins and McDowell?

2. A CLOSER LOOK AT THE CRUCIAL TEXTS ON *EPIEIKEIA*

One possible objection to be raised against a particularist or incommensurabilist interpretation of *epieikeia* could be based on the claim that Aristotelian *phronēsis* is a merely instrumental kind of practical rationality, directed only towards the means necessary for an end. Taken this way, the context-sensitivity of *phronēsis* would be restricted to the instrumental level, whereas the ends of a valuable human life would be unambiguously identified by virtue. But it is far from clear whether such an instrumentalist view of *phronēsis* is correct; there are also evidences in favour of a more comprehensive role for practical deliberation.[21] Another line of argument is this: Aristotle may simply be seen as following Plato's legal epistemology, which is simultaneously context-sensitive and generalist. Particularly in the *Statesman*, Plato prefers a competent individual to the rigid rule of laws (294a), but it seems implausible that he does so on the basis of a moral particularism. Although nowhere utilizing the word *epieikeia* to appeal to a perfect personal knowledge distinct from written rules, Plato outlines a competence quite similar to Aristotelian *epieikeia*: he introduces a twofold 'art of measurement' (*metrētikē*) whose second part is concerned with 'the mean, and the fit, and the opportune and the due, and with all those words, in short, which denote a mean or standard removed from the extremes' (πρὸς τὸ μέτριον καὶ τὸ πρέπον καὶ τὸν καιρὸν καὶ τὸ δέον καὶ πάνθ' ὁπόσα εἰς τὸ μέσον ἀπῳκίσθη τῶν ἐσχάτων, 284e6–7).[22] This competence can deal with the shortcomings of written law. What he describes as the insufficiency of the law is that it does not perfectly comprehend 'what is noblest and most just for all' and that it 'therefore cannot enforce what is best'. Plato tells us that 'the differences of men and actions, and the endless irregular movements of human things, do not admit of any universal and simple

[21] See e.g. Anagnostopoulos 1994: 77.

[22] Here and in what follows the translation is from Jowett 1953.

rule, and no art whatsoever can lay down a rule which will last for all time' (294b2–6). Apparently, the *metrētikē* under discussion is the competence to find the mean and the fit which makes Plato's perfect leader superior to the written laws. As we are told in the *Statesman*, laws are no more than necessary substitutes for the perfect knowledge of the man who possesses full insight. Plato's political personalism, however, is certainly not founded on a particularist idea of decision-making. The underlying Platonic epistemology tends to favour an absolute expert who is in possession of an ideal type of abstract knowledge, not of practical experience. What Plato seems to have in mind is a sort of infallible and invariant knowledge, not a radically context-dependent Wittgensteinian capacity for deliberation and judgement. But Aristotle certainly does not follow Plato in the ideal of an intellectually perfect ruler. And we saw Aristotle's appreciation of practical experience, which is without parallel in Plato. So it is illegitimate to infer from Plato's position to Aristotle's; we must consider Aristotle's texts more closely. There are four passages which are of special interest for the practice of *epieikeia*, one of which can be found in the *Nicomachean Ethics*, and three in the *Rhetoric*:

(1) In *EN* 5.10, there is a short passage in which Aristotle investigates cases suffering from overgeneralization. If the lawgiver has formulated a rule too simply, leaving out too many details, then *epieikeia* consists in 'correcting what has been left out' (*epanorthoun to elleiphthen*). This passage is omitted in Wiggins' translation which I quoted above (p. 145). It runs as follows:

> When the law speaks universally (*katholou*), then, and a case arises on it which is not covered by the universal statement, then it is right, when the legislator fails us and has erred by over-simplicity, to correct the omission – to say what the legislator himself would have said had he been present, and would have put into his law if he had known. (1137b19–24)

Epieikeia is here described as the capacity to judge as if the legislator himself had been present and had knowledge of the case in question. The competence to adapt given enactments to a context may mean that equity is a faculty to expand the range of written laws by adding distinctions which are not explicitly mentioned in the law. It might also be interpreted as an addition of written laws formulated in the spirit of the legislator. At any rate, it seems clear that Aristotle means an amplification, not a transformation or an abandoning of written laws. The person who is in possession of *epieikeia* is able to continue the work begun by the lawgiver by precisely representing his intentions. The passage clearly causes some difficulties for a particularist reading of equity as it doesn't speak of a principal limitation of generalized rules. We should be aware of the fact that *epieikeia*, here, does not signify an ability relative to the individual who practises it or dependent on the relevant circumstances for a fair judgement. Regarding this text, one might propose the following thought experiment. If two or more persons who both possess *epieikeia* were in exactly the same situation, would they, according to Aristotle, come to the same conclusion? Given that all other aspects of a situation were the same, would there be a sort of individual agent-relativity or context-dependency? As far as the text under consideration suggests, Aristotle believes that their judgements would be identical; otherwise it would not make sense to say that the *epieikēs* is capable of judging as if the legislator were present. I think there is even something more in the statement that the *epieikēs* supplements the law in the spirit of the lawmaker: it seems as if the competence described by Aristotle always achieves its goal according to an accepted standard. We have no indication that *epieikeia* would lead, even sometimes, to the abolition of a written law.

(2) In *Rh.* 1.13, Aristotle speaks of *epieikeia* in his discussion of just and unjust behaviour, and he considers it as one form of unwritten justice. He defines *epieikeia* in this context as 'justice against the written law' (*estin de epieikes to para ton gegrammenon nomon dikaion*). The meaning of the '*para*' in this definition must be rather 'against' than 'besides' since Aristotle sharply stresses the difference between written and unwritten forms of justice.[23] Thus, in contrast to his explanations in the *Nicomachean Ethics*, Aristotle does not seem to consider it as a supplement to written laws, but rather as something genuine, a phenomenon in its own right. The domain of *epieikeia* is that which has been left out (*to elleima*, 1374a26) of written laws. The decisive passage is this:

> Its existence [i.e. the existence of equity] partly is and partly is not intended by legislators; not intended, where they have noticed no defect in the law; intended, where they find themselves unable to define things exactly, and are obliged to legislate as if that held good always which in fact only holds good usually; or where it is not easy to be complete owing to the endless possible cases presented, such as the kinds and sizes of weapons that may be used to inflict wounds – a lifetime would be too short to make out a complete list of these. If, then, a precise statement is impossible and yet legislation is necessary, the law must be expressed in wide terms; and so, if a man has no more than a finger ring on his hand when he lifts it to strike or actually strikes another man, he is guilty of a criminal act according to the written words of the law; but he is innocent really, and it is equity that declares him to be so. (1374a28–b1)

[23] Rapp 2002: vol. 2, 501–2 draws attention to 1375a34–5, where Antigone is said to have buried her brother 'against the law of Creon, but not against the unwritten law' (παρὰ τὸν τοῦ Κρέοντος νόμον, ἀλλ' οὐ παρὰ τὸν ἄγραφον).

As Aristotle tells us, the imperfection of laws and the need for equity have two different aspects: one according to the intention of lawgivers (a voluntary one: *hekontōn*), the other against their intention (an involuntary one: *akontōn*). In the second case, lawgivers simply ignore or neglect the shortcomings of their generalized formulations, whereas in the first case, they foresee these defects and leave room for corrections and improvements. Legislators (at least the non-ignorant among them) accept their inability to determine a law exactly, but since they know that they at least have to give a provisional formula, they limit it to standard cases (*hōs epi to polu*: 1374a31). It seems clear that unintentional shortcomings of legislation are the sort of thing that a particularist has in mind; someone who formulates abstract rules may not think of the limits of this enterprise. But what about cases of intentional inclusion of *epieikeia*? Can the particularist make sense of them? If the legislator foresees the need for equity, might that mean that he is aware of the fundamental failures of written law? That does not seem very plausible. It is more convincing to assume that the lawgiver leaves room for new rules or for the context-sensitive application of rules. If this is correct, it provides an argument for a generalist reading of equity.

Also in this passage, Aristotle explains the impossibility of giving general laws by claiming that a problem arises 'because of infinity' (*di'apeirian*). What Aristotle means is that even a whole human life would not suffice to determine all relevant factors. His example in the quoted passage is that of beating a person with a metal object: lawgivers rightly distinguish this criminal act according to its gravity from the act of simply beating a person. But, as Aristotle contends, in the case of beating a person with a finger ring, one has to make an exception from the more general rule. Beating someone this way must equitably be judged much less severely. The claim that 'a lifetime would not be enough to give a complete list' of cases can be taken to go in the same direction. It presupposes that there could be abstract rules, even if it might be impossible to spell out every detail in advance. Moreover, the example of the finger ring gives us a clear indication how Aristotle understood the insufficiency of generalized rules: a law which may read 'Do not hurt anybody by beating them' must be differentiated from one that forbids beating anybody with a piece of metal; and this last example must itself be distinguished from an enactment which makes exceptions, e.g. a finger ring. What Aristotle apparently wants to say is that the severity of a criminal act depends on the objects involved in it.[24]

[24] Regarding this interpretation, I follow Shiner 1987: 179.

These observations again support what I called an applicationist view since even exceptions to a rule can be generalized.

(3) In the next text, Aristotle emphasizes the more traditional and popular feature of equity: the principle of charity and benevolence. *Epieikeia* here is understood as forgiveness, leniency and mercy. Aristotle follows in this respect, for example, orators like Antiphon (2.213) and Isocrates (15.4); we find the expression used in this sense in Plato, *Laws* 757e1. But Aristotle, unlike Plato, affirms and appreciates this personal quality. In *Rhetoric* 1.13, he gives a list of typical elements of equity:

> From this definition of equity it is plain what sort of actions, and what sort of persons, are equitable or the reverse. Equity must be applied to forgivable actions; and it must make us distinguish between criminal acts on the one hand, and errors of judgement, or misfortunes, on the other. (A 'misfortune' is an act, not due to moral badness, that has unexpected results; an 'error of judgement' is an act, also not due to moral badness, that has results that might have been expected; a 'criminal act' has results that might have been expected, but is due to moral badness, for that is the source of all actions inspired by our appetites.) Equity bids us be merciful to the weakness of human nature; to think less about the laws than about the man who framed them, and less about what he said than about what he meant; not to consider the actions of the accused so much as his intentions, nor this or that detail so much as the whole story; to ask not what a man is now but what he has always or usually been. It bids us remember benefits rather than injuries, and benefits received rather than benefits conferred; to be patient when we are wronged; to settle a dispute by negotiation and not by force; to prefer arbitration to litigation, for an arbitrator goes by the equity of a case, a judge by the strict law, and arbitration was invented with the express purpose of securing full power for equity. The above may be taken as a sufficient account of the nature of equity. (1374b2–23)

Aristotle enumerates these features of *epieikeia* to support the orator who wants to make use of it for a speech in court. He gives us a list of examples of equity: typical contexts of use are cases in which forgiveness is needed, cases in which one must distinguish mere mistakes or accidents from unjust acts, and cases of human weakness. Then he characterizes equity as the ability to look at the lawgiver's intention and not at the wording of the law. What follows is an analysis of the wrongdoer's motives: *epieikeia* means to look less at an act than at the intentions behind the act, less at a part of someone's behaviour than at the whole, less at an isolated deed than at someone's general character. Finally, Aristotle provides a list of acts which are typical for the equitable: acts of forgiveness and de-escalation. Particularly, the equitable person demands less than his strict juridical right. Generally speaking, he accepts his own disadvantages to realize a higher-order form of justice.

What seems crucial for our controversy concerning particularist and generalist accounts of *epieikeia* is this: the opposition proposed in *Rhetoric* 1.13 between misfortunes (*hamartēmata* and *atuchēmata*) on the one hand and criminal acts (*adikēmata*) on the other apparently is part of a casuistic typology, not part of a particularist argument. It would clearly only favour a particularist reading of equity if Aristotle's examples were similar to those used by Wiggins or McDowell: incommensurable commitments of individual agents, conflicts between virtues, or the need to relativize virtues. The cases he discusses are, however, such that the motives of an agent must carefully be considered in order to find the right judgement. In our passage, Aristotle does not go beyond the limits of case-rule deliberations. These observations are corroborated by the study of Anagnostopoulos: as his thorough investigations show, Aristotle's thesis that practical philosophy remains always and necessarily inexact results from the action-guiding purposes which he firmly connects with practical knowledge.[25] So Aristotle does not wish to exclude general practical knowledge at all, but he claims that it is insufficient as long as it does not reach the level of concrete agency. Now, since concrete actions have to do with an infinite number of aspects of reality, there can be no appropriate practical generalizations. Thus, the insufficiency of practical knowledge is due solely to its required concreteness, not caused by a principal impossibility of general rules.

(4) The last text which I would like to take into consideration moves in quite a surprising direction: it treats equity in conjunction with an unwritten universal law. Far from defending a sort of particularism or contextualism, it seems to presuppose a version of Natural Law theory. The text from *Rhetoric* 1.15 reads as follows:

> If the written law tells against our case, clearly we must appeal to the universal law, and insist on its greater equity and justice. We must argue that the juror's oath 'I will give my verdict according to honest opinion' means that one will not simply follow the letter of the written law. We must urge that the principles of equity are permanent and changeless, and that the universal law does not change either, for it is the law of nature, whereas written laws often do change. This is the bearing of the lines in Sophocles' *Antigone*, where Antigone pleads that in burying her brother she had broken Creon's law, but not the unwritten law. (1375a28–33)

The first thing to note is that Natural Law does not play any role within the account of equity given in *EN* 5.10, in spite of the fact that Aristotle

[25] Cf. Anagnostopoulos 1994.

spoke of a *phusikon dikaion* in *EN* 5.7. We don't find any support for the assumption that the equitable person, in doing his job of correcting and supplementing the law, may be inspired by a universal moral law. It seems probable that the idea of a dual Natural Law that has normative force for the positive legislation of the individual state is totally absent in the *Nicomachean Ethics* – maybe even in the entire *Corpus Aristotelicum*.[26] The treatment of what Aristotle calls *phusikon dikaion* in *EN* 5.7 does not provide us with any clear evidence for this concept, so well known from later tradition. But there are, on the other hand, unambiguous statements in the *Politics* and the *Rhetoric* which may be interpreted as traces of an Aristotelian concept of Natural Law. In *Politics* 1, Aristotle defends the theory of a 'natural slavery' of certain persons and a 'natural dominance' of others.[27] And in *Rhetoric* 1.10 and 1.13–15, he develops a point of view common to all humans; it is situated beyond the laws of particular communities but has, nevertheless, normative significance for them.

There are, however, several aspects that weaken the alleged importance of these passages. First of all, we have to keep in mind that the *Rhetoric* is written for the purposes of orators; that the perspective of a common law of mankind may in fact be attractive for orators, but may not necessarily be identical to Aristotle's own view. The reference to Natural Law may be, in Aristotle's eyes, a good strategy for a convincing speech in court without leading to an attractive philosophical position. Next, there is no indication for an Aristotelian use of *nomos* in the sense of 'moral law'.[28] Moreover, we have no clear information about what Aristotle may have taken to be the prescriptions of a possible Natural Law. There is no positive account of rules which can be seen as valid for all human beings. The unwritten laws which Sophocles' Antigone is referring to stem from the religious, not the moral sphere. In addition, there may be rules of conduct based on customs, conventions and traditions such as the principles of kindness, hospitality or philanthropy, which can be said to be of universal importance (e.g. *EN* 1155a21–2). But one would make too much of them by calling them prescriptions of Natural Law. Finally, we should note that, on a close reading, Aristotle is treating the universal law (which is supposed to be common to mankind) and *epieikeia* as alternatives, as becomes clear in *Rhetoric* 1375a27–9. Thus Natural Law is not the kind of object one can refer to as an *epieikēs*. As already indicated by Brunschwig, we must consider the legislator whom Aristotle talks about in *EN* 5.10 and

[26] This has been made plausible e.g. by Schroeder 1981 and Striker 1996c.
[27] For a number of further examples see Miller Jr 1995 and Cooper 1996.
[28] For this point, see Kraut 2002: 105.

in *Rhetoric* 1.13, as someone who gives rules for his community, not laws of universal importance.[29] Hence equity corrects and supplements his laws on a context-dependent basis, even if an equitable agent can refer to the unwritten part of a tradition.

Having considered the most important features discussed by Aristotle, the two opposed interpretations of *epieikeia* may still be possible, but the second one seems much more plausible: (a) In practical deliberation, general rules or laws are impossible since the subject matter does not permit them. The conditions which are inherent in every situation are context-dependent and differ from case to case. Generalizations being thus excluded, all we can give are rules of thumb or radically individual proposals for good or virtuous actions. According to this interpretation, *epieikeia* is not a compensation of the unavoidable defects of law, but it is already the ruling force behind the lawgiver's ability to give provisional rules and to decide on individual cases. (b) General and abstract laws and rules mostly are (or at least can be) adequate guidelines for human behaviour. But what cause some difficulties are (i) a certain variation under unforeseeable concrete conditions, and (ii) the rigorous and non-indulgent application of the rules by imperfect judges or rulers. Neither of these two objections implies that there is a fundamental defect with laws or rules. Generalizations are not questionable in themselves. Objection (i) does nothing more than raise the problem of which rule to apply, and objection (ii) does nothing more than ask the question of how strictly we should apply the rule.

3. FURTHER EVIDENCE AGAINST A PARTICULARIST INTERPRETATION

I would like to discuss some additional aspects which support the criticism of a particularist or incommensurabilist view. Taken together, there is, in my opinion, sufficient evidence to reject such a reading of *epieikeia*. Nevertheless, I will come to the conclusion that there is some truth in this reading and that we should not go so far as to regard Aristotle as a true specimen of a moral generalist. My claim will be that what Aristotle maintains is a kind of context-sensitive universalism, not a contextualism with universalist additions.

A first point of importance which can be advanced against a particularist reading is the following: Aristotle maintains a relevant number of generalized rules, moral principles which are, in his view, valid without

[29] Cf. Brunschwig 1996.

qualification. Terence Irwin provides a remarkable list of moral generalizations, e.g. the principle that everyone is necessarily oriented towards happiness as his final goal, or the advice that virtue always consists in finding the right mean between excess and deficiency.[30] There are, obviously, such 'universalist', rule-based elements as the arithmetical and geometrical principles of determining justice in *EN* 5. One might even claim that Aristotle possesses a rule of an extremely generalized form, namely the principle 'same standards for the same cases, different standards for different cases' formulated in *EN* 5 and *Politics* 3.[31] As Brunschwig argues convincingly, the knowledge of the *epieikēs* is itself rule-guided, namely by a type of second- or higher-order knowledge.[32] It contains, according to Brunschwig, both 'that-rules' and 'how-rules'. A that-rule is based on the knowledge *that* a law must be rectified, a how-rule contains the knowledge *how* it must be transformed.

This may bring us to the question of what Aristotle means exactly when he composes the formula *hōs epi to polu*. On a close reading, provided in particular by Georgios Anagnostopoulos (1994) and Irwin (2000), this question leads to a couple of further objections against a particularist reading. The first thing to note is that 'valid for most cases' describes the normal case and not the most frequent one. This implies that regularities can be formulated even if one has to keep in mind that there are relevant exceptions. It does not mean that all rules occurring in practical contexts are only statistically true or, even worse, that all rules are only approximately correct. When Aristotle declares that moral philosophy is an inexact discipline, he doesn't want to separate it from a generalized form of knowledge. In *Metaphysics* 6.2 we are informed that even theoretical knowledge (*epistēmē*) does include that which holds true for most cases (*hōs epi to polu*, 1027a20–1). As the famous opening chapter of the *Metaphysics* claims, pure *empeiria* is deficient compared to *technē* which includes knowledge of causes (*dioti*, 1.1, 981a28–30). Furthermore, there can be no doubt that Aristotelian epistemology sees generality as perfectly possible; apodeictic knowledge is in some cases a sort of general knowledge (*An. post.* 1.4). But Aristotle restricts the possibility of generality to cases of immaterial entities: namely concerning the objects of mathematics, of astronomy (at least the fixed stars), and the concepts and theorems of theoretical philosophy. Even if Aristotle's invariantism concerning theoretical philosophy cannot be transferred to practical deliberation, it would not be correct to say that it depends on

[30] Irwin 2000: 111. [31] *EN* 5.3, 1131a10–b15; *Pol.* 3.9, 1280a8–15, 3.12, 1282b18–23.
[32] Cf. Brunschwig 1996.

mere perception. On the contrary, particular *aisthēsis* is described in *EN* 6.8 and 11 as a relevant part of *phronēsis* but it is always combined with abstract and general forms of knowledge. According to *EN* 10.9, the education of single individuals is superior to the supervision of all citizens since the teacher knows which exceptions should be made in a particular case. But nevertheless, mere experience is insufficient compared to a knowledge of the universal (1180b11–23). In the same way, legislation practised by an experienced lawgiver is valuable and even advantageous, but in addition some general knowledge is needed (1181a9–b11).

I would like to advance to a further argument against the particularist reading. Aristotle describes in several passages of the *Nicomachean Ethics* and the *Eudemian Ethics* a fully virtuous person whom he calls *spoudaios*, *phronimos*, or *epieikēs*. This person is characterized as someone who does not act voluntarily wrongly (*EN* 1128b22–32; *EE* 1228a5–7) and as having a practical reason by which he always possesses truth and is never deceived (*EN* 1141a3–4). Aristotle tells us that the *epieikēs* is always capable of acting correctly; he has no reason to be ashamed of his conduct. Now, if Aristotle defended a sort of particularism, these statements would be at odds with some typical convictions of an incommensurabilist: namely that there can be no single and objective best solution valid for everyone, that contingencies sometimes even force us to choose what we think to be a second-best solution, or that it may be unavoidable to commit a mistake and become tragically guilty. Furthermore, certain problems are, according to a strict particularist, completely unforeseeable for an agent, even by a person endowed with the best moral insight available. But to be sure, such descriptions of our condition as agents can hardly be reconciled with the picture of the fully virtuous person drawn by Aristotle. His view is apparently based on two convictions: first, that practical deliberation always has a clear and unambiguous solution, and second, that contingencies never prohibit the *epieikēs* from acting adequately (or at least as well as possible under the given conditions). Now there is a well-known passage in *EN* 6.7 in which Aristotle discusses the relationship between generality and particularity in practical deliberation:

> Practical wisdom (*phronēsis*) on the other hand is concerned with things human and things about which it is possible to deliberate; for we say this is above all the work of the man of practical wisdom, to deliberate well, but no one deliberates about things invariable, nor about things which have not an end. And that [i.e. the end] must be a good that can be brought about by action. The man who is without qualification good at deliberating is the man who is capable of aiming in accordance with calculation at the best for man of things attainable by action. Nor

is practical wisdom concerned with universals only – it must also recognize the particulars; for it is practical, and practice is concerned with particulars. This is why some who do not know, and especially those who have experience, are more practical than others who know; for if a man knew that light meats are digestible and wholesome, but did not know which sorts of meat are light, he would not produce health, but the man who knows that chicken is wholesome is more likely to produce health. Now practical wisdom is concerned with action; therefore one should have both forms of it, or the latter in preference to the former. (1141b8–22)

In this text we are informed of what is meant by practical deliberation according to Aristotle: the practical syllogism which contains a first general premiss and a second particular one. Aristotle discusses the relative importance of both kinds of knowledge. But even if it is right to say that the quoted passage prefers in a sense the particular knowledge to the general, what is crucial, for our purposes, is that the procedure described here fits into the generalist or applicationist view. Hence, though Aristotle emphasizes that, in practical deliberation, knowledge based on experience may count more than theoretical knowledge, we find in the text some support for the generalist reading. As the example of the chicken illustrates, Aristotle thinks that knowledge of particulars gains its importance by being integrated into the procedure of the practical syllogism.[33]

If the particularist interpretation were correct, it would follow that, for Aristotle, context-based practical deliberations and decisions must be principally preferable to abstract and detached ones. He must have regarded it as advantageous to take into consideration as many details and singular facts as possible. But it is the opposite view that we find at the beginning of *Rhetoric* 1.1. Aristotle here speaks of the relationships between abstract law, its application by a judge, and the necessity to formulate singular decrees:

Now, it is of great moment that well-drawn laws should themselves define all the points they possibly can and leave as few as may be to the decision of the judges; and this for several reasons. First, to find one man, or a few men, who are sensible persons and capable of legislating and administering justice is easier than to find a large number. Next, laws are made after long consideration, whereas decisions in the courts are given at short notice, which makes it hard for those who try the case to satisfy the claims of justice and expediency. The weightiest reason of all is that the decision of the lawgiver is not particular but prospective and general, whereas members of the assembly and the jury find it their duty to decide on

[33] One should also note that, in *EN* 6.8, 1141b24–8, Aristotle describes the relationship between the generalized *politikē* and the particularized *phronēsis* in terms of mutual completion, not in terms of conflict. The ruling competence (*architektonikē*) is the more general one.

definite cases brought before them. They will often have allowed themselves to be so much influenced by feelings of friendship or hatred or self-interest that they lose any clear vision of the truth and have their judgement obscured by considerations of personal pleasure or pain. (1354a31–b11)

As this passage shows, written law is, for Aristotle, in a sense even the prevailing form of justice; the good legislator should leave as few cases as possible to the judge. For this, Aristotle gives us three reasons. The first is that competent judges are too rare to build jurisprudence mainly on them. This remark is apparently consistent with the high appreciation Aristotle has for the *epieikēs*. But it seems hardly compatible with the particularist idea that cases cannot be adequately discerned without examining their circumstances in some detail. Secondly, the decisions made by judges may suffer from a lack of deliberation, whereas laws are brought about by a long deliberative process. If there were a particularist intention behind Aristotle's text, this statement would be, at the very least, inappropriate. Note that it claims the priority of general rules on the basis of practical deliberation; but practical deliberation is precisely what seems to be the central domain of particular decrees. Thirdly, judges are too much caught by context-based factors to be able to achieve a fair result. The third statement is an especially clear case for a generalist reading; it contrasts generalized and particularized judgements and claims the superiority of the former.

To corroborate these observations, let us take a brief look at one of Aristotle's most important statements concerning the role of invariant institutions in a state. In *Politics* 3.15–16, Aristotle reports possible objections raised by egalitarian democrats against the principle of monarchy. These critics, he tells us, prefer the rule of law in comparison to the rule of individuals (1287a20–32). One might call the two options under Aristotle's consideration 'political legalism' and 'political personalism'. The view defended by the egalitarians is a legalist one. The anti-monarchists raise several objections to the idea of political personalism. Firstly, personalism violates the principle of natural equality among citizens. Since all citizens are equal by nature, they have to be treated equally. This excludes, they contend, a personalist distribution of political functions. Secondly, a legalist view has, in their opinion, the advantage of replacing the rule of individuals by the rule of law. The reason why this is advantageous is that law is some kind of invariant order. It sees political functions as devoted to the service of law. Even if an institutionalist, the legalists continue, might have to concede that laws are possibly incomplete, it holds equally true that individuals may be lacking knowledge of given cases. One cannot, the legalists conclude, assume that individuals' competence will always cover more cases than laws do. Furthermore, one can correct or improve laws if experience shows the need to do so. And finally, an inherent danger wherever individuals are ruling is that their government is influenced by their egocentric wishes and desires. Therefore, law can be characterized as 'reason without striving' (*aneu orexeōs nous*, *Pol.* 1287a32).

Regarding this detailed report on political legalism, it is difficult, but not impossible, to determine what was probably Aristotle's own opinion. A passage in the *Nicomachean Ethics* (5.6, 1134a35–b8) parallels this theme of *Politics* 3.16 and confirms the fear that a sort of tyranny threatens as a consequence of political personalism. Akin to Plato's concerns in the *Republic* and the *Laws*, Aristotle raises the suspicion that governing individuals are always tempted to follow their own interests. Thus far Aristotle is opposed to personalism. We can also accept as Aristotelian the conviction that the law can be improved and extended to cases which in the past were neglected. On the other hand, it would be going too far to assume that Aristotle shares the idea that law is a sort of pure reason which is not contaminated by desire. Aristotle criticizes the anti-monarchist view for its strict refusal of personalism: they correctly oppose, in his eyes, the rule of one single individual but do not correctly reject the idea of a multitude of counselling people. The crucial passage is this:

> And at this day there are magistrates, for example judges, who have authority to decide some matters which the law is unable to determine, since no one doubts that the law would command and decide in the best manner whatever it could. But some things can, and other things cannot, be comprehended under the law, and this is the origin of the next question, whether the best law or the best man should rule. For matters of detail about which men deliberate cannot be included in legislation. Nor does anyone deny that the decision of such matters must be left to man, but it is argued that there should be many judges, and not one only. For every ruler who has been trained by the law judges well. (*Pol.* 3.16, 1287b15–26)

At first glance, the passage seems to give some support for a particularist reading of Aristotle since it suggests the existence of principal limits of written laws and legalism. But on a close reading, what Aristotle is claiming here is not the superiority of political personalism compared to legalism. On the contrary, he appreciates the ruler only if this person is trained by the law. As he says in *Politics* 3.15, people who govern must also possess some universal knowledge, not only experience.[34] In this sense, it is decisive to establish good laws; but these are deficient since neither one nor many

[34] 1286a16–17: ἀλλὰ μὴν κἀκεῖνον δεῖ ὑπάρχειν τὸν λόγον, τὸν καθόλου, τοῖς ἄρχουσιν.

legislators are able to anticipate all relevant cases (*Pol.* 3.11, 1282b1–6). The necessary supplements possibly advanced by a multitude of free citizens must, therefore, always be according to the law; they must be restricted to cases where law is lacking (*ekleipein*: *Pol.* 3.16, 1286a36–7).

Thus, it is not the contextualized ability to judge particular cases that seems crucial here, but the competence to follow the laws and to apply them to situations which have not been foreseen by the legislator. Aristotle clearly prefers a situation in which well-educated and rule-guided individuals decide on the basis of prudent deliberations to an underdetermined political personalism and to a rigid rule of law. That precisely seems to be the combined model he also has in mind in his descriptions of the role of *epieikeia*.

4. CONCLUDING REMARKS AND A PROPOSED SOLUTION

According to the particularist line of interpretation, Aristotelian equity would have to play a fundamental role as a deliberative capacity which is decisive for an agent's moral orientation. This claim does certainly contain some truth. Aristotle indeed holds that general practical knowledge is unavoidably and necessarily insufficient since it cannot make determinations about the particular case. But it is precisely the particular case for which it is made. Nevertheless, I think that there is strong evidence that, *pace* Wiggins and McDowell, a particularist reading of *epieikeia* cannot be defended. Aristotle does not believe that practical generalizations and particular contexts are unable to be reconciled. Thus, the shortcomings of this interpretation are too extensive. To be convincing, the particularist interpretation would have to show that Aristotle is indifferent or even hostile towards moral generalizations and that he principally defends the claim of vagueness and incommensurability of rules. Wiggins and McDowell should have provided some evidence for the contention that the laws of the *polis* are, in Aristotle's account of justice, nothing but pragmatic rules of thumb. There are, however, no sufficient indications that this view is correct.

According to the competing line of interpretation, i.e. the generalist one, we may consider Aristotelian equity as a mere compensatory ability. Equity, taken in this sense, enters the scene as soon as written law is lacking, but not before. It means, then, the competence to fill up the gaps of the written laws and to apply the laws correctly. This interpretation seems convincing insofar as it can deal with a great part of the relevant textual details. It seems particularly appropriate regarding Aristotle's claim that the *epieikēs* is able to share the intention of the legislator and follow his spirit whenever supplementation of the law is needed.

Should we therefore simply draw the conclusion that it might be best to adopt the applicationist reading? Maybe, on a second view, things look a little different; Aristotle shows a strong preference for a morally perfect person instead of a mere rule of rigid laws. If one tries to make sense of this without falling into the trap of particularism, one should try to find out what causes the overriding character of *epieikeia* in the face of written rules. Equity seems to be rather a fundamental capacity to practise justice, not a mere compensation or a stopgap. It characteristically brings together knowledge of rules and a context-sensitive form of leniency.

This brings me finally back to the question how closely related the two different aspects of *epieikeia* and *epieikēs* are. Is it one or two moral ideals that Aristotle has in mind when he speaks of *epieikeia* and the *epieikēs*? Is there a rather technical ideal, seen as the capability to judge on difficult cases, and, separated from this, a more conventional one, i.e. to be concessive if the situation requires indulgence? We saw that *epieikeia* has two fundamental significations: on the one hand it means to adopt the view of the situation which justice requires, even if justice differs from the written law; on the other hand it means that the person who possesses it demands for himself less than he is entitled to. I think that what is crucial for the concept of the *epieikēs* is not so much the juridical competence to supplement the law as the second aspect he mentions. What really counts for Aristotle is the personal ideal of having a perfect character, a character determined by gentleness and benevolence. This is the reason why Aristotle can combine the two different aspects and why he emphasizes the perfection of being equitable. Even if a law is pertinent, there can be numerous cases in which it should be applied defensively. As we saw, several Aristotelian examples are introduced to show that, sometimes, the voluntary character of wrongdoing has to be put into question, or that it isn't appropriate to demand that the wrongdoer pay the full price. In a very telling passage of *EN* 6.11, he says:

> What is called judgement, in virtue of which men are said to 'be sympathetic judges' and to 'have judgement', is the right discrimination of the equitable. This is shown by the fact that we say the equitable man is above all others a man of sympathetic judgement, and identify equity with sympathetic judgement about certain facts. And sympathetic judgement is judgement which discriminates what is equitable and does so correctly; and correct judgement is that which judges what is true. (1143a19–24)

In the concept of equity, the two features of juridical competence and of appropriate indulgence are not arbitrarily combined. Law is in a sense justice, according to Aristotle, but what is even better than lawfulness is benevolence. That is the reason why Aristotle says, in *EN* 5.10, that 'the equitable is just, and better than one kind of justice – not better than absolute justice but better than the error that arises from the absoluteness of the statement.' Aristotle is primarily defending a personal ideal, even if he fully acknowledges the importance of general rules.[35]

[35] I would like to thank Ryan Bremner for many helpful corrections and improvements.

CHAPTER 8

Aristotle on the benefits of virtue (Nicomachean Ethics *10.7 and 9.8)*

Jan Szaif

1. INTRODUCTION

Ancient virtue ethics assumes that all persons have a natural concern for their own life and well-being. It holds that the ability to lead a good life is grounded on certain excellent qualities and dispositions of one's character and intellect. Those qualities or dispositions are called *aretai* – 'virtues' as the term is traditionally if problematically translated.[1] A crucial question for ancient virtue theory is: does the set of 'virtues' that enable a person to lead a good life have to include attitudes like justice and generosity? Or are the intelligent, self-controlled, resolute egoists who see other people as mere instruments, or obstacles, to their own well-being equally or even better suited to leading a good life?

The speech of Callicles in Plato's *Gorgias* is a famous and forceful defence of the attitude of moral egoism. A theoretical elaboration of the view that all human beings are ultimately egoists is set forth in Glaucon's speech in Plato's *Republic* 2. Aristotle follows Socrates' and Plato's footsteps in depreciating a sort of egoism that seeks fulfilment in the augmentation and gratification of bodily pleasures or the amassment of wealth and social prestige. He unequivocally affirms the value of virtues like justice and generosity and states that behaviour exhibiting those virtues has to be motivated by the acknowledgement of their value and, hence, is clearly different from a strategic *pretence* of justice or generosity. But he also extols, like Plato before him, the philosophical life, and one has to wonder if the philosophers, whose life-form and enjoyments are focused on their own philosophical insights, might not quite as well be conceived of as moral egoists who care for other people only insofar as those others are helpful to their own philosophical fulfilment.

[1] I will also translate *aretē* as 'virtue', at least in the case of the ethical *aretai* (excellent character dispositions), just to preserve the terminological continuity of 'virtue theories', which undoubtedly include the ancient philosophical theories of human *aretē*.

This question of moral egoism can even be raised with regard to the performance of the ethical virtues. It is the requirement that the motivation for virtuous action has to be based on the acknowledgement of its intrinsic value[2] which opens the possibility for such virtues to be founded on a more sophisticated kind of moral egoism. In order to explain why, I need to comment on some general features of, and open questions about, Aristotle's theory of the teleology of human actions.

According to Aristotle, the virtuous action is, in a certain sense, self-referential. It is so because the value of a course of action that consists in its ethical correctness and fineness is supposed to provide an ultimate reason for that action. Thus the ethically desirable action is, in some sense, *chosen for its own sake* or, what seems to be the same for Aristotle, *because of its inherent value.* (Aristotle often uses the term '*kalon*' to name this ethical value – with the connotation that such an action is valuable, fine and also pleasing from the point of view of sound ethical judgement. The corresponding ethical motivation is called 'acting for the sake of what is *kalon*'.)[3]

The ethical correctness of an action includes this self-referential structure. But of course there has to be some foundation for its value that goes beyond its self-referentiality. The inherent value of the action must be rooted in some other features of the action that precede the acknowledgement of its value. Emotional reactions and ensuing actions are ethically correct, according to Aristotle, if they are as they 'ought to be' in a number of different respects that have to be distinguished as the type of action requires it. Let's take the case of a generous action as an example. Here those respects would include that it has the right beneficiaries, provides the right kind of gift and chooses the right timing (*EN* 4.1, 1120a23–6). If and only if the action is right in all those respects, and provided it be chosen on account of

[2] A note on my usage of the terms 'intrinsic value' or 'inherent value': it will turn out that, in the Aristotelian conception, the value of an action which makes it desirable 'in itself' can include the reference to some desirable external consequences. The intrinsic value of an action *qua* virtuous action can hence supervene in some way on a set of properties that includes relational (extrinsic) properties.

[3] For acts to count as grounded on virtue, they have to be chosen 'because of what they are (*di'auta*)': *EN* 2.4, 1105a32; 'for their own sakes (*autōn heneka*)': 6.12, 1144a13–20; 'for the sake of what is *kalon* (*tou kalou heneka*)' or 'because (*hoti*) it is *kalon*': 3.7, 1115b10–15, 21–4; 8, 1116b2–3, 1117a16–17; 9, 1117b9; 11, 1119a18; 12, 1119b15–18; 4.1, 1120a23–5; 2, 1122b6–7. The passages in 3.7 and 4.2 emphasize that this is a mark of virtue in general (cf. also *EE* 3.1, 1230a26–33). An action's being just (*diakaion*) can likewise be treated as an intrinsically motivating quality from the point of view of the virtuous agent (e.g. *EN* 5.5, 1134a1–2); but this quality can also be subsumed under the *kalon* together with all the other virtue predicates (cf. 9.8, 1168b25–8). On '*kalon*' as naming the intrinsic value property of an action, not a consequence, compare e.g. Ross 1964: 204; Gauthier and Jolif 1970: vol. 2, *ad* 1115b12–13.

this correctness, is it an action how it 'ought to be'. Then, and only then, does it qualify as something fine or noble (*kalon*) in the ethical sense of this word.[4]

But what about the purpose (*hou heneka*) which is also mentioned as one of the relevant respects of the 'how it ought to be' (2.6, 1106b21–2)? In the case of a generous action one would expect this action to aim at helping somebody who needs and deserves help (without requesting a return). Yet in his treatise on generosity (or liberality), as in his other treatises on particular virtues, he consistently specifies the purpose to be pursued as that which is *kalon* (*tou kalou heneka*),[5] and when we further notice that Aristotle equates this expression with the alternative phrase 'because it [the action] is *kalon*',[6] we cannot doubt that the motivating ground of a virtuous action as such is supposed to be its inherent value as a *kalon*. That is why we are allowed to speak of the self-referentiality, or self-motivating nature, of the virtuous action. On the other hand, an act of generosity has an external effect and aims at producing that effect. In his *treatise* on generosity this becomes explicit when he calls acts of generosity both instances of *eu poiein (tina)* – doing good (to somebody) – and of noble activity (*kala prattein, kalē praxis*) (4.1, 1120a11–15). We know from other passages that explain the terminological distinction between *poiēsis* and *praxis*[7] that the former term names an activity that effects or brings about some external result which is its purpose, while *praxis*, in this context, signifies an instance of human behaviour which can bear an intrinsic moral quality (e.g. the property *kalon*) that would render the action self-motivating. Generous behaviour somehow includes both: insofar as it exhibits a virtue, it is *praxis*, an instance of *to kalon* and thus an end in itself; but insofar as it is, or is

4 The theory of the different aspects of the correctness of an emotional reaction, or a feeling of pleasure or pain, or an ensuing tendency to act is part of his theory of virtue as being and tracking some sort of *mean* between excess and deficiency in our reactions and actions (see *EN* 2.3, 1104b21–4; 2.6, 1106b21–2, 1107a4). He equates *to kalon* with *to deon*, i.e. 'that which *ought* to be (felt or done)', and with what is correct (*orthon*), or is grounded in or exhibits the right kind of *logos* (reason, reasoning, proportion). The *deon* or *hōs dei* can be spelled out in a list of different aspects of how it ought to be. The talk of *to deon* and its aspects occurs frequently in his analysis of the ethical virtues (e.g. 3.7, 1115b12–24; 11, 1118b21–7, 1119a11–20; 12, 1119b15–19; 4.1, 1120a23–b4, 1121a1–4, a8–b12 *et passim*). An interesting attempt to further elaborate Aristotle's conception of those aspects of correctness can be found in Müller 2004.

5 *EN* 4.1, 1120a23–5, 27–9, 1121b3–5; cf. e.g. 3.7, 1115b12–13; 8, 1116b31, 1117a8; 3.12, 1119b16; 4.2, 1122b6–7, 1123a24–5.

6 *EN* 3.7, 1116a11–15, b2–3; 8, 1116b2–3, 1117a17; 9, 1117b9; *EE* 3.1, 1230a31–2. These examples are from the treatise on courage, but 4.1, 1121b4–5 has the same implication; see also n. 3 above.

7 *EN* 6.2, 1139b1–4; 4, 1140a2–6; 5, 1140b6–7; *Pol.* 1.4, 1254a5–8. In a phrase like *kala prattein* the grammatical object (*kala*) does not designate some external object or effect of the action, but the act done as something which is *kalon* (cf. Ebert 1976).

wedded to, an act of *poiēsis*, it has an external purpose. So, it seems that we encounter a duality of *underived* ends for the same action, one other-regarding and one self-regarding. But, on the other hand, it is a standard doctrine of Aristotle's that the ends pursued by acts of *poiēsis* are only *means* for enabling performances of valuable *praxis* (*eupraxia*) which are ends in themselves.

The situation is further complicated because virtuous action can have not only an external but also an 'internal' purpose, besides being somehow self-motivating *qua* virtuous action. The desirable internal consequence is the agent's *eudaimonia*, i.e. the overall excellence of the agent's life-performance which can be increased by fitting acts of virtue. Let's call the latter type of consequence the *internal teleology* of virtuous actions and the former their *external teleology*. Already in the case of activities that have only an internal teleology in addition to their inherent desirability (like acts of contemplation) the question arises what the true motive of the activity is. Is it self-motivating or motivated because of that desired internal consequence? We get into even deeper waters when, in addition, an external desirable consequence comes into play.

Now, in the first case (inherent desirability plus internal teleology) the congruence of the two motivational sources can be explained by pointing out that excellent performances contribute to the excellence of the overall life-performance roughly the way parts constitute a whole. The idea is that a life is good only if the person succeeds in tracking and realizing types of activity that can confer value upon this life. So the concern for *eudaimonia* naturally, as it were, seizes upon actions that have inherent value and hence self-motivating force. The acknowledgement of their inherent value is not compromised by the fact that they are also desired as constituents of a eudaimonic life-performance, because they can fulfil this function only on account of their inherent value and desirability.

The issue is more intricate, though, in the second case (virtuous actions with inherent desirability plus internal teleology plus external teleology) since, for us at least, part of the moral value of such actions seems to depend on the seriousness of the other-regarding concern. The crucial question here is: how can the other-regarding motivations connect with rational self-regarding concern without the latter cancelling or compromising the former? Commentators on Aristotle's ethics today often are confident that other-regarding concern is part of what makes up Aristotelian virtue and that there is no problem of incompatibility between other-regarding and self-regarding concerns if the agents define the desired value of their lives by the standards of virtue. I will call this the *Compatibility Thesis (CT)*.[8] Yet it remains a controversial issue since other-regarding and self-regarding motivations seem to be opposite motivational pulls. One wonders what really *drives* the individual act of generosity: concern for one's own excellence or genuine concern for the beneficiary?[9]

Moreover, it is not even clear yet if Aristotle himself was interested in that sort of compatibility. To be sure, the acknowledgement that someone is worthy as an object of one's own generosity is, as we have seen, part of what constitutes a genuine act of generosity, but that does not necessarily imply that one has to really care about that other person, or any other person at all. The other person might just serve as a welcome circumstantial element in the situation occasioning but not motivating the generous action. The motivation for generous actions could thus be entirely based on one's interest in increasing or preserving the intrinsic value of one's own life-performance. Accordingly, the attitude underlying those seemingly altruistic exploits of virtue might turn out to be but another example of a more sophisticated type of egoism. In view of the aesthetic connotations of the leading value term *kalon*, this might be seen as resulting from a kind of aesthetics of behaviour.

The example of generosity that I have used allows for a conveniently straightforward exposition of the question how other-regarding concern fits into a theory of virtuous action as 'choiceworthy in itself'. But this problem is equally relevant, for example, for Aristotle's theory of justice as

[8] See for instance Annas 1993: 260 (commenting on *EN* 9.8), 'The agent acts out of self-concern, but where this is concern for oneself as a rational agent aiming at the fine, this will take the form of other-directed and moral action.' For the related issue if the intrinsic desirability of an action (the quality that makes it an appropriate constituent of a valuable life) is compatible with genuine other-regarding concern, see also Broadie 1991: 422, 'There is no difficulty in reconciling the assumption that the good person engages in the right or noble practical action just because it is noble or right, with the supposition that he seeks a result beyond his action; for it is the nature of practical action to be directed to getting something changed;' Korsgaard 1996: 216, 'If we take Aristotle to hold a double-aspect theory of motivation, however, there is no problem at all. ... It is the whole package – the action along with the purpose, sacrificing your life for the sake of your country – that is chosen for its own sake.' For a more sceptical stance on the significance of other-regarding concern in Aristotle's ethics cf. de Vogel 1985.

[9] The question of how genuine other-regarding concern fits into a theory of moral action as self-motivating can also be raised with regard to modern deontological theories in the Kantian vein. A once influential philosophical attack against the idea that moral action is self-motivating in view of its inherent rightness and value, claiming that this idea leads to a position of moral complacency, can be found in Scheler 1954: 49, 140–1 *et seq*. Today, the issue of how individual altruistic concern or caring fits into a general and abstract theory of moral rightness is often discussed by adherents of virtue ethics under the heading of the moral 'schizophrenia' which supposedly results from the disparity of real life motives based on caring and abstract moral reasoning, following Stocker 1976 (a perhaps not very successfully argued but often quoted paper).

a virtue (in view of the importance of the various types of this virtue for the common good) and of courage (in view of the prime application of courage to actions in war on behalf of the city community).

Aristotle does not always show so little interest in the motivational significance of other-regarding concern as in his analysis of the singular virtues. There is, to start with, the phenomenon of genuine friendship, about which Aristotle affirms that it is akin to and based on virtue (8.1, 1155a3–4), and also that it is an attitude of genuine caring for some other person.[10] He holds that a prime expression of this attitude is generous acts of giving.[11] The end served by such a generous action, if understood as an act of genuine friendship, is the well-being of the friend for its own sake. *Doing good* (*eu poiein*) is a way to live this friendship. Does that mean that some of these generous acts are self-motivating actualizations of generosity, while others belong to the manifestations of friendship and are for the sake of the friend? The two sets rather seem to overlap. In his theory of generosity, Aristotle maintains that one of the aspects of 'how it ought to be' is the right choice of beneficiaries, and one can already assume that friends in need are the exemplary beneficiaries of generosity.[12] This becomes explicit in the treatise on friendship: it is even suggested here that one of the reasons why an excellent life cannot do without friends is that there are no better-suited objects of generosity than friends (9.9, 1169b11–16). So by an act of *eu poiein* one can realize both an actualization of generosity, self-motivated in view of its inherent excellence, and an act of friendship inspired by genuine caring for the other person.

There is another context in Aristotle's ethics where the altruistic aspect of virtuous behaviour comes to the foreground. In *EN* 5.1 he sets out a conception of 'universal justice', which is explicated as comprising all ethical virtues insofar as they are applied in our behaviour toward others and to the benefit of others or the common good (1129b25–30a14). At the same time, universal justice is also identified with the attitude of the law-abiding citizen, on the supposition that the laws are designed so as to serve the common good and to educate the citizens accordingly (1129b11–19). Aristotle's theory of law is not positivistic. He assumes that law has an essential purpose, viz. the well-being and flourishing of the community of citizens, which provides rational criteria for the goodness and justice of the body of laws. Law would lose its force to command the loyalty of citizens endowed with practical reason (*phronimoi*) if it turned out to be against the common interest.

[10] Cf. n. 33 below. [11] e.g. 8.1, 1155a5–9; 13, 1162b6–8; 9.8, 1169a18–b2; 9, 1169b10–22; 11, 1171b12–25.

[12] Cf. the casual remark in 4.1, 1122a11 and Gauthier and Jolif 1970: vol. 2, *ad* 1120a25–6.

Hence justice, in the sense of the virtue of law-abidingness, is teleologically connected with the common good, and ethically reflective persons abide by the law because they take an interest in the common good. Now, since Aristotle (following Plato), emphasizes the educational role a good body of laws should assume,[13] he can interpret all acts of virtue, to the extent that they serve the common good, as being in accordance with the law. All such acts can thus be understood as expressions of a law-abiding attitude for the sake of the common good as served by the laws. That includes acts of generosity – not because they are literally prescribed by the law (that would no longer be generosity), but rather because they match with the spirit of the laws[14] and the purpose of education as defined by the law. (The concept of justice as universal virtue serving the common good could also be connected with the theory of civic virtue in *Politics* 3.4, since civic virtue implies the wish to foster the public well-being and is at the same time, at least in its highest form, said to be identical with the virtue of a human being as such (cf. 7.14, 1333a11–12), i.e. virtue as dealt with in the ethical treatises. But that is not something I can further develop here.)

Thus it should be clear that altruistic aspects of motivation do not drop out of Aristotle's description of the motivational set-up of the virtuous and reasonable agent. But one wonders how it all fits together: his theory of the self-motivating nature of virtuous action, his conception of the subordination of virtuous action under the ultimate aim of *eudaimonia* according to the general teleology of human action and practical reasoning, and finally his description and justification of the altruistic elements of virtue as applied in friendship and citizenship. This is a vast topic that cannot be fully explored here. I want to shed some light on it, though, by discussing two exemplary passages in the *Nicomachean Ethics*.

In my comments on the significance of friendship for a complete understanding of the teleology of virtuous actions, I hinted at the possibility that an act of giving might at the same time function as an act of friendship, rooted in genuine other-regarding concern, *and* as an act of generosity desirable both in itself and in view of the desired excellence of one's own

[13] *EN* 2.1, 1103b2–6; 5.1, 1129b19–25; 2, 1130b22–9; 10.9, 1179b31–1180b28; *Pol.* 7.14, 1333a11–16, 8.1.

[14] In his discussion of the advantages of the institution of private property Aristotle affirms that the use or benefits of private property should be shared (*Pol.* 2.5, 1263a21–40). Those acts of having other people share in the benefits should not be prescribed by law but left to the owners' virtue (this virtue obviously being generosity). However, the lawgiver should aim at educating the citizens accordingly (probably so as to foster concord and unity among the citizen body liable to disintegration through great inequalities in wealth). This is an important example of how generosity, though not directly prescribable by law, can and should be set up as an educational goal by the laws. For more details cf. Szaif 2005a: 54–7.

life. So friendship might serve as a kind of inlet for altruism into Aristotle's ethics and as a way of showing how those two motivational sources can integrate. Yet in a famous chapter in the Nicomachean version of the treatise on friendship, where he talks about the relation between self-love and concern for others (*EN* 9.8), his argumentation rather seems to confirm the egoistic nature of his ethics. The upshot of this passage appears to be that seemingly altruistic actions to the benefit of others actually are to the greater advantage of the agent, because their intrinsic ethical value (*to kalon*) elevates the agent's life-performance and thus represents a greater benefit accruing to the agent than the external good conferred upon the recipient. On the other hand, a passage in the equally famous and important chapter *EN* 10.7 seems to contradict these assumptions by stating that the highest kinds of ethically valuable action are not choiceworthy in themselves but only in view of the external benefits that result from them. Since this passage indicates that the specific dignity of those highest exploits of ethical virtue lies in their importance for the public well-being, it confirms the altruistic teleology of such actions. Yet in the end, this passage too seems to have an egoistic upshot since the fact that those acts serve an external purpose seems to provide the very reason for denying the status of perfect *eudaimonia* to a life-form defined by that type of activity.

I am going to call the passage in 10.7 'passage A' (1177b1–26) and that in 9.8 'passage B' (1169a18–b2). Either passage poses a puzzle insofar as it seems to contradict some other important aspect of the Aristotelian theories of virtue and friendship. My aim is to show how those puzzles can be solved and how and to what extent the arguments of both passages are open for a reading that does justice to the basic self-regarding concern of human agents without falling into the position of moral egoism. I will first set out the puzzles and then elaborate the solutions.

2. THE PUZZLE POSED BY *EN* 10.7, 1177B1–26: ARE THE SUPREME KINDS OF NOBLE ACTION ONLY INSTRUMENTALLY CHOICEWORTHY?

Passage A is part of Aristotle's second treatise on the good life (*eudaimonia*)[15] in the *EN* (10.6–9). Before addressing this passage, I first want to discuss a relevant point in the preceding stretch of text. Aristotle starts his second

[15] I will consistently avoid translating *eudaimonia* as 'happiness' because that term tends to be understood as a name for a certain way of *experiencing* one's own life or situation, and that is not implied in the meaning of the Greek term. Put in a nutshell, *eudaimonia* is the kind of life a sensible person would wish to be able to lead or enjoy. A hedonist would of course suggest that the good life is the life that feels good. But that is a specific theoretical viewpoint about the true nature of a good human life not yet implied in the meaning of the term *eudaimonia* as it is used by ancient philosophers.

treatise on *eudaimonia* in 1176a33–b9 by claiming that *eudaimonia* is, first, a type or mode of activity (*energeia*) rather than an acquired disposition (*hexis*) of one's soul (a point familiar to us from book 1), yet, secondly, not an activity which is necessary/necessitated (*anankaia*) and desirable only in view of some other goal (*di' heteron hairetē*) but one that is choiceworthy in itself (*kath' hautēn hairetē*). The second claim is argued for by drawing a connection between *eudaimonia* and self-sufficiency. The point of this seems to be that activities that are undertaken *only* so as to ensure or provide some external good indicate a state of want (*endeēs*) incompatible with the self-sufficiency characteristic of *eudaimonia*. The talk of 'necessitated actions' too refers to actions which are chosen *only* as means to some other indispensable end.[16] Thus we encounter here a twofold distinction of activities:

D-2 (1) activities choiceworthy in themselves;
(2) activities choiceworthy for something else and necessitated.

He goes on to say that those activities are choiceworthy in themselves 'from which nothing is sought beyond themselves' and identifies them with the class of actions that are 'grounded on virtue' (*kat' aretēn*). These in turn are identified with 'doing what is fine/noble and good (*ta kala kai spoudaia prattein*)'. Aristotle does not specify here the kinds of actions that would qualify as 'doing what is fine/noble and good'. But elsewhere this expression would be typically applied to actions based on ethical virtue. Now, it may seem puzzling that virtuous actions are classified as actions 'from which nothing is sought beyond themselves'. After all, virtuous actions often, and quite typically, have external effects that are part of their specification (as in the case of generous acts). Yet we have seen that Aristotle, when talking about virtuous acts *as such*, does not treat the external effects as motivating reasons. So we do not yet have to worry at this point about Aristotle's consistency.

In book 1 (7, 1097a25–b6, cf. 6, 1096b8–19) Aristotle has set out an (at least) *threefold* division by taking into account that there are activities and states that can be both desirable in themselves and because of 'something else', i.e. some other desirable end they serve. Thus there are:

D-3 (1) things desirable only in themselves and never relative to something else;
(2) things desirable both in themselves and relative to something else;
(3) things desirable only because of something else.

[16] It is typical for Aristotle to contrast such activities as are necessitated and constrained (*anankaia*) with what is *kalon* and done for its own sake and at leisure: e.g. *Pol.* 4.4, 1291a17–18; 7.13, 1332a7–18; 14, 1333a30–6, a41–b3; 8.3, 1338a11–13, a30–32; *EN* 4.1, 1120b1; 8.1, 1155a28–9; 9.2, 1165a4; 10, 1171a24–6; see also *Met.* 5.5, 1015a20–6; *Part. an.* 1.1, 639b11–40a10.

The clear case of an item in class (1) is *eudaimonia*. Virtuous activities, on the other hand, belong to class (2) because they have intrinsic value in view of their being virtuous, but can also serve some other end. Now, the 'other end' Aristotle has in mind here is the highest good, *eudaimonia* (1097b4–6): insofar as virtuous activities contribute to the excellence of a whole life, they are related to that highest good as their consequence and, hence, desirable also in view of that consequence.

How can the twofold division (D-2) in 10.6 be projected onto D-3? Has Aristotle simply forgotten that he has already elaborated a more differentiated analysis in *EN* 1.6 and 1.7?[17] Aristotle often disregards certain differentiations that he has reached elsewhere but would not serve his current argument. This is all right as long as it does not lead to contradictions. If we want to get a clearer idea about how D-2 compares to D-3 we have to bear in mind that the activities chosen for the sake of 'something else' are also called necessitated activities in D-2. This indicates that they would fall into the third class of D-3: choiceworthy *only* in view of the end they serve. That is also confirmed later on by his calling them unleisured activities. The 'something else' (*heteron*) served by such an activity is an *external* end or good, whereas the 'something else' served by the activities of the second class in D-3 is an *internal* good: the person's *eudaimonia*. The good life, to be sure, is 'something else' relative to individual virtuous activities even if those are thought to constitute the good life, because a whole is not identical with any single part of it. But it is not *external*. In other words, D-2 compares intrinsically valuable activities with activities whose value consists only in some external consequence (which may in turn provide some useful means to one's own *eudaimonia* – but that would only be an indirect connection between the 'necessitated' activity and one's own good life). D-3, on the other hand, introduces an internal consequence into the picture, the contribution of an intrinsically valuable activity toward the constitution of a good life – an aspect disregarded but not contradicted by D-2. (When I speak of certain activities 'constituting' a good life, that of course does not mean that a good life has to be composed only of such activities. A life is constituted as a *good* life by activities through which a person lives up to the leading value and 'target' (*skopos*[18]) which defines the life-form that person has chosen.)

After this introductory passage and a passage on the significance of playful activities, Aristotle's argument takes a crucial step forward in 1177a12–18

[17] Cf. Gauthier and Jolif 1970: vol. 2, *ad* 1177b1–4.

[18] Cf. 1.2, 1094a23–5; *EE* 1.2, 1214b6–11; 2.10, 1126b29–30; *Pol.* 7.2, 1324a32–5; 13, 1331b29–34.

by retrieving from book 1 the concept of *eudaimonia* as activity in accordance with the best, or most superior and highest-ranking, virtue in us. The activity according to the superior virtue in us is then identified with the activity of the best thing (*ariston*) in us, namely the *nous* (intellect), according to its *proper* virtue (which we know to be *sophia*). That activity is then called perfect (*teleios*[19]) *eudaimonia* and identified as *theōria* (intellectual contemplation).[20]

The subsequent text (1177a19–b26), which contains our passage A, is meant to adduce further evidence for the claim that the activity of *theōria* alone is constitutive of (perfect) *eudaimonia*. It does so partly by way of a comparison of *theōria* with excellent practical activity. First, it allocates the following characteristics to *theōria*.

Theōria is

(1) the most superior or highest-ranking form of activity (*kratistē*);
(2) most continuous (*sunechestatē*);
(3) most pleasant (*hēdistē*);
(4) self-sufficient (*autarkēs*) to the highest degree;
(5) the only activity loved for its own sake;
(6) involving leisure whereas the most excellent kinds of practical activities (activities in politics and in war) are unleisured.

Point (5) reappears as a premiss in the argument in support of (6). Therefore I treat (5) and the argument in support of (6) as one argument whose intended conclusion is that practical activity cannot qualify as perfect *eudaimonia*. I will quote that argument as my passage A, dividing it up into three chunks:

A-1 (5) And this [sc. activity of contemplation] alone would seem to be loved for its own sake; for nothing arises from it apart from the contemplating, while from practical activities we gain (*peripoioumetha*) more or less apart from the action. (1177b1–4)[21]

[19] Today we often encounter the translation 'complete' for *teleios*. This is a possible translation for *teleios*, but it should not serve as the default translation because *teleios* in Greek, especially in an ethical context, has a strong evaluative connotation which gets lost when translated as 'complete'. The traditional translation 'perfect' also has the advantage of being non-tendentious on the issue of the 'dominant end' or 'inclusive end' reading. The perfection of a life-form can be construed as the most inclusive or as the highest-ranking unfolding of valuable human capacities.

[20] The term 'contemplation' for *theōria* is not meant to designate some kind of mystical vision or religious meditation but rather the activity of entertaining thoughts about objects of philosophical and scientific knowledge accompanied by understanding (cf. Burnyeat 1981 about understanding). It is different from the activity of the researcher who is still trying to achieve complete understanding (cf. *EN* 10.7, 1177a26–7).

[21] The translations are after Ross 1984 and Rackham 1934. See also n. 15 above.

Here, we seem to encounter distinction D-2 again. But its application is puzzling. The claim that *only* activities of contemplation (*theōria*) are loved (or appreciated) for their own sake must seem strange in view of Aristotle's frequent assertions earlier on that virtuous activities in general are desirable in themselves. On the other hand, the way he describes the activities that belong to the second class fits in with the way the second class was characterized in 10.6. For he mentions the intention to *gain* something apart from the action, i.e. some external good or benefit (gaining it *for oneself* as the Greek verb form suggests), and this is indeed a characteristic of actions that are 'necessitated' by some want or need. But then it seems that passage A-1 operates with a false dilemma. For it would turn out that self-motivated acts of virtue fit neither into the second class, which contains only necessitated actions, nor into the first class, which is supposed to contain only acts of contemplation. This is obviously a very unsatisfactory piece of reasoning on Aristotle's part.[22] The next step of the argument, which relates to (6), will roughly pursue the same line. But it will support this with more elaborate reasoning.

A-2 (6) And *eudaimonia* is thought to involve leisure; for we are busy that we may have leisure, and make war that we may live in peace. Now (*men oun*), the practical virtues are exercised in politics or in warfare; but the actions concerned with these [sc. politics or warfare] seem to be unleisurely. Warlike actions are completely so (for no one chooses to be at war, or provokes war, for the sake of being at war . . .); but the activity of the politician also is unleisurely, and aims at securing something beyond the mere participation in politics – positions of authority and honour,[23] or [sc. *alternatively*][24] *eudaimonia* for himself and his fellow citizens,

[22] To avoid such a consequence, Kraut 1989: 191–2 suggests a different mapping of D-2 onto D-3. He suggests that the lower class in D-2 comprises all the activities that are chosen *not only* for the sake of themselves. That would remove our problems with the argument in A-2. But it would not fit in with the way D-2 was introduced in *EN* 10.6, since there it was suggested that the upper class of D-2 could be identified with the class of activities grounded on or actualizing virtue (*hai kat' aretēn praxeis*). Moreover, it would only shift the problem to another place. Aristotle claims that the activities in the lower class of D-2 are necessitated (1176b3, cf. n. 16 above) and unleisured (1177b17–18). So in the end, we would not have to worry, maybe, about why he restricts the upper class to acts of contemplation, but instead we would have to explain why all other activities except contemplation are supposed to be unleisured and necessitated. That is not consistent with his standard doctrine either.

[23] Here I follow Rackham's translation, which seems to me to catch the sense of this clause better than Ross's.

[24] The '*ge*' in this clause should be translated not as 'at all events', as Ross does, but as emphasizing that the disjunctive clause introduces an alternative (cf. *LSJ* art. γε, II.3.b). The sentence implies a distinction between two kinds of political activity and their different goals. First he mentions 'positions of authority and honour', secondly the well-being or *eudaimonia* of the agent and his fellow citizens. Politicians who see power and honour as their leading goal have not yet understood the true purpose of politics, as Aristotle has pointed out in *EN* 1.5, while those committed to the true purpose of politics would desire positions of authority and honour only as a necessary means.

this *eudaimonia* being different from political activity, and evidently sought as something different.[25] (1177b4–15)

I will interpret the argumentative content of A-2 shortly, but first I want to quote its sequel in A-3. For the stretch of argument introduced by a '*men oun*' in A-2 is not yet complete. It has only set out that and why political and warlike activities are unleisured and thus not by themselves constitutive of *eudaimonia*. To become complete, the argument still has to point out that *theōria*, by contrast, is leisured (*en tēi scholēi*). Also we want to know why warlike and political activities, and not some other types of action, should be picked out as the activities in which the practical virtues excel. The structure of Aristotle's argument is, however, somewhat obscured by the fact that these additional elements of his reasoning in support of (6) are added in a subsequent conditional sentence which also reiterates crucial points of the whole preceding argumentation and then introduces the final conclusion that contemplative activity is the perfect form of *eudaimonia*. More precisely, this sentence starts with two complex antecedents, the first of which still comments on practical activity as being unleisured, while the second reiterates the positive attributes of *theōria* that have been set out so far.[26] It is followed by the consequent which gives the intended conclusion, and by an additional antecedent reminding us of the requirement that the life-span has to be complete in order for this life to count as an instance of human *eudaimonia*. The if-clauses are not just hypothetical but give plausible reasons. In my quotation I will leave out all other attributes apart from the characteristics (5) and (6):

A-3 So if [1st antecedent] among actions displaying the virtues those in politics and war stand out as pre-eminent in nobility and grandeur, and yet they are unleisurely, aim at some end and are not desirable for their own sake,
and if, on the other hand [2nd antecedent], the activity of the intellect seems to aim at no end beyond itself, . . . , and . . . leisuredness, . . . , and all the other attributes of blessedness are evidently those connected with this activity,
it follows [consequent] that this [sc. activity of the intellect] will be the perfect (*teleia*) human *eudaimonia*,

[25] This final clause, which Ross (more or less closely followed by the more recent translators of the *Nicomachean Ethics*) translates as 'and evidently sought as something different', can also be interpreted in a very different way as in Rackham ('indeed we are clearly investigating it as so distinct'). Gauthier and Jolif 1970 see it as a doublet of the preceding clause and conjecture that it might derive from a second redaction by Aristotle's own hand.

[26] He takes up not only the points (1) to (6) listed above but also the specific 'seriousness' of the contemplative activity, which harks back to the discussion of serious and playful pursuits in *EN* 10.6, 1176b9–1177a11.

provided [additional antecedent] it be allowed a complete (*teleion*) term of life, for nothing that belongs to *eudaimonia* is imperfect/incomplete (*ateles*). (1177b16–26)

Since the argument in support of (6) draws on point (5), one can treat both claims and the argumentation connected with them as one argument. In reconstructing this argument, we have to spell out some implicit premisses as well. I list these preceded by ‘0’.

(0a) There are only two general kinds of human activity that can qualify a human life as good: *theōria* and virtuous activity.

(0b) In order to determine which of those two forms of activity amounts to the *most perfect* life (perfect *eudaimonia*), one has to compare *theōria* with the highest kind of virtuous activity.

(0c) If an activity turns out to be choiceworthy not for its own sake but only for the sake of something else and (hence) to be unleisured, it cannot be an activity constitutive of *eudaimonia*.

(1) Among actions displaying the virtues, those in politics and war stand out as pre-eminent in nobility and grandeur (1177b16–17).

(2) Actions in politics and war are unleisured, aim at some ulterior end and are not desirable for their own sake (1177b17–18).

(3) *theōria* is chosen only for its own sake and is leisured activity (1177b20, 22).

Conclusion: *theōria* does, whereas virtuous activity does not, qualify as constitutive of the most perfect human life (perfect *eudaimonia*).

What are the Aristotelian justifications for these premisses? I concentrate on the four middle premisses from (0b) to (2) which are crucial for his argument on the value of ethical activities.

Premiss 0b – This important if implicit assumption seems fairly plausible. If indeed a life committed to the achievements of ethical virtue were the best human life-form, and there is, among the ethical activities, a distinction between higher and more noble ones and those which are noble but to a lesser degree, then the highest-ranking ethical activities would be the most perfect *eudaimonia*. After all, the eudaimonic quality of a life is not to be decided, in the first instance, on how it feels to lead such a life but on its objective value as a human life-form. (It is one of the achievements of character virtue according to Aristotle that the good activities also feel good, i.e. are enjoyable for the agent.[27]) Thus, if activities to the benefit of the whole city community are the most valuable form of ethical practice, they rather than ethical behaviour in a merely private context would qualify as perfect *eudaimonia*. So if one wants to decide the issue in favour of *theōria*, one has to compare it with these public forms of ethical activity and to show that the latter cannot qualify as perfect *eudaimonia*.

Premiss oc – The value of a life-performance derives primarily, according to Aristotle, from the quality of the activities a person engages in. Some activities have only instrumental value in that they provide some important external goods which in turn are necessary or useful for the activities that have intrinsic value. It is only the latter that can confer intrinsic value upon a life and render it choiceworthy in itself. Thus it is a necessary condition for a type of activity to function as a *constituent* of good life (*eudaimonia*) that it be intrinsically, and not only instrumentally, valuable.[28]

Premiss oc combines the two characteristics (1) that an activity is chosen only for its instrumental value, and (2) that it is unleisured. The distinction between leisurely and unleisured activities is more fully elaborated in some chapters of the treatise on the ideal political constitution (*Pol.* 7.3, 14–15; 8.3). Put in a nutshell, an unleisured activity is an activity that we take on only because of a threat to some indispensable or important external goods necessitating action. If people who are able to live a good life engage in such inferior activities, they do it only so as to provide for or preserve the means for doing what they really want to do. The entailment relation suggested in the *Politics* seems to be such that the fact that an activity is unleisured entails that it is undertaken for some other, external end (and hence cannot be constitutive of *eudaimonia*, e.g. *Pol.* 8.3, 1238a4–6). The

[27] Compare e.g. *EN* 1.9, 1099a11–21; 2.3, 1104b3–13; 3.4, 1113a25–b2; 9.9, 1170a14–16; 10.5, 1176a10–22; *EE* 7.2, 1236b39–1237a2.

[28] These statements are independent from the position on the inclusive vs. dominant-end debate. Even the dominant-end version (which seems to be unequivocally asserted in *EN* 10, cf. Kenny 1992; Kraut 1989) needs to specify some specific kind of intrinsically valuable activity which constitutes a eudaimonic activity. Inclusiveness (cf. Lawrence 1997 on that) can mean that other valuable activities, namely the engagements of ethical virtue, are parts of *eudaimonia* (apparently the favoured point of view of the *EE*), or that even other types of goods are additional components of the structured aggregate of goods that somehow makes up a good life (e.g. enjoyment, cf. *EN* 10.4, or certain external social goods with more than instrumental significance, especially loved ones and the city community, cf. 1.8–10). Irrespective of the degree of 'inclusiveness' in the conception of *eudaimonia*, it cannot be doubted that intrinsically valuable activities (some or all) are the core of *eudaimonia* for Aristotle. On *eudaimonia* as ultimate purpose see e.g. *EN* 1.4, 1095a17–20; 7, 1097a33–b6, b20–1; 6.5, 1140a25–8; *EE* 1.7, 1217a20–2; *Pol.* 7.13, 1331b39–40; *eudaimonia* as constituted by intrinsically valuable activities but only aided by activities and goods with merely instrumental value: e.g. *EE* 1.2, 1214b11–27; *EN* 1.7, 1097b1–6; *Pol.* 7.8, 1328a21–5. A survey of Aristotle's terminology, ethical teleology and epistemology of the human good and goods can be found in Szaif 2004.

passage I am currently commenting on rather suggests a reverse entailment relation. When Aristotle gives his reason why the engagements in war are unleisured he points out that no one would desire war for its own sake. In the case of political activity, both aspects are connected by an 'and' (*kai*, 1177b12) which can, and probably should, be read as a *kai explicativum*, indicating that it is the fact that an activity is directed toward some external end which supports the claim that it is unleisured. So here the fact that an act is chosen only to help some other end is supposed to entail that it is a case of unleisured activity (and hence cannot be eudaimonic). This reversal of the entailment-relation does not pose a problem since it is plausible to assume that those two characteristics are *equivalent*.

Premiss 1 – Already at the beginning of *EN* 1 (1.2, 1094b7–11), Aristotle has stated that those among the ethical activities which serve not only one's own well-being but the well-being of the political community are the finest and most noble. The political community of free citizens completes the process of human socialization and provides the framework for the most elevated human activities (including science and philosophy).[29] That is why there is no aim more noble for virtuous activity than the well-being of this community. So if the life of ethical achievements were the best form of human life, this would apply to a life devoted to the communal good in the first place. A similar connection with the well-being of the community is suggested by Aristotle's explanation of why courage is specifically related to actions in war. Aristotle's argumentation in *EN* 3.6 aims at showing that acts of 'courage', in the most proper sense of this word, are related to the risk of death that one incurs while fighting in a war. The reason he gives is that war is the most important and noble risk (*megistos kai kallistos kindunos*, 1115a30–1), and a death sustained under such circumstances is hence a 'beautiful/noble death' (*kalos thanatos*, 1115a33). He does not spell out why war is the most significant and noble way to risk one's life, but it is rather obvious that this is connected to the fact that one is risking one's life to save the whole community. Consequently, the specific dignity of courageous actions in war is grounded on the same kind of purpose as that of politics, sc. the preservation and well-being of the *polis*.

Premiss 2 – An unleisured activity is, as mentioned above, an activity that serves some other purpose and that no rational person would choose for its own sake. Any kind of labour that nobody would undertake except as a necessary means of ensuring the basic commodities of life falls under

[29] Cf. *Pol.* 1.2, 1252b27–30; 3.9, 1280b39–81a4; 7.1, 1323a14–21; *EN* 1.13, 1102a5–15; see also 2.1, 1103b2–5; 10.9; *Pol.* 7.13, 1332a28–b11.

this rubric. Engagements in war also are a clear example, since no one with good sense would want or instigate war just in order to exhibit his own virtue. This is a point explicitly argued in passage A-2:

For no one chooses to be at war, or provokes war, for the sake of being at war; anyone would seem utterly bloodthirsty if he turned friendly states into enemies in order to bring about battle and slaughter. (1177b9–12)

One might wonder why people who want to excel in virtue and think that they could perform particularly well in a war should not desire a war to occur. (This attitude has not been so unfamiliar in the course of history.) But Aristotle could reply that truly courageous people are motivated to risk their lives in war out of their concern for the *polis* they belong to. Therefore it would be a perversion of that concern if they actually longed for a war that endangered their own city. But we have to note also that there is a difference between warlike activities and the inferior labours in that the former do, whereas the latter do not, provide the opportunity for exploits of virtue. That is why the latter are not mentioned at all in 10.7. They are disqualified right away as possible constituents of a good life.

While it is clear that nobody in a sound state of mind would desire action in war for its own sake, this sort of claim is much more problematic in the case of political activities. The *polis* community and its well-being is a good in itself dependent on the good performance of the citizens who hold the political offices. Why would Aristotle want to deny that wealthy people in a position of leisure could freely and rationally opt for a political career as their way of leading an excellent life that fully unfolds their virtuous capacities and intentions to the benefit of a worthy object of concern? His argumentation relies on the assumption that political activities are choiceworthy only in view of their external results, since only on the basis of that claim is it plausible to classify them as unleisured activities (cf. *premiss oc*). Otherwise the argument from attributes (5) and (6) against the eudaimonic character of a life-form defined by such activities would fail.

In this connection, it is an important detail that political activity is said to have a goal which is different from the political activity itself (1177b13–15). This goal is specified as one's own well-being and that of the citizens. Now, that turn of phrase actually names two goals. As to the well-being of the citizen community, it is trivially true that it is not identical with one's political activity. As to the benefit from political activity for one's own well-being, there are at least two ways of understanding that. One would be that the virtuous political activity is constitutive of a certain excellent life-form.[30] But in that case the political activity, taken as a life-form, would indeed be identical with one's chosen form of a good life (or the core of it). So that cannot be the meaning here. The positive effect of the political commitment on one's own well-being, as envisaged in this passage, can consist only in some *causal* connection (for instance the fact that by helping the community to be in a good shape and serve the right purposes one also ensures the right kind of environment for one's own dedication to philosophy). Now, on this assumption political activities would indeed fulfil the criterion of an unleisured activity since they would be undertaken only as a means of providing or preserving some external conditions for a different type of life-form. But then the question arises: why does Aristotle disregard the possibility that virtuous persons may identify with the role of responsible political agents as their way of leading a valuable life?

The outcome of this argument is very puzzling in at least two regards. First, it seems to show too much since virtuous activity, and especially the life-form of the virtuously motivated politician, is soon going to be declared the second-best kind of *eudaimonia* (10.8), but as such, it should be an activity choiceworthy in itself.[31] To be sure, the *conclusion* of this argument is only about *perfect eudaimonia*. As such it does not exclude the possibility that a life dedicated to public activities might provide a less perfect degree of *eudaimonia*. But in the *argument* itself public activities have been characterized as unleisured, i.e. as motivated only by their external consequences, and it is hard to see how this characterization leaves open the possibility for the political life to count as a second-best kind of *eudaimonia*. Secondly, the argument runs against Aristotle's virtue-theoretical understanding of how the characteristic of being *kalon* confers intrinsic value and desirability on such a kind of activity. Both difficulties are connected because in order to establish the ethically motivated political life-form as a second-best type of human *eudaimonia*, one has to acknowledge the intrinsic value of this type of activity. That seems to be denied in passage A. It therefore gives rise to the following puzzle:

Puzzle I: The argumentation in 1177b1–26 (passage A) claims that ethical virtue excels most in virtuous political and warlike actions and that those, though noble (*kalon*), are not undertaken for their

[30] In the *EE*, it is very clearly affirmed that the politician who has the appropriate understanding of his life-form engages in noble activities (*kalai praxeis*) for their own sakes (1.5, 1216a24–6, cf. 1.4, 1215b3–4). *EN* 1.5 likewise hints at the idea that the right kind of political activity aims at being a practice of virtue (1095b26–1096a2).

[31] Cf. Kraut 1989: 191.

own sakes. Thus it apparently contradicts a central tenet of Aristotle's ethics: that the virtuous person chooses an action which is *kalon* for its own sake.

3. THE PUZZLE POSED BY *EN* 9.8, 1169A18–B2: ARE THE (APPARENTLY ALTRUISTIC) ACTIONS OF FRIENDSHIP INHERENTLY EGOISTIC?

In *EN* 9.8, Aristotle raises the question whether one should love oneself more than any other person. First he introduces two arguments pro and contra, the argument contra relying on the common understanding of selfishness as morally bad (1168a29–35), while the argument in favour of the priority of self-love draws on an interpretation of certain common opinions and sayings in the light of his earlier argument in 9.4 which set out how other-regarding love is in some way derived from self-love (1168b1–10). He then proceeds to a more systematic account which, in a way, salvages both positions as partial truths and dissolves the apparent contradiction. The clue to the solution is that there are two types of self-love: (1) a natural and reasonable pro-attitude toward oneself which provides the reason why people care about themselves and about the quality of their lives; (2) selfish behaviour which seeks to gain undeserved advantages in external goods but is based on a misconception of what is truly important for leading a good life. Reasonable self-love knows that it is the intrinsic value of virtuous actions which renders one's life a good and noble life – a life as reasonable and virtuous persons wish to lead. The behaviour that springs from this attitude is therefore sharply distinct from that of the selfish person who believes that external advantages, even if gained by unfair or disgraceful means, can enhance one's life. On that basis Aristotle can state that the common disapproval of self-love is directed against this kind of selfishness and is fully justified as to that. At the same time he can uphold the priority of the concern for oneself.

> With the bad man therefore, what he does clashes with what he ought to do,[32] but what the good man ought to do he does; for the intellect (*nous*) always chooses what is best for itself, and the good man obeys his intellect. (1169a15–18)

So far the argumentation could be summarized as maintaining that self-love has priority but also emphasizing that this does not imply what is commonly called selfishness:

[32] The 'ought (*dei*)' in this and the next clause is not strictly moral in the modern sense but relates to what the requirements of reasonableness in a given situation are.

(1) Although the love for another person, if genuine, is built upon a genuine pro-attitude toward that person and his well-being, rendering this external goal an end in itself for the loving person, this pro-attitude cannot be as intensive as that implied in the rational person's self-love. This would imply that if there should arise a conflict between the integrity of my own life and the possibility of some virtuous and beneficial action in the interest of the other person, the interest in preserving my own integrity would prevail.

(2) But such a conflict cannot arise! It cannot arise since people who give are in fact always the winners since they get the better part – getting *to kalon* while giving a mere external benefit – enhancing the quality of their own life-performance immediately while relinquishing only some external tool for a possible enhancement of their life-performance.

This latter point is well set out in the passage I call passage B:

> It is true of the good man too that he does many acts for the sake of his friends and his country, and if necessary dies for them; for he will surrender both wealth and honours and in general the goods that are objects of competition, gaining for himself nobility; since he would prefer a short period of rapture to a long one of mild enjoyment, a year of noble life to many years of ordinary existence, and one great and noble action to many trivial ones. Now those who die for others doubtless attain this result; and thus they choose great nobility for themselves. They will forgo wealth too on condition that their friends will gain more; for while a man's friend gains wealth he himself achieves nobility; and thus he assigns the greater good to himself. The same too is true of honour and office; all these things he will sacrifice to his friend; for this is noble and laudable for himself. . . . In all spheres of praiseworthy conduct, therefore, it is manifest that the good man assigns to himself the greater share in what is noble. In this sense then, as has been said, one should be a lover of self; but in the sense in which most men are one ought not. (1169a18–b2)

The problem with this argumentation is that it sounds as if altruism in the case of friendship were *just a particularly clever form of egoism*. But that would seem incompatible with his description of the attitude of genuine friendship in *EN* 8 as based on genuine, non-instrumental benevolence.[33]

The argumentation in passage B is not limited to the case of individual friendship. As the clearest example of altruistic action, passage B mentions

[33] See *EN* 8.2, 1155b31; 3, 1156a6–19, 1156b7–12; 4, 1157a30–1, b3; 9.4, 1166a2–6; compare also Aristotle's idea that the friend is for me 'another (my)self' (*EE* 7.12, 1245a29–30; *EN* 9.4, 1166a31–2; 9, 1169b6–7, 1170b6–7), meaning a similarity of attitude between one's self-regarding concern and the concern for this specific other person (cf. 9.4, 1166a29–32; 9, 1170b5–7; 12, 1171b33–4). On the general character of the theory of perfect friendship and the meaning of the 'other self' formula cf. Price 1989: 103–30; Szaif 2005b: 37–56.

the case of 'giving one's life' for the sake of one's friends or one's own city community (*polis*). This allows for a particularly neat comparison with the argument of passage A (in 10.7) about political and warlike actions. The shared example of both passages is that of courageous actions in war on behalf of one's city. But while in A the warlike action is treated as altruistic, as being motivated by a goal that is different from one's own *eudaimonia*, sc. the well-being of the city, passage B seems to view it as but another example of this trade-off in which the giving part always gets the better deal and knows it in advance. With regard to passage B we can thus formulate a second puzzle:

Puzzle II: The claim that benevolent agents acting for the benefit of their friends or city community assign to themselves, by those very acts, the higher kind of good appears to indicate that such acts are in reality motivated by self-interest. This claim seems incompatible with Aristotle's analysis of genuine friendship and civic virtue as based on other-regarding concern.

4. SOLUTION TO PUZZLE II: THE COMPATIBILITY AND CONNECTEDNESS OF OTHER-REGARDING AND SELF-REGARDING CONCERNS IN THE CASE OF VIRTUOUS ACTIONS

As I have set out in my introduction, it is by now a widely shared view that in Aristotle's model of how a rational and virtuous person acts, there is no real conflict between altruistic and egoistic motivation, or self-love and other-regarding concern. I called this the *Compatibility Thesis* (CT). In my introduction I also remarked that Aristotle's treatises on the singular virtues do not talk about the concern for others as a relevant element for virtuous action at all. So on the basis of those treatises one might doubt whether Aristotle was interested in any version of CT at all. Passage B, however, belongs to the treatise on friendship and talks about actions for the benefit of friends, and here at least we can expect Aristotle to come up with some version of CT, since other-regarding concern is constitutive for genuine friendship and should therefore also inform virtuous acts towards our friends. Yet his argumentation in passage B seems to lead back into egoism, and that is the core of our second puzzle.

The whole issue is connected with certain value-theoretical assumptions that may be spelled out as follows:

(1) There is objective intrinsic value, and human activities can instantiate such value.

(2) Rational self-love aims at instantiating value in one's own life as a whole through activities with intrinsic value.
(3) The class of activities that instantiate intrinsic value includes virtuous activities with a genuinely benevolent other-regarding intention.

Premiss (3) is the critical one for CT. The supporters of CT among the modern interpreters of Aristotle understand the other-regarding intention as a genuine concern for the other person. Yet it could be given a much weaker interpretation. Thus the exact moral implications of CT are far from clear. I want to illustrate that by introducing two possible interpretations of CT that stand, as it were, at opposite ends of a range of possibilities. (It is important to see that the act of entertaining a reason functions as a cause if the action is a rational one, i.e. the outcome of practical deliberation. This is at least the way Aristotle understands rational action.)

Interpretation 1: The dominant reason or rational cause for helping out a friend is that by doing so one's own life-performance is embellished. This attitude actually bears the danger that one starts looking for such opportunities and welcomes other people's misery in this perspective. But as long as that includes the acknowledgement that the beneficiaries of my actions are worthy objects of altruistic action and that this is the reason why helping them embellishes my life-performance, that attitude may still be seen as one way of spelling out CT. But of course such a person would be very self-centred.

Interpretation 2: The, so to speak, *active* cause of the action is one's wish to help. But one's awareness of the fact that this activity does not impair the integrity of one's own life (and on the contrary rather supports it) is also causally relevant since in the case of incompatibility with one's integrity there would be an overriding reason against such an action. In other words, the two causal factors would be combined so that one would operate analogously to a driving force, the other analogously to a stabilizing cause that prevents the interposition of a possible obstacle. The attitude of caring for the other person would indeed provide the driving motive, but the awareness of the fittingness of such a kind of action for one's overall life-performance would still be a causally relevant background factor. That would be an elaboration of CT much more in line with the intuitions on moral motivation many of us today share.

So Aristotle's suggestion in passage B, that other-regarding virtuous actions do not conflict with reasonable self-love because they are valuable aspects of one's performance in life, can be developed in very different ways. At one pole, there is the narcissistic person who acknowledges the intrinsic value of certain other persons but views them just as beautiful and fitting elements in a world centred around him, and as suitable points of reference for his own wonderful exploits of virtue and generosity. At the other pole, there are those who are helpful and committed out of a genuine concern for others, though their rush into benevolent action would still be controlled by the concern for the integrity of their own lives.

Now, we should not expect Aristotle's 'virtuous man' (*spoudaios*), who is also a man of practical reason (*phronimos*), to fit right away into the picture evoked by interpretation 2. At least the treatises on *eudaimonia* and the highest human good, and also his treatises on 'greatness of soul' (*megalopsuchia*) and on *phronēsis*, let us expect that the integrity of one's life is more than just a background concern for the Aristotelian *phronimos*. But what I want to show is that the Aristotelian virtuous person is also not to be approximated to the type described in interpretation 1, although passage B might invite such a misunderstanding. Aristotle's conception of genuine friendship and of its great significance for a good life, and also his conception of civic virtue and justice, withstand such a narcissistic misunderstanding, and our task is to show why the argumentation in B is not inconsistent with genuine other-regarding concern.

It may seem inconsistent with it because he describes the generous acts to the benefit of friends or the courageous acts on behalf of the city as if they were a trade-off in which the giving party is always the winner. But the question Aristotle wants to answer here is whether there is a conflict *in principle* between self-regarding and other-regarding motivation. His answer is that there isn't.

One might raise the following objection, though: does not the fact that the virtuous person chooses to procure for the friend only an *external* good, not the higher good of some ethical *kalon*, show the element of latent egoism irreconcilable with altruistic motivation? But this objection fails. For it is not possible to hand over, as it were, an instance of the ethical *kalon*, because the ethical *kalon* is an internal good constituted by the right kind of motivation and corresponding *praxis*. It can come into being only through an agent's own decision-making and acting.

To be sure, the objection could be reformulated so that it refers to the *opportunity* for noble action: would not altruism require that the opportunity for such action be yielded to the friend? Aristotle, anticipating this objection in passage B,[34] acknowledges that a virtuous person might do that but then points out that even so this person could not help getting the

[34] *EN* 9.8, 1169a32–4: 'It may even be the case that he gives up actions to his friend and that it is nobler for him to become the cause of his friend's acting than to act himself.'

better part out of it because that act of yielding would be even nobler than the action the opportunity for which has been yielded to the friend.[35]

Because of that win-win situation, virtuous altruistic action and its corresponding motivation can harmonize with the concern for the value of one's own good life. The overridingness of self-love does not have to imply more than overridingness of the concern for the integrity of one's own life, but this integrity can never be vitiated by reasonable acts of altruism.

5. A POSSIBLE SOLUTION FOR PUZZLE I: THE MOTIVATION FOR COMMUNITY-RELATED COMMITMENTS FROM THE VIEWPOINT OF THE PHILOSOPHICAL FORM OF LIFE

How can it be that, in passage A, Aristotle excludes the achievements of virtue in politics and war from the class of activities undertaken for their own sake? Is that not utterly incompatible with his general theory of virtuous action and his remarks in passage B about the self-regarding benefits of virtuous altruistic actions?

There seem to be only two ways of saving Aristotle's consistency on such a very basic point. One way would be to interpret the crucial text (1177b18) as if Aristotle had said that one chooses political activity *not only* for its own sake.[36] But that is not what he says.

I therefore prefer to argue for the following solution: In 10.7, Aristotle describes the motivational situation from the point of view of a life devoted to philosophy. What reason could a philosopher have for engaging in politics or war? None, unless the situation forces him to do so. And when I speak of the situation forcing the philosopher into a certain kind of action

[35] Of course, the attempt to let the other do the action could be reciprocated as well, as when two people mutually try to let the other one pass through a doorway first, and in theory that would be the starting point of an infinite regress preventing the action from ever taking place. But in practice that does not seem to be a real problem.

[36] Kraut 1989: 190–2, for instance, interprets 1177b18 as if it stated that those actions were chosen not *only* because of themselves. But such an 'only' is not in the text (as Kraut acknowledges), and the way he wants to insert it into the implied meaning, namely through a different interpretation of the meaning of D-2, only shifts but does not solve the problem, as I have pointed out above (n. 22). Broadie 1991: 423 suggests that he is describing here not the attitude that ideally the politician should assume but 'a divergent *de facto* attitude', i.e. the attitude that real politicians happen to have. But Aristotle's argumentation here is not about *de facto* politicians but about the status *in principle* of political activity, as the highest form of virtuous activity, in comparison to the philosophical life-form. Some interpreters (cf. D. Frede 1998: 280; Wolf 2002: 248–9) suggest that his assessment in this passage is based on a different understanding of *autarkeia* compared to that in *EN* 1.7. Yet it seems that the reference to *autarkeia* belongs to a different part of the argumentation in 10.7. The argument regarding the attributes (5) and (6) of *theōria* does not depend on the understanding of *autarkeia*. Irwin's translation would avoid the problems, but it does not match with the unequivocal semantic import of the two crucial clauses in 1177b1–4 and b18 (cf. Kraut 1989: 90, n. 18).

to the benefit of the community, I do not have in mind some force exerted by the society on the philosopher. I mean rather something like the force of a moral obligation arising from a certain situation and exerting itself on a person who is endowed with the relevant ethical virtues.[37] Aristotle's philosopher has a moral identity as well: '. . . but insofar as he is a human being and living in the society of others, he chooses to engage in virtuous action' (1178b5–6). The standard case (in the Greek context) would be that the philosopher is a citizen of the city-state he lives in. Obviously, as citizen of an ancient Greek city, he would act unjustly if he tried to evade his obligation to serve the city in a war. The philosophers are supposed to have a good character and good practical judgement.[38] Living a life of human beings (*anthrōpeuesthai*, 1178b7) and hence embedded into social and political frameworks, they will not only exhibit justice, moderation etc. in their behaviour toward others, but also commit themselves to politics or war if the circumstances demand it. But that will not be the purpose of their

[37] Wolf 2002: 246–53 also tries to explain the claim in 10.7 that political activity, even if virtuous, is not desirable in itself, as due to the fact that Aristotle is here assuming the perspective of the philosopher. Her position differs from mine, though, in that she suggests (referring to 1178b5–6) that philosophers would engage in politics to a limited extent only so as to preserve the political framework necessary for their own philosophical leisure (249–51), following Cooper 1975 to some extent. This would mean that their political commitments would be only self-serving. But I do not think that that would be a consistent position for Aristotle to hold. If Aristotle's philosophers, who are supposed to be endowed with the ethical virtues, perceive that there is a need for them to engage in the politics of their city, they will do so according to the teleology of right political action, because otherwise their ethical virtue and *phronēsis* would not be genuine. The inherent purpose of political activity and right attitude of someone who holds a public office is to serve justice and the common well-being (*EN* 5.6, 1134b1–8; 6.8, 1141b23–33; *Pol.* 3.12, 1282b14–18), and hence to help all citizens to realize the best life possible for them (*Pol.* 7.2, 1324a23–5).

[38] One may wonder why philosophers are supposed to have the ethical virtues and *phronēsis*. Can you not be a good philosopher without being a good fellow human and good citizen? There is a simple way for stating Aristotle's case based on *EN* 6.13. The philosopher's life with its focus on philosophy has to be organized by *phronēsis* (1145a6–11), because organizing a life is, by definition, the task of *phronēsis* (cf. 6.5). But *phronēsis* can only come in one package with all the character virtues (1144b30–45a2). – Yet this conclusion cannot be more convincing than its premisses. Why can *phronēsis*, as the rational foundation for leading *any* kind of really good life, be had only in a package with all the character virtues? Based on *EN* 6, especially 6.12–13, one can try to develop an answer by starting from the premiss that *phronēsis* can fulfil its task (i.e. provide a correct orientation for how to live a good life) only on the basis of a correct understanding of the objective values that matter for a human life, together with the ability to find out how, in the particular situations of one's life, those leading values can be realized or approximated. The second required premiss would be that this sort of understanding cannot fully develop and become operative without a congruent development of the character virtues that make the person *enjoy* the values realized by excellent activities. The unequivocal commitment to a life of philosophy and science (not for some extrinsic purposes) would depend on such a correct understanding of the significance and order of human values, aided by the right character development. As based on that kind of understanding, it would not only acknowledge the superiority of the objects and achievements of contemplation but also the intrinsic value of ethical virtues (and by the same token acquire the characteristic motivational patterns that dispose one to moral behaviour).

lives. Although they acknowledge the intrinsic value of such actions, they will not identify them as constituents of their own *eudaimonia*.[39] Therefore such actions, especially commitments in politics and war, would indeed be unleisured activities from their point of view, i.e. activities they are compelled to undertake as virtuous citizens in order to ensure some necessary external means and conditions of good human life not only for their own sakes, but also for the sake of the entire city community (cf. 1177b14).

For people who opted for a life that gains its value from the noble character of their political activities, the situation would be very different. To be sure, their own well-being and integrity would not be identical with that of the *polis*. But by making themselves useful to the *polis* they would, by the same token, also achieve their own 'happiness', not just by helping to create the right social conditions for good human life but by living a good life through those excellent activities. Being in a position of leisure, they would choose public engagements as their way of personal accomplishment. They would understand their activity as a form of *eu poiein* (doing good) causally benefiting the community, which at the same time, as a form of *kalē praxis* (noble activity), contributed to their own good life by constituting it. (Hence, in their case, those activities would belong in the upper class of D-2.)

This is the way the benefits of a life dedicated to public commitments will be described in 9.8. But in passage A (10.7) we are *not* supposed to see things from the point of view of that merely second-best form of life. Passage A describes the teleology of human activities from the point of view of those who search for and create the defining value of their lives in the pursuit of philosophical inquiry. For Aristotle, this life-form and its point of view is not just one option beside others. It is the choice of the best life a human being can accomplish because there is no more elevated activity than science and philosophy, as Aristotle tries to show by drawing on an ontological conception of value that singles out the theoretical intellect as the most valuable part in us, able to reach out for the most important and elevated objects (10.7–8, 1177b26–1178a23).

We know already why that does not imply that the philosophers' behaviour toward others will be egoistic. One might even suggest that

39 Cf. Heinaman 1988: 51–3; Kenny 1992: 86–92. There are four combinatory possibilities here that have been covered by recent scholars (and I will mention just a few): Aristotle in book 10 might hold that the acts of ethical virtue either are a part of the *eudaimonia* of the philosopher (I), or are not (II); and he might take those acts to have value for the philosophers either *only* as a means to contemplative activity (A), or also intrinsically (B). I-A is supported by Keyt 1983 and Cooper 1987; I-B by Gauthier and Jolif 1970: vol. 2, 860–6; II-A by Kraut 1989: 23–7 *et seq.*; II-B by Heinaman 1988 and Kenny 1992, and also in this article.

Aristotle's philosophers can be more clearly altruistically motivated in their ethical behaviour. To be sure, the philosophers, if anyone, will be able to appreciate the intrinsic value that such actions have and can confer upon a life as a whole. But they won't need that as a source of value for their own lives, because they have a life-form which is even better. Thus for people who seek value through ethical exploits, ethically valuable activities will always be an expression not only of their other-regarding concerns, but also of their self-love, while Aristotle's virtuous philosophers could act purely altruistically when the situation challenges them to perform such activities, performing them as a compelling human requirement, not as a constituent of their own *eudaimonia.*

There remains, however, a doubt regarding the consistency of this result with Aristotle's general theory of virtue. The development of a virtuous character includes the acquisition of a certain understanding of *negative* value, as part of the process of moral learning which is described by Aristotle in other contexts. The philosophers who are also just and courageous would, if they dodged some incontrovertible obligation toward their fellow citizens, knowingly harm their own personal value, and thus the value of their life-performance as a whole. It seems that this consideration, if pursued further, would lead toward a more inclusive understanding of *eudaimonia.*

CHAPTER 9

Epicurean 'passions' and the good life

David Konstan

In this essay, I investigate the status of the *pathē* (plural of *pathos*) in Epicurean psychology. It will emerge that Epicurus had a very narrow view of the significance of this term, in comparison with its use among his contemporaries (and some of his followers). What is more, this restriction has important consequences for Epicurus' understanding both of the emotions and of the goal of life in general.

In popular as well as philosophical literature of the late fifth century onward, *pathos* is the normal Greek word for 'emotion'. The term nevertheless retained a wide range of connotations, and if it came to refer specifically to emotion only in 'the 420s and probably later' (Harris 2001: 84), it was not limited to this meaning either in everyday or scientific usage. For example, the word often bears the sense of an accident or misfortune, as well as the neutral significance of a condition or state of affairs. In philosophical language, *pathos* may signify a secondary quality as opposed to the essence of a thing (cf. Aristotle, *Met.* 5.21, 1022b15–21; Urmson 1990: 126–7). Even in the domain of psychology, *pathos* might well include sensations such as pleasure and pain, and also desires or appetites, which we do not necessarily classify as emotions in the strict sense of the term – nor did Aristotle. Thus, in the *Rhetoric to Alexander* (7.5), formerly thought to be by Aristotle but now commonly ascribed to Anaximenes and dated slightly earlier than Aristotle's own *Rhetoric*, we find *pathē* illustrated by contempt, fear, taking pleasure (*hēsthentes*), feeling pain (*lupēthentes*) and desiring (*epithumountes*); elsewhere (7.14), the list of characteristic *pathē* embraces passionate love, anger, drunkenness and ambition (*erōs*, *orgē*, *methē* and *philotimia*). In the *Nicomachean Ethics*, Aristotle himself adopts a somewhat wider usage, in which he includes desire in the broad sense among the *pathē*, e.g. at 2.5, 1105b21–3: 'I call *pathē* desire (*epithumia*), anger, fear, confidence, envy, joy (*chara*), love, hatred, longing, competitiveness, pity and in general those things upon which attend pleasure and pain' (cf. 7.3, 1147a14–15; for *pathos* complemented by *epithumia*, 7.9, 1151b8–9; also *EE* 2.2, 1220b12–13).

Aristotle is more precise, however, in the *Rhetoric*, where he offers his most detailed analysis of the several *pathē*. Here, Aristotle makes it clear that pleasure and pain (*hēdonē* and *lupē*) are elements or components of *pathē*, properly speaking: 'Let the emotions be all those things on account of which people change their minds and differ in regard to their judgements, and upon which attend pain and pleasure, for example anger, pity, fear and all other such things and their opposites' (*Rh.* 2.1, 1378a20–3); and this account is confirmed in the *Nicomachean Ethics* as well, where Aristotle describes the virtues as being about actions and *pathē*, and adds that 'pleasure and pain attend on every *pathos* and every action' (2.3, 1104b14–15). The *pathē* that Aristotle discusses in the *Rhetoric* include anger, the satisfaction that assuages anger, love and hate, fear and confidence, shame, gratitude, pity, envy and competitiveness, among others. Some of these are characterized by a desire, for example anger (a desire or *orexis* for revenge) and love (a wish that the loved one may prosper); but simple desires in the sense of appetites – hunger, thirst and the like – are not treated as *pathē*.[1]

More particularly, Aristotle in the *Rhetoric* treats pleasure and pain, that is, *hēdonē* and *lupē*, as sensations or *aisthēseis*:

> . . . since feeling pleasure is in the perception of some experience (*pathos*), and *phantasia* is a weak kind of perception (*aisthēsis*), some *phantasia* of what one remembers or expects always occurs in a person when he remembers or expects something . . . Thus, it is necessary that all pleasures are either present in perception or arise in remembering things that have happened or in expecting things that will happen. (1.11, 1370a27–34)[2]

In respect to *pathos*, as with a number of other technical terms, Epicurus went his own way, and indeed seems almost deliberately to have turned Aristotle's account on its head. *Pathos* appears principally as one of three (or perhaps four) basic epistemological capacities that Epicurus calls 'criteria'. Thus, Diogenes Laertius, in his summary of Epicurus' teaching, reports that 'in the *Canon*, Epicurus says that the criteria of truth are sensations (*aisthēseis*) and preconceptions (*prolēpseis*) and the *pathē*, and some Epicureans add the imaginative projections of thought (τὰς φανταστικὰς ἐπιβολὰς τῆς διανοίας)' (10.31). Epicurus associates sensations and *pathē* in

[1] For Plato's usage, see Solmsen 1961: 151–7.

[2] On the relationship between *phantasia* and *aisthēsis* in Aristotle, see *De an.* 3.3 and *Insomn.* 2, 459a15–19, where *phantasia* is said to be a motion that arises from (or as a result of) the activity of perception. Solmsen 1961: 157 affirms that Aristotle makes *aisthēsis* 'a cognitive power inferior only to the activities of νοῦς'. It is conceivable that Aristotle's account, in *De an.* 3.7, 430a26–431a8, of *aisthēseis* as determining what is or is not the case, whereas the pleasant and unpleasant condition what one seeks and avoids, had an influence on Epicurus.

several passages in the *Letter to Herodotus* (37–8, 55, 63, 82; cf. *Sent.* 24). For example, he writes (38): 'For it is necessary to look to the primary concept behind each sound . . . Then we must observe everything in accord with the *aisthēseis*, and, simply, the attendant projections whether of thought or of some other of the criteria, and so too the occurrent *pathē*' (cf. *Ep. Pyth.* 116). It is clear that the *pathē* operate alongside *aisthēseis* and certain processes of thought, and together provide us with all the information we have concerning the world.

The *aisthēseis* have received considerable attention from scholars, especially in connection with Epicurus' doctrine that 'all sensations are true' (see e.g. Taylor 1980; Everson 1990; Striker 1996b). Leaving this puzzle aside, what we know about *aisthēseis* is that they do not involve reason (*aisthēsis* is *alogos*, D.L. 10.31) or memory (*mnēmē*), and that they are associated with the five senses (*Ep. Hdt.* 68). The *pathē* are evidently distinct from the *aisthēseis*, but what precisely are they? According to Diogenes Laertius (10.34), the Epicureans 'say that there are two *pathē*, pleasure (*hēdonē*) and pain (*algēdōn*), which exist in every animal, the one pertaining to what is one's own (*oikeion*), the other pertaining to what is foreign (*allotrion*), by which choices and avoidances are distinguished'. For Epicurus, then, the *pathē* are what inform us about the affective value of things in the world – whether they are to be pursued or shunned – whereas the *aisthēseis* inform us about how things appear physically.[3]

In a recent survey of 'Epicurean Epistemology', Elizabeth Asmis (1999: 275–6) offers a subtle and detailed analysis of the role of the *pathē* in Epicurus' psychology. I cite it in extenso, both because of its clarity and because I find myself in disagreement with certain elements of her interpretation. She writes:

Epicurus joins 'feelings' (*pathē*) to perceptions as a basis of inference. In his survey of Epicurean canonic, Diogenes Laertius (10.35) states that there are two feelings, pleasure and pain, by which choice and avoidance are judged . . . But this does not imply that pleasure and pain are not also a criterion of truth. For they determine action by serving as a measure of what truly is good and bad . . . The basic difference between these two measures of truth is that feelings are acts of awareness of inner states, whereas perceptions are directed at what is external to us. As a type of canon, the feelings are not simply altered conditions of the sense organ; they include an awareness of the condition. Epicurus agreed with others that every act of perception

[3] Epicurus also uses the term *pathos* in connection with the senses (e.g. *Ep. Hdt.* 52–3). It is conceivable that this usage reflects a distinction between the impact of the acoustic stimuli, which consist of material films or *eidōla* (in Latin *simulacra*), and sensation proper, which is something more than the mere physical collision of the image-bearing atoms and the auditory apparatus. But I suspect rather that Epicurus is simply using *pathos* in a way that is equivalent to *aisthēsis* here; cf. Koenen 1997: 169.

depends on an alteration of the sense organ; and this may be called a feeling. In addition to being moved, the sense organ may have a feeling of being moved; and this constitutes a criterion of truth. At the most general level, this criterion is a feeling of pleasure or pain. Subsumed under these feelings is the whole range of bodily sensations, such as feeling sated or hungry or having a pain in the stomach, and the entire range of emotions, such as anger, sadness, or joy . . . One highly controversial claim supported by reference to feelings is the claim that the mind is situated in the heart. Like the Stoics (though with a different logical apparatus), the Epicureans sought to determine the location of the mind by the 'evident' fact that the heart is where we feel fear, joy and other emotions . . . Since the mind is the seat of the emotions, this feeling shows that the mind is located in the heart.

Let me isolate four of Asmis' claims for closer attention: (1) 'feelings are acts of awareness of inner states, whereas perceptions are directed at what is external to us'; (2) 'feelings are not simply altered conditions of the sense organ; they include an awareness of the condition'; (3) 'Subsumed under these feelings is the whole range of bodily sensations, such as feeling sated or hungry or having a pain in the stomach, and the entire range of emotions, such as anger, sadness, or joy'; (4) 'feeling shows that the mind is located in the heart.'

First, then, let us consider the pleasure we derive from agreeable music – one of Epicurus' own examples of kinetic pleasure (*On the Goal*, quoted in Cicero, *Tusc.* 3.41), and clearly quite different from pleasures of replenishment, such as those which derive from satisfying hunger or thirst. Why is the *pathos* associated with listening to music more 'internal' than, say, the auditory sensation, which also, as we have seen, involves a *pathos*? We perceive the pleasing quality of the music, just as we hear the pitch and rhythm of the music, not of the locus where the sensory organ is affected. Second, is there a distinction between a *pathos* as a condition of an organ, and as the awareness of that condition? I am inclined to think that Epicurus would not have recognized such a division; certainly, there is no direct evidence that he did. Rather, the alteration in the sense organ (in which, as we shall see, the psyche is implicated) just is the awareness of pleasure.[4]

Asmis' third point involves the inclusion of the emotions among the *pathē*, so that a pain in the stomach associated with the feeling of hunger is subsumed under the same category as anger and joy. We may consider this item together with the last, that the feelings testify that the mind is located in the chest or heart. The evidence for this last proposition is a scholium incorporated into the text of Diogenes Laertius 10.66 = fr. 311

[4] See Glidden 1980: 184 on 'the material identity of these *pathē* with atomic motions in our bodies'; but note the criticisms of Mitsis 1988: 45–6.

Usener, which reads as follows: 'He says elsewhere that it [the soul] is made up of very smooth and round atoms, which differ greatly from those of fire; and one part of it is non-rational (*alogon*), and dispersed throughout the rest of the body; but the rational part (*to logikon*) is in the chest (*thōrax*), as is evident from fears (*phoboi*) and from joy (*chara*).' Now, to say, with Asmis, that 'feeling shows that the mind is located in the heart' is to beg the question of whether emotions may be classified under *pathē*, since the 'feelings' in question are not pleasure and pain, which we know to be *pathē*, but rather fears and joy. These latter pertain to the rational part of the soul; that is why our awareness of them in the chest proves that the rational part of the soul is located there. I presume that Epicurus appeals to fears and joy because they are more palpable than thoughts, and are more commonly felt to inhabit the region of the heart. But his argument goes also to show that these two emotions, if we may call them that, are specifically situated in *to logikon* (the term *to logikon* does not seem to occur elsewhere in Epicurean writings, at least according to the *Glossarium Epicureum* = Usener 1977). As I shall indicate in a moment, that is not the locus of what Epicurus calls *pathē*.

First, however, I cite the evidence of Lucretius to show that he confirms Epicurus on this matter quite precisely.[5] The passage is toward the beginning of Book 3 (136–51); I quote the translation of Long and Sedley (1987: vol. 1, 66–7), inserting the Latin words where relevant:

> My next point is that the mind (*animus*) and the spirit (*anima*) are firmly interlinked and constitute a single nature, but that the deliberative element (*consilium*) which we call the mind (*animum mentemque*) is, as it were, the chief, and holds sway throughout the body. It is firmly located in the central part of the chest. For that is where fear and dread (*pavor ac metus*) leap up, and where joys (*laetitiae*) caress us: therefore it is where the mind (*mens animusque*) is. The remaining part of the spirit (*anima*), which is distributed throughout the body, obeys the mind (*mens*) and moves at its beck and call. The mind by itself possesses its own understanding and its own joys (*sibi gaudet*) while nothing is affecting either the spirit (*anima*) or the body. And just as, when our head or eye is hurt (*laeditur*) by an attack of pain (*dolor*), the agony is not shared (*non . . . concruciamur*) by our whole body, so too the mind (*animus*) sometimes itself suffers pain (*laeditur*) or waxes with joy (*laetitia*) while the rest of the spirit (*anima*) throughout the limbs and frame is receiving no new stimulus.

Lucretius goes on to explain that when the mind (*mens*) is affected by a very great fear (*metus*), the spirit (*anima*) as a whole shares the sensation (152–3), while physical impacts such as a wound from a spear affect the

[5] Contrast Mehl 1999: 272–87, who argues that Lucretius makes rather a mess of things.

mind (*animus*), for example by producing mental confusion (*mentis aestus*) (168–76).

I note first that the familiar contrast in Lucretius between *animus* and *anima*, while it produces an agreeable jingle,[6] may serve to obscure Epicurus' precise characterization of these parts, of which Lucretius himself is perfectly well aware. He chooses the term *consilium* as the proper equivalent to Epicurus' *to logikon*; he explicitly says that he will call this *animus* or *mens*, which are more natural in Latin. The word *nous* does not seem to occur in Diogenes Laertius' tenth book, and I suspect that Epicurus avoided it as a technical term (cf. *Glossarium Epicureum* s.v.). Lucretius' *anima*, in turn, renders Epicurus' *psuchē*. The *psuchē* is the locus of *aisthēsis*, which, as we have seen, is specifically said to be *alogos*, and lacking in memory or *mnēmē*. Like Epicurus, Lucretius calls in witness two emotions, fear (*pavor ac metus* = *phoboi*) and joy (*laetitiae* = *chara*) to show that the *consilium* is located in the chest. Just as *chara* is distinct from the *pathos hēdonē*, so too Lucretius employs the term *laetitia* rather than *voluptas* for the emotion that resides in the *consilium*. The body is affected by pain: *dolor* renders Epicurus' term *algēdōn*, which, unlike *lupē*, the term favoured by Aristotle, connotes a specifically physical or corporeal sensation. Epicurus, again, seems to have avoided the term *lupē*, though he employs the participial form of the verb *lupeisthai* to designate mental distress.[7] The body, however, cannot feel pain, or anything, on its own; it is only in combination with *psuchē* that it experiences the *pathē*, whether pleasure or pain. Thus, in the *Letter to Herodotus* (63–4) Epicurus writes:

> And indeed one must keep in mind that the soul (*psuchē*) has the primary responsibility for perception (*aisthēsis*). But (the soul) would not in fact have gained this [responsibility] if it were not somehow covered by the rest of the aggregate. But the rest of the aggregate, having provided for the soul this responsibility, itself too has obtained a share in this attribute from the soul, although it does not have a share in all the things that the soul possesses.

Like the *psuchē*, the rational element can also suffer: Lucretius applies the verb *laeditur* to both; but its distress resides in fear itself, which seems to

[6] Boyancé 1958: 135 notes that the Latin jingle reproduces that between *logikon* and *alogon*, the two parts of the *psuchē* indicated by the scholion to the *Ep. Hdt.* 67 and by Aëtius 4.4.6 = fr. 312 Usener, DK 68 A 105, no. 160 in Arrighetti, 1973: 516.

[7] Cf. *Sent.* 3 and 10, where *to algoun* and *to lupoumenon* are evidently distinct, and neither is compatible with the presence of *hēdonē* (cf. Diano 1974: 168); for *lupeisthai* = 'grief', see D.L. 10.119; at 10.125 the three mentions of *lupein* presumably reflect an opponent's words. Note Seneca, *Ep.* 99.25: *est aliqua voluptas cognata tristitiae*, where 'grief' or 'sadness' seems the sense, as opposed to *dolor*; Cic. *Tusc.* 3.61 translates *lupē* as *aegritudo*, and this seems right. Contra Diano 1974: 178, who describes the pleasures and pains of the soul as 'gioie e tristezze, χαραί e λύπαι'.

serve as the contrasting term to *chara* or *laetitia*. Thus, in the proem to Book 2, Lucretius famously declares that 'nature demands nothing for itself but that pain (*dolor*) be absent from the body, and that the mind (*mens*) enjoy a pleasing sensation (*iucundo sensu*) with the removal of anxiety and fear (*cura . . . metuque*)' (17–19). Lucretius contrasts the pain of the body with that of the mind, and this is a natural enough way to speak, but in a sense it is not wholly accurate. Both pain in the sense of *algēdōn*, and the distress of fears or *phoboi*, are perceived by the soul in the larger sense in which *psuchē* includes both the non-rational and the rational parts; likewise, both pleasure as *hēdonē* and joy, or *chara*, are psychological affects. The difference between them is better expressed as that between non-rational vs. rational affects: the former are the *pathē*; the latter do not seem to have a special name in Epicurean theory, but it is reasonable to dub them emotions.[8]

The *pathē*, then, are a function of the *psuchē* or *anima*, and are not rational in the sense that they do not involve the logical element or mind. The *pathē* of pleasure and pain function automatically, and do not depend on *logos*; according to Diogenes Laertius (10.137 = fr. 66 Usener), Epicurus cited as proof that pleasure (*hēdonē*) is the goal (*telos*) the fact that 'animals, as soon as they are born, are satisfied with it [pleasure] but they are in conflict with suffering (*ponos*) by nature and apart from reason (*logos*). We thus avoid pain (*algēdōn*) by our own *pathē* (*autopathōs*).' The twin emotions of fear and joy, on the other hand, belong specifically to the *consilium* or *logikon*, and they are distinct in category from the *pathē*.[9]

What, then, is the status of *chara* or *laetitia* in Epicurus' system? To begin with, we may say that *chara* ought not to be confused with the goal or *telos*, which is variously described either as *hēdonē* (e.g. D.L. 10.11; cf. 10.131, where *hēdonē* is defined as 'neither feeling pain (*algein*) in the body nor being disturbed (*tarattesthai*) in the soul (*psuchē*)'; 10.137), or as *ataraxia*, 'freedom from perturbation' (cf. *Ep. Pyth.* 85; D.L. 10.128, where ataraxy is defined similarly to *hēdonē* as 'suffering neither pain (*algein*) nor anxious fear (*tarbein*)'), but never as *chara* or joy.

Diogenes Laertius reports (10.136 = fr. 2 Usener) that, in his book *On Choices* (*Peri haireseōn*), Epicurus affirmed that 'ataraxy and freedom from trouble (*aponia*) are katastematic pleasures (*hēdonai*); but *chara* and good

[8] Diano 1974: 252 asserts that 'πάθη nel senso specifico di "passioni" s'incontra negli scritti epicurei di frequente', citing frs. 221 and 548 Usener; his other evidence does not derive from Epicurus himself, however, and I suspect that a change occurred in usage in the later school, for example in Philodemus (see below).

[9] In this, I agree essentially with Diano 1974: 168, save that I speak of the rational and non-rational parts of the soul, whereas Diano speaks of the soul vs. the body.

cheer (*euphrosunē*) are regarded as kinetic activities.'[10] Erler and Schofield (1999) offer an interpretation of this passage which has the great merit of making clear the distinction between *chara* and *hēdonē*, but with which I find myself in disagreement over the fundamental character of these affects. Erler and Schofield first explain the difference between static or katastematic pleasures, and those that are kinetic or dynamic. The essence of katastematic pleasure, they write (1999: 656), 'is simply that it is a stable condition . . . When the body is in such a *katastēma*, it is entirely free of pain; hence the designation of *aponia* as a katastematic pleasure. We must suppose that *ataraxia*, the katastematic pleasure of the soul, is achieved when it attains an analogous condition of stable psychic harmony.'[11] Erler and Schofield then continue: 'What matters most for Epicurean ethics in the end is not katastematic pleasure itself, but the joy and delight it gives us. For joy and delight are forms of awareness, or *pathē*, as katastematic pleasure is not' (here they cite the passage from Diogenes Laertius quoted above). And they conclude: 'From one point of view, therefore, Epicurus' disagreement with Aristippus is much less than he makes it appear, since the greatest pleasure remains strictly speaking a kinetic pleasure, namely our delight in *aponia* and *ataraxia*.'

Now, it will be clear from what I have said that I disagree about applying the label *pathos* to joy and delight. Beyond the question of labels, however, there is a substantive issue here. The *pathē* are very elementary forms of awareness, operating at the level of the non-rational *psuchē*. They constitute the physiological basis of approach and avoidance, and are instinctive, pertaining as much to animals as to human beings. In themselves, they admit of no deliberation, no reasoning. The sense in which the *pathos* of pleasure or *hēdonē* constitutes the goal or *telos* for Epicureanism is, as I understand it, just by virtue of the fact that it is the thing to which all living creatures are naturally attracted, just as they are repelled by its opposite, *algēdōn*.[12] Of course, one is aware of such pleasure, just as one

[10] Reading κατὰ κίνησιν ἐνέργειαι (nom. pl.) with Long and Sedley 1987: vol. 2, 124–5; the mss. give κατὰ κίνησιν ἐνεργείᾳ, 'kinetic by virtue of activity'. Purinton 1993: 288–90 defends the dative; cf. Giannantoni 1984: 28.

[11] Cf. Diano 1974: 170, and contrast Giannantoni 1984: 44.

[12] Alberti 1994 argues, rightly in my view, that Epicurus located the highest good in pleasure, not in virtue (contra Mitsis 1988; Annas 1987; Annas 1993); the virtues are not pleasurable in themselves. Cf. Cicero, *Fin.* 1, where Torquatus (29–31) makes it clear – against later Epicureans who think that reason plays some part in our knowledge of the highest good – that pleasure is the criterion for choice for every animal; animals do not choose rationally. All that reason or *logismos* does, apart from getting rid of false opinions (198–9), is to choose among immediate pleasures with a view to the long-term pleasurable state (194–7): 'È sempre dunque la ragione, e non la virtù, a determinare qual'è la condotta richiesta per conseguire il fine del piacere' (201). Hence, 'la teoria etica epicurea si pone al di fuori della cosiddetta "etica della virtù"' (202).

is aware of sensations or *aisthēseis* without the mediation of higher-order reasoning in the *logikon* part of the soul. This awareness is as much a feature of katastematic pleasure as it is of kinetic pleasure: one simply is conscious of the *pathos* constituted in and by stability and the absence of pain or perturbation in the body or soul.

Joy or *chara*, however, is not the same as pleasure at all, any more than fear, the negative condition of the *logikon* or rational part of the soul, is the same as pain. The important thing is to recognize that *phobos* and *chara* are both kinetic activities of the rational soul. Fear is the sign of a disturbance or *tarachē*, of course; what then is joy a sign of? There is no evident reason for supposing that it constitutes awareness of the katastematic or stable condition of the body or soul. Let us pursue the analogy with fear. We understand fear as involving not simply the awareness of an unpleasant sensation, but rather as a complex emotion involving a judgement concerning the nature of the object to which it corresponds, or which evokes it. In this sense, fear is very much like an Aristotelian emotion. Aristotle's definition of fear runs as follows:

> Let fear be a kind of pain (*lupē*) or disturbance (*tarachē*) deriving from an impression (*phantasia*) of a future evil that is destructive or painful; for not all evils are feared, for example whether one will be unjust or slow, but as many as are productive of great pain or destruction, and these if they are not distant but rather seem near so as to impend. For things that are remote are not greatly feared. (*Rh.* 2.5, 1382a21–5)

Fear involves the sensation of pain, but not just that; it also depends on evaluation or calculation – what Epicurus would call *epilogismos* (D.L. 10.73) – of the nature of an impending evil: that it is indeed harmful or productive of pain. The sensation of pain is incorrigible; that is in the nature of a *pathos*. Fear, however, is subject to reasoning and argument. It may indeed have a valid cause, in which case it is justified, or it may not – as in the case of the fear of death, according to Epicurus. It is esssential to fear that it pertain to the rational part of the soul, for if it did not, there would be no possibility of eliminating it by the therapy of philosophy.

I take it that *chara* or joy is also a rational emotion, which responds to an impression of something deemed to be pleasant. As such, it too should be corrigible, and hence able to be mistaken. One may, for example, imagine oneself acquiring a large fortune, and think oneself perfectly secure as a result. If one is thinking of security against death, this will be a false kind of joy, dependent on what Epicurus calls empty belief or *kenodoxia* and motivated in large part by a fear that is itself irrational. It will also prompt desires that are insatiable in nature, leading to a reciprocally reinforcing cycle of empty fears and desires (see Konstan 1973: 3–34). If, however, one anticipates rather the kind of tranquillity that is possible for human beings, and which resides in the absence of pain and the freedom from mental perturbation, then it is a proper and rational joy.[13] Erler and Schofield's claim that 'what matters most for Epicurean ethics in the end is not katastematic pleasure itself, but the joy and delight it gives us', is thus misleading. The *telos* or goal of Epicurean philosophy is not *chara*, but ataraxy (combined with the absence of physical pain). To the extent that the condition of non-perturbation is pleasurable, the awareness of it takes the form of a *pathos*, and is experienced in the irrational part of the *psuchē*.[14]

Whether or not it is the case, as I have suggested, that Epicurus deliberately restricted the use of the term *pathos* to the non-rational sensations of pleasure and pain, as opposed to emotions such as fear that entail rational judgements, Philodemus, in his treatise *On Anger*, clearly does refer to anger (*orgē*) as a *pathos*, although the term most often seems to carry a negative connotation.[15] Philodemus in this essay draws a sharp distinction between *orgē*, which he, like Aristotle, considers a legitimate response to harm or insult, and what he calls *thumos*, which is excessively intense. Thus, Giovanni Indelli (2004: 104) explains:

With *orgē*, Philodemus designates the true and proper feeling of anger, without further specifications. When it is caused (as happens in the greater part of the cases) by particular actions or behaviors, when, that is, it is not *kenē orgē* ('empty *orgē*'), it need not, for the Epicureans, be repressed, because it is considered something

[13] Cf. πᾶσα διὰ σαρκὸς ἐπιτερπὴς κίνησις ἐφ' ἡδονήν τινα καὶ χαρὰν ψυχῆς ἀναπεμπομένη (fr. 433 Usener = Plut. *Non posse suaviter vivere* 2, 1087 B; partially quoted also in fr. 552 Usener); I expect this is a somewhat garbled reference to the distinction between *hēdonē* and *chara*, the latter specific to the rational part of the *psuchē*. So too Cicero, *Fin*. 3.35: *quamquam Stoici communi nomine corporis et animi* ἡδονήν *appellant, ego malo laetitiam appellare quasi gestientis animi elationem voluptariam*; this passage seems decisive for the technical distinction recognized by the Epicureans. Lucretius employs *voluptas* somewhat more freely, sometimes in connection with tranquillity of mind (3.40, 6.94); cf. *divina voluptas . . . atque horror* (3.28–9). Venus, understood as sexual pleasure, is *hominum divomque voluptas* (1.1; cf. 2.172–3, and 4.1057, 1075, 1081, 1085, 1114, 1201, 1207, 1263), and Lucretius speaks too of the *voluptas* that derives from 'sweet (*suavis*) friendship' (1.140–1). At 2.258, *voluptas*, like *hēdonē*, is the cause of attraction. On *voluptas* as the sensation associated with the return of matter in the body to its proper place, see 2.963–8, and cf. 3.251, 4.627–9 on pleasures of the senses.

[14] Whether animals (other than human beings) have emotions depends on whether they are considered rational. Aristotle, like the Stoics, held that they are not (cf. Fortenbaugh 2002: 94). Epicurus' position on the rationality of animals is not entirely clear, but Polystratus, the third head of the Garden (D.L. 10.25), denies to animals the possibility of either recalling or anticipating events, including their own prior or future states of pleasure and pain (coll. I–VII = Indelli 1978: 109–11). For further discussion, see Konstan 2006.

[15] e.g. 3.23: τοῖς ὀργ[ίλοις] πάθεσιν; 6.13: τὰ δ' ἐν τῇ ψυχῇ πάθη διὰ τὴν ἡμετέραν ψευδοδοξίαν παρακολοθοῦντα, where *pathos* refers to passion resulting from false opinion; 15.17; 26.11; 40.36; 43.8; passages cited from Indelli 1988.

natural and rationally controllable, in contrast to *thumos*, characterized by a fundamental irrationality, since the latter is the product of instinct and not of *logismos* ('calculation').[16]

Now, it is unlikely that excessive or uncontrolled anger is 'a product of instinct'. Jeffrey Fish (2004: 121) argues that 'there is reason to believe that only in Philodemus' school, even among the Epicureans, was any theory of anger like this taught'.[17] Even if this is so, and despite the damage to the text, Philodemus would not have described an instinctive or non-rational response as 'empty'. A *pathos* in this sense is, as we have seen, always correct and incorrigible. If anger is 'empty' or 'vain', it must mean that it is based on, or involves, the addition of opinion: it is the *doxa* that is false, and this pertains to *to logikon*, not to the *alogon meros* or non-rational part of the *psuchē*.

More than any other philosophical school in antiquity, and in pronounced contrast to Aristotle in particular, the Epicureans were concerned with emotions that appear to have no reasonable object in the world: emotions, that is, and above all fear, that are elicited by false beliefs about the nature of an ostensibly threatening or harmful event. Epicurus designated these emotions as 'empty' (*kenos*), in the sense that they depend on vain opinion. Aristotle noted in passing that people may experience fear even when there exists no immediate cause in the environment (*De an.* 1.1, 403a23–4), but he did not suggest that such fear was a pervasive cause of human malaise; as William Harris (2001: 16) states in respect to anger, 'Aristotle and all the other classical authors who defined anger agreed, in effect, that it was an emotion with a specific object.' But for the Epicureans, emotions elicited by events that do not justify them were a primary object of attention. Thus, analogously to the distinction between two kinds of anger drawn by Philodemus, Diogenes of Oenoanda discriminates two types of fear (fr. 35.II Smith): 'As a matter of fact this fear is sometimes clear, sometimes not clear – clear when we avoid something manifestly harmful like fire through fear that we shall meet death by it, not clear when, while the mind is occupied with something else, it [fear] has insinuated itself into our nature and [lurks] . . .' (tr. Smith 1993: 385).

The Epicurean emphasis on the vanity of the object of fear, in particular in the case of the fear of death, made it essential to locate fear and other emotions in the rational part of the soul, where the direct and incontrovertible evidence provided by sensation and the *pathe* was embellished by

[16] Cf. Indelli 1988: 24; Indelli 2004: 105–6; Fish 2004: 114, citing 44.5–35.

[17] Fish suggests (2004: 133, n. 46) that Philodemus may have derived his view from his teacher Zeno; cf. also Procopé 1993: 378–86.

the addition of belief. Nancy Sherman (2000: 155) has observed that on Aristotle's 'appraisal-based' view of the emotions, 'emotional shifts are the result of cognitive shifts.' But, she adds, this intellectualist approach constitutes a limitation to his theory: 'What Aristotle doesn't explore is why some emotions don't reform at the beck and call of reason' (156). Sherman extends her critique to ancient Greek and Roman thought as a whole: 'The question Ancient moral psychology leaves us with (though the Ancients never ask it) is, why doesn't persuasion work? That is, why doesn't rational discourse undo irrational emotions?' These are the very questions, as Sherman notes, that 'underlie Freud's project' (157).

In the Hellenistic period, however, some philosophical schools did pose the question why certain emotional responses seem to be resistant to amelioration. The Epicureans in particular held that people are commonly mistaken about the causes of their emotions, and more particularly are universally consumed by the fear of death, a fear they either conceal or misrecognize. To help rid human beings of this anxiety, they elaborated a complex doctrine involving two levels of the soul, the one irrational and the seat of sensations and feelings or *pathē*, the other rational and the locus of those emotions that depend essentially on belief. In addition, they examined how such false beliefs arose in the course of human history, and why they persist in the face of argument, thanks to the vicious circle of mutually reinforcing fears and desires. The roots of Epicurus' theory in many ways lie in the tradition represented by Plato and Aristotle, but he gave their insights a radically new twist. His doctrine of the *pathē* is a crucial element in this development.

CHAPTER 10

Moral responsibility and moral development in Epicurus' philosophy

Susanne Bobzien

1. MORAL RESPONSIBILITY

For the purpose of this paper, I assume that if a person is morally responsible for an action, this is a necessary and sufficient condition for moral appraisal of that person for that action. For instance, if the action is morally wrong, moral blame is in order. Other morally relevant responses that are sometimes connected with moral responsibility are praise, pardon, shame, pride, reward, punishment, remorse.

I now introduce two quite different concepts of moral responsibility: one grounded on the causal responsibility of the agent for an action, the other on the ability of the agent to do otherwise. The one based on the agent's causal responsibility considers it a necessary condition for praising or blaming an agent for an action, that it was the agent *and not something else* that brought about the action. The question of moral responsibility becomes one of whether the agent was the or a cause of the action, or whether the agent was forced to act by something else. On this view, actions or choices can be attributed to agents because it is in their actions and choices that the agents, *qua* moral beings, manifest themselves.

The second idea of moral responsibility considers it a prerequisite for blaming or praising an agent for an action that the agent could have done otherwise. This idea is often connected with the agents' sentiments or beliefs that they could have done otherwise, as well as the agents' feelings of guilt or regret, or pride, for what they have done. Some philosophers consider the causal indeterminedness of the agent's decision to act as necessary to warrant that the agent could have done otherwise.

Early versions of this paper have been presented at the Institute for Classical Studies in London, at Cornell University, and at a meeting of the Cambridge Philological Society, and I am grateful to my audiences for their stimulating discussions. Special thanks go to David Blank, Charles Brittain and David Sedley for their most helpful comments. It is my pleasure to dedicate this paper to Dorothea Frede, from whose wisdom, kindness and generosity I have benefited many times over the past two decades.

Depending on what conception of moral responsibility philosophers have, they will have to produce different reasons if they want to show that or how moral responsibility is preserved or integrated in their philosophical systems.

With a concept of moral responsibility based on causal responsibility, philosophers have to show that agents themselves (and not something else) are the causes of their actions; and they have to determine what characteristics an agent needs to have in order to be the sort of cause of an action to which responsibility can be attributed.

With a concept of moral responsibility based on the agent's ability to do otherwise, philosophers will have to show that in their systems agents are in fact capable of acting or of deciding and acting otherwise than they do. In this first section I set out to show that our sources univocally suggest that Epicurus had a concept of moral responsibility based not on the agent's ability to do otherwise, but on the agent's causal responsibility.

There are only a few texts that provide information about Epicurus' concept of moral responsibility. The most important information comes from Epicurus' *On Nature* book 25. In this book Epicurus considers three different causal factors that are involved in human behaviour:

1. Our *original constitution* (*hē ex archēs sustasis*; sometimes Epicurus simply uses *archē*), or nature (*phusis*); i.e. the package of soul atoms we come with, and which in part differs from person to person.
2. The *environment* (*ta periechonta*); most commonly, the environment influences our behaviour via our perception of it; e.g. when I perceive that it is starting to rain heavily, I will open up my umbrella.
3. *Us ourselves*, or, as Epicurus also says, 'the cause from ourselves' (*hē ex hēmōn aitia*)[1] or 'that through ourselves' (*to di' hēmōn autōn*), etc.[2]

When our initial constitution and our environment together (i.e. nature and nurture, as it were) fully determine what we do, then our actions are the result of necessity.[3] When we ourselves are causally involved in the actions, then they are not the result of necessity.

Epicurus takes the fact that we blame each other, and try to reform each other, as an *indication* that the cause of our actions lies in ourselves, or that the actions happen through ourselves:

[1] Cf. also Laursen 1997: 47.

[2] Τὴν ἐξ ἑαυτοῦ αἰτίαν; τὸ δι' ἡμῶν αὐτῶν; ἔχοντας ἐν ἑαυτοῖς τὴν αἰτίαν; τὸ ἐξ ἡμῶν αὐτῶν πραττόμενον; ἡ ἐξ ἡμῶν γεννομένην <αἰτία> (Laursen 1997: 45; 697.4). With 'us' or 'we' Epicurus refers to human beings.

[3] Long and Sedley 1987 (= LS) 20 C 2, Laursen 1997: 28.

(2) [And we can invoke against the argument that our behaviour must be caused by our initial constitution or by environmental factors] by which we never cease to be affected, [the fact that] we rebuke, oppose, and reform each other as if we have the cause also in ourselves, and not only in our initial constitution and in the mechanical necessity of that which surrounds and penetrates us[4,5] (LS 20 C 2)

The concept of blame presupposes that the beings that are blamed were themselves causally responsible for their actions. It *makes no sense* to blame individuals for certain events, if those events came about through necessity, and the individuals were forced in bringing them about.[6]

Moreover, Epicurus thinks, we have a *preconception* that we are the causes of our actions

(8) . . . using the word 'necessity' of that which we call ' . . . by ourselves', he is merely changing a name; but *he* [i.e. Epicurus' opponent] *must**[7] *prove that we have a preconception of a kind which has faulty delineations when we call that which [comes] through ourselves causally responsible.*[8] (Epicur. *Nat.* 25, 34.28 in Arrighetti 1973 (= Arr.), Laursen 1997: 37)

(4) . . . when he blames or praises. *But if he were to act in this way, he would be leaving intact the very same behaviour* [i.e. praising and blaming] *which we think* of as concerning ourselves, in accordance with* our preconception of the cause;*[9,10]

A preconception is some kind of veridical general conception or true opinion that we have acquired empirically, by having repeatedly the same sort of perceptual experience.[11] Preconceptions are self-evident.[12] Epicurus, it seems, holds that we acquire the preconception of us as causes precisely through our observations that human beings, including ourselves, are praised and blamed for their actions. And given that Epicurus thinks we have such a preconception, and that all preconceptions are self-evident, we

[4] Namely by means of perception, cf. Epicur. *Nat.* 25, Laursen 1997: 33, LS 20 C 1, quoted below.

[5] (2) ἐστήκει, ὧν οὐ . . . ἀπολειπείτα πάθη τοῦ γίνεσθαι, . . . νουθετεῖν τε ἀλλήλους καὶ μάχεσθαι καὶ μεταρυθμίζειν ὡς ἔχοντας καὶ ἐν ἑαυτοῖς τὴν αἰτίαν καὶ οὐχὶ ἐν τῇ ἐξ ἀρχῆς μόνον συστάσει καὶ ἐν τῇ τοῦ περιέχοντος καὶ ἐπεισιόντος κατὰ τὸ αὐτόματον ἀνάγκῃ.

[6] Cf. LS 20 C 3.

[7] I follow Laursen's reading, Laursen 1997; '*' indicates differences from the text in LS.

[8] (8) . . . φ ἡμῶν αὐτῶγ καλούμενον τῶι τῆς ἀνάγκης ὀνόματι προσαγορεύειν ὄνομα μόνομ μετατίθεται * δεῖ δ' ἐπιδῖξαι ὅτι τοιοῦτο τι ω μοχθηρ[οί εἰσι τύ]ποι προειληφότες τὸ δι' ἡμῶν αὐτῶν αἴτιογ καλοῦμεν, ούτιδ . . .

[9] I follow Laursen's reading (cf. next footnote). However, I do not quite understand what it means. I hope it still means the same as what Sedley 1983 suggested, viz. that our observation of blaming and praising produces our preconception of us as causes of our actions.

[10] (4) μεμφόμενος ἢ ἐπαινῶν ἀλλ' εἰ μὲν τοῦτο πράττοι, τὸ μὲν* ἔργον ἂν εἴη καταλείπων ὃ ἐφ'ἡμῶν αὐτῶν κατὰ* τὴν τῆς αἰτίας πρόληψιν, ἐννοοῦμεν*.

[11] Cf. D.L. 10.33.

[12] Cf. D.L. 10.33, ἐναργές.

can surmise that he thought it to be self-evident that we are the causes of our actions.

Two other passages from *On Nature* 25 suggest that what makes an action blame- or praiseworthy or exempted from blame and praise, is *not* the fact that it is a *physical event* of a certain kind, *but* that it has *causal factors* of a certain kind:

> And if, on account of the cause which is now already out of itself, it actually goes to what is similar to the original constitution, and this is a bad one, then we censure it at times even more, but rather in an admonitory way . . .[13] (Epicur. *Nat.* 25, 34.25 Arr., Laursen 1997: 31)

and:

> (1) But many naturally capable of achieving such and such results fail to achieve them, because of themselves, not because of one and the same causal responsibility of the atoms and of themselves. (2) And with these we especially do battle, and rebuke them . . . because they behave in accordance with their disordered original nature, as we do with the whole range of animals. (3) For the nature of their atoms has contributed nothing to some of their behaviour, and degrees of behaviour and dispositions, but it is their developments which themselves possess all or most of the causal responsibility for certain things.[14] (Epicur. *Nat.* 25, 34.21 Arr., LS 20 B 1–3, Laursen 1997: 19; tr. Long and Sedley 1987, modified)

Thus, if an action of a certain kind is caused by the initial constitution of a person, in response to the environment, then the person is – presumably – not to be reproached. Thus if, say, toddler Tina throws a tantrum for not getting a toy, she is presumably not to be morally blamed. However if an action *of the same kind* is caused by Tina herself, and thus not by the initial constitution, then she is to be blamed for it. For example, if Tina keeps having tantrums about trivia as an adult, presumably she *is* to be blamed for them.

One last passage concerned with moral responsibility comes from the *Letter to Menoeceus*:

> [he says that some things happen by necessity,] others by chance, and others again because of us, since necessity is not accountable to anyone, and chance is an unstable

[13] ἂν δὲ καὶ βαδίζῃ διὰ τὴν ἑαυτοῦ ἤδη αἰτίαν εἰς τὸ ὅμοιον τῃ ἐξ ἀρχῆς συστάσει φαύλῃ οὔσῃ, ἔτι μᾶλλον ἐνίοτε κακίζομεν, ἐν νουθετητικῷ μέντοι μᾶλλον τρόπῳ . . .

[14] πολλὰ δὲ καὶ τῶνδε καὶ τῶν[δε φ]ύσιν ἔχοντα ἀπεργαστικὰ [γί]νεσθαι δι᾽ ἑαυτὰ οὐ γίνεται ἀ[πε]ργαστικὰ (οὐ διὰ τὴν αὐτὴν αἰτία[ν] τῶν τε ἀτόμων καὶ ἑαυτῶν), οἷς δὴ καὶ μάλιστα μαχόμεθα καὶ ἐπιτιμῶμεν .[.].οῦντες κατὰ τὴν ἐξ ἀρχῆς [τ]αραχώ[δ]η φύσιν ἔχοντα, κα[θά]περ ἐπὶ τῶν πάντων ζῴων. [*οὐ]θὲν γὰρ αὐτοῖς συνήργηκεν εἰς ἔνια ἔργα τε καὶ μεγέθη ἔργων καὶ διαθέσεων ἡ τῶν ἀτόμων φύσις ἀλλ᾽ αὐτὰ τὰ ἀπογεγεννημένα τὴν πᾶσαν ἢ τὴν πλείστην κέκτηται αἰτίαν τῶνδέ τινων, ἐκ δ᾽ ἐκείνης ἔνιαι τῶν ἀτόμων κινήσεις ταραχώδεις κινοῦνται, οὐχὶ διὰ τατ[. . . . πά]ντως [διὰ δὲ τῶ]ν [παρεμ]π[ι]πτόν[των . . . ἐκ τοῦ περι]έχοντος

thing to watch, whereas that because of us is without master, and culpability and its opposite are naturally attached to it. (Epicur. *Ep. Men.* 133–4)[15]

Here we learn that Epicurus distinguished between three types of events: those that happen by necessity, those that happen by chance, and those that happen because of us (*gignesthai par' hēmas*). He adds two pieces of information about the things that come to be because of us. First, they are said to be without master. By this I take Epicurus to mean that it is we who bring the events about and not something else; in particular not fate, which he called master (or rather mistress) just the sentence before. Second, the things that happen because of us are said to have praiseworthiness and culpability naturally attached to them. This suggests that they are precisely those things for which we can be held morally accountable. Taking the two points together, it – again – appears that I can be held *morally* responsible for something, when I am somehow *causally* responsible for its occurrence. And I assume that those things that come to be because of us (*gignesthai par' hēmas*) are those of which we ourselves are the causes.

There is, then, one element all these passages on moral responsibility have in common: they connect the concept of moral responsibility with us as *causal factors* of the things for which we are considered morally accountable. We thus need to see what it is that makes *us* the causes of our behaviour – as opposed to the mere combination of our initial constitution (or atoms) and our environment. In the surviving evidence, Epicurus never directly addresses this question, but his *On Nature* 25 gives some hints how he would have answered it.

If we are the cause of an action, this involves, first, that we are not forced in bringing it about (LS 20 C 10, *Ep. Men.* 133); second, that we have an impulse (*hormēma*) or desire (*prothumia*) to perform that action; and third, that we act in accordance with that impulse or desire (LS 20 C 9–11). Fourth, the most important element seems to come from Epicurus' gloss on what it is that something comes to be because of us (*gignesthai par' hēmas*):

Hence at some point* it is unqualifiedly *because of* (*para*) us that the development comes to be now of this kind or that kind; i.e. the things which on account of the pores flow in of necessity from what surrounds us at some point come to be [of this kind or that kind] *because of* (*para*) us, or rather *because of* (*para*)

[15] [ἃ μὲν κατ' ἀνάγκην γίνεσθαι λέγει], ἃ δὲ ἀπὸ τύχης, ἃ δὲ παρ' ἡμᾶς, διὰ τὸ τὴν μὲν ἀνάγκην ἀνυπεύθυνον εἶναι, τὴν δὲ τύχην ἄστατον ὁρᾶν, τὸ δὲ παρ' ἡμᾶς ἀδέσποτον ᾧ καὶ τὸ μεμπτὸν καὶ τὸ ἐναντίον παρακολουθεῖν πέφυκεν.

our beliefs from ourselves.[16] (Epicur. *Nat.* 25, 34.26 Arr., LS 20 C 1, Laursen 1997: 32–3)

It seems (if, as I suggest we should, we understand the 'or rather' (*kai*)[17] in the last sentence as epexegetic) that if something comes to be because of us, then it does so because of *our own beliefs* (*doxai*).[18] *If* this is so, we can infer several things about Epicurus' concept of moral responsibility.

First, this suggests that if we are morally responsible for something (actions, characteristics), then we must *have* certain beliefs; and hence *be capable of* having beliefs; these requirements preclude very little children and some animals from being responsible for their behaviour, since they do not have beliefs. This squares with Epicurus' view, as elsewhere attested, that wild animals are not to be held responsible for their behaviour.[19]

Second, our beliefs must be somehow causally involved in bringing about the actions and dispositions that 'come to be because of us'. Now we know that, for Epicurus, beliefs are indeed causally involved in most of our behaviour.[20] By beliefs (*doxai*) Epicurus does not intend – or at least not primarily – that e.g. when I sit down, I probably think 'I should sit down' just beforehand. Beliefs (*doxai*) are not (just) volatile, momentary, thoughts of this kind, but are lasting, and firmly held by the individual; they make up a fundamental part of our mental dispositions; they underlie or are part of our dispositions to experience emotions, and they determine what kinds of desires we will have, and hence what we do. For example, if I believe that thunder is a form of divine punishment, then this will invoke certain fears in me, which in turn will make me tend to react in certain ways to external factors like thunderstorms. We can thus understand

[16] ὥστε παρ' ἡμᾶς π[οθ']* ἁπλῶς τὸ ἀπογεγεννημένον ἤδη γείνεσθαι, [τ]οῖα ἢ τοῖα, καὶ τὰ ἐκ τοῦ περιέχοντος κ[α]τ' ἀνάγκην διὰ τοὺς πό[ρους] εἰσρέο[ν]τα παρ' ημᾶς π[ο]τε γε[ίνε]σθαι καὶ παρὰ τ[ὰς] ἡμε[τέρα]ς [ἐ]ξ ἡμῶν αὐτ[ῶν] δόξ[ας. *This is Laursen's reading.

[17] Laursen's tentative reading in papyrus 1056 is ἤ, which also supports an epexegetical interpretation.

[18] David Sedley has suggested to me that 'happens (or comes to be) *depending on* us' captures γίνεσθαι παρ' ἡμᾶς better than 'happens (or comes to be) *because of* us'. I disagree. I take the παρὰ in γίνεσθαι παρ' ἡμᾶς in the general sense illustrated in LSJ C III 7, with possible alternative translations 'happens on account of us' 'happens through us' or 'happens with us being the cause'. Phrases like 'this happened depending on me' seem to strain the English, and generally I believe that the use of παρὰ + acc. together with γίνεσθαι makes 'depending on us' a less desirable translation. In any case, I believe the causal reading I give to παρὰ + acc. is justified by the fact that this is the best reading for the grammatically parallel παρὰ τ[ὰς] ἡμε[τέρα]ς [ἐ]ξ ἡμῶν αὐτ[ῶν] δόξ[ας in the very same clause, in which, I believe, Epicurus must have used παρὰ in the same sense as in the immediately preceding παρ' ἡμᾶς π[ο]τε γε[ίνε]σθαι καὶ.

[19] Laursen 1997: 31.

[20] e.g. *Ep. Men.* 132; D.L. 10.149 = *Sent.* 30; see also Furley 1967: 202 and Mitsis 1988: 141.

why Epicurus thought that our beliefs play an essential role for our moral responsibility. (Switching to the level of atoms, we can describe this as follows: the atomic structure of our mind is in part determined by the beliefs we hold. For our beliefs *are* certain structures of the atoms in the mind which make it possible that certain external influences can enter our mind (and be thought, and reacted upon), whereas others cannot. For the latter there will be no pathways or channels of the right shape, that is of the shape that would be needed for it to be possible for them to enter the mind. I picture this process analogously to that of perception, as described by Epicurus.)

Third, it seems that the fact that Epicurus emphasizes that the beliefs are the agents' *own* beliefs (τ[ὰς] ἡμε[τέρα]ς [ἐ]ξ ἡμῶν αὐτ[ῶν] δόξ[ας), implies at the very least that the agents must have *thought* the beliefs themselves, and that they must have *accepted* them in some way. However, presumably what Epicurus has in mind is something stronger. For instance, he may have envisaged a distinction between on the one hand beliefs that a person simply took over from others, without thinking them through, and on the other, beliefs that the person thought through, and then adopted as their own, on the basis of some rational grounds for the belief.[21]

Not all the details of Epicurus' conception of moral responsibility are then clear. But all passages connect the concept of moral responsibility with us as being *causally responsible* for the things for which we are morally responsible. There is no trace of a concept of moral responsibility which takes it to be a necessary condition that we (the same persons, in the same circumstances) are capable of deciding or acting otherwise than we do. On the contrary, it seems that Epicurus held that when we are the causes of our actions, then how we react to external stimuli at any given time will depend fully on us as we are at the time when we set out to act,[22] i.e. on our overall mental disposition, including our beliefs, at that time.[23] That is, if in two situations my overall mental disposition were the same, I would in my actions necessarily react in the same way to the same external stimuli. There is – in this sense – no possibility for us to act 'out of character'.

[21] Cf. the distinction between false assumptions (ὑπολήψεις ψευδεῖς) and προλήψεις about the gods, *Ep. Men.* 124; see also Mitsis 1988: 141, n. 27; cf. further 'if we do not grasp what the canon is, i.e. that which judges all things that come to be through beliefs, but irrationally follow the tendencies of the many, everything with respect to which we investigate will be lost' (Laursen 1997: 43–4; context and Greek in section 3 below).

[22] At least nothing in the sources is incompatible with the assumption.

[23] See also Phld. *Ir.* 32 and cf. Annas 1992: 180–1 and Mitsis 1988: 141.

Let us now turn to the topic of moral development and its connection with moral responsibility.[24] I call an individual a 'moral being', if they can in principle be held morally responsible for at least some of their behaviour. We can then distinguish two different issues concerning moral development:

1. The development of someone from not being a moral being (i.e. not to be held morally responsible for anything) to their being a moral being (being held morally responsible – in principle – for something). There is thus a conceptual connection between moral responsibility and moral development.
2. The development of a moral being from their present state to being morally better or morally worse (in some particular respect or overall); for Epicurus, the important case is that of becoming morally better, i.e. of moral improvement or moral progress.

2. MORAL DEVELOPMENT I: HOW DO WE BECOME MORAL BEINGS?

Our first question is 'How do we become moral beings?' or 'What does our transition from the non-moral or pre-moral stage of our lives to the moral stage consist in?' Following what I just said, we can also rephrase this question as 'How do we become beings who are morally responsible for our behaviour?' For philosophers who think that we are morally responsible for an action if we could have done otherwise, this question boils down to: 'When and how do we become capable of doing otherwise than we do?' For instance, such philosophers presumably do not consider toddlers as capable of doing otherwise (in the relevant sense), but consider 18-year-olds as having that capacity. (The question, however, is rarely asked in this fashion.) By contrast, for philosophers like Epicurus, who think that we are morally responsible for our actions when we ourselves are the *causes* of our actions, the question amounts to: 'When and how do we ourselves become causally responsible for our actions?'[25] Roughly, Epicurus' answer to this question appears to be this: we become causally responsible for our actions when our mind has developed to a point at which we are capable of consciously adopting, as our own, beliefs that do not square with our initial constitution, and can internalize these beliefs so

[24] One can talk about the moral development of individuals as well as of groups of people, such as societies or communities. In this paper, I am interested exclusively in the moral development of individuals.

[25] There is to my knowledge *no* evidence that Epicurus ever considered a question like 'When or how do we become able to do otherwise?' On the other hand, there is *some* evidence that he asked when and how we become causes of our actions.

that they in turn causally influence our actions. But let us proceed more slowly.

Let me first remind you of the very basics of Epicurus' ethics. In a nutshell, and ruthlessly simplified, it comes up to this:

- The end (*telos*) which all human beings do and should aim at is a life of happiness (*eudaimonia*), above all in the form of tranquillity (*ataraxia*),[26] that is freedom from mental disturbance (*tarachē*). For Epicurus such happiness consists in pleasure[27] and the absence of pain.
- It is the task of ethics to aid us in achieving happiness.
- The core of Epicurean ethics is a complex theory of desires, pains and pleasures, which enables us to grasp with our intellect which of all the many pleasures and pains to choose, and which to shun, so that we can attain tranquillity.[28]
- It turns out that as a matter of fact we can reach such tranquillity only if we are virtuous.[29] However, virtue is understood strictly as a means to the end pleasure.[30]

So far Epicurus' ethics in a nutshell. Back to moral development.

First, what do we know about Epicurus' view of the mental constitution of human beings very early on, say, at birth?[31] We have at birth two different kinds of atomic substructures in our mind: those which we all share, and those in which we differ. Our minds are all *equal*, for example, in so far as from birth we all aim at obtaining pleasure and avoiding pain.[32] We do so instinctively, not as the result of deliberation, since we cannot deliberate yet.[33] Our minds *differ* from each other, for instance, in that we have different emotional tendencies, different dispositions for experiencing certain emotions, and for behaving accordingly. Thus, in terms of atoms, if we have more fire-like atoms in the nature of our mind, we get angry more easily; if we have more air-like atoms in the nature of our mind, we are more easily afraid; and if there is an abundance of breath-like atoms, we are naturally calm.[34] These tendencies are morally relevant, since

[26] *Ep. Men.* 128, 131. [27] e.g. *Ep. Men.* 129. [28] e.g. *Ep. Men.* 127–32.

[29] *Ep. Men.* 132; D.L. 10.140.

[30] D.L. 10.138. As we take medicine for the sake of health, so we choose the virtues on account of pleasure and not for their own sake.

[31] Lucr. 3.344–7: *anima* and body are combined already in the mother's womb.

[32] Cf. D.L. 10.137, the so-called 'cradle argument'.

[33] Cf. D.L. 10.137, 'naturally and without reason' (φυσικῶς καὶ χωρὶς λόγου); also Cic. *Fin.* 1.30.

[34] '(4) The mind also has that kind of heat which it takes on when it boils with anger and the eyes shine with a fiercer flame; it has plenty of cold wind, the companion of fear, which excites fright in the limbs and rouses the frame; and it has that state of the still air which is found in a tranquil chest and in a calm face. But there is more heat in those with fierce hearts and angry minds which easily boil over with anger. A prime example is the lion, which regularly bursts its chest with roaring

they later co-determine how successful we will be when trying to achieve tranquillity.

Next, how does the mind develop from birth to adulthood? Lucretius writes:

> Furthermore, we perceive that the mind is born jointly with the body, grows up jointly with it, and ages jointly with it. For just as infants walk unsteadily with a frail and tender body, so too their accompanying power of mental judgement is tenuous. Then when they have matured to an age of robust strength, their judgement is greater and their mental strength increased.[35] (Lucr. 3.445–50)

This passage suggests a *gradual* development of the mind, starting in early childhood, leading to a more fully developed intellect and capacity for reasoning at the onset of adulthood.

There is some evidence that Epicurus thought some of our mental development to be necessitated by the initial constitution of our minds – both concerning developments based on elements shared by all humans, and developments based on elements that differ across individuals. Thus in *On Nature* 25 he writes:

> But if in the mind the first constitution expels something from the development, this sort of thing not being developed from necessity *all the way* to these particular things; but on the one hand to the point where it has come to be a soul, or rather a soul which has a disposition and motion of such a size, this sort of thing being developed *from necessity* from these sorts of things; and on the other hand to the point . . . (34.24 Arr., Laursen 1997: 28, my emphasis, text continued below)[36]

We may perhaps think of these necessitated developments as a kind of genetically directed 'maturing' of the mind. (Thus in this way it is determined that an individual develops a soul, and that that soul has a disposition and motion of a particular size.) We can imagine that with age our minds unfold to greater and greater complexity (in the combination of the atoms), and this means that we acquire more and more capacities and dispositions.

and groaning and cannot contain the billows of rage in its chest. But the cold mind of stags is more windy, and quicker to rouse through their flesh those chilly gusts which set the limbs in trembling motion. The nature of cattle, on the other hand, is characterized more by calm air. Neither does ignition by the smouldering brand of anger ever over-excite it and cloud it with blind darkness, nor is it transfixed and numbed by the icy shafts of fear. It lies midway between stags and fierce lions. (5) Likewise the human race' (Lucr. 3.289–307, LS 14 D 4–5).

[35] Praeterea gigni pariter cum corpore et una / crescere sentimus pariterque senescere mentem. / Nam velut infirmo pueri teneroque vagantur / corpore, sic animi sequitur sententia tenuis. / Inde ubi robustis adolevit viribus aetas, / consilium quoque maius et auctior est animi vis.

[36] Κἂν κατὰ διάνοιαν δέ τι ἐκβιάζηται ἡ πρώτη σύστασις τοῦ ἀπογεγεννημένου, μὴ ἐξ ἀνάγκης μέχρι τωνδί τινων ?ἐξ ἀνάγκης ?τοιοῦδε ἀπογεννωμένου ἀλλὰ μέχρι μὲν τοῦ ψυχὴν γενέσθαι ἢ καὶ τοσαυτηνὶ διάθεσιν καὶ κίνησιν ἔχουσαν ψυχὴν ἐξ ἀνάγκης ?τοιοῦδε ἀπογεννωμένου ἐκ τῶν τοιουτωνί, μέχρι δὲ . . . (text continued in n. 49 below)

For instance, we all learn how to speak (a complicated business);[37] we all develop some 'preconceptions' (e.g. of horses and cows);[38] we all learn to reason.[39] Despite genetic pre-programming, these ongoing differentiations of our minds still mostly require certain environmental conditions in order to be realized: if we perceived nothing, we would not obtain any preconceptions of things; and if no one around us spoke a language, nor would we.[40] The dispositions we develop will at least in part vary from person to person, owing to the differences in our initial constitutions – and this will be so even when the environments are similar. Moreover, all these developments take a certain time – thus we won't learn how to speak before the approximate age of one; and we won't learn how to reason properly before adolescence.[41] In this context, Epicurus considers time and age as causes;[42] that is – I take it – as factors we can use rightly in explanations in answer to questions like 'Why can't she speak yet?' 'She's not yet one.'

In addition, differences in the environment will influence us in such a way that different individuals turn out differently, even where their initial natures do not vary significantly; thus, only when we perceive kangaroos, will we obtain a preconception of kangaroos, and only when people around us speak Greek, will the language we learn as a child be Greek.[43] Moreover, Epicurus is known to have recommended that one should watch over the young, so that they do not develop maddening desires.[44] Thus he thought that different external influences on children make them develop different desires. Hence, before reaching the age of morality, education and environment generally are factors that will influence our chances to become moral.

Epicurus' recommendation to watch over the young also exemplifies that there is one very important way in which the environment may have an influence even on our pre-moral mental development. Once we can speak and start having thoughts, we will be able to, and will indeed, take in the views or beliefs of other people around us, in particular of parents, teachers, peers. Thus we are likely to take in the views that death is bad and to be feared, that the soul is immortal, that there is punishment in the afterlife, and more such nonsense. We will initially take these views in without questioning them, and will unreflectively internalize them; they will determine our desires and fears, and how we react to new, incoming influences, just as our preconceptions will. Thus if I have been told and

[37] Inferred from Lucr. 5.1028 ff. on the origin of language.
[38] Inferred from D. L. 10.33.
[39] Lucr. 3.445–50, quoted above, LS 19 B.
[40] Again inferred from Lucr. 5.1028 ff., LS 19 B.
[41] e.g. Lucr. 3.445–50, quoted above.
[42] Cf. Laursen 1997: 28–9 and 42–5.
[43] Cf. Mitsis 1988: 147.
[44] *Sent. Vat.* 80.

now believe that thunder and lightning are a form of divine revenge, and I have a predominantly air-like mind, this will invoke fear of thunderstorms in me, and I will behave accordingly.

So our mental development is a rather complicated affair. But however complex our mind becomes, before we are *ourselves* the causes of our actions, for Epicurus, everything we become and do is a function of hereditary and environmental factors. That is, we are fully determined or necessitated by a combination of those two factors.[45] And as long as this is so, we cannot be held morally responsible for our behaviour.[46]

How do we have to envisage the transition from this pre-moral stage to that of us as moral beings (i.e. as causal factors of our actions)?

We can assume that Epicurus believed that we all have the innate potential for becoming moral beings. For first he thinks that we can all morally improve (a point I will get to later). And second, he seems to think that one of those features of mental development that we all share is that of becoming a cause of our actions.[47] For this, as I said earlier, we need to have 'our own beliefs', and these have to be causally relevant for what we do.[48]

Epicurus implies also that we need to reach a certain age or stage of maturity, a stage at which our mind has developed a sufficient complexity, in order for it to be possible that we are causes ourselves (this is the continuation of the text from *On Nature* 25 quoted above):

> . . . on the other hand, to the point where [it has come to be] this kind of soul or that, this sort of thing being developed not from necessity, or rather this sort of thing being developed not by necessity whenever there is advancement in age, but from itself being able – or [from] the cause which comes from itself – [to develop? to become? to bring about?] something else as well . . . (34.24 Arr., Laursen 1997: 28)[49]

In this passage internal necessitation and lack thereof do not concern individual actions or volitions, but what a person's soul *comes to be like*. The emphasis is on the non-necessity of mental development, and in particular on the fact that we ourselves (or the cause from ourselves) are causally responsible for the *changes in our soul*, and that *these changes* are not necessary.[50]

45 LS 20 C 2; also Laursen 1997: 28. Our development is necessary as long as we aren't causes ourselves.

46 LS 20 C; and inferred from Laursen 1997: 28.

47 Laursen 1997: 43–5; also 28.

48 LS 20 C 1; also Laursen 1997: 43–5; LS 20 B 5–7 (Laursen 1997: 22).

49 . . . μέχρι δὲ τοῦ τοιανδὶ ψυχὴν ἢ τοιανδὶ οὐκ ἐξ ἀνάγκης τοιοῦδε ἀπογεννωμένου ἢ οὐκ ἐπειδὰν προβῆ γε τῇ ἡλικίᾳ τοιοῦδε ἀπογεννωμένου κατ' ἀνάγκην ἀλλ' ἐξ ἑαυτοῦ δυναμένου καὶ τῆς ἐξ ἑαυτοῦ αἰτίας καὶ ἄλλο . . . (text continued from n. 36 above).

50 Cf. Bobzien 2000: section 6.

One fragmentary passage from *On Nature* 25 seems to suggest that we become causes ourselves at the moment when there is in us a certain development that differs qualitatively from (what is there in) the atomic structure of our mind, and we make this new development part of our 'nature' or mind, as it were.

> (5) In this way whenever something is developed which takes on some distinctness from the atoms in a way that pertains to judgement[51] – not in the way as from a different distance – he receives the causal responsibility which is from himself; (6) and then he immediately imparts this to his first natures and somehow makes the whole of it into one. (7) That is why those who cannot correctly make such distinctions confuse themselves about the adjudication of causal responsibility. (Epicur. *Nat.* 25, 34.22 Arr., LS 20 B 5–7, Laursen 1997: 22; tr. Long and Sedley 1987, modified)[52]

What exactly this means, I do not know. But it seems to me that R. W. Sharples is right, when he says about this passage:

> The obvious, indeed inevitable way of interpreting this in the atomic context is to say that we, by thought and effort, can modify our character, and hence also the atomic structure of our minds . . . the downwards causation in the passage . . . may thus relate to the process by which we modify our characters, and not to the explanation of free choice by volition causing atomic swerves.[53]

Regarding the details, I believe Epicurus' idea could have been something like this: we ourselves become causes at the moment at which we – consciously – identify with an incoming idea or thought which is not in keeping with the beliefs we have so far taken in from our environment 'unthinkingly', as it were, and in accordance with the original nature of our mind. More precisely, when we identify with this new thought, we incorporate it into our mind, and thus change our mental dispositions; as a result, from then on our actions can be caused by behavioural dispositions that are at least partially the result of our identifying with something that was not part of our original constitution.[54] (Earlier in *On Nature* 25, Epicurus mentions

[51] Or 'in a discriminating way'.

[52] (5) οὕτως ἐπειδὰν ἀπογεννηθῆ τι λανβάνον τινὰ ἑτερότητα τῶν ἀτόμων κατά τινα τρόπον διαληπτικόν, οὐ τὸν ὡς ἀφ' ἑτέρου διαστήματος, ἰσχάνει τὴν ἐξ ἑαυτοῦ αἰτίαν, (6) εἶτα ἀναδίδωσιν εὐθὺς μέχρι τῶν πρώτων φύσεων καὶ μίαν πως ἅπασαν αὐτὴν ποιεῖ*. (7) ὅθεν δὴ καὶ οἱ μὴ δυνάμενοι κατὰ τρόπον τὰ τοιαῦτα διαιρεῖν χειμάζουσιν αὑτοὺς περὶ τὴν τῶν αἰτιῶν ἀπόφασιν. (Laursen 1997: 22

[53] Sharples 1991–3: 186.

[54] This is then a quasi-empirical proof that it is not our original nature. Another passage (LS 20 B 1–4, Laursen 1997: 19–20, in fact just before the one quoted) deals with the point that, once we are causes ourselves, even if the behaviour is the same as that of our original nature would have been, we are responsible, since we (not our original nature) are the cause. Generally, thus it would presumably suffice, if we *were capable of* incorporating 'alien' elements into our mind, whether or not we actually do so.

that at some point in our life we become able to 'think ourselves by means of ourselves'.[55] So it is tempting to assume that only when we are able to 'think ourselves by means of ourselves' will we be able to have beliefs that are our own – not just absorbed 'unthinkingly', from others.)[56] At that point, thus, the disposition is no longer – fully – the result of internal and external necessity, but in part the result of conscious, rational influencing. When, then, someone acts from such a disposition, *they* are the cause of the action, and no longer 'the atoms', i.e. those of their initial constitution. Of course nothing guarantees that the incoming thoughts we identify with are correct – they, too, may be based on cultural prejudice. Equally, if we rethink some of our culturally induced beliefs, nothing prevents us from ending up retaining false beliefs, or replacing false beliefs by false beliefs.

In another passage in *On Nature* 25 – which is rather badly preserved – Epicurus may refer to the same kind of development:

> And the same thing was both generated as permanent and was a kind of seed, as I say, leading from the origin[al nature] to something else, and when this is present, we think or form beliefs . . . and there is much that [happens] with [our] nature helping, and much [that happens] when [our] nature is not helping, and there is something that [happens] when our nature is rearranged by us. (34.31 Arr., Laursen 1997: 44–5; context and Greek in section 3 below)

This passage – at least as I have reconstructed it following Laursen – suggests that all human beings, at some point, reach a developmental stage at which they start thinking and forming opinions.[57]

Epicurus seems to assume then that – in the normal course of events – at some point during the process of their growing up every person reaches this stage of development where they start 'thinking for themselves'. Yet, it is unclear whether the quoted passages describe a unique event in a person's life, or a gradual process in which a person changes or confirms (part of) their beliefs one by one upon reflection over a longer period of time. If this is a unique event, we may consider our becoming moral beings as instantaneous. If it is a gradual process, Epicurus could have

[55] Laursen 1995: 46–7: ἐν] [ἑ]αυτῷ κατὰ τὸ ὅμοιον καὶ ἀδιάφορον ἑαυτὸν [ῥ]ηθήσεται διανοεῖσθαι.

[56] Laursen himself suggests in Laursen 1995: when we 'think ourselves by means of ourselves' we have the mental faculty of 'subsequent reasoning' (45–6); 'this makes it possible to realize one's real goal (τέλος)' (46); 'reason is acquired by time . . . at a comparatively late stage, we acquire the capacity for a reasoned consideration of our state as a whole' (47), but then, strangely, continues the last sentence thus, 'that is, we become moral philosophers'. In my view, it is much more likely that at that point we have become adult, rational beings.

[57] The end of the passage suggests the possibility that we ourselves rearrange the atoms in our minds, which plausibly could be our changing our dispositions as a result of our adopting new beliefs – see also section 3 on this point.

thought that we become moral beings when we ourselves become causes of something for the first time (since we then have the capacity for becoming causes ourselves); or else, our becoming morally responsible could itself be a gradual process. This last possibility seems to me the most exciting, as it seems both a very modern idea, and to come closest to the truth.[58]

3. MORAL DEVELOPMENT II: HOW CAN WE BECOME MORALLY BETTER?

Let us assume that we are now moral beings (as opposed to pre-moral beings). How can we then *develop* morally according to Epicurus? In particular, how can we become morally better?

Theories of moral responsibility based on the agent's ability to do otherwise tend to spend little time on the question of moral development. When they deal with it, they may connect measures for moral improvement with an agent's freedom of decision in two ways: (i) Agents need to be given a maximum of relevant information for mental storage that they can make use of at times when they have to make a moral decision. Relevant information here covers anything that enables them to find out what the morally right thing to do is. (ii) Agents need to strengthen their will – or whatever it is that decides freely – so that in a situation of choice, in which they know what the right thing to do is, they will actually decide to do the right thing, instead of satisfying some adverse more immediate desire.

By contrast, theories of moral responsibility that are based on the agents *qua* rational agents as the cause of their behaviour tend to display substantial interest in the question of moral development. There is one simple reason for this: if the assumption is that how a person acts or reacts in a given situation depends fully on that person's mental dispositions at the time, then moral improvement becomes a question of how one can alter one's mental dispositions in such a way that one will react in the morally right way to external stimuli. This is the only possible way of getting oneself to act differently or better than one tends to do at present. For there is no way of 'deciding or acting out of character' at the very moment one has to decide what to do: one's decision is a function of the overall state of one's mind.

In line with his concept of moral responsibility, this is the approach to moral development Epicurus took. He believed that, in order to make moral progress, one has to change one's mental dispositions:

[58] Remember that Lucretius, in the passage quoted above, describes the development of our rationality as if it were gradual.

> . . . Likewise the human race. Even though education may produce individuals equally well turned out, it still leaves those *original traces of each mind's nature.* And we must not suppose that faults can be completely eradicated, so that one person will not plunge too hastily into bitter anger, another not be assailed too readily by fear, or the third type not be over-indulgent in tolerating certain things. There are many other respects in which the various *natures and consequently the behaviours* of human beings must differ, but I cannot now set out their hidden causes, nor can I find enough names for all the shapes of primary particles from which this variety springs. But there is one thing which I see I can state in this matter: so slight are *the traces of our natures which reason cannot expel from us,* that nothing stands in the way of our leading a life worthy of the gods.[59] (Lucr. 3.307–22, tr. Long and Sedley 1987, modified, my emphasis)

The relevant points in this passage are these: the initial nature of a human mind includes certain morally relevant dispositions, which are present in different people in various strengths. Through education people's minds can develop in such a way that these differences are by and large evened out. The reason is that by the use of our intellect we can modify our mental dispositions to a large extent. This passage corroborates the assumption that the Epicureans worked with a model of disposition-dependent agency on several counts. First, it makes it clear that Lucretius took a person's mind to include that person's character dispositions (3.309). Second, it implies that Lucretius thinks that one's nature determines one's behaviour; and third, that in order to change one's behaviour, one has to change one's nature, that is, the nature of one's mind, by the use of one's intellect.

The last sentence of the Lucretius passage suggests that our original nature cannot be expelled completely, but that most of it can. This expelling can only consist in some change of the *dispositions* (or atomic structure) of our mind. In support of this assumption, Diogenes Laertius' report of Epicurus' view that 'someone who has once become wise never again takes on the opposite *disposition*'[60] implies that in order to become wise, and that is morally good, one has to change one's mental disposition. Accordingly, the major part of Epicurus' ethics is geared to the development of the

[59] Sic hominum genus est. Quamvis doctrina politos / constituat pariter quosdam, tamen illa relinquit / *naturae cuiusque animi vestigia prima.* / Nec radicitus evelli mala posse putandumst, / quin proclivius hic iras decurrat ad acris, / ille metu citius paulo temptetur, at ille / tertius accipiat quaedam clementius aequo. / Inque aliis rebus multis differre necessest / naturas hominum varias moresque sequaces; / quorum ego nunc nequeo caecas exponere causas / nec reperire figurarum tot nomina quot sunt / principiis, unde haec oritur variantia rerum. / Illud in his rebus video firmare potesse, / usque adeo *naturarum vestigia* linqui / parvula *quae nequeat ratio depellere nobis,* / ut nil impediat dignam dis degere vitam (my emphasis).

[60] τὸν ἅπαξ γενόμενον σοφὸν μηκέτι τὴν ἐναντίαν λαμβάνειν διάθεσιν μηδὲ πλάττειν ἑκόντα (D.L. 10.117). Cf. also the passages in *Nat.* 25 about changing or developing one's disposition (διάθεσις).

individual's behavioural dispositions. Since the end to which all human behaviour should be above all directed is tranquillity (*ataraxia*), it follows that, in order to improve one's behaviour, one has to try to develop one's mind in such a way that one's emotions, desires and actions will become conducive to attaining tranquillity.

With regard to the opportunities for moral improvement, there is variation across individuals. Epicurus starts out with the optimistic belief that everyone can morally improve[61] and get to a life of true pleasure and tranquillity,[62] and that it is never too late to start trying to morally improve.[63] However, moral improvement will not be equally easy for everyone, nor will the development be of the same kind. The starting situations of individuals can vary quite significantly, as is clear from the Lucretius passage on fire-, air- and breath-like atoms.[64] At the point when people have become moral beings, some of them will be closer to a life of tranquillity, others further away. This will depend (a) on the education and external influences they have been exposed to up to then, and (b) on the fact that their natures are different in morally relevant ways. Thus it will be more difficult for someone with a very irascible nature to get to the *right degree* of irascibility, than for someone of a calmer nature. But both can succeed.[65]

A passage in a letter by Seneca confirms that Epicurus considered the question whether humans and their natures are susceptible to moral improvement, and shows that he distinguished three types of human beings with respect to their moral progress:[66]

1. Some people's nature is such that they can acquire tranquillity by their own impulse and efforts. (Apparently, Epicurus was thought to fall in this class.)

[61] *Ep. Men.* 122. [62] Lucr. 3.320–2.

[63] 'Let no one be slow to seek wisdom when he is young or weary in the search of wisdom when he is old; for no age is too early or too late for the health of the soul.' Μήτε νέος τις ὢν μελλέτω φιλοσοφεῖν, μήτε γέρων ὑπάρχων κοπιάτω φιλοσοφῶν· οὔτε γὰρ ἄωρος οὐδείς ἐστιν οὔτε πάρωρος πρὸς τὸ κατὰ ψυχὴν ὑγιαῖνον, etc. (*Ep. Men.* 122).

[64] Lucr. 3.289–307, quoted in section 2. [65] Lucr. 3.307–22.

[66] Sen. *Ep.* 52.3–4: (3) Quosdam ait Epicurus ad veritatem sine ullius adiutorio exisse, fecisse sibi ipsos viam. Hos maxime laudat, quibus ex se impetus fuit, qui se ipsi protulerunt. Quosdam indigere ope aliena, non ituros, si nemo praecesserit, sed bene secuturos. Ex his Metrodorum ait esse; egregium hoc quoque, sed secundae sortis ingenium. Ne hunc quidem contempseris hominem, qui alieno beneficio esse salvus potest; et hoc multum est, velle servari. (4) Praeter haec adhuc invenies genus aliud hominum ne ipsum quidem fastidiendum eorum, qui cogi ad rectum conpellique possunt, quibus non duce tantum opus sit, sed adiutore, et, ut ita dicam, coactore. Si quaeris huius quoque exemplar, Hermarchum ait Epicurus talem fuisse. Itaque alteri magis gratulatur, alterum magis suspicit; quamvis enim ad eundem finem uterque pervenerit, tamen maior est laus idem effecisse in difficiliore materia.

2. Others (want to do the right thing – *velle servari* – but) need some moral role-model, as it were, 'to show them the way' – which way, once they have found it, they will follow faithfully. (Metrodorus was placed here.)
3. Others again need someone to actively encourage them and perhaps even to force them along. (Hermarchus is an example of this case.)

Epicurus does not doubt that individuals of all three types can morally improve.[67]

How then do we have to imagine the mental process of moral development in detail? We know that the mind of adult human beings (or of moral beings) encompasses their individual 'initial constitution' or nature,[68] preconceptions, and also a set of beliefs that are *their own* in the sense that by means of them the individual can become causally responsible for their behaviour. The mind further includes some conception of the end (*telos*), namely that it consists in pleasure.[69] The person's set of beliefs will determine their emotions and desires,[70] and it will ordinarily include true and false beliefs, and among the false ones what Epicurus calls empty beliefs, i.e. beliefs that are counterproductive to reaching tranquillity – such as beliefs about vengeful gods.[71]

Moral improvement will then consist in the main in restructuring[72] a person's system of concepts and beliefs, in the light of the end (*telos*), and in strengthening the new, true beliefs, and thus aligning the accompanying habits.[73] False and empty beliefs will have to be first identified, and then measures will have to be taken so that the person gives them up and replaces them by true beliefs.[74]

Epicurus was aware of the fact that my simply pointing out to myself (or having it pointed out to me) that a belief of mine is incorrect will not make me abandon it. Just saying to myself 'The belief that death is an evil is false' is unlikely to suffice to change that belief and the desires and emotions tied to it. One obvious reason for this should be the fact that we

[67] Did Epicurus distinguish more than these three types? Possibly. Could they all morally improve at least to some degree? Most probably yes; see *Ep. Men.* 122 and below.

[68] Cf. also Lucr. 3.289–322.

[69] Cic. *Fin.* 1.55, LS 21 U 1; Cic. *Fin.* 1.29–39, LS 21 A 4. Some Epicureans hold that this preconception of pleasure is understood by mind and reasoning.

[70] *Ep. Men.* 132.

[71] D.L. 10.144 = *Sent.* 15; D.L. 10.149 = *Sent.* 29–30; Porph. *Marc.* 31, 34 8P = 239 in Arrighetti 1973: 567.

[72] κατακοσμουμένης, Laursen 1997: 45; μετακοσμήσει, LS 20 C 10, Laursen 1997: 39.

[73] συνεθίζειν (accustom oneself to, make it a habit), *Ep. Men.* 124, 131; μελετᾶν (train, exercise oneself, practise), *Ep. Men.* 122; 'Accustom yourself to believe that death is nothing to us', Συνέθιζε δὲ ἐν τῷ νομίζειν μηδὲν πρὸς ἡμᾶς εἶναι τὸν θάνατον, followed by reasons for why we should believe this. *Ep. Men.* 124.

[74] See e.g. *Ep. Men.* 124.

do not have beliefs in isolation, but that our beliefs are interconnected in complicated ways. Changing one's beliefs about something will thus take some time; and it will usually involve a plurality of causal factors.

Epicurus seems to have given some thought to the question what different causal factors can be involved in moral improvement, as (yet another) fragmentary passage from *On Nature* 25 suggests (the information most relevant here is found after the first lacuna):[75]

> But often both [the considerations of the end itself and the origin(al natures)?] actually are equally causally responsible, even without the ones having been attracted by the others, or without [the ones] being attracted [by the others] and forcing many such things to happen because of time and age and other causes. Hence both the consideration of the end itself and the origin[al nature] were causally responsible, but we were, too. The [causal factor] from us was the perception[76] of the fact that if we do not grasp what the canon is, i.e. that which judges all things that come to be through beliefs, but we irrationally follow the tendencies of the many, everything with respect to which we investigate will be lost and excess . . . (lacuna of *c*.3 words[77]). And the same thing was both generated as permanent and was a kind of seed, as I say,[78] leading from the origin[al nature] to something else, and when this is present, we think or form beliefs . . . and there is much that [happens] with [our] nature helping, and much [that happens] when [our] nature is not helping, and there is something that [happens] when our nature is rearranged by us; but there is also something that [happens] when [our nature] itself leads the way (lacuna of *c*.3 words) [not only] matured, but also because the things which flow in from the environment take the lead to improvement, and do not merely follow . . .[79] (Laursen 1997: 43–5)

75 I provide the context, since I refer to individual phrases from that context below.

76 For this perception to become the causal factor *from us*, we must somehow have adopted it, retained it, made it our own (see above, section 2). Perhaps Epicurus' use of ἐπαίσθησις instead of the simple αἴσθησις hints at that fact?

77 Some phrase expressing the general idea that excess will follow or will be the result or will reign would make sense here.

78 ὥσπερ ληρῶ would translate roughly as 'as I keep ranting about'. However, I just don't believe this is what Epicurus intended to say at this point. Maybe, he wrote ὥσπερ λέγω, 'as I say', referring to 'seed', which is Epicurean terminology, in which the word is used metaphorically; or, perhaps, in Hellenistic times the meaning of ληρῶ had been watered down, so that it sometimes simply meant 'I say'.

79 . . . νον πολλάκις δὲ καὶ τὴν αὐτὴν ἀμφότερα κέκτηται μὲν αἰτίαν καὶ μὴ συνεπεσπασμένα τὰ ἕτερα ὑπὸ τῶν ἑτέρων μηδὲ συνεπισπώμενα καὶ βιαζόμενα παρά τε χρόνους πολλὰ τῶν τοιούτων συνπίπτειν καὶ ἡλικίας καὶ ἄλλας αἰτίας. ὅθεν καὶ τὸ τοῦ τέλους αὐτοῦ ἐπιλόγισμα εἶχε μὲν καὶ ἡ ἀρχὴ τὴν αἰτίαν εἴχομεν δὲ καὶ ἡμεῖς. ἦν δὲ τὸ ἐξ ἡμῶν ἐπαίσθησις τοῦ "εἰ μὴ ληψόμεθα τίς ὁ κανὼν καὶ τὸ ἐπικρεῖνον πάντα τὰ διὰ τῶν δοξῶν περαινόμενα ἀλλ' ἀκολουθήσομεν ἀλόγως ταῖς τῶν πολλῶν φοραῖς, οἰχήσεται πάντα καθ' ἃ διερευνώμεθά τι καὶ ὑπεροχή . . ." [lacuna of *c*.3 words] τὸ δ' αὐτὸ καὶ ἀΐδιον ἐγεννήθη καὶ σπέρμα ἦν τι ὥσπερ ληρῶ, ἐξ ἀρχῆς πρὸς ἕτερον ἀγωγόν, παρόντος δὲ τούτου νοοῦμεν ἢ δοξάζομεν . . . πολὺ δὲ αὐτό ἐστιν μὲν ὃ συνεργούσης τῆς φύσεως, ἔστι δ' ὃ οὐ συνεργούσης, ἔστι δ' ὃ κατακοσμουμένης ὑφ' ἡμῶν, ἔστι δὲ καὶ αὐτῆς προηγουμένης τι [lacuna of *c*.3 words] ἐπαυξόμενον ἀλλὰ καὶ διὰ τὰ ἐκ τοῦ περιέχοντος ἐπεισιόντα τὰς καθηγεμονίας εἰς τὸ βέλτιον*, οὐ μόνον τὰς συνακολουθήσεις λαμβάνοντα * The reading of εἰς τὸ βέλτιον ('to the better') is uncertain.

First, Epicurus seems to think that in some cases of moral improvement one's original nature (or constitution) functions as a causal factor, in others it does not.[80] One way this nature can be influential may simply be that the nature of a person's mind 'matures', or develops further.[81] Then, presumably, our natural instinct to pursue pleasure may be helpful for adopting the belief that we should pursue pleasure.[82] By contrast, if someone who is by nature very irascible wants to reduce their irascibility, *that* aspect of their nature will not be of much help.

Epicurus equally seems to acknowledge that we ourselves may restructure our nature (and thus, I assume, some of the atoms in our mind) up to a certain point.[83] This should mean that certain of our beliefs which we have adopted as our own, and which make up 'us' as causes,[84] are used in order to get rid of certain *other* beliefs – beliefs which we took in either unreflectively from others, in accordance with our initial nature,[85] or as the result of inaccurate reasoning.

For example, if I have many air-like atoms in my soul, I will have readily embraced the views that the gods use lightning to punish sinful mortals and hence I fear thunderstorms; but now my newly acquired beliefs about the true nature of the gods allow me to get rid of some of those views. For this method to work, presumably I will first have to come to realize the true nature of the gods, for example that they have better things to do than being concerned with earthly events. Then, I have to realize that if this is so, the gods will not waste their time hurling lightning. However, in order actually to lose my fear of thunderstorms, I will have to thoroughly convince myself that there are no grounds for having it.[86] For this I may have to rehearse the arguments against the existence of vengeful gods repeatedly, and as many such arguments as possible, and especially so, when the clouds get darker. I will also have to cultivate a replacement set of true beliefs, which, if firmly held, will provide me with the dispositions and desires needed to reach tranquillity.

Finally, Epicurus also acknowledges environmental impacts on our moral development; as we have seen earlier, not many people will be able to

[80] Laursen 1997: 45, 'there is much that [happens] with [our] nature helping, and much [that happens] when [our] nature is not helping'.

[81] Laursen 1997: at the end of 45, 'matured', 'grown' (ἐπαυξόμενον). ἐπαυξάνω also occurs at [5] VIII 8; [34.27] 8; [34.31] 31 Arr. Cf. also Epicurus calling times and ages 'causes' just before, Laursen 1997: 43.

[82] Cf. 'the consideration of the end itself', Laursen 1997: 43.

[83] Laursen 1997: 45, 'and there is something that [happens] when our nature is rearranged by us'.

[84] See above, section 1.

[85] Cf. Laursen 1997: 43, 'we irrationally follow the tendencies of the many'.

[86] βέβαιος ('firm'), Epicur. *Ep. Hdt.* 63; *Ep. Pyth.* 85; *Sent.* 40; Laursen 1997: 46–7, κατανοεῖν, see below.

restructure their belief system all by themselves.[87] Most people need some help from outside. They *may* realize that the end is a life of pleasure, which takes the form of tranquillity,[88] and that they are not in its possession, and somehow do not succeed in getting there. In order to succeed, they have to change their environment. For example, they could join the Epicurean school, and receive the required guidance which will help them to shed their empty beliefs, and replace them by a set of true beliefs; in this way they may establish new dispositions, and come closer to a life of tranquillity. Note that education of this kind constitutes a special way in which the environment has an influence on us.

As we have seen earlier,[89] for Epicurus, ordinarily our reactions to external influences will be determined either by our nature or by ourselves *qua* causes,[90] and our overall mental dispositions will not change as a result of our reactions to our environment. (For instance, if I have many air-like atoms, and hear a thunderstorm coming, then I will get frightened, and hide under a blanket, say. But my dispositions won't change. Next time there's a thunderstorm I'll be under the blanket again.)

The special case on the other hand is one in which environmental influences can also 'take the lead to the better', as Epicurus says.[91] In particular, we should assume from what else we know about Epicurus' ethics that if we are externally influenced by *teaching*, we can get rid of ingrained false beliefs, and can, by so changing our dispositions, also change our behaviour. Thus if someone provides me with a convincing scientific explanation of thunder, I may eventually stop being frightened; hence not go into hiding any more.

Moral development, whether self-caused or triggered by others, consists thus primarily in the change of one's mental dispositions, in particular one's beliefs. There is a passage in *On Nature* 25 which suggests that Epicurus may have made an attempt at explaining such a process on the atomic level of the mind. (This passage is rather lacunose in character and its first two sentences are fragmented, but the text is still full enough to offer some interesting information.)

. . . of [speech] sounds and thinking and thoughts and representations of the everlasting or non-everlasting disturbance or happiness in the soul [being/is/are?]

87 Sen. *Ep.* 52.3–4.

88 Perhaps even there help is required in some cases? Remember the third category of people in the passage from Seneca's letter.

89 Above, in section 1.

90 LS 20 C 1.

91 If the – uncertain – reading 'to the better' or 'to improvement' (εἰς τὸ βέλτιον) is correct. Laursen 1997: 45, 'but there is also something that [happens] when [our nature] itself leads the way (lacuna of *c.*3 words) [not only] matured, but also because the things which flow in from the environment take the lead to improvement' (context and Greek above).

the cause for hunting down, little by little, the principle, or canon or criterion. For these things lead to the consideration of the criterion, and from the criterion it[self] . . . perception . . . considera[tion] . . . to the investigation little by little of the things I mentioned earlier. For these things furnished each other with their cause and use[92] and each thought coming in immediately pulled along in turn the other thought, at first coming in little by little and flowing out again quickly, then being understood more and more, in part because of the natural cause of the growth and of loss of fluidity,[93] in part because of that [cause] which comes to be from ourselves.[94] (Laursen 1997: 46–7)

I very tentatively suggest that one idea underlying this gap-ridden passage is as follows: when other people say something to us (i.e. something that can be thought), very fine atomic structures enter our mind from outside and leave it again,[95] being thought by us only briefly, while they were there; and at first they may leave hardly a trace in the mind. But this may happen repeatedly with the same sort of thought, and thus the thought can be understood better each time. It will be connected with other thoughts, which 'pull it along' as Epicurus puts it, so that when we think one thing, we think another also (i.e. some sort of association theory of learning). In part owing to ourselves as causes (perhaps as focusing on it, or connecting it with other thoughts that are our own already), the new thought is, it seems, eventually anchored in the mind, and becomes part of it (by leaving a durable impression, and thus having changed the atomic structure of the mind permanently).[96] The thought has thus become a belief of ours, and at the same time our behavioural dispositions have changed.[97]

[92] i.e. one makes use (takes advantage of) the other.

[93] Or loss of flaccidity: the idea may be that when the soul gains in firmness and structure, because more and more (hopefully correct) thoughts are being adopted and integrated as beliefs, the more easily a new thought is interconnected with these and retained and understood.

[94] . . . ψόφων τε καὶ νοήσεων καὶ ἐπινοημάτων καὶ φαντασμάτων καὶ τῆς αἰωνίας κατὰ ψυχὴν ὀχλήσεως ἢ εὐδαιμονίας ἢ μὴ αἰωνίας τὴν αἰτίαν τοῦ θηρεύειν τὴν ἀρχὴν καὶ κανόνα καὶ κριτήριον καὶ κατὰ μικρόν. ταῦτά τε γὰρ εἰς τὸν ἐπιλογισμὸν τοῦ κριτηρίου ἦγεν καὶ ἐκ τοῦ κριτηρίου αὐτ. . ἐπαισθα[±5/6 ἐ]πιλογι . . . εἰς τὴν κατὰ μικρὸν ὧνπερ ἔνπροσθεν εἶπα διερεύνησιν. ἀλλήλοις γὰρ ταῦτα τὴν αἰτίαν καὶ χρείαν παρείχετο καὶ ἐναλλὰξ ἑκάτερον παρενπίπτον ἐπεσπάσατο εὐθὺς τὸ ἕτερον ἐπινόημα κατὰ μικρὸν πρῶτον ἐγγεινόμενον καὶ ταχέως ἐκρέον, εἶτα μᾶλλον μᾶλλον κατανοούμενον, τὰ μὲν διὰ τὴν φυσικὴν αἰτίαν τῆς ἀπαυξήσεως καὶ ἀπαλλάξεως πλαδαρότητος, τὰ δὲ διὰ τὴν ἐξ ἡμῶν γεινομένην καὶ . . .

[95] Atoms are not mentioned in so many words in the passage. However, Epicurus' talk of thoughts 'coming in' (i.e. into the soul, which consists of atoms) and 'flowing out', and of 'growth' and 'loss of fluidity' suggests that atomic structures are at issue (cf. also Lucr. 3.510–16). This is in any case what we would expect in line with Epicurus' materialist view of the soul – except perhaps adherents of Sedley's emergentist interpretation of Epicurus' psychology (e.g. Long and Sedley 1987: vol. 1, 109–11), an interpretation to which I have provided an alternative above in section 2 and, in more detail, in Bobzien 2000.

[96] Cf. also *Ep. Pyth.* 85, 'firm belief' (πίστιν βέβαιον).

[97] Cf. also Lucr. 3.510–16 for the possibility of change of our mind: such change involves either adding or taking away atoms, or changing the structure of the present atoms.

It is in this light, I suggest, that one has to understand the method of philosophizing and teaching philosophy in the Epicurean school. The practice of memorizing the canon of Epicurean philosophy by repeating it again and again to oneself and others,[98] is on this interpretation in no sense a 'mindless' enterprise. The repetition is meant to increase one's understanding of new beliefs (especially those that are incompatible with the ones one has so far held) and thus to increase the firmness with which one holds those beliefs (they have to make a 'lasting impression' in the mind, quite literally).[99] Similarly, the Epicurean practice of producing a number of different arguments to prove the same point becomes comprehensible in this way. (Recall the twenty-nine or so proofs for the mortality of the soul in Lucretius, book 3.) For the new beliefs have to be integrated and harmonized with one's other beliefs – and here different arguments for them will lead to connections with different beliefs. All this is needed, since only if one firmly holds the new beliefs will they be able to result in a change of one's desires and emotions, and thus lead to a change in what actions one tends to perform.[100]

4. CONCLUDING REMARKS

Let me finally return briefly to the subject of moral responsibility. From what we have seen about Epicurus' ideas of moral development and moral progress, it is clear that at any time the state of an adult human's moral dispositions is *only in part* the result of their own critical restructuring of their mind. We are not causally responsible for the initial constitution of our mind, but this constitution will determine, for instance, whether our moral progress will be faster or slower, effortless or arduous. Similarly, we are not causally responsible for the surroundings we find ourselves in initially, nor are we *ever completely* causally responsible for our environment; but this environment, too, will be a causal factor in our moral development. Consequently, both our nature and our past and present environment will – indirectly – *co*-determine what sort of *actions* we perform, and hence also whether we should be blamed or praised for our actions. Thus not only will the calm-natured offspring of a family of Epicureans growing up within

[98] Cf. e.g. Epicur. *Ep. Hdt.* 35–6.

[99] The many repetitions in Lucretius' *On the Nature of Things* may be intended to serve the same purpose.

[100] For the importance of reason in the process of moral improvement cf. e.g. Lucr. 3.321, 'reason' (*ratio*); Epicur. *Ep. Men.* 124–5, 'correct understanding' (γνῶσις ὀρθή); 132, 'reasoning' (λογισμός) and D.L., 10.117 and 120.

a circle of Epicurean friends have a much smoother and shorter path to a life of tranquillity than the fire-natured, irascible youth who grew up in a society that indulges in luxury and fervently teaches religious superstition; the latter will also be likely to deserve blame for a much larger proportion of their actions.

This is a fact about which we find no sign of worry in Epicurean writings, nor, as far as I am aware, in any other philosophical writings from antiquity.[101] Epicurus simply seems to accept that blame is attached to those actions of moral beings of which they are themselves the main causal factor, regardless of how far the overall disposition of their mind is a result of their rational reflection and belief, and how far the result of necessitating factors.[102] The agents can be blamed for their actions, because they were not in any sense forced to bring them about and because the actions are not the outcome of a 'mindless' co-operation of nature and nurture; rather they result from the agents' own beliefs, which in turn determine their desires and emotions.

What is, however, important here is the fact that, for Epicurus, ethics does not have the function of developing or justifying a moral system that allows for the effective allocation of praise and blame. The function of ethics – and in fact of the whole of philosophy[103] – is rather to give *everyone* a chance to morally improve; that is, a chance to understand that in order to reach true happiness, one has to learn to distinguish between pleasures conducive to that end and pleasures distracting from it; and in the course of this, to give up prejudicial and irrational beliefs which one has unthinkingly absorbed from the social surroundings one lives in. Epicurean ethics is thus exclusively forward-looking. It takes praise and blame for actions as in principle justified, based on the rationality of the agent. But praise and blame are not themselves a topic of ethics.[104] Human failure is taken into account only as a starting point for moral progress towards a life of happiness and tranquillity.

[101] Cf. Bobzien 1998: section 6.3.6.

[102] He does, though, make the interesting distinction between 'respect' one should have for people who approach tranquillity with difficult starting positions, and congratulations to those who had it easy; cf. Sen. *Ep.* 52.4.

[103] Sext. Emp. *Math.* 11.169; Epicur. *Ep. Pyth.* 85; *Sent.* 11–13.

[104] The role of the swerve is not to justify moral praise and blame for individual actions, but to make it possible that our mental constitution, and in particular our beliefs, can change in response to environmental influences; see Bobzien 2000.

CHAPTER 11

'Who do we think we are?'

Brad Inwood

Dorothea Frede's contributions to the study of Greek ethics are rooted in both an intimate knowledge of Greek culture and civilization and a powerful understanding of the philosophical issues of the modern world. She does not lose sight of what makes the ancient Greeks remote and foreign, but equally she attends to those features of Greek ethics which connect it to our own philosophical concerns. Thus (as in so many other ways) she has been a model to emulate. The Greeks made major contributions to the question of personal identity as we still understand it, despite the considerable differences between their cultural context and ours. It is an honour to dedicate to Professor Frede this brief consideration of Empedocles' contribution to a still vital philosophical question.

In approaching this question, I have two closely connected aims. First, I want to show that Empedocles, in the fifth century BC, had a deep and serious interest in the question of personal identity, an issue shaped for us by the influence of Locke.[1] Second, I want to argue, partly on the basis of this Empedoclean contribution to the issue, that we should accept the readings of the primary scribe of the newly recovered Strasbourg papyrus of Empedocles[2] at the three critical points where this ancient text transmits the letter θ rather than the letter ν which we would expect from the evidence

An early version of this paper was read to the January 2005 meeting of the American Philological Association in Boston, in a session on 'The New Empedocles' organized by David Sider. In addition to valuable suggestions from the audience at that session, I received particularly helpful discussion after the session from Dirk Obbink and Margaret Graver. In a preliminary form this paper benefited from critical comment by Jennifer Whiting. I am also grateful to the Centre for Advanced Study in the Behavioural Sciences for the perfect working conditions they provided.

1 As indicated, for instance, by the way Williams in 'Personal identity and individuation' (Williams 1973: ch. 1) begins from the chapter of Locke on which I will focus here. In the following Locke's *Essay* will be quoted from Woolhouse 1997.

2 The papyrus was purchased for the Deutsches Papyruskartell in 1904, assigned for study to Alain Martin in 1990 and identified as Empedoclean in 1994. The initial publication was by Martin and his collaborator Oliver Primavesi in Martin and Primavesi 1999.

of the indirect tradition.[3] In each case the presence of θ affects the sense of the lines in question by compelling us to accept that Empedocles' aim is to call into question the identity and nature of human beings over time and to make an important point about human responsibility. There are non-philosophical reasons for accepting the reading of the primary scribe of the earliest known text of Empedocles, but here I will concentrate on the philosophical reasons for welcoming this new evidence and taking it at face value.

Empedocles is justly famous for a great many things, not least of which is the sensational biography which he somehow managed to generate;[4] he is also the originator of the four-element theory in Western cosmology and physics, indeed the first thinker to clearly articulate the idea of an element as an unchangeable building block of the natural world. Despite all of that, my focus here will be on only one aspect of his thought, his challenge to ideas about personal identity, an aspect of his philosophical endeavour that has not yet been properly appreciated, in some measure because the tools of his challenge include a theory of reincarnation or metempsychosis.[5] This is a theory that we regard as highly unlikely to be true and one which can therefore be readily marginalized. Reincarnation, for most of us, is a theory as familiar as it is implausible; we seem to have lost sight of the potential relevance of it to contemporary discussions of personal identity.[6] Hence we fail, I think, to appreciate how systematic Empedocles' concerns about identity were and how central this concern was to his philosophical activity.[7] And if we take account of how explicit his interest in the issues

[3] The θs are written in the first hand of the papyrus at ensemble a(i) 6 = B 17 line 36 and a(ii) 17 = B 17 line 56; and in fragment 38/20 line 2 as improved by the reading of ensemble c; in each case a second hand has written ν as a suggested correction, thus producing a text that matches what is quoted by the ancient authors who are the main source of evidence for Empedocles' poem. Some modern scholars urge that we accept the reading of the second hand rather than that of the first. See, e.g., Mansfeld and Algra 2001 and Trépanier 2003. Laks 2002, in a very sophisticated and careful discussion of issues which do not directly touch on my immediate concerns, accepts the θs. See also Curd 2001: 44–8 and Wildberg 2001: 51.

[4] See D.L. 8.51–77 and more generally fragments DK 31 A 1–A 19.

[5] Although not the originator of this theory, his is the earliest well-attested version of it.

[6] In claiming that there is a relevance of Empedoclean reflection to issues still of live philosophical interest I do not intend to assimilate ancient problems with our own. A. O. Rorty 1990: 21-2 points correctly to the 'dramatically discontinuous changes in the characterization of persons' and to the 'differences in practices that involve the concept of personhood'. Morton 1990: 39-40 similarly emphasizes the differences. There is, however, abundant room for a degree of similarity as well and this chapter is intended only to put one or two of them on the table, mostly as an aid to appreciating a particularly important historical feature of Empedocles' thought.

[7] Wright 1990, for example, has nothing to say about the issue even in a volume of essays devoted to the concept of persons in ancient and modern philosophy. Clark 1990: 205 accomplishes more with his brief reference to 'the occult self that Empedocles . . . called *daimōn* and Plato identified with the undying intellect'.

was, then the fact that the scribe (as opposed to the subsequent corrector) of the papyrus points to the same concern will be less strange; the centrality of Empedocles' concern about personal identity and the new papyrological evidence reinforce each other.

The question of personal identity is still a matter of philosophical interest in our modern philosophical tradition, and for us the key historical text is John Locke's *An Essay Concerning Human Understanding*, book 2, chapter 27 ('Of identity and diversity'). Persuasively arguing that the conditions of identity are different for inert material objects, for plants and for animals (sections 3–6), Locke goes on to distinguish the unity of a *man* from that of a *person* and that of a mere *substance* (section 7): since the ideas are different, so too are the identity conditions. With the pathbreaking clarity that has made his analysis of the issue central ever since, Locke defines conditions for the identity of persons distinct from those for the identity of men. Although I may be a substance, a man and a person, my sameness considered under each of these 'ideas' is not the same. Personal identity emerges as not just a distinct philosophical concern. It is also the central concern both epistemologically and morally. For as Locke shows, when it comes to questions of responsibility, reward and punishment we work primarily with the forensic idea of a 'person' rather than with the (more or less) biological idea of 'man' (sections 18 and 26). The key to personal identity is continuity of self-awareness; and when human law holds a person accountable for things of which he is not conscious, owing to drunkenness perhaps, Locke recognizes this as a practice justified by practical epistemic limitations. The law cannot be certain that the malefactor does not have and can never come to have an awareness of what he did and so must punish anyway. But on Judgement Day, 'wherein the secrets of all hearts shall be laid open, it may be reasonable to think, no one shall be made to answer for what he knows nothing of; but shall receive his doom, his conscience accusing or excusing him' (section 22). Judgement Day is the circumstance under which perfect transparency about self-awareness may be assumed; deprived of Locke's Christian apparatus, we would turn instead to a robust counterfactual or a thought experiment to get the same result.

In the course of this discussion, Locke gives due consideration to reincarnation and transmigration, among other things. In section 14 he assesses the conditions for personal identity in a case where the same immaterial soul comes to inhabit a new body with 'no remaining consciousness of what it did in that pre-existent state, either wholly separate from body, or informing any other body'. In such a case, if awareness of a former life is truly impossible, then we have a different person, 'personal identity reaching no further than consciousness reaches'. If, however, even minimal continuity of consciousness is present between two distinct incarnations of the soul, then identity of persons is established.[8] Similarly, in section 16 Locke imagines himself having 'the same consciousness, that I saw the Ark and Noah's flood, as that I saw an overflowing of the Thames last winter, or as that I write now'. In such a case that ancient observer of Noah's ark would be the same person as the living philosopher, just as Socrates and the Mayor of Quinborough would be the same if they shared identity of consciousness (section 19).

Reincarnation was not a live religious or philosophical option in Locke's own day, but resurrection at Judgement Day was. With his criterion for identity of personhood, Locke is well positioned to take a stand on the difficult question of how the person judged on that final day could be the same as the person whose life is at issue now. At the beginning of section 15 he notes that sameness of consciousness in the soul being judged is a sufficient criterion of sameness to permit ascriptions of responsibility and therefore moral judgement. The theological claim that the reassembly of precisely the same flesh is necessary for Judgement Day to proceed is implicitly denied without impugning the justness of God's final judgement.

Given the importance of Pythagorean, Platonic and even Empedoclean theories of reincarnation in Christian eschatological debates, it is hardly accidental that Empedocles should seem relevant to the questions of personal identity raised by Locke, partly against that background. But so far there has been insufficient attention paid to this aspect of Empedocles' thought and too little inclination to see how his bold theory permeated so many aspects of his philosophy. It is also important to remember that his poem is virtually the earliest detailed evidence we have for 'Pythagorean' theories of reincarnation. A fresh look at Empedocles will confirm the centrality of these issues and show why we should welcome the fresh evidence of the Strasbourg papyrus without hesitation.

In order to show that this claim of a philosophical concern with personal identity is not mere retrojection onto Empedocles of later concerns, we should consider briefly some of the background. There is a definite Homeric precedent for this issue, broadly conceived. For even if we set aside Bruno Snell's[9] worry about the unity of Homer's man – the idea that Homer

[8] 'But let him *once* find himself conscious of *any* of the actions of Nestor, he then finds himself the same person with Nestor.'

[9] Snell 1975.

somehow lacked a robust conception of the person and saw each agent as a bundle of distinct psychological modules – there are still questions about who a person is in Homer. The *Nekuia* of *Odyssey* 11 forces us, the audience of the poem then and now, to think hard about who we are, about our own identity and continuity in this life and the next. Are we only our body on the earth, acting and suffering? Is it still 'us' when our shade lingers on in the realm of Hades, aware but impotent, burdened perhaps with regretful memories of our active life but still tragically aware that we are the same person? Is Achilles' robust physical body so much a part of himself that he should aspire to get it back at the cost of his active role as a noble warrior? Or are heroism and undying glory really what it means to be Achilles, so that he would no longer be himself if he embraced the life of a landless serf?

Similarly, without raising the issue of death and reincarnation, the legend of Tiresias shows that early Greek reflection explored in its own way the boundaries of personal identity.[10] In a turn of events that Locke might have welcomed as an illustration of the potential independence of the consciousness that makes a person and the bodily sameness that makes a man, Tiresias (without dying) had the chance to live in both a man's and a woman's body and retained awareness of both incarnations, a self-consciousness sufficient to permit comparison of the sexual pleasure available to each sex.

Pythagoras, of course, raises the issue more acutely – and so, no doubt, do the more shadowy Orphic or proto-Orphic thinkers who lurk in the background of the archaic age. Issues about evidence are difficult, of course, but the elegies of Xenophanes provide unimpeachable and virtually contemporary evidence. 'They say that once, when someone was beating a puppy, he came by, took pity on him and spoke as follows: "Stop, don't hit him, for truly it is the soul of a man who is a friend. I recognized it when I heard him cry out"' (D.L. 8.36). Even if we doubt the evidence from Heraclides of Pontus (D.L. 8.5) – which includes the full list of names that Pythagoras had held in his various incarnations – we can be confident that memory of previous lives did play a central role in his thinking about successive lives. It is likely this which is behind Empedocles' reference to a great man who 'easily saw each of all the things which are in ten or twenty lifetimes' (6/129.5–6).[11] The Xenophanes anecdote reveals not just a conviction that souls get reused in new bodies, even those of different species, but that in a sense which matters most for morality there is some sort of sameness of a person in the two different bodies. The puppy has the soul

[10] Apollod. *Bibl.* 3.70–2; Ov. *Met.* 3.316–38.

[11] I cite Empedocles from my own second edition (Inwood 2001); the Diels/Kranz number comes after the slash, so that 6/129 indicates my fragment 6, Diels/Kranz fragment 129. Line numbers follow the period.

of a man who is a friend and that soul has brought with him enough of his old personality that the vocalizations reveal his identity.

This anecdote certainly confirms some sort of concern with issues of personal identity, but it would be rash to think of it as a straightforward bit of evidence. For in it, we find a strange twist of theory being attributed to Pythagoras. The puppy is *not* said to be aware that he has the same soul that Pythagoras' old friend had (although neither is this denied). So it is not clear that on Lockean criteria the puppy and the old friend really are the same *person*; yet they are clearly supposed to be bearers of the same soul. In this anecdote Pythagoras was able to detect the sameness of the recycled soul, so there seems to be a considerable degree of continuity of which the puppy itself might not have been aware. Would Pythagoras be justified in treating the puppy as his old friend because of that continuity, even if the puppy did not itself have the continuity of awareness that defines our sense of personal identity? Xenophanes presents him in that light. In philosophical satire there can be muddle, and in this case I find it very difficult to decide who should be thought of as the victim of the confusion: the pup, Pythagoras or Xenophanes.

Turning to the legend of Pythagoras' own lives, more clearly relevant to the issue as Locke framed it (especially in section 14), Pythagoras' own soul, according to the account of Heraclides, was not only the same through all of its lives, but it remembered details of its previous lives so well that, when it was Hermotimus, it was able to use those memories to prove the continuity of his own identity with Euphorbus. Pythagoras himself in his various incarnations clearly met Lockean criteria for personal identity, though if Xenophanes is to be believed it isn't necessarily the case that every reincarnated soul would do so.

In recounting these familiar facts I want to emphasize the evident interest in the continuity of personhood in various forms. The interest of Achilles' situation comes not from the survival of his soul in Hades, but from the fact that he is still the same person; the story of Pythagoras and the puppy absolutely depends on the fact that the puppy *still is* his friend, that is, is still the same soul as when he had only two legs and a more articulate vocal apparatus, whether or not Lockean criteria for personal identity are met. We are not dealing here with the preservation of life-stuff in the manner of the recycling theory of Plato's *Phaedo*. In many cases at least there is no river of *Lēthē* to drink from which might complicate if not undo the sense of continuity with other lives.[12]

[12] As my interest is only with Empedocles I will not discuss the complicated questions raised by the various Platonic treatments of reincarnation in a range of dialogues. For an argument that Platonic soul can usefully be understood in terms of personhood, see Long 2005.

Thus when Empedocles comes on the scene we can be confident that issues of personal identity and the continuity of moral personhood were familiar to him, at the very least from two of his most important influences, Homer and Pythagoras. And it was enough of an issue for the readers of philosophical poetry that Xenophanes could make play with it. And what Empedocles does is to pick up this idea and make it central to his poem or poems.[13]

Let us begin with what I take to have been the beginning of the poem. In fragment 1/112 some sort of concern with personhood is placed front and centre in the proem.[14] How else to describe the impact of saying 'I go among you all as a deathless god, no longer mortal' while he is manifestly supposed to be embodied and in a real sense an *ordinary* person? That, I suspect, is the force of adding 'honoured just as I seem' (*tetimenos hōsper eoika*). The speaker here is both what he seems *and* a god, at the same moment and in the eyes of the same observers. Who, or what, is this speaker? No answer is needed here – the question is what counts, as Empedocles forces on his readers a challenging set of concerns.[15] Who, Empedocles is asking his audience, is it that is speaking to them? And if the speaker isn't who he seems to be, how are the audience to understand themselves?

The toughness of this question is reflected in the acknowledgement that these pronouncements of his are going to be hard to accept (2/114). The *egō* of this fragment is perhaps more of a *prophētēs* than a god; it is certainly dissonant with the audience's expectations and with their understanding of themselves. This weirdness of identity is echoed again in 7/113 where Empedocles distinguishes himself as superior to 'men who die many times'. He both claims that men in general (the audience) die more than once – strange enough, one supposes, and certainly enough to make his audience wonder about their own continuity – and he marks himself off as being better than they are. The foundation for this superiority is, I suggest, the continuity of recollection that he has achieved in emulation of his master Pythagoras (6/129). It is a real death, of the kind that Empedocles escapes, if one sees only the pathetic scraps of one's experiences that are available to

[13] In what follows nothing depends on whether Empedocles wrote one or two poems. Critical analysis of our traditional evidence for Empedocles *and* the new evidence of the papyrus both show that the questions at issue were all present in one poem even if there was also a second one with a different title. See Inwood 2001: 8–21.

[14] I am following my own reconstruction of the ordering of the fragments. It cannot be regarded as certain and if it is shown that, for example, 1/112 was not in the proem the discussion which follows would need a certain amount of cosmetic revision, but nothing substantial.

[15] Similar issues are raised, perhaps, when Heraclitus says 'immortals mortals, mortals immortals' each living the life of the other (DK 22 B 62).

those who don't maintain continuity of memory (8/2). Forgetful men may die many times, but they are swift to their dooms if they don't retain memory and continuity of consciousness. The moral of the story is becoming clearer: every soul gets reused in a new life, no doubt, but to go on being yourself some special conditions need to be met. When Empedocles dismisses other men as *ephēmerioi* (9/3, 10/131) he is not denying that their souls come back in new bodies (after all, they cannot be ephemeral in that sense if they aren't going to be *poluphthereis*); but they are not themselves because they lose the thread of identity owing to their lack of connected consciousness – and so they are ephemeral.

There is in Empedocles' poem an explicit epistemological requirement on one's ability to be oneself over time. On my reconstruction of the poem we are scarcely out of the introduction and already the central questions are those which deal with the continuity of who we are. Ordinary people are muddled, unaware of the history of the souls they bear and so failing to be the continuous persons they could, in principle, have been. Empedocles, by contrast, *knows* who he is and thereby attains the continuous personhood of which we all presumably are capable.

It is this, I think, which enables Empedocles to claim (in 11/115) that he is an exile. If his story about punishment for some primal sin is right, then all souls go through the wanderings he outlines, but most fail to be aware of it. They, then, are not exiles in the way that Empedocles is, precisely because they lack the continuous personhood that he has attained. Empedocles claims to be a refugee (*phugas theothen kai alētēs*) because he has remembered, has maintained the continuity of his experience. Continuous memory is clearly the main key to personal identity in Empedocles, and this issue recurs many times throughout the fragments we have. Even more interesting, in my opinion, is that Empedocles emphasizes that he has retained this sense of identity not just through the human incarnations that Pythagoras claimed for himself, but even across those boundaries of species alluded to by Xenophanes.

Indeed, Empedocles goes a step further: his *identity* as himself has been preserved, because he has retained the memory of it, even across the boundary between plants and animals.[16] For Empedocles has been not just a boy and a girl, not just a fish of some sort and a bird, but also a bush (111/117).

[16] This is a move which Locke, with his strong commitment to the difference between plants and animals, could not have accepted, though he seems also to avoid close consideration of the prospect that we might cross the boundary between 'brute' animals and conscious ones. This is perhaps a reflection of his Christian and Cartesian legacy; Plato remained Empedoclean in his openness to the migration of souls around the animal kingdom.

His sense of who he is seems to be so firmly anchored in memory and continuity of experience that his very flesh can be treated as alien to who he really is (113/126). This alienation from one's own body is perhaps what is being indicated by the references to entering a cave (119/120), which is such an unfamiliar place to be in that it occasions lamentation (115/118).

And yet this alienation from his own body does not constitute moral detachment from his deeds when being a different species. In the new and improved version of 124/139.6 the terrible alimentary actions undertaken by the wandering *egō* are no longer ambiguous. They are not human deeds, as they would have been if we read *cheilesi*, lips. They are the deeds of some awful beast he has been (perhaps a mountain-roaming lion, 135/127), for they are done with claws (*chēlais*). Empedocles, then, is morally responsible not just for the actions of unwitting murder he committed when offering flesh sacrifice (128/137), but for all that he in his continuity of personhood has done.

Nevertheless, it seems certain that Empedocles does not free his misguided fellows (who do not remember their previous lives and so fail to be continuous in their personal identities) from responsibility for their deeds.[17] For the circulation of 'souls' from one body to another is presented as a punishment inflicted on souls in general, not just on the self-aware who achieve continuous personhood. Empedocles preaches to his benighted fellows that they should strive to become aware of their continuity – not so that they may then *become* responsible for the misdeeds of their former lives for the first time but rather so that they may become *aware of the responsibility* they already bear and so finally begin to deal with its consequences. If we are unaware of our past lives we aren't the person who did the deeds of those lives, but we are still held to account for those deeds. The continuity of personhood which Empedocles has achieved is, he suggests, something that all of us can in principle attain. By becoming aware of the continuity of our soul-body exploits we become multi-lived persons able to see where we fit in the world.

Empedocles, it seems to me, has not just learned a doctrine of reincarnation from the Pythagoreans. He has seized upon it as something important enough to place squarely at the centre of his poetic message about human morality and human awareness. But the message is unsettling. We are in

[17] Locke, of course, takes a different view about ordinary forensic punishment. The law necessarily holds drunkards who *may* be unaware of their misdeeds accountable, because certainty about the agent's awareness cannot be achieved. But when certainty is possible, as on Judgement Day, 'wherein the secrets of all hearts shall be laid open', the strict criterion of continuity of awareness will be employed (*Essay* 2.27.22; see above).

some sense the same person even if we don't recall our former lives. We remain responsible for what we have done even in other bodies that we may not recall. How can this be? Isn't this disturbingly like holding me responsible for what my grandfather did? I think any hearer of this poem has to begin wondering who he really is, just as Aeschylus' audience is bound to wonder about the responsibility Agamemnon bears for what he did while shouldering the yoke of necessity.[18] The criterion for personal identity that we see in Empedocles is broadly Lockean (though we may prefer to claim that Locke's is broadly Empedoclean), but there is clearly an interesting difference in the idea of personal responsibility. Empedocles obviously does not share Locke's forensic conception of a person, nor is he interested in preserving a sense of fairness in the moral evaluations which flow from his metaphysics of personhood. He is, though, interested in something missing from Locke's account. He concentrates on the possibility that other humans, who lack the consciousness of their multi-bodied lives that he has attained, may yet attain that awareness. That won't change their responsibility for their actions and choices, but it will bring a degree of transparency to their moral lives, a transparency which plays a central role in the moral aspiration which Empedocles urges on his audience.

For Locke there was a sharp boundary between the realm of persons and that of mere animals, let alone the realm of mere corpuscular substances. Here Empedocles' views are in the sharpest possible contrast to those of Locke. For in Empedocles there is another issue which raises questions of personhood, one that connects not at all to Locke but, surprisingly, very closely to reincarnation in his own theory.[19] Let us look afresh at the other theme in the Empedoclean fragments which raises questions of personal identity. This is the question of how we as persons are related to our elemental parts, the earth, air, fire and water (even love and strife,

[18] Aesch. *Ag.* 218.

[19] Interestingly, Empedocles seems to lack completely any interest in how one might justify claims of continuous personal identity on the elemental level during one normal lifetime. As some sort of reductionist about our person, regarding us as just equivalent to our elemental make-up, Empedocles might be expected to worry intensely about how we can remain one despite our material flux (as, arguably, the Stoics later did); Dirk Obbink and Margaret Graver raised this issue with me in different ways. Locke certainly thought that such flux was relevant to the identity conditions for mere substances. Locke, however, had no trouble in articulating identity conditions for plants and animals which compensated for the flux of their matter (*Essay* 2.27.1–6) and my suggestion is that Empedocles did not need the implicit precedent of Aristotle to warrant a similar assumption, though it was almost certainly an under-theorized assumption unsupported by further argument. Hence I am not trying to impute a theory to him, merely to explain why we should not be surprised if a certain issue did not occur to him. At the worst, we might conclude that he ought to have raised the issue and that if he had it would have created a provisional conflict with his awareness-based theory of personal identity, a conflict that he would have had to resolve or else modify parts of his theory.

perhaps, though nothing turns on this as far as I am concerned) which make us up. This too is an issue very much on the surface of Empedocles' thinking and it is closely connected to his concern with reincarnation (so we see him concerned with both synchronic and diachronic questions about who we are). For example, in 22/9 he refers in the context of his element theory to 'the things mixed to make up a man' and 'the things mixed to make up the race of wild beasts or bushes or birds'. It is surely no accident that the relation of humans to the elements is apparently the same as that of the beasts, bushes and birds which they have been in other incarnations. Just as I *am* still the beast that once prowled the forest primeval, so too I *am* the elements which make up the compound which is wrongly said to come to be. A contemporary philosopher might describe this as a reductive identity with my components (and the reductionism is visible also in 98/98 as well as in the fragments of a more overtly Parmenidean character), but it was certain to raise eyebrows in the fifth century BC (as it would have in Locke's day as well) to claim that I simply *am* the compound of my parts. And this, again, is not an accidental or one-off reference. We see the same correlation of the species singled out in Empedocles' own history of incarnations with element theory in 26/21, 27/23, 28/26 and especially in 38/20.6–7.

This point about reductionism could be laboured longer and supported with observations about Empedocles' views on how humans normally misunderstand what life and death really are (24/15), about the centrality of the reductive elements to the thoughts, pleasures and pains (92/107) which make up our conscious mental life (see also 93/106–96/105). But there would be little benefit in lingering over the point. It is time to return to the question of the new papyrus. It is worth recalling a few facts about this remarkable new document. It consists of the recoverable portions of a piece or pieces of papyrus originally used as a funerary wreath in an Egyptian tomb; folded into an appropriate long, narrow shape, the papyrus was covered with copper and gold and the resultant wreath placed on the body in a tomb. It had been purchased from an Egyptian antiquities dealer, and when it was properly restored by Martin and Primavesi the various pieces of broken papyrus were assembled into four relatively substantial pieces (ensembles a–d), two smaller assemblages, and a few even smaller scraps. The plates in Martin and Primavesi 1999 make clear how much hard work is involved in gaining useful information about Empedocles' poem, and work continues among specialists on the physical reconstruction of the papyrus. The four major ensembles, however, do tell us a good deal. Ensemble a overlaps with 25/17 and extends it with portions of almost 40 additional lines of text, some so short as to be quite uninformative. Ensemble b expands on 83/76 with parts of three additional lines and shows that Plutarch quoted the lines he did cite in the wrong order, ensemble c includes 38/20, and ensemble d includes and extends 124/139, providing a fuller but still controversial context for lines familiar from the indirect tradition and improving the reading in several places. All in all the papyrus gives us just over 70 lines or partial lines of text and in many places it gives us a text different from that of the 'indirect' tradition (the texts quoted by other ancient authors which have until now been the only evidence for Empedocles' poetry). For the most part the papyrus confirms or slightly modifies what we already believed, but the occasional presence of the letter θ in place of the letter ν provided by the indirect tradition raises the issues which interest me here. The fact that a corrector has apparently gone through the papyrus indicating that the θ is wrong and that the papyrus should have the ν familiar to us from the indirect tradition has made the entire question even more controversial. If Empedocles wrote 'we' instead of 'it' or 'they' it means that his poem was more involved with the fate of persons and was less purely cosmological than had previously been thought on the basis of the indirect tradition.

But if Empedocles really did have on the surface of his authorially intent mind questions that we would identify as those of personal identity in both areas of his thought (synchronic and reductionist as well as diachronic and Lockean), then the otherwise baffling 'we' that turns up in the new papyrus fragments makes reasonable sense – in fact, it would even be predictable. And if that is so, then any hesitations we might have about accepting the θs of the first hand will have to be justified on non-philosophical grounds. Indeed, the objections to them will have to be strong enough to rebut the obvious philosophical good fit of the text as transmitted by the first hand of the direct tradition. I would not, then, rest my defence of the θs on a rigid preference for the primary tradition nor on a mechanical and false assumption that the first hand is always more likely to be right than a corrector. The reason for accepting the reading is not just that it is in textual terms primary; it is also philosophically superior in exactly the ways that the rest of the evidence would predict. Let's look briefly at the *loci* in question.

The first-person plurals occur in what is now the extension of fragment DK 31 B 17 (a(i) 6 = B 17 line 36 and a(ii) 17 = B 17 line 56; this is my 25/17) and in fragment 38/20 line 2 as improved by the reading of ensemble c. With the new readings of the papyrus we now find ideas like these in 25/17:

But these very things are, and running through each other
they become different at different times and are always, perpetually alike
. . . . *we* come together into one cosmos [i.e., orderly compound],
. . . . to be many from one,
from which all things that were, that are and will be in the future
have sprung: trees and men and women
and beasts and birds and water-nourished fish,
and long-lived gods first in their prerogatives [lines 34–41]
. . . and in the very middle . . . *we* come together to be one alone. [line 56]

and this in fragment 20:

This is very clear in the bulk of mortal limbs:
at one time *we* come together into one by love,
all the limbs which have found a body in the peak of flourishing life;
at another time again, being divided by evil quarrels,
they [the limbs] wander, all of them separately, about the breakers of life.

Although in some of these cases we cannot be certain of the run of argument in the whole passage, owing to the highly fragmentary state of the new papyrus, and although there will for a very long time be room for challenges to the currently available reconstructions, there is clearly a provisional fit between the 'we' readings and the surrounding contexts that is more than adequate to justify the claims made here. So in conclusion, I want to restate my case in a general way.

The appearance of 'we' in these passages should not be surprising (as it has been to some) and hence hesitations about accepting the evidence of the original scribe of the papyrus rather than the corrector's hand need not arise on the grounds of the sense of the lines. One of Empedocles' great accomplishments in his entire poem is to force his audience to reassess who 'we' really are, to re-examine what constitutes the personhood to which human beings have come to feel so desperately attached. And he does so in a manner which grows out of the earlier Greek tradition but (I think) far transcends it in sophistication. Empedocles uses his own rather special case as an example in his argument about personal identity and the prospects for moral improvement. Now a god, he has himself been 'a boy and a girl and a bush and a bird' and some kind of fish. He has also been the ravening beast who tore apart flesh with his claws in order to have food, and yet was not destroyed for his sin but only pitifully banished to a hard life among the mortal elements instead. Empedocles has a theory about what makes up a human being and so can make sense of this experience, but ordinary men don't realize 'who is who' – like the fools who slaughter their own family members in their ignorance. Even without the new readings of the papyrus, which suggest that our very identity as persons is open to question and challenge, we can tell that Empedocles forced his audience to re-evaluate who 'they' really are. The evidence of the papyrus merely provides further indication of *how* he does so. This new evidence should be welcomed on philosophical as well as on palaeographical grounds.

General bibliography

ABBREVIATIONS

AGPh	*Archiv für Geschichte der Philosophie*
AJPh	*American Journal of Philology*
AncPhil	*Ancient Philosophy*
BACAP	*Proceedings of the Boston Area Colloquium in Ancient Philosophy*
BICS	*Bulletin of the Institute of Classical Studies*
CQ	*Classical Quarterly*
GS	*German Studies*
JHS	*The Journal of Hellenic Studies*
JHPh	*Journal of the History of Philosophy*
JPh	*The Journal of Philosophy*
OSAPh	*Oxford Studies in Ancient Philosophy*
PAS	*Proceedings of the Aristotelian Society*
PCPhS	*Proceedings of the Cambridge Philological Society*
PhR	*The Philosophical Review*
PhRdschau	*Philosophische Rundschau*
RMeta	*The Review of Metaphysics*
TAPhA	*Transactions of the American Philological Association*
ZPhF	*Zeitschrift für philosophische Forschung*

Alberti, A. (1994) 'Ragione e virtù nell'etica epicurea', in *Realtà e ragione: studi di filosofia antica*, ed. A. Alberti. Florence: 185–216.

Algra, K., J. Barnes, J. Mansfeld and M. Schofield (eds.) (1999) *The Cambridge History of Hellenistic Philosophy*. Cambridge.

Allen, R. E. (1991) *The Dialogues of Plato*, vol. 2: *The Symposium*. New Haven.

Anagnostopoulos, G. (1994) *Aristotle on the Goals and Exactness of Ethics*. Berkeley.

Annas, J. (1981) *An Introduction to Plato's Republic*. Oxford.

(1985) 'Self-knowledge in early Plato', in *Platonic Investigations*, ed. D. J. O'Meara. Washington, DC: 111–38.

(1987) 'Epicurus on pleasure and happiness', *Philosophical Topics* 15: 5–21.

(1992) *Hellenistic Philosophy of Mind*. Berkeley.

(1993) *The Morality of Happiness*. New York.

(1999) *Platonic Ethics Old and New*. Ithaca, NY.

(2002) 'What are Plato's "middle" dialogues in the middle of?', in Annas and Rowe (2002), 1–23.
Annas, J. and C. Rowe (eds.) (2002) *New Perspectives on Plato, Modern and Ancient.* Cambridge, MA.
Armstrong, D., J. Fish, P. A. Johnston and M. B. Skinner (eds.) (2004) *Vergil, Philodemus, and the Augustans.* Austin, TX.
Arrighetti, G. (ed.) (1973) *Epicuro: Opere.* 2nd edn. Turin.
Asmis, E. (1999) 'Epicurean epistemology', in Algra *et al.* (1999), 260–94.
Barnes, J. (ed.) (1984) *The Complete Works of Aristotle. The Revised Oxford Translation.* Princeton.
Bobzien, S. (1998) *Determinism and Freedom in Stoic Philosophy.* Oxford.
(2000) 'Did Epicurus discover the free-will problem?', *OSAPh* 19: 287–337.
Boyancé, P. (1958) 'La Théorie de l'âme chez Lucrèce', in Classen (1986), 131–50.
Brandwood, L. (1990) *The Chronology of Plato's Dialogues.* Cambridge.
Broadie, S. (1991) *Ethics with Aristotle.* New York.
(2005) 'On the idea of the *summum bonum*', in Gill (2005), 41–58.
Brown, L. (1997) 'What is "the mean relative to us" in Aristotle's Ethics?', *Phronesis* 42: 77–93.
Brunschwig, J. (1996) 'The Aristotelian theory of equity', in *Rationality in Greek Thought*, eds. M. Frede and G. Striker. Oxford: 115–55.
Burnyeat, M. F. (1976) 'Plato on the grammar of perceiving', *CQ* 26: 29–51.
(1981) 'Aristotle on understanding knowledge', in *Aristotle on Science*, ed. E. Berti. Padua: 97–139.
(ed.) (1990) *The Theaetetus of Plato*, with tr. by M. J. Levett rev. by M. Burnyeat. Indianapolis.
(2000) 'Plato on why mathematics is good for the soul', in *Mathematics and Necessity: Essays in the History of Philosophy*, ed. T. J. Smiley. Oxford: 1–82.
(2002) 'Plato on how not to speak of what is not', in *Le Style de la pensée: recueil de textes en hommage à Jacques Brunschwig*, eds. M. Canto-Sperber and P. Pellegrin. Paris: 40–66.
(2003) 'Apology 30b2–4: Socrates, money and the grammar of *gignesthai*', *JHS* 123: 1–25.
Bury, R. G. (ed.) (1932) *The Symposium of Plato*, with intr. and comm., 2nd edn. Cambridge.
Castagnoli, L. (2001). 'L' ἔλεγχος di Agatone. Una rilettura di Platone, *Simposio* 199c3–201c9', *Dianoia* 6: 39–84.
Chang, R. (ed.) (1997) *Incommensurability, Incomparability, and Practical Reason.* Cambridge, MA.
Clark, S. R. L. (1990) 'Reason as *daimōn*', in Gill (1990), ch. 8.
Classen, C. J. (ed.) (1986) *Probleme der Lukrezforschung.* Hildesheim.
Clay, D. (1975) 'The tragic and comic poet of the *Symposium*', *Arion* n.s. 2: 238–61, repr. in *Essays in Ancient Greek Philosophy*, eds. J. P. Anton and A. Preus. Albany, NY (1983), 186–202.
Cooper, J. M. (1970) 'Plato on sense-perception and knowledge (*Theaetetus* 184–6)', *Phronesis* 15: 123–65.

(1975) *Reason and Human Good in Aristotle*. Cambridge, MA.
(1987) 'Contemplation and happiness: a reconsideration', *Synthese* 72: 187–216.
(1996) 'Justice and rights in Aristotle's *Politics*', *RMeta* 49: 859–72.
(ed.) (1997) *Plato: Complete Works*, with intr. and notes. Indianapolis.
Cornford, F. M. (1939) *Plato and Parmenides*. London.
(1941) *The Republic of Plato*. Oxford.
(1957) *Plato's Theory of Knowledge*. London.
(1965) 'Mathematics and dialectic in the *Republic*, VI–VII', in *Studies in Plato's Metaphysics*, ed. R. E. Allen. London: 61–95.
Cross, R. C. and A. D. Woozley (1964) *Plato's Republic: A Philosophical Commentary*. London.
Curd, P. (2001) 'A new Empedocles', *BACAP* 17: 27–49.
Dancy, J. (2004) *Ethics without Principles*. Oxford.
Denyer, N. (ed.) (2001) *Plato: Alcibiades*, with intr. and comm. Cambridge.
Diano, C. (1974 [orig. 1939–42]) 'La psicologia d'Epicuro e la teoria delle passioni', in C. Diano, *Scritti Epicurei*. Florence: 129–280.
Dirlmeier, F. (ed.) (1956) *Aristoteles: Nikomachische Ethik*, tr. with comm. Berlin.
Dixsaut, M. (1997) 'What is it Plato calls "thinking"?', *BACAP* 13: 1–27.
Ebert, T. (1976) 'Praxis und Poiesis: zu einer handlungstheoretischen Unterscheidung bei Aristoteles', *ZPhF* 30: 12–30.
Erler, M. and M. Schofield (1999) 'Epicurean ethics', in Algra *et al.* (1999), 642–74.
Everson, S. (1990) 'Epicurus on the truth of the senses', in *Epistemology*, ed. S. Everson. Cambridge: 161–83.
Fine, G. (1990) 'Knowledge and belief in *Republic* V–VII', in *Epistemology: Companions to Ancient Thought 1*, ed. S. Everson. Cambridge: 85–115.
(1993) *On Ideas*. Oxford.
Fish, J. (2004) 'Anger, Philodemus' good king, and the Helen episode of Aeneid 2.567–589: a new proof of authenticity from Herculaneum', in Armstrong *et al.* (2004), 111–38.
Fortenbaugh, W. W. (2002 [orig. 1975]) *Aristotle on Emotion*, 2nd edn. London.
Frede, D. (1978) 'The final proof of the immortality of the soul in Plato's *Phaedo* 102a–107a', *Phronesis* 23: 27–41.
(1985) 'Rumpelstiltskin's pleasures: true and false pleasures in Plato's *Philebus*', *Phronesis* 30: 151–80.
(1986) 'The impossibility of perfection: Socrates' criticism of Simonides' poem in the *Protagoras*', *RMeta* 39: 729–53.
(1989) 'The soul's silent dialogue: a non-aporetic reading of the *Theaetetus*', *PCPhS* 215: 20–49.
(ed.) (1993a) *Plato: Philebus*, tr. with intr. and notes. Indianapolis.
(1993b) 'Out of the cave: what Socrates learned from Diotima', in *Nomodeiktes: Greek Studies in Honor of Martin Ostwald*, eds. R. M. Rosen and J. Farrell. Ann Arbor: 397–422.
(1997) 'Glück und Glas . . . Martha Nussbaum über die Zerbrechlichkeit des Guten im menschlichen Leben', *PhRdschau* 44: 1–19.

(1998) 'Der "Übermensch" in der politischen Philosophie des Aristoteles: Zum Verhältnis von *bios theoretikos* und *bios praktikos*', *Internationale Zeitschrift für Philosophie* 2: 259–84.
(1999) 'Plato on what the body's eye tells the mind's eye', *PAS* 99: 191–210.
(2002) 'Comments on Annas [2002]', in Annas and Rowe (2002), 25–36.
(2003) 'Stoic determinism', in *The Cambridge Companion to the Stoics*, ed. B. Inwood. Cambridge: 179–205.
(2006) 'Pleasure and pain in Aristotle's ethics', in *The Blackwell Guide to Aristotle's* Nicomachean Ethics, ed. R. Kraut. Oxford: 255–75.
Frede, M. (1987) 'Observations on perception in Plato's later dialogues', in *Essays in Ancient Philosophy*, ed. M. Frede. Oxford: 3–8.
Furley, D. (1967) 'Aristotle and Epicurus on voluntary action', in D. Furley, *Two Studies in the Greek Atomists*. Princeton: 159–237.
Gagarin, M. (1969) 'The purpose of Plato's *Protagoras*', *TAPhA* 100: 133–64.
Gauthier, R. A. and J. Y. Jolif (1970) *Aristote, l'Éthique à Nicomaque*, with intr., tr. and comm., 2 vols., 2nd edn. Louvain.
Georgiadis, C. (1987) 'Equitable and equity in Aristotle', in Panagiotou (1987), 159–72.
Giannantoni, G. (1984) 'Il piacere cinetico nell'etica epicurea', *Elenchos* 5: 25–44.
Gill, C. (ed.) (1990) *The Person and the Human Mind: Issues in Ancient and Modern Philosophy*. Oxford.
(ed.) (2005) *Virtue, Norms and Objectivity*. Oxford.
Glidden, D. (1980) 'Epicurus and the pleasure principle', in *The Greeks and the Good Life*, ed D. Depew. Fullerton, CA: 177–97.
Gomez-Lobo, A. (1977) 'Plato's description of dialectic in the *Sophist*', *Phronesis* 22: 29–47.
Gulley, N. (1971) 'Socrates' thesis at *Protagoras* 358b–c', *Phoenix* 25: 118–23.
Harris, W. V. (2001) *Restraining Rage: The Ideology of Anger Control in Classical Antiquity*. Cambridge, MA.
Hawtrey, R. S. W. (1981) *A Commentary on Plato's Euthydemus*. Philadelphia.
Heinaman, R. (1988) 'Eudaimonia and self-sufficiency in the *Nicomachean Ethics*', *Phronesis* 33: 31–53.
(2003) 'Plato: metaphysics and epistemology', in *From the Beginning to Plato*, ed. C. C. W. Taylor. London: 356–93.
Hooker, B. and M. Little (eds.) (2000) *Moral Particularism*. Oxford.
Hunter, R. (2004) *Plato's Symposium*. Oxford.
Hursthouse, R. (1980/1) 'A false doctrine of the mean', *PAS* 81: 57–72.
(1999) *On Virtue Ethics*. Oxford.
Indelli, G. (ed.) (1978) *Polistrato: Sul disprezzo irrazionale delle opinioni popolari*, with tr., La scuola di Epicuro 2, Naples.
(ed.) (1988) *Filodemo: L'ira*, with tr., La scuola di Epicuro 5, Naples.
(2004) 'The vocabulary of anger in Philodemus' *De ira* and Vergil's *Aeneid*', in Armstrong *et al.* (2004), 103–10.
Inwood, B. (2001) *The Poem of Empedocles*, 2nd edn. Toronto.
Irwin, T. H. (1986) 'Aristotle's conception of morality', *BACAP* 1: 115–43.
(1995) *Plato's Ethics*. New York.

(2000) 'Ethics as inexact science: Aristotle's ambitions for moral theory', in Hooker and Little (2000), 100–29.

Jowett, B. (ed.) (1953) *The Dialogues of Plato*, tr. with intr., 4 vols. 2nd edn. Oxford.

(tr.) (1984) *Aristotle: Politics*, in Barnes (1984), 1986–2129.

Kahn, C. (2002) 'On Platonic chronology', in Annas and Rowe (2002), 93–127.

Kenny, A. (1992) *Aristotle on the Perfect Life*, Oxford.

Keyt, D. (1983) 'Intellectualism in Aristotle', in *Essays in Ancient Greek Philosophy*, vol. 2, eds. J. P. Anton and A. Preus. Albany: 364–87.

Koenen, M. (1997) 'Lucretius' olfactory theory in *De rerum natura* IV', in *Lucretius and his Intellectual Background*, eds. K. A. Algra, M. H. Koenen and P. H. Schrijvers. Amsterdam: 163–77.

Konstan, D. (1973) *Some Aspects of Epicurean Psychology*. Leiden.

(2006) *Lucrezio e la psicologia epicurea*, tr. I. Ramelli. Milan.

Korsgaard, C. M. (1983) 'Two distinctions in goodness', *PhR* 92: 169–95.

(1996) 'From duty and for the sake of the noble: Kant and Aristotle on morally good action', in *Aristotle, Kant and the Stoics: Rethinking Happiness and Duty*, eds. S. Engstrom and J. Whiting. Cambridge: 203–36.

Kraut, R. (1989) *Aristotle on the Human Good*. Princeton.

(1993) 'In defense of the grand end', *Ethics* 103: 361–74.

(2002) *Aristotle: Political Philosophy*. Oxford.

Laks, A. (2002) 'Reading the readings: on the first person plurals in the Strasburg Empedocles', in *Presocratic Philosophy. Essays in Honour of Alexander Mourelatos*, eds. V. Caston and D. W. Graham. Aldershot: 127–38.

Laursen, S. (1995) 'The early parts of Epicurus *On Nature*, 25th book', *Cronache Ercolanesi*: 5–109.

(1997) 'The later parts of Epicurus *On Nature*, 25th book', *Cronache Ercolanesi*: 5–82.

Lawrence, G. (1997) 'Nonaggregatability, inclusiveness, and the theory of focal value: *Nicomachean Ethics* 1.7, 1097b16–20', *Phronesis* 42: 32–76.

Long, A. A. (2005) 'Platonic souls as persons', in *Metaphysics, Soul and Ethics in Ancient Thought: Themes from the Work of Richard Sorabji*, ed. R. Salles. Oxford: ch. 8.

Long, A. A. and D. N. Sedley (eds.) (1987) *The Hellenistic Philosophers*, 2 vols. Cambridge.

Long, A. G. (2004) *Character and Dialectic: The Philosophical Origins of the Platonic Dialogue*, unpub. Ph.D. dissertation: University of Cambridge.

MacIntyre, A. (1981) *After Virtue*. Notre Dame, IN.

Makin, S. (1990–1) 'An ancient principle about causation', *PAS* 91: 135–52.

Mansfeld, J. and K. Algra (2001) 'Three Thētas in the Empédocle de Strasbourg', *Mnemosyne* 54: 78–84.

Manuwald, B. (ed.) (1999) *Platon: Protagoras*, tr. and comm. Göttingen.

Martin, A. and O. Primavesi (1999) *L'Empédocle de Strasbourg*. New York.

Matthews, G. B. (1999) *Socratic Perplexity*. Oxford.

McCabe, M. M. (2000) *Plato and his Predecessors: The Dramatisation of Reason*. Cambridge.

(2001) 'Developing the good: prolepsis or critique in the *Euthydemus*?', *Plato: Electronic Journal of the International Plato Society* 2.
(2005a) 'Out of the labyrinth: Plato's attack on consequentialism', in Gill (2005), 189–214.
(2005b) 'Does your Plato bite?' in *Agonistes*, eds. J. Dillon and M. Dixsaut. London: 103–15.
McDowell, J. (1979) 'Virtue and reason', *The Monist* 62: 331–50.
(1996) 'Deliberation and moral development in Aristotle's ethics', in *Aristotle, Kant, and the Stoics: Rethinking Happiness and Duty*, eds. S. Engstrom and J. Whiting. Cambridge: 19–35.
McKirahan, R. (1984) 'Socrates and Protagoras on σωφροσύνη and justice. *Protagoras* 333–334', *Apeiron* 18: 19–25.
Mehl, D. (1999) 'The intricate translation of the Epicurean doctrine of ψυχή in book 3 of Lucretius', *Philologus* 143: 272–87.
Miller, Jr, F. D. (1995) *Nature, Justice, and Rights in Aristotle's Politics*. Oxford.
Mitsis, P. (1988) *Epicurus' Ethical Theory: The Pleasures of Invulnerability*. Ithaca, NY.
Morton, A. (1990) 'Why there is no concept of a person', in Gill (1990), ch. 2.
Müller, A. W. (2004) 'Aristotle's conception of ethical and natural virtue: how the unity thesis sheds light on the doctrine of the mean', in Szaif and Lutz-Bachmann (2004), 18–53.
Nehamas, A. (2004) '*Episteme* and *logos* in Plato's later thought', in A. Nehamas, *Virtues of Authenticity*. Princeton: 224–48.
Nightingale, A. W. (2004) *Spectacles of Truth in Classical Greek Philosophy*. Cambridge.
Nussbaum, M. C. (1990) *Love's Knowledge: Essays on Philosophy and Literature*. New York.
Panagiotou, S. (ed.) (1987) *Justice, Law, and Method in Plato and Aristotle*. Edmonton.
Payne, A. (1999) 'The Refutation of Agathon: *Symposium* 199c–201c', *AncPhil* 19: 235–53.
Penner, T. (1973) 'The unity of virtue', *PhR* 82: 35–68.
Penner, T. and C. Rowe (2005) *Plato's Lysis*. Cambridge.
Politis, V. (2004a) *Aristotle and the Metaphysics*. London.
(2004b) '*Aporia* and searching in the early Plato', in *Socrates, 2000 Years since his Death*, ed. V. Karasmanis. Delphi: 303–17.
Price, A. W. (1989) *Love and Friendship in Plato and Aristotle*. Oxford.
Procopé, J. (1993) 'Epicureans on anger', in *Philanthropia kai Eusebeia: Festschrift für Albrecht Dihle zum 70. Geburtstag*, eds. G. W. Most, H. Petersmann and A. M. Ritter. Göttingen: 363–86.
Purinton, J. S. (1993) 'Epicurus on the telos', *Phronesis* 38: 281–320.
Rackham, H. (ed.) (1934) *Aristotle: The Nicomachean Ethics*, with tr. Cambridge, MA.
Rapp, C. (ed.) (2002) *Aristoteles: Rhetorik*, tr. with comm., 2 vols. Berlin.
Roberts, W. R. (tr.) (1984) *Aristotle: Rhetoric*, in Barnes (1984), 2152–2269.

Robinson, R. (1953) *Plato's Earlier Dialectic*. Oxford.
Rorty, A. O. (1990) 'Persons and *personae*', in Gill (1990), ch.1.
Ross, D. (ed.) (1957) *Aristotelis Politica*. Oxford.
(1964) *Aristotle*. Oxford.
(tr.) (1984) *Aristotle: Nicomachean Ethics*, rev. by J. O. Urmson, in Barnes (1984), 1729–867.
Rowe, C. (1998). *Plato: Symposium*. Exeter.
Scheler, M. (1954) *Der Formalismus in der Ethik und die materiale Wertethik*, 4th edn. Bern.
Schroeder, D. N. (1981) 'Aristotle on Law', *Polis* 4: 17–31.
Scott, D. (1995) *Recollection and Experience*. Cambridge.
(2005) *Plato's Meno*. Cambridge.
Sedley, D. N. (1983) 'Epicurus' refutation of determinism', in ΣΥΖΗΤΗΣΙΣ: *studi sull'epicureismo greco e romano offerti a Marcello Gigante*. Naples: 11–51.
(1996) 'Three Platonist interpretations of the *Theaetetus*', in *Form and Argument in Late Plato*, eds. C. Gill and M. M. McCabe. Oxford: 79–103.
(1998) 'Platonic causes', *Phronesis* 43: 114–32.
(2003) *Plato's Cratylus*. Cambridge.
(2004) *The Midwife of Platonism: Text and Subtext in Plato's Theaetetus*. Oxford.
Segvic, H. (2000) 'No one errs willingly: the meaning of Socratic intellectualism', *OSAPh* 19: 1–45.
Sharples, R. W. (1991–93) 'Epicurus, Carneades and the atomic swerve', *BICS*: 174–90.
Sherman, N. (1989) *The Fabric of Character*. Oxford.
(2000) 'Emotional agents', in *The Analytic Freud: Philosophy and Psychoanalysis*, ed. M. P. Levine. London: 154–76.
Shiner, R. A. (1987) 'Aristotle's theory of equity', in Panagiotou (1987), 173–91.
Silverman, A. (2002) *The Dialectic of Essence*. Princeton.
Smith, M. F. (ed.) (1993) *Diogenes of Oenoanda: The Epicurean Inscription*. Naples.
Smith, N. (2004) 'Did Plato write the *Alcibiades*?', *Apeiron* 37: 93–108.
Snell, B. (1975) *Die Entdeckung des Geistes: Studien zur Entstehung des europäischen Denkens bei den Griechen*, 4th edn. Göttingen.
Solmsen, F. (1961) 'αἴσθησις in Aristotelian and Epicurean thought', in Classen (1986), 151–72.
Sorabji, R. (1980) *Necessity, Cause, and Blame*. London.
Stenzel, J. (1940) *Plato's Method of Dialectic*, tr. D. J. Allen. Oxford.
Stocker, M. (1976) 'The schizophrenia of modern ethical theories', *JPh* 73: 453–66.
Stokes, M. C. (1986) *Plato's Socratic Conversations: Drama and Dialectic in Three Dialogues*. London.
Striker, G. (1996a) *Essays on Hellenistic Epistemology and Ethics*. Cambridge.
(1996b) 'Epicurus on the truth of sense impressions', in Striker (1996a), 77–91.
(1996c) 'Origins of the concept of natural law', in Striker (1996a), 209–20.
Szaif, J. (2004) *Naturbegriff und Güterlehre in der Ethik des Aristoteles*, in Szaif and Lutz-Bachmann (2004), 54–100.

(2005a) 'Aristoteles: eine teleologische Konzeption von Besitz und Eigentum', in *Was ist Eigentum? Philosophische Positionen von Platon bis Habermas*, eds. A. Eckl and B. Ludwig. Munich: 43–58.

(2005b) *Freundschaft und Moral: über Freundschaft als Thema der philosophischen Ethik*. Bonn.

Szaif, J. and M. Lutz-Bachmann (eds.) (2004) *Was ist das für den Menschen Gute?/ What is Good for a Human Being?* Berlin.

Taylor, C. C. W. (1980) '"All perceptions are true"', in *Doubt and Dogmatism*, eds. M. Schofield, J. Barnes and M. Burnyeat. Oxford: 105–24.

(ed.) (1991) *Plato: Protagoras*, with tr. and notes, 2nd edn. Oxford.

Trépanier, S. (2003) '"We" and Empedocles' cosmic lottery', *Mnemosyne* 56: 385–419.

Urmson, J. O. (1990) *The Greek Philosophical Vocabulary*. London.

Usener, H. (ed.) (1887) *Epicurea*. Leipzig.

(1977) *Glossarium Epicureum*, eds. M. Gigante and W. Schmid. Rome.

Vlastos, G. (ed.) (1956), *Plato: Protagoras*, B. Jowett's tr. rev. by M. Ostwald with intr. by G. Vlastos. Indianapolis.

Vogel, C. de (1985) 'Selbstliebe bei Platon und Aristoteles und der Charakter der aristotelischen Ethik', in *Aristoteles: Werk und Wirkung*, vol. 1, ed. J. Wiesner. Berlin: 393–426.

White, F. C. (1989) 'Love and beauty in Plato's *Symposium*', *JHS* 109: 149–57.

White, N. P. (1992) 'Plato's metaphysical epistemology', in *The Cambridge Companion to Plato*, ed. R. Kraut. Cambridge: 277–310.

Wiggins, D. (1997) 'Incommensurability. Four proposals', in Chang (1997), 52–66.

Wildberg, C. (2001) 'Commentary on Curd', *BACAP* 17: 50–6.

Williams, B. (1973) *Problems of the Self*. Cambridge.

(1985) *Ethics and the Limits of Philosophy*. London.

(2003) 'Plato's construction of intrinsic goodness', in *Perspectives on Greek Philosophy: S. V. Keeling Lectures in Ancient Philosophy*, ed. R. W. Sharples. Aldershot: 1–18.

Wright, M. R. (1990) 'Presocratic minds', in Gill (1990), ch. 9.

Wolf, U. (2002) *Aristoteles' Nikomachische Ethik*. Darmstadt.

Woolhouse, R. (ed.) (1997) *John Locke: An Essay Concerning Human Understanding*. London.

Young, C. M. (1988) 'A delicacy in Plato's *Phaedo*', *CQ* 38: 250–1.

Zeyl, D. (1980) 'Socrates and hedonism: *Protagoras* 351b–358d', *Phronesis* 25: 250–9.

List of publications by Dorothea Frede

BOOKS

(1970) *Aristoteles und die 'Seeschlacht': Das Problem der Contingentia Futura in* De interpretatione *9*. *Hypomnemata* vol. XXVII. Göttingen.
(1993) *Plato*: Philebus, *Translated, with Introduction & Notes*. Indianapolis.
(1997) *Platon*: Philebos, *Übersetzung und Kommentar*. Platon, Werke vol. III 2. Göttingen.
(1999) *Platons* Phaidon: *Der Traum von der Unsterblichkeit der Seele*. Darmstadt.

BOOKS EDITED

— and R. Schmücker (1997) *Ernst Cassirers Werk und Wirkung: Kultur und Philosophie*. Darmstadt.
— and A. Laks (2002) *Traditions of Theology: Studies in Hellenistic Theology, its Background and Aftermath*. Papers presented at the 8th Symposium Hellenisticum, Villeneuve-d'Ascq, France, 1998. Philosophia Antiqua vol. LXXXIX. Leiden.
— and K. Pawlik (2002) *Forschungsfreiheit und ihre ethischen Grenzen*. Referate gehalten auf der Tagung der Joachim Jungius-Gesellschaft Hamburg am 19. und 20. Oktober 2001. Veröffentlichung der Joachim Jungius-Gesellschaft der Wissenschaften Hamburg, Nr. 93. Göttingen.
— and B. Inwood (2005) *Language and Learning: Philosophy of Language in the Hellenistic Age*. Papers presented at the 9th Symposium Hellenisticum, Hamburg, Germany, 2001. Cambridge.

CONTRIBUTIONS TO BOOKS

(1985) 'Aristotle on the limits of determinism: accidental causes in *Metaphysics* E 3', in *Aristotle on Nature and Living Things: Philosophical and Historical Studies presented to David M. Balme*, ed. A. Gotthelf. Pittsburgh: 207–25.
(1986) 'Heidegger and the scandal of philosophy', in *Human Nature and Natural Knowledge: Essays Presented to Marjorie Grene on the Occasion of her Seventy-Fifth Birthday*. Boston Studies in the Philosophy of Science vol. LXXXIX, eds. A. Donagan, A. N. Perovich, Jr, M. V. Wedin. Dordrecht: 129–51.

(1988) 'The moment of vision and bad faith: the problem of an authentic present in Martin Heidegger', in *Gedankenzeichen: Festschrift für Klaus Oehler zum 60. Geburtstag*, eds. R. Claussen and R. Daube-Schackat. Tübingen: 57–63.
(1989) 'Constitution and citizenship: Peripatetic influence on Cicero's political conceptions in the *De re publica*', in *Cicero's Knowledge of the Peripatos*. Rutgers University Studies in Classical Humanities vol. IV, eds. W. W. Fortenbaugh and P. Steinmetz. New Brunswick: 77–100.
(1992) 'The cognitive role of phantasia in Aristotle', in *Essays on Aristotle's* De Anima, eds. M. C. Nussbaum and A. Oksenberg Rorty. Oxford: 279–95.
(1992) 'Disintegration and restoration: pleasure and pain in Plato's *Philebus*', in *The Cambridge Companion to Plato*, ed. R. Kraut. Cambridge: 425–63.
(1992) 'Necessity, chance, and "what happens for the most part" in Aristotle's *Poetics*', in *Essays on Aristotle's* Poetics, ed. A. Oksenberg Rorty. Princeton: 197–219.
(1993) 'Die Aktualität der antiken Ethik in der gegenwärtigen Philosophie', in *Die Antike in der europäischen Gegenwart*. Referate gehalten auf dem Symposion der Joachim Jungius-Gesellschaft der Wissenschaften Hamburg am 23. und 24. Oktober 1992. Veröffentlichung der Joachim Jungius-Gesellschaft der Wissenschaften Hamburg, Nr. 72, ed. W. Ludwig. Göttingen: 135–50.
(1993) 'Heidegger and the question of being', in *The Cambridge Companion to Heidegger*, ed. C. B. Guignon. Cambridge: 42–69.
(1993) 'Out of the cave: what Socrates learned from Diotima', in *Nomodeiktes: Greek Studies in Honor of Martin Ostwald*, eds. R. M. Rosen and J. Farrell. Ann Arbor: 397–422.
(1995) 'Die wundersame Wandelbarkeit der antiken Philosophie in der Gegenwart', in *Die Wissenschaften vom Altertum am Ende des 2. Jahrtausends n. Chr.* 6 Vorträge gehalten auf der Tagung der Mommsen-Gesellschaft 1995 in Marburg, ed. E.-R. Schwinge. Stuttgart: 9–40.
(1996) 'The hedonist's conversion: the role of Socrates in the *Philebus*', in *Form and Argument in Late Plato*, eds. C. Gill and M. M. McCabe. Oxford: 213–48.
(1996) 'How sceptical were the Academic sceptics?', in *Scepticism in the History of Philosophy: A Pan-American Dialogue*. International Archives of the History of Ideas vol. CXLV, ed. R. H. Popkin. Dordrecht: 1–25.
(1996) 'Mixed feelings in Aristotle's *Rhetoric*', in *Essays on Aristotle's* Rhetoric, ed. A. Oksenberg Rorty. Berkeley: 258–85.
(1996) 'The philosophical economy of Plato's psychology: rationality and common concepts in the *Timaeus*', in *Rationality in Greek Thought*, eds. M. Frede and G. Striker. Oxford: 29–58.
(1996) 'Platon, Popper und der Historizismus', in *Polis und Kosmos: Naturphilosophie und politische Philosophie bei Platon*, ed. E. Rudolph. Darmstadt: 74–107.
(1997) 'Mündlichkeit und Schriftlichkeit: Von Platon zu Plotin', in *Logos und Buchstabe: Mündlichkeit und Schriftlichkeit im Judentum und Christentum der Antike*, eds. G. Sellin and F. Vouga. Tübingen: 33–54.

(1997) 'Die ungerechten Verfassungen und die ihnen entsprechenden Menschen', in *Platon, Politeia*. Klassiker auslegen vol. VII, ed. O. Höffe. Berlin: 251–70.

(1998) 'Ficino über das gute Leben im platonischen *Philebos*', in *Die Renaissance und ihre Antike: die Renaissance als erste Aufklärung I*, ed. E. Rudolph. Tübingen: 35–56.

(2001) 'Aquinas on *phantasia*', in *Ancient and Medieval Theories of Intentionality*. Studien und Texte zur Geistesgeschichte des Mittelalters vol. LXXVI, ed. D. Perler. Leiden: 155–83.

(2001) 'Heidegger und die Eigentlichkeit des Todes', in *Bilder vom Tod: Kulturwissenschaftliche Perspektiven*. Interethnische Beziehungen und Kulturwandel vol. XLIV, ed. D. Drecklé. Münster: 9–27.

(2001) 'Meditationen über Sein und Sinn: philosophischer Probleme', in *Was ist ein 'philosophisches Problem'?*, eds. J. Schulte and U. J. Wenzel. Frankfurt am Main: 42–53.

(2001) 'Not in the book: how does recollection work?', in *Plato's* Phaedo. Proceedings of the Second Symposium Platonicum Pragense, eds. A. Havlíček and F. Karfík. Prague: 241–65.

(2001) 'Staatsverfassung und Staatsbürger in der Politik des Aristoteles', in: *Aristoteles, Politik*, ed. O. Höffe. Berlin: 75–92.

(2002) 'Comments on [J.] Annas ['What are Plato's "middle" dialogues in the middle of?']', in *New Perspectives on Plato, Modern and Ancient*, eds. J. Annas and C. Rowe. Cambridge, MA: 25–36.

(2002) 'Einführung', in *Forschungsfreiheit und ihre ethischen Grenzen*. Referate gehalten auf der Tagung der Joachim Jungius-Gesellschaft Hamburg am 19. und 20. Oktober 2001. Veröffentlichung der Joachim Jungius-Gesellschaft der Wissenschaften Hamburg; Nr. 93, eds. D. Frede and K. Pawlik. Göttingen: 9–18.

(2002) 'Die Einheit des Seins: Heidegger in Davos – kritische Überlegungen', in *Cassirer – Heidegger: 70 Jahre Davoser Disputation*, eds. D. Kaegi and E. Rudolph. Hamburg: 156–82.

(2002) 'Platon und die Augen des Geistes als Zugang zur Wahrheit', in *Interpretationen der Wahrheit*, ed. G. Figal. Tübingen: 82–111.

(2002) '*Sensus communis* und "Synästhetik" bei Thomas von Aquin', in *Synästhesie: Interferenz – Transfer – Synthese der Sinne*, eds. H. Adler and U. Zeuch. Würzburg: 149–66.

(2002) 'Theodicy and providential care in Stoicism', in *Traditions of Theology: Studies in Hellenistic Theology, its Background and Aftermath*. Papers presented at the 8th Symposium Hellenisticum, Villeneuve-d'Ascq, France, 1998. Philosophia Antiqua vol. LXXXIX, eds. D. Frede and A. Laks. Leiden: 85–117.

(2003) 'Aristoteles über Leib und Seele', in *Kann man heute noch etwas anfangen mit Aristoteles?*, eds. Th. Buchheim, H. Flashar, R. A. H. King. Darmstadt: 85–109.

(2003) '*Stichwort*: Sein: Zum Sinn von Sein und Seinsverstehen', in *Heidegger-Handbuch: Leben – Werk – Wirkung*, ed. D. Thomä. Stuttgart: 80–6.

(2003) '*Stichwort*: Wahrheit: Vom aufdeckenden Erschließen zur Offenheit der Lichtung', in *Heidegger-Handbuch: Leben – Werk – Wirkung*, ed. D. Thomä. Stuttgart: 127–34.

(2003) 'Stoic determinism', in *The Cambridge Companion to the Stoics*, ed. B. Inwood. Cambridge: 179–205.

(2004) 'Dialektik in Platons Spätdialogen', in *Platon verstehen: Themen und Perspektiven*, ed. M. van Ackeren. Darmstadt: 147–67.

(2004) 'Grenze und Unbegrenztheit – Das gute Leben in Platons *Philebos*', in *Grenzen und Grenzüberschreitungen*, XIX. Deutscher Kongress für Philosophie, Bonn, 23.–27. September 2002, Vorträge und Kolloquien, ed. W. Hogrebe. Berlin: 62–75.

(2004) '*On Generation and Corruption* I, 10: on mixture and mixables', in *Aristotle's* On Generation and Corruption, *book 1*, eds. F. de Haas and J. Mansfeld. Oxford: 289–314.

(2004) 'Die Orphik: Mysterienreligion oder Philosophie?', in *Der Orpheus-Mythos von der Antike bis zur Gegenwart*, ed. C. Maurer-Zenck. Frankfurt am Main: 229–45.

(2004) 'Das Philosophie-Curriculum in Platons *Staat*', in *Ethisch-philosophische Basiskompetenz*, ed. J. Rohbeck. Dresden: 40–64.

(2004) 'Platons Dialoge als "Erinnerungen": Zur Methodik der Platondeutung', in *Semantik und Ontologie: Beiträge zur philosophischen Forschung*. Philosophical Research vol. II, eds. M. Siebel and M. Textor. Frankfurt am Main: 281–303.

(2004) 'Platon: Eine Ethik des guten Lebens', in *Klassiker der Philosophie heute*, eds. A. Beckermann and D. Perler. Stuttgart: 17–37.

(2005) 'Citizenship in Aristotle's *Politics*', in *Aristotle's* Politics: *Critical Essays*, eds. R. Kraut and S. Skultety. Lanham, MD: 167–84.

(2006) 'Pleasure and pain in Aristotle's ethics', in *The Blackwell Guide to Aristotle's* Nicomachean Ethics, ed. R. Kraut. Oxford: 255–75.

(2006) 'Platons Essentialismus – ein hoffnungsloser Fall von Anachronismus?', in *Antike Philosophie verstehen/Understanding Ancient Philosophy*, eds. M. van Ackeren and J. Müller. Darmstadt: 131–47.

(2006) 'Platons Dialoge als Hypomnemata – Zur Methodik der Platondeutung', in *Platon im nachmetaphysischen Zeitalter*, eds. G. Schiemann, D. Mersch, G. Böhme. Darmstadt: 41–58.

(Forthcoming) 'Das mathematische Curriculum in Platons *Staat*', in *Wissen und Bildung in der antiken Philosophie*, eds. C. Rapp and T. Wagner. Stuttgart.

(Forthcoming) 'Auf Taubenfüßen: Über Natur und Ursprung des *orthos logos* in der Aristotelischen Ethik', in *Handlung – Wille – Willensschwäche: Grundfragen der Aristotelischen Handlungstheorie*, eds. K. Corcilius and C. Rapp. Stuttgart.

(Forthcoming) 'Platon und die Freie Wille', in *Hat der Mensch einen Freien Willen?* eds. U. van der Heiden and H. Schneider. Stuttgart.

ARTICLES IN PERIODICALS

(1971) 'Theophrasts Kritik am unbewegten Beweger des Aristoteles', *Phronesis* 16: 65–79.

(1972) 'Omne quod est quando est necesse est esse', *AGPh* 54: 153–67.

(1974) 'Comment on Hintikka's paper "On the ingredients of an Aristotelian science"', *Synthese* 28: 79–89.

(1978) 'The final proof of the immortality of the soul in Plato's *Phaedo* 102a–107a', *Phronesis* 23: 27–41 (repr. in *Essays on Plato's Psychology*, ed. E. Wagner. Lanham, MD (2001): 281–96).

(1982) 'The dramatization of determinism: Alexander of Aphrodisias' *De fato*', *Phronesis* 27: 276–98.

(1985) 'Rumpelstiltskin's pleasures: true and false pleasures in Plato's *Philebus*', *Phronesis* 30: 151–80 (repr. in *Plato*, ed. G. Fine. Oxford (2000): 827–54).

(1985) 'The sea-battle reconsidered: a defence of the traditional interpretation', *OSAPh* 3: 31–87.

(1986) 'The impossibility of perfection: Socrates' criticism of Simonides' poem in the *Protagoras*', *RMeta* 39: 729–53.

(1987) 'Beyond realism and anti-realism: Rorty on Heidegger and Davidson', *RMeta* 40: 733–57.

(1989) 'The soul's silent dialogue: a non-aporetic reading of the *Theaetetus*', *PCPhS* 215: 20–49.

(1992) 'Accidental causes in Aristotle', *Synthese* 92: 39–62.

(1992) 'Fatalism and future truth', *BACAP* 6 [1990]: 195–227.

(1998) 'Plato, Popper, and historicism', *BACAP* 12 [1996]: 247–76.

(1998) 'Der "Übermensch" in der politischen Philosophie des Aristoteles: Zum Verhältnis von *bios theoretikos* und *bios praktikos*', *Internationale Zeitschrift für Philosophie* 2: 259–84.

(1999) 'Der Begriff der *eudaimonia* in Platons *Philebos*', *ZPhF* 53: 329–54.

(1999) *Heideggers Tragödie: Bemerkungen zur Bedeutung seiner Philosophie*. Berichte aus den Sitzungen der Joachim Jungius-Gesellschaft der Wissenschaften e.V. Hamburg, Jhg. 17,1. Göttingen.

(1999) 'Plato on what the body's eye tells the mind's eye', *PAS* 99: 191–209.

(2001) *Bruno Snell und die Gründung der Joachim Jungius-Gesellschaft der Wissenschaften*. Veröffentlichung der Joachim Jungius-Gesellschaft der Wissenschaften Hamburg, Nr. 91. Göttingen.

ARTICLES IN ENCYCLOPEDIC WORKS

(1996) 'Aristoteles [6, Sohn des Nikomachos, aus Stageira]', in *Der Neue Pauly* 1: 1134–45.

(1997) 'Alexander of Aphrodisias', in *Encyclopedia of Classical Philosophy*, ed. D. J. Zeyl. Westport: 20–3.

(1997) 'Aristocles', in *Encyclopedia of Classical Philosophy*, ed. D. J. Zeyl, Westport: 57.

(1999) 'Chorismos', in *Religion in Geschichte und Gegenwart* 2: 176.

(1999) 'Lust', in *Der Neue Pauly* 7: 518–20.

(2001) 'Schicksal', in *Der Neue Pauly* 11: 156–8.

(2002) 'Wille', in *Der Neue Pauly* 12/2: 511–13.

(2003) 'Alexander of Aphrodisias', in *The Stanford Encyclopedia of Philosophy (Winter 2003 Edition)*, ed. E. N. Zalta, URL = http://plato.stanford.edu/archives/win2003/entries/alexander-aphrodisias/

(2003) 'Plato's Ethics: An Overview', in *The Stanford Encyclopedia of Philosophy (Fall 2003 Edition)*, ed. E. N. Zalta, URL = http://plato.stanford.edu/archives/fall2003/entries/plato-ethics/

(Forthcoming) 'Beweis', 'Definition', 'Grund/Begründung', in *Lexikon: Platon und die platonische Tradition*, ed. C. Schäfer. Darmstadt.

(Forthcoming) 'Platon', in *Handbuch für politische Philosophie und Sozialphilosophie*, eds. W. Hinsch, S. Gosepath, B. Rössler. Berlin.

BOOK REVIEWS

(1971) Wieland, W., *Die Aristotelische Physik*, *GS Section I: Philosophy and History* 4: 178–80.

(1972) Nebel, G., *Sokrates*, *GS Section I: Philosophy and History* 5: 40–1.

(1972) Wolff, M., *Fallgesetz und Massebegriff*, *GS Section I: Philosophy and History* 5: 173–75.

(1975) Leszl, W., *Logic and Metaphysics in Aristotle*, *Gnomon* 47: 340–9.

(1976) Bos, A. P., *On the Elements: Aristotle's Early Cosmology*, *JHPh* 14: 227–9.

(1976) Hintikka, J., *Time and Necessity*, *PhRdschau* 22: 237–42.

(1977) Ebert, Th., *Meinung und Wissen in der Philosophie Platons*, *PhRdschau* 24: 209–15.

(1978) Barnes, J., *Aristotle's* Posterior Analytics, *PhR* 87: 288–91.

(1984) 'Could Paris (son of Priam) have chosen otherwise? On R. W. Sharples: Alexander of Aphrodisias *On Fate*', *OSAPh* 2: 279–92.

(1985) Ferber, R., *Platos Idee des Guten*, *RMeta* 39: 353–5.

(1986) Burger, R., *The* Phaedo: *A Platonic Labyrinth*, *AJPh* 107: 121–3.

(1986) Wieland, W., *Platon und die Formen des Wissens*, *PhR* 95: 464–7.

(1987) Reale, G., *The Systems of the Hellenistic Age: A History of Ancient Philosophy*, vol. III, *RMeta* 41: 159–61.

(1988) Allen, R. E., *Plato's* Parmenides, *PhRdschau* 35: 86–95.

(1988) Hägler, R.-P., *Platons* Parmenides, *PhRdschau* 35: 76–86.

(1989) White, M. J., *Agency and Integrality*, *AncPhil* 9: 126–30.

(1990) Mitsis, Ph., *Epicurus' Ethical Theory*, *AJPh* 111: 561–6.

(1990) Okrent, M., *Heidegger's Pragmatism*, *Philosophy and Phenomenological Research* 50: 619–24.

(1995) Benardete, S., *The Tragedy and Comedy of Life: Plato's* Philebus, *JHPh* 33: 331–3.

(1997) 'Glück und Glas . . . Martha Nussbaum über die Zerbrechlichkeit des Guten im menschlichen Leben', *PhRdschau* 44: 1–19.

(1998) *Grundriss der Geschichte der Philosophie: die Philosophie der Antike*, vol. IV: *Die hellenistische Philosophie*, ed. H. Flashar, *Klio* 80: 521–5.

(1998) 'Logik, Sprache und die Offenheit der Zukunft in der Antike. Bemerkungen zu zwei neuen Forschungsbeiträgen', *ZPhF* 52: 84–104.
(2004) 'Ein neuer Reiseführer zu Platon: von Kutschera, F., *Platons Philosophie*', *Deutsche Zeitschrift für Philosophie* 52: 811–19.
(2005) 'Book Notes: Plato and Socrates', *Phronesis* 50: 79–94.
(2006) 'Book Notes: Socrates and Plato', *Phronesis* 51: 91–108.

Index locorum

[1] In the book, Epicur. *Nat.* 25 is quoted from the most recent edition of the relevant papyri by Laursen 1995 and 1997. Here, Arrighetti 1973 (= Arr.) and Long and Sedley 1987 (= LS) references are given, since these editions are more widely available; Laursen includes Arrighetti numbers.

[2] Us. = Usener 1887.

Index nominum et rerum